Hannibal for Dinner

Hannibal for Dinner

Essays on America's Favorite Cannibal on Television

EDITED BY KYLE A. MOODY *and*
NICHOLAS A. YANES

McFarland & Company, Inc., Publishers
Jefferson, North Carolina

Also of Interest: *The Iconic Obama, 2007–2009: Essays on Media Representations of the Candidate and New President,* edited by Nicholas A. Yanes and Derrais Carter (McFarland, 2012)

LIBRARY OF CONGRESS CATALOGUING-IN-PUBLICATION DATA

Names: Moody, Kyle A., 1983– editor. | Yanes, Nicholas A., 1982– editor.
Title: Hannibal for dinner : essays on America's favorite cannibal on television / edited by Kyle A. Moody and Nicholas A. Yanes.
Description: Jefferson, North Carolina : McFarland & Company, Inc., Publishers, 2021 | Includes bibliographical references and index.
Identifiers: LCCN 2020057830 |
ISBN 9781476666426 (paperback : acid free paper) ∞
ISBN 9781476641621 (ebook)
Subjects: LCSH: Lecter, Hannibal (Fictitious character),
1933– | Harris, Thomas, 1940– Television adaptations. | Hannibal (Television program : 2013-2015) | Thrillers (Television programs)—United States—History and criticism.
Classification: LCC PN1992.77.H336 H36 2021 | DDC 791.45/72—dc23
LC record available at https://lccn.loc.gov/2020057830

BRITISH LIBRARY CATALOGUING DATA ARE AVAILABLE

ISBN (print) 978-1-4766-6642-6
ISBN (ebook) 978-1-4766-4162-1

Front cover images © 2021 Shutterstock

———

Printed in the United States of America

McFarland & Company, Inc., Publishers
Box 611, Jefferson, North Carolina 28640
www.mcfarlandpub.com

To my wife, children, and family:
Thank you for your tireless support.

To my mentors and all those who taught me
in some way over the years: Thank you for
your continued support. I hope to
carry on your great work.

To Bryan Fuller and the writers, producers, cast,
and all who worked on *Hannibal*: We hope you
enjoy our design. Everybody in this book
certainly loved yours.
—Kyle A. Moody

To my friends, mentors, and teachers:
Thank you all for your continued support.

To Bryan Fuller and the entire *Hannibal* team,
may you all continue to cook up and serve
incredible stories for decades to come.
—Nicholas A. Yanes

Table of Contents

Acknowledgments

Kyle A. Moody: There are far too many people to acknowledge on this long and strange trip through *Hannibal*'s many twists and turns, so if I fail to properly address all those who helped foster this book's long journey to publication I apologize in advance.

I want to thank my wife and my rock Maricruz for always being there for me. Whether it was proofreading work, offering advice and support, or simply placing that hand on my shoulder when I always needed it, you have never wavered in your support for me. I wouldn't have completed this journey without you. I also thank my children, both of whom make every day better than the last. You make me laugh and relax and remember that this design would be far less interesting without you as a part of it.

This journey was made possible by all the honorable academics who supported me throughout my education and training. From my beginning years at Western Kentucky University to my master's degree in mass communication at Miami University, I had a sturdy foundation of powerful academics and teachers that gave me strength, wisdom, and courage to pursue my dreams. To Dr. Marjorie Yambor, Dr. Karen Schneider, Dr. Bruce Drushel, Dr. Ronald Scott, Dr. Lisa McLaughlin, Dr. David Sholle, Dr. Howard Kleiman, Dr. Ron Becker, Dr. David Sholle, and Dr. Judith Weiner, I cannot thank you enough for the inspiration to seek out truth and joy within the hallowed halls of the academy. You guided me and gave me strength to enter a Ph.D. program. I was lucky to walk in your footsteps, and I look forward to where my journey takes me next with your guidance.

The University of Iowa School of Journalism and Mass Communication has been a major factor in my growth as a scholar and as a human being. When I walked into the building in 2009, I could not have foreseen where this odyssey would take me. It was through the strength of character and overwhelming support provided by the excellent faculty that I was able to make it through this program, and I am lucky to have worked with them all. In particular, Dr. David Perlmutter (now at Texas Tech) and Dr. Venise Berry were invaluable as advisors and mentors. They taught me how to write and how to reach higher in the academy. I was also able to navigate my teaching assistantship with the help of Dr. Frank Durham, Dr. Gigi Durham, and Dr. Julie Andsager. I was extremely fortunate to work with Dr. André L. Brock and Dr. Bonnie Sunstein during my time at Iowa. They taught me about fieldwork, rhetoric, qualitative analysis, and critical pedagogy. It was an absolute thrill to write this book as a culmination of my studies. Finally, I want to thank Jon Winet and Nikki JD White at Iowa's Digital Scholarship and Publishing Studio. I would not have made it in my final year without your help in addressing public social media, event management, and interactive learning mechanisms during my assistantship. You make me proud to have been a Hawkeye, and you made the University of Iowa a wonderful place to earn my doctorate.

I've been blessed to have many peers along the way, all of whom have done much to keep this dude writing and thinking. To J.J. Sylvia IV, Rob Carr, Shawn Harmsen, Samuel Tobin, Jeff Warmouth, Joseph Wachtel, Rauf Arif, Lamia Zia, Marilda Oviedo, Ulysses Youngblood, Catherine Buell, Jennifer Berg, Sean Goodlett, Mary Baker, Randy Howe, Charles Sides, Wayne Munson, Viera Lorencova, Adam Rugg, Josh Pederson, James Carviou, Ben Morton, Jennifer Turchi, and countless others, I would not have made it without you. You have been there for me when I needed it, and you have helped me go further than I ever thought possible.

Finally, I must thank my ever-patient friend and colleague Nicholas A. Yanes for being a coeditor on this excellent work. I've been friends with Nick ever since we met in our respective doctoral programs at the University of Iowa. We have always pushed each other, sometimes competed with each other, and strove for more every day. Whether it was spending long nights addressing formatting or collecting important documents for publishing, or just arguing about comic books and movies long into the day over bourbon, this book would not have happened without him. Working with him has been hugely rewarding, and at times it feels like he has been the Hannibal to my Will. I have been deeply lucky to call you a coeditor, and even luckier to call you a friend, Nick.

Nicholas A. Yanes: Like all people who have written an acknowledgment section for a text that they have worked on, I have to take a moment to shine a spotlight on those who have greatly helped me on this project. As expected, I'm perpetually thankful to my family and friends (both real and imaginary) for providing moral support for this endeavor. I'd like to also thank Thomas Harris, Bryan Fuller, Martha De Laurentiis, Hugh Dancy, Mads Mikkelsen, Laurence Fishburne, Gillian Anderson, and everyone who worked on *Hannibal* for bringing this show into existence.

Every successful academic stands on the shoulders of the fantastic mentors that they've had along the way. From my undergraduate time at Florida Atlantic University's Harriet L. Wilkes Honors College to the now gone, but not forgotten American Studies Program at Florida State University, I have been fortunate to have had phenomenal professors who invested greatly into my future. To Dr. Christopher Strain, Dr. Laura Barrett, Dr. John Fenstermaker, Dr. Amanda Porterfield and Dr. Margaret (Peggy) Wright-Cleveland, you are the five professors I had that inspired, encouraged and guided me towards going for my Ph.D. And on the subject of a Ph.D., I'd like to also thank the University of Iowa's Dr. Laura Rigal, Dr. Brooks Landon, Dr. David Dowling, and Dr. Deborah Whaley. They are faculty members who helped me grow as an academic and have continued to offer me mentorship even after I've earned my doctorate. So, know these two things, whatever I do, it's your fault, and thank you.

And I'd finally like to thank Kyle A. Moody. As a friend for nearly a decade, Kyle has been an accomplice in many of my misadventures and bad ideas. So, I am deeply grateful he took a chance to join on me on the never-ending hangover that is creating and publishing an academic book. Here's to several more decades of great stories coming from bad ideas.

Introduction

The Hors d'Oeuvre

KYLE A. MOODY *and* NICHOLAS A. YANES

Bryan Fuller's *Hannibal* ends with the main characters William Graham and Hannibal Lecter falling off a cliff. The two men are covered in blood after they have just killed Francis "The Great Red Dragon" Dolarhyde; an act of violence that was depicted with deeply sexual overtones. Stunned by the beauty of blood in the moonlight, Graham and Lecter embrace one another just as Graham pulls the pair off a bluff toward the violent waters deep below. While we don't know for sure what happens to the pair, viewers are left with an image of Gillian Anderson's Bedelia Du Maurier in a beautiful dress sitting before a decorated dinner table with her left leg having been amputated, cooked, and on display as a meal.

Hannibal's ending was like the series as a whole: a cinematically beautiful and narratively breathtaking experience that left us (Moody and Yanes) wanting more. The hunger to continue to enjoy this world that Fuller created is what inspired us to begin this project. Unfortunately, we both encountered unexpected personal difficulties. We say this because we have been blown away by not just the quality of work contributors gave us, but because we are extremely humbled by the professionalism and patience the academics in this collection showed. Academic projects have a tendency to take longer than initially expected, but we are still so grateful that every person in this project understood the effort we were investing. For that, we are forever grateful to the contributors in this collection.

This work would not have been possible without the excellent contributions by all our authors and also by those who put together their work in a timely fashion. Our authors focused on crime, romance, mythology, food, gender and sexuality, fan studies, and the gothic nature of a show. Not too bad for a program that lasted three seasons and barely made a dent in broadcast or DVR ratings. This speaks to the devoted nature of *Hannibal*

1

fans and their intense interest in the show, which was more than just a television series. *Hannibal* was art that inspired devotion and interest, and these essays highlight the diversity of content within the program.

Lisa Rufus explores how bodies become constructions of power and representative character in the initial essay. Her examination of Dr. Hannibal Lecter's choice to display his work as a sort of calling card reflects how our culture associates actions with visual representation. This is also linked to the visual artistry of the show, which is predicated on adaptation of the work of Thomas Harris while also expanding the palette of content available on the show.

Kirsty Worrow's essay "My Darling Cannibal: The Mechanics of Perverse Allegiance in *Hannibal*" explores how *Hannibal*'s production team carefully formed a unique bond with its audience that promoted Hannibal Lecter to a protagonist role. Her argument is that the narrative itself is concocted around upending expectations for the audience, which only extends the tension inherent within the story of Lecter and Will Graham. She connects Lecter to Romantic Gothic stories and argues that the story has been elevated to this through the reflexive interaction of text, producer and spectator.

Nicole Michaud Wild's essay "Empathy for the Audience: *Hannibal*, the Fannibals and What Happens When a Show Takes Its Fandom Seriously" is a fantastic addition to fan studies scholarship, highlighting how the intersection between production and fandom increased audience viability and visibility during production. The emergence of "Fannibals" also highlighted the intersection of LGBTQ+ content within the program, which was entirely intentional based on creator Bryan Fuller's background.

Samantha McLaren highlights "Bodies That Change: Transformation, Body Dysmorphia and the Malleability of Identity in Bryan Fuller's *Hannibal*." Her work explores the ways in which the body functions in *Hannibal* as both a site for transformation and as a material that is susceptible to being transformed. Her essay discusses how Lecter's human subjects are dismantled and repurposed for his own benefit—along with those of the viewer—then examines the resemblances between Lecter's view of ethics and aesthetics and that displayed in Gothic texts of the fin-de-siècle period. She convincingly argues that these texts, like *Hannibal*, are often deeply preoccupied with the threats and possibilities inherent in transgressing the realm of the unified human subject.

Naja Later's essay "Cannibalizing Hannibal: The Horrific and Appetizing Rewriting of *Hannibal* Mythology" explores how the medium of television itself was ideal for a recreation of Harris' work. The remixing of content to fit the medium of television and Fuller's ideal is part of the greater revision of *Hannibal*'s source material, along with placing political and social changes within the text of the story. This content sits comfortably alongside continually evolving intellectual property, and the revisions only benefit the narrative.

Megan Fowler takes a different approach to adaptation in her essay "'If I saw you every day, forever, I'd remember this time': Deconstructing Gender Performance and Heteronormativity Through Adaptation." This essay analyzes the ways in which the *Hannibal* TV series as an adaptation "queers" the original Hannibal film and book franchise by reproducing dialogue and re-framing of Hannibal Lecter's heterosexual love interest Clarice Starling with male lead Will Graham in her position. Fowler argues that *Hannibal* "gender-bends" Clarice's feminist protagonist into the male Will, helping to push the adaptation into new territory while maintaining the authorial intent of Harris. Moreover, the asexual but undeniably romantic relationship between Will and Hannibal helps to create new queer meanings from the original franchise.

Lorianne Reuser's essay "Go with the Flow: Will Graham and Liminality in Bryan Fuller's *Hannibal*" explores the meaning of time and consciousness within the program.

Vittoria Lion's essay "Eating Exquisite Corpses and Drinking New Wine: The Chesapeake Ripper as the Authentic Surreal Murderer" places the first season's alter ego of Hannibal within the role of other serial killers in the popular consciousness. Her work explores the identity of serial murderers and their representation within popular fiction such as *Hannibal*. Lion's essay vacillates between actual serial killings and the fantastical methods of *Hannibal*'s criminal class, illustrating how the empathy illustrated by Will Graham pushes the reader to understand if not embrace the outré villains of the program.

Megan McAllister's focus on "Food Culture in *Hannibal*" allows for a unique perspective into the appetizing representation of cannibalism onscreen. The prominent utilization of food within the show not only illustrates character for the titular character, but is also meant to be a wry commentary on the proceedings within the narrative. This places the show within a bigger framework of popular culture. Food culture grew in stature during the production of the show due to socially mediated communication platforms such as Instagram, so the program gained new viewership through its loving depiction of *haute cuisine* onscreen.

Anamarija Horvat's essay "Matchless in His Irony: Divinity and the Aesthetics of Death in Bryan Fuller's *Hannibal*" focuses on the intense relationship between death and representation of godhood within the show. Hannibal's use of religious iconography is tied with his death tableaus during the program. This is matched with the linkage between divinity and worship that many of the cannibal's admirers express to him, particularly during the second season. Horvat's work focuses on how aesthetic horror can also be linked to artistic beauty and depth.

Sarah Cleary's essay, "It's a Matter of Taste: Bourdieu and the Impeccably Mannered Anthropophagite," explores the relationship between cultural capital and Hannibal's focus on squelching rudeness in all its forms. The link between taste and victims illustrates how the morality on display in the show pushes Hannibal into a place of protagonism, in spite of his overwhelming focus on being the representative cannibal within the show. In fact, the program goes out of its way to depict Hannibal as structured and confident, while also keeping his vision of a society that is set up around culture he sees fit to reproduce.

Simon Bacon's "Stranger in a Strange Land: *Hannibal* as an Adaptation of Stoker's and Browning's *Dracula*" places the program within the narrative canon of societally approved monsters, illustrating how Lecter's vampiric qualities and "otherness" makes him an extension of Stoker and Browning's classic text. Bacon also illustrates how Hannibal creates a newer form of society through his actions, essentially rewriting the moral code of his area.

Olimpia Calì's "Pygmalion of a Broken Mind: Physical and Mental Desire in Will Graham and Hannibal Lecter's Relationship" "explores how Will Graham's broken mind becomes a means of reconfiguration, especially for Hannibal as he reconstitutes Will's experiences into his own narrative." This is largely because Will is seen by Hannibal as a potential friend and replicate of himself. For this reason, Hannibal starts to push Will to his limits, manipulating his mind and his thoughts until Will cannot understand what is real and what it is not. While Hannibal should help Will to heal from his mental disease, Hannibal instead makes him feel worse and develops a symbiotic relationship in which Will needs him even though he understands that Hannibal is dangerous to his mind.

Building on this collection's examinations of adaptation, Evelyn Deshane's contribution "Gender/Animal Suits: Adapting Buffalo Bill from *The Silence of the Lambs* to NBC's *Hannibal*" takes on the near impossible task of linking the iconic Buffalo Bill to the series without explicitly mentioning them. Not only was this a difficult character to bring to television after their ground-breaking appearance in *The Silence of the Lambs*, but Deshane manages to connect this character to real world people they are based on, showing how the series is much more than an endlessly referential text.

The end of the book examines what *Hannibal* means for a variety of cultural forces, emphasizing how the show illustrates changes within particular industrial and social areas. Evan Hayles Gledhill's text "Queer(y)ing Adaptation: Bryan Fuller's *Hannibal* as Slash Fiction Gothic Romance" argues that Fuller nominally pushes the show into unexplored territory for mainstream television by combining the gothic romance with the traditions of slash fiction. She states that Fuller is attempting to challenge normative values of and in quality television series and queer fiction's place in the margins of the mainstream.

In his essay, "An Art Form That Honors Aesthetic and Taste: The Art of Murder and the Art of Television in *Hannibal*," Michael Fuchs touches on a question for the ages: Can television be considered "art"? His discussion of the visual grammar of *Hannibal* is based on the idea that it is a remediation of painting and high culture artifacts. This is a key to understanding both the artistic merits of the show and the bigger academic lessons *Hannibal* can teach us.

Finally, coeditor Kyle A. Moody's text illustrates how the relationship between Fannibals and show creator and showrunner Fuller is expanded through Twitter and other media. The use of social media as a means of connecting with audiences is now expected for the televisual medium, with Fuller exemplifying this usage to highlight how his voice has been used to translate Harris's texts. It is also a means of emphasizing the shifting nature of the showrunner, from a quiet guiding voice to the visible production leader that must interact with the public. *Hannibal* illustrates how Fuller's evolution and growth in Hollywood is also commensurate with his values, creating a unique intersection of LGBTQ+ growth and visibility for creators through programming.

In addition to these amazing contributions, this collection also contains original interviews with one of *Hannibal*'s executive producers, Martha De Laurentiis, as well as two writers who worked on the show, Tom de Ville and Nick Antosca. Martha De Laurentiis has a history in entertainment production going back to the early 1980s and was a producer on the films *Hannibal* (2001), *Red Dragon* (2002), and *Hannibal Rising* (2007). In addition to writing for the *Hannibal* television show, Tom de Ville has also written for *Urban Gothic* and *Stan Lee's Lucky Man*. Nick Antosca has written for *Hannibal* and has worked on shows such as *Teen Wolf*, *Last Resort*, and *Believe*. After writing for *Hannibal*, he has gone on to create the shows *Channel Zero* and *The Act*. While these interviews may lack the academic rhetoric other contributions in this book have, the Q&As with these creators provide an important look at the production of *Hannibal* specifically and television in general. These illustrate how the professional interests and creative impulses of the *Hannibal* team are linked with the greater academic studies that the show has produced.

Overall, we hope that this book highlights the myriad ways Bryan Fuller's *Hannibal* inspired its academic fans and allowed fans to recontextualize the franchise that Hannibal Lecter cooked for us.

As we finish this book, it has been announced that Alex Kurtzman will be spearheading a television show for CBS tentatively titled *Clarice*, a sequel to *The Silence of the Lambs* that focuses on Clarice Starling and avoids the use of the world's most famous cannibal. The creative team that Kurtzman and CBS put together to bring *Clarice* to life are entitled to have a clear slate for them to create their own version of whatever mental palace Thomas Harris's work inspires. However, we do hope that a legacy of Fuller's opus that echoes in *Clarice* will be that this franchise is not just a standard procedural crime drama. *Hannibal* showed that this franchise is elastic and that its characters and stories could be updated to reflect a myriad of complex and deep themes. This is because Dr. Hannibal Lecter isn't just a cannibal, he's an artist; Lecter isn't just a criminal, he is a being who has so perfected himself that he compares himself to humans as we compare ourselves to cattle. In short, the Hannibal Lecter franchise could be used to serve the entertainment equivalent of fast food, but it is at its core a gourmet meal served at a Michelin 3-star restaurant. Whatever form it takes, we look forward to seeing Hannibal's next design.

Giving Voice to the Unmentionable

How Hannibal Lecter Uses Bodies
in the Television Series Hannibal

Lisa Rufus

When we first encounter Doctor Hannibal Lecter in Bryan Fuller's television series *Hannibal*, we do not see him; we hear him. Hannibal's introduction in the episode "Apéritif" is accompanied by the introduction to Johann Sebastian Bach's *Goldberg Variations*. The *Aria Da Capo*, referred to in Thomas Harris' novels and heard in three of the five film adaptations is, in essence, Hannibal's theme song.

The *Aria* plays over the polished sheen of a black marble table top. The camera tilts up slowly to reveal a beautifully presented meal, and we hear the clink of silverware against an expensive porcelain plate. The camera draws us closer to Hannibal as one would approach any predatory carnivore: cautiously, without making eye contact. He skewers a piece of liver from his plate onto a fork, lifts it to his mouth, and eats. Light from above casts shadows down his face. With hollowed sockets and sunken cheeks Hannibal looks straight towards us. He knows we are watching. He seduces us into becoming accessories to his crimes and we comply most willingly.

Although he does not say a word, this brief scene contains valuable information about this incarnation of Hannibal Lecter. For those familiar with the character, the sight of the meal prompts us to recall that Hannibal's preferred source of protein is morally problematic. The exquisite elements of *mise-en-scéne* are emblematic of Hannibal's renowned rarefied tastes and aesthetic sensibilities.

In his essay "Hannibal at the Lectern" John Goodrich notes that previous manifestations of the character, such as Hannibal in *Red Dragon*, have been "impossible to evaluate" due to the fact that the character has been imprisoned for much of his story, thus leaving his actions "severely limited."[1] But in the television series, we are given the opportunity to witness Hannibal during the prime of his criminal career, free from judicial suspicion, and as a practicing psychiatrist.

Goodrich also says, "If we want to understand who the character is, we need to understand what needs he serves in his actions."[2] These new conditions pose new questions: Who is this new Hannibal Lecter and how does he differ from past versions of the character?

Hannibal's motives are not exposited via voiceover from the eponymous character's inner monolog. Hannibal keeps his thoughts private, leaving the audience to seek other means to inquire into his character. The audience can do this through the observations of Will Graham as he gets to know Hannibal while they work together, and also as Will creates psychological profiles of the Chesapeake Ripper and Copycat Killer by examining their crime scenes.

John Douglas and Corrine Munn tell us that crime scenes can elicit a great deal of information regarding a person's behavior: "The same forces that influence normal everyday conduct also influence the offender's actions during an offense."[3] With this in mind, this essay focuses on how Hannibal uses the bodies of his victims by means of adaptation, transformation, communication, and consumption and what the findings can tell us about how series creator, Bryan Fuller, has constructed the "very well-tailored person suit" worn by his version of Hannibal Lecter.[4] The bodies of Hannibal's murder victims are presented with a terrific theatricality and are viewed by characters in the diegesis as aesthetic objects. This artistic reconceptualization of the corpse speaks volumes about the nature of the character and warrants further academic discussion.

Narrative television's extended story temporality, particularly seriality, grants more time for the audience to spend with the character—much more than the mere sixteen minutes that Hannibal Lecter was seen on screen during the film *The Silence of the Lambs*. *Hannibal*'s thirteen-episode season provides the audience with a greater insight into the public and private personae of the psychiatrist/cannibal as we see him form relationships with some characters and manipulate others. The extra time allows for more opportunities for Hannibal to interact with bodies and for the program's highly stylized visuals to flaunt Hannibal's appetite for beautiful things. By using forensic investigation techniques, we are also given the opportunity to study Hannibal's criminality including his *modus operandi* and construction of crime scenes—much can be revealed in how a murderer interacts with their victims after death. Together, these circumstances have a pivotal effect on how we view Hannibal Lecter as what we already know about the character is both amplified and complicated by the television series.

Adaptation

> **WILL:** This Copycat is an avid reader of Freddie Lounds and TattleCrime.com. He had intimate knowledge of Garret Jacob Hobbs' murders, motives, patterns; enough to recreate them and arguably, elevate them to art.[5]

When constructing a psychological profile of a killer, former FBI Profiler John Douglas gives us this advice: "If you want to understand the artist, you have to look at the painting."[6] Body placement, victimology, cause of death, each individual element of a crime scene, each brushstroke, can be studied to provide insight into the killers' motivations and character.

During the first season of *Hannibal*, we are shown the bodies or parts of bodies of nineteen of Hannibal Lecter's victims (not including Miriam Lass), many of which are presented with a macabre extravagance. The FBI does not know that Hannibal is responsible for these killings, so they are attributed to an unidentified "Copycat." Following a close analysis of Hannibal's crime scenes, a pattern emerges—the way Hannibal stages the bodies of his victims is similar to the *modi operandi* of other killers seen in the first season. But Hannibal is no mere copycat.

Linda Hutcheon defines adaptation as an "acknowledged transposition of a recognisable other work or works [and a] creative and an interpretive act of appropriation/salvaging."[7] With this definition in mind, we can examine how Hannibal uses bodies as adaptations by focusing on the murders of Cassie Boyle in episode one, and Jeremy Olmstead in episode six. These victims have been selected for analysis because Cassie Boyle is the first victim we see from this adaptation of Hannibal, and the murder of Jeremy Olmstead is one of the murders that appear both in the novels and in the television series which allows us to make a comparison. Analyzing the bodies of Olmstead and Boyle also provide the opportunity to track the evolution of a creative concept as Hannibal is influenced by outside forces and how these are reflected in his works.

Midway through the first episode "Apéritif," our screen is filled with the image of a pecking raven.[8] The sound of the bird's throaty call is accompanied by the hollow chimes of tolling tubular bells. Another raven flaps its black wings to seek balance. Through a series of quick, fragmented edits we are shown the source of their fare. Placed in the middle of a field is the murdered body of Cassie Boyle, impaled on the head of a trophy stag. Her naked body is bolstered by flesh-piercing antlers while her lifeless limbs hang. Her feet are suspended in the air—fingertips caress the rocks on the ground. Haloed by the afternoon sun, her head hangs back, mouth partly open as if mid-breath. The birds perch on her bare thigh and ribs and puff their feathers. The crime scene investigators respectfully shoo them away.

The dramatic display of Cassie Boyle's naked corpse impaled on a stag's head against a background of yellow grasses and a crisp blue sky makes for a unique image. Cinematographer James Hawkinson brings beauty to a dark, horrible place. Her lungs have been ripped out. The antler piercings have left trails of dried blood down Cassie's cold skin. The image is truly horrific, yet it is also visually stunning.

While the head of the FBI's Behavioral Science Unit, Jack Crawford incorrectly thinks that Boyle was murdered by the same person who killed Elise Nichols earlier in the episode, Special Agent Will Graham has interpreted the crime scene differently: "Whoever tucked Elise Nichols into bed didn't paint this picture." Jack asks, "You think this was a copycat?"[9] But Jack's description of the author of these killings is crude: the word *copy* conjures images of cheap knock-offs and "being secondary."[10]

If we apply Hutcheon's definition of adaptation to Hannibal's staging of Cassie Boyle's corpse, it becomes clear that Cassie Boyle's murder is not just a copy but an adaptation of how Garret Jacob Hobbs murdered Elise Nichols. During an autopsy earlier in "Apéritif" Beverly Katz reports that Elise's body had also been pierced by deer antlers and her organs had been removed.

Hannibal has adapted the *modus operandi* of Hobbs, but has also added his own flair to his presentation of the corpse by placing rocks at the base of the stag head and staging her body as if it were a trophy, thus performing the "creative and interpretive act of appropriation/salvaging" that Hutcheon described.[11] A key feature of Hannibal's post mortem interactions with the bodies of his victims is that the product of adaptation is different to its source material. As mentioned before, Hannibal does not merely copy, he reinterprets the original texts and adds his own signature, making them his own works.

This is very similar to the Greek concept of *imitatio* which is "not slavish copying; [but] it is a process of making the material one's own."[12] D.A. Russell's writings on *imitatio* also help describe the compulsion for artistic dominance we see in Hannibal Lecter: "You must make the thing 'your own' … and the way you do this is to select, to modify, and at all costs to avoid treading precisely and timidly in the footsteps of the man in front."[13] If Hannibal were to slavishly copy the works of other serial killers and follow timidly in their footsteps, then his adaptations would be indistinguishable from others and bland—one thing Hannibal is not.

During a lecture Will gives on the Copycat he notes the differences between Hobbs' method and that of the Copycat: "The killer who did kill [Cassie Boyle] wanted us to know he wasn't the Minnesota Shrike, he was better than that."[14] Jack notes in "Relevés" that the Copycat goes "further" than the original killings.[15] One of the goals of *imitatio* is that the new author must "surpass their predecessors."[16] Hannibals' killings surpass their source materials: they are more artful, more complete, and more gruesome than those of any other killers we encounter in the season. Jack notes in "Relevés" the Copycat goes "further" than the original killings and provides the adaptations with something more.[17] He rips out Cassie Boyle's lungs while she's still alive; he decapitates Dr. Donald Sutcliffe's head from the jaw; he savagely eviscerates Andrew Caldwell, then harvests his organs. All of Hannibal's killings, all graphically represented, are more brutal and sadistic than those whom he adapts because *this* Hannibal is more brutal and sadistic than any the audience has seen before. He uses corpses as a way to express his artistic bent and, as Will Graham recognizes, "elevate[s] them to art."[18] The number of Hannibal's victims, and the fastidious level of detail he employs to create these macabre masterpieces, clearly demonstrates that his art brings him pleasure. He relishes the awe his creations inspire, particularly how Will sees them as aesthetic objects to be admired and appreciated.

Another notable alteration to Hobbs' method is that Hannibal has placed the dead body of Cassie Boyle in the middle of a field. This is in stark contrast to what Hobbs did to his other victims. Will asks Jack if they have found any remains of the missing eight girls that are presumed to murdered by Hobbs, to which Jack says they have "no bodies. No parts of bodies. Nothing that comes out of bodies."[19] Garret Jacob Hobbs' philosophy towards killing is a holistic one and he believes that all parts of a corpse should be put to use: "[W]e will honor every part of [Elise Nichols]. None of her will go to waste. Eating her is honoring her. Otherwise it's just murder."[20] Hannibal deviates from this rationale as he does not honor the body, nor the life, of Cassie Boyle, he only uses her liver. The rest of her is propped up in a field like a prize, dishonored and murdered. This kind of ostentatious behavior is because, as Thomas Fahy says, Lecter's "crimes are, in part, all about visibility."[21] Hannibal puts Cassie Boyle's corpse in a field so it can be seen. He sees the corpse as a thing of beauty and like all things of beauty they should be looked upon, worshipped.

Hutcheon likens the process of adaptation to evolution particularly in the way an object mutates and adjusts to suit its new environment.[22] Hannibal's theatrical display of bodies evolves as the character is represented in different media and one that is greatly intensified in the television series.

Of the nineteen murders committed by Hannibal that are discussed in the first season of *Hannibal*, eight of these are adaptations of the works of four other killers. However, there is one victim whose murder is not an adaptation of another killer's work but of a drawing. "Wound Man" is the name given to a medieval sketch that was used as a point of anatomical reference during and after the fourteenth century. The sketch, tells Boyd Hill, is "a figure illustrating various blows and lacerations to the human body by weapons such as clubs and knives."[23] Described by Karl Sudhoff as a "Saint Sebastian distorted into a surgical grotesque," the Wound Man's accompanying text prescribes specialized treatment for each type of wound portrayed on the body.[24] Hutcheon tells us, before an adaptation is attempted, one must first "have their own personal reasons for deciding first to do an adaptation and then choosing which adapted work and what medium to do it in."[25]

In the novel *Hannibal* (1999), Clarice tells Warden Moody about Hannibal's sixth murder victim and former patient who was also named Jeremy Olmstead and presented in a similar fashion to Jeremy Olmstead of the television series: "He left him hanging from a peg board with all sorts of wounds in him. He left him like a medieval medical illustration called Wound Man. He's interested in medieval things."[26]

Hannibal's interest in medieval things carries over to the television series and with it, a preoccupation with the study of wounded and wounding bodies. We see Jeremy Olmstead's corpse during a flashback in episode six, "Entrée." The events in the flashback occurred two years earlier. His body lies on a table in his workshop surrounded by lathes, jigsaws, and busy benches. The monochromatic palette adds a horrifying filter to what is shown to the audience. Pools of blood on the concrete floor are thick and tarry, along with the punctures and slashes on Jeremy's torso. His corpse resembles a metal-shop worker's pincushion. Hammers, pliers, iron rods, screwdrivers, all protrude from his flesh.

When adapting a text, one may use the original medium or select a different platform. This "transcoding" incorporates the physical qualities of the new medium.[27] The corpse of Jeremy Olmstead has been adapted into a real-life rendering of Wound Man with a radical change in medium from paper and pencil to a human body and sharp objects.

Hannibal eviscerates his victims and turns their corpses into pageantry because it brings him pleasure. This indulgent aspect of Hannibal's nature, while evident in previous incarnations, whether directly witnessed or indirectly reported, is dramatically expanded upon in the television series and its graphic depiction of Hannibals' victims.

Manipulation

> **WILL:** I've been sleepwalking, experiencing hallucinations. Maybe I should get a brain scan.[28]

In his book *Palimpsests: Literature in the Second Degree*, Gérard Genette discusses what must be done in order to achieve a successful adaptation: "in order to imitate a text it is inevitably necessary to acquire at least a partial mastery of it, a mastery of that specific quality which one has chosen to imitate."[29] Hutcheon also agrees that a deep level of engagement with a text is crucial before attempting to adapt it, "for the adapter is an interpreter before becoming a creator."[30] To Hannibal, Will Graham is a text and throughout the first season Hannibal gains a mastery of Will's composition. Hannibal instigates his process of physiologically and psychologically manipulating Will Graham in the pilot episode by using another serial killer as a catalyst.

Hannibal becomes curious about Will during their first meeting together with Jack Crawford, and he is quick to fashion a foundational theory of Will's psyche: "I imagine what you see and learn touches everything else in our mind. Your values and decency are present yet shocked at your associations, appalled at your dreams. No forts in the bone arena of your skull for the things you love."[31] Will is visibly stunned that Hannibal can tell so much about him after such a brief encounter and leaves the room. While Will's empathy disorder frightens him, Hannibal realizes potential in his unique mindset as something to be crafted and exploited. But Hannibal must first understand how Will's mind works before he can mold it.

In "Apéritif" Will Graham suspects pipe-fitter Garret Jacob Hobbs as the murderer of eight girls. When alone, Hannibal calls Hobbs to warn him that the FBI is on to him. Hannibal's warning has dual functions. First, as a keen student of human behavior, Hannibal is curious as to how Hobbs, an established killer, will react now that the FBI is coming to apprehend him. Second, Hannibal is also curious as to how Will Graham will act in the impending situation and to see whether or not Will has the capacity to take a human life. Hannibal's curiosity results in the death of two people. Hobbs slits his wife's throat and tries to do the same to his daughter, Abigail, but Will shoots Hobbs and saves Abigail's life. Hannibal walks into the blood-soaked kitchen in time to see Hobbs' bullet-ridden body slump dead on the floor.

Will refuses to participate in any structured form of psychiatric therapy in order to deal with this traumatic event, but he does agree to have "conversations" with Hannibal.[32] Through these conversations Hannibal learns about Will and how his mind works. Subtly and perniciously, Hannibal suggests to Will that he may not be true to his nature. Later, Hannibal explains to his own psychiatrist, Dr. Bedelia Du Maurier, his intentions regarding Will Graham. "He has flaws in intuitive beliefs about what makes him who he is. I'm trying to help him understand."[33]

While Will vehemently attests to the horror he felt shooting Hobbs, Hannibal is not so sure of Will's conviction. Hannibal tugs at Will's moralistic view on killing as being "the ugliest thing in the world" and offers a loophole: "It's the inevitability of there being a man so bad that killing him felt good."[34] Will confesses, "I liked killing Hobbs."[35]

Will's mental state deteriorates throughout the first season. In episode ten, "Buffet Froid," he has an MRI scan under the watchful eye of neurologist Dr. Donald Sutcliffe, who is also a colleague of Hannibal's. The scan shows that Will is suffering from anti NMDA-receptor encephalitis, a debilitating disease that affects cognitive functions and causes hallucinations and black outs. Untreated, the disease can be fatal; however, Hannibal persuades Sutcliffe to withhold Will's diagnosis from him for professional gain. "A doctor has to weigh the ultimate benefit of scientific study. Even in these times, we know so little about the brain. There are great discoveries to be made."[36] As a direct result of Hannibal Lecter's actions, Will's distress physically manifests as high-grade fevers, loss of time, disorientation, and ultimately a neurological seizure.

He suffers great physical and psychological pain and Hannibal does nothing to ease it. Hannibal takes advantage of Will's weakening mental state and incorporates it into part of his process of manipulating Will's mindset as he becomes more malleable and less resistant to change.

But why does Hannibal do this to Will Graham? What needs are served by manipulating Will into believing that he enjoys killing? John Goodrich has an explanation for similar behaviors witnessed between Hannibal and Clarice Starling in both *The Silence of the Lambs* and in the novel *Hannibal* and that is, quite simply, "to stave off loneliness."[37] Goodrich continues, "This is the basic, fundamental need for companionship. Lecter knows he is unlikely to meet anyone like himself, and so he must make someone."[38]

The persona Hannibal shares with the public is relatively open. He is a member of Baltimore's cultural elite—he attends symphonies and hosts dinner parties for other members. But his private persona, the one he has hidden for so long, is closed off to the world. The Chesapeake Ripper is not able to share the success of his latest killings with anyone, let alone argue their aesthetic merits. He wants to share with Will the power that God feels when he drops a roof on praying grandmothers. Hannibal and Will are connected by the tremendous isolation they deal with in their private lives. Hannibal is transforming Will, helping him seek out what Hannibal believes to be his true self, so he can experience a mutual relationship with someone who can know him as Hannibal and as the Chesapeake Ripper.

During one of their sessions, Bedelia comments on Hannibal's inability to form relationships: "It must be so lonely." Hannibal is quick to retort, "I have friends, and the opportunities for friends."[39] The themes of friendship and loneliness weave their way through the episode until we see how cognizant Bedelia is when Will misses an appointment with Hannibal.

The heaviness of the "Lacrimosa" from Mozart's *Requiem Mass* fills the scene in "Sorbet" with its melancholic weight as Hannibal opens his office door to an empty waiting room. He sits back at his desk in his even emptier office. Ascending and descending violins pine as Hannibal places his hand on his telephone, but he does not use it. He then checks his appointment book: "W. Graham 7:30pm." Will is late. Hannibal leaves his office in Baltimore, Maryland, and we next see him in Will Graham's office in Quantico, Virginia. Hannibal drives interstate to remind one of his patients of his twenty-four hour cancellation policy, something he could have easily achieved over the telephone. But Will is not just one of his patients, as Hannibal tells Bedelia in a later episode, "Will is my friend."[40]

After lengthy fireside conversations, a bond forms between the two men. Despite Hannibal's sadistic methods to reveal Will's true nature, he feels that he is doing the best for Will. But as Will is slowly molded into the ideal self that Hannibal projects on to him, he begins to see the motivations of the enigmatic Chesapeake Ripper.

Communication

> **WILL:** [H]e's telling us how to catch him. Actually, he's telling you. Where was the last place you saw a severed arm, Jack?[41]

In her book *Detecting Men: Masculinity and the Hollywood Detective Film*, Philippa Gates discusses how, in the world of crime fiction, the body can be "read as a text."[42] Serial killers use a "code or language" that is ingrained in the killer's work which, "if analysed and interpreted correctly, gives clues to the killer's identity...."[43] The investigator becomes a "semiotician" as he/she begins to comprehend the killer's language resulting in the body becoming "a mode of communication for the two … one as author (killer) and the other as reader (the detective).[44] In the television series *Hannibal*, Hannibal sends messages to the FBI and he prefers to communicate via corpses.

In "Entrée" the camera begins high above Dr. Lecter's workspace, allowing us a moment to admire the neat arrangement of items on his polished wooden desk. Leather-bound journals, a marble inkwell, a silver letter opener shines like a scalpel in the lamplight—all tools used to communicate one's thoughts. In his left hand is a small tablet computer from which he reads Criminal Justice Journalist Freddie Loundes' website, Tattle-Crime.com.

Freddie's article is about another serial killer and permanent resident in the Baltimore State Hospital for the Criminally Insane, Dr. Abel Gideon. When he is taken to the hospital wing for treatment, he kills a nurse. He impales her body with IV stands, legs from beds and chairs, and other pointed implements close at hand. The spikes and poles prop up the dead nurse's corpse; blood drenches her once-white whites. The image is eerily familiar to the staging of Cassie Boyle's corpse.

The article is part of a plan hatched by Will and Jack Crawford to flush the Chesapeake Ripper out in the open. A precognizant Will predicts the Ripper's response to another killer taking credit for his work: "If he is a plagiarist, the real Chesapeake Ripper is going to make sure everybody knows it."[45]

Freddie's voiceover discusses the possibility that Abel Gideon could be the Chesapeake Ripper. Like Hannibal, we know this is not true. Hannibal reads on, his right elbow rested on the table, hand up close to his face. Non-diegetic bells toll, creating a hollow sense of unease; the more Freddie reads, the more bells we hear. Her voice continues, "Maybe, just maybe, Gideon is the most sought-after serial killer at large; a killer who has eluded the FBI for years and has baffled their most gifted profilers. That serial killer? None other than the Chesapeake Ripper."[46] Behavior-wise, the only clue to his internal turmoil is the *flick, flick, flick* of his thumbnail against his index finger. His stoic demeanor is also betrayed by the accompanying soundtrack which gives us a truer representation of Hannibal's state of mind. The cacophony of bells builds while a single high G is struck repeatedly in a *prestissimo* beat, nagging, becoming louder, more incessant like a vexing mosquito after lights out. In the fireplace behind him, flames rage on his behalf. Incited by Freddie's fabricated words, Hannibal responds to the article exactly how Will predicted. However, Hannibal does not use any of the items on his desk to impart this information.

Jack, Will, and Katz are called to an abandoned astronomical observatory where they find the arm of Jack's trainee agent who went missing two years prior. Curiously, the amputated limb does not exhibit any signs of decomposition—it must have been surgically removed recently. Next to the arm is a cream card flecked with the textual imperfections often seen in hand-made paper. Written with a fountain pen in exquisite cursive is a question: "What do you see?" Jack "sees" that this is not the work of Gideon—that Gideon is not the Chesapeake Ripper.

Later in the first season, Hannibal uses another body to communicate with the FBI. In "Rôti" we see psychiatrist Dr. Carson Nahn lying dead on a cold, steel table in the morgue. Next to Dr. Nahn is the corpse of Dr. Paul Carruthers, Gideon's former psychiatrist. They share identical wounds—a total frenectomy or "Colombian Necktie." However, Dr. Nahn possesses an additional wound: his arm has been amputated. Jack thinks Gideon, who recently escaped custody, is responsible for both deaths. Will successfully interprets the murdered corpse of Dr. Nahn as if it were a letter from the

Chesapeake Ripper and concludes: "Abel Gideon didn't kill this man."[47] Gideon only killed Dr. Carruthers.

By looking closer into the circumstances of these two communiqués we can learn more about this latest incarnation of Hannibal Lecter. The messages that Hannibal sends, using the bodies of Miriam Lass and Dr. Nahn, are both "written" after Gideon threatened to hijack his celebrity. In the killings of a nurse and Dr. Caruthers, Gideon blatantly copies Hannibal's technique. During an interview with Will and Alana, Gideon says, "I am the Chesapeake Ripper."[48] He takes credit for Hannibal's works twice, and both times Hannibal must act to reclaim his authorship. The Chesapeake Ripper has become a brand, Hannibal's brand. As with other brands, his is quickly recognizable. He takes great pride in being the Ripper: a name that is frequently seen on mastheads instilling fear among the reading public and the FBI. Gideon, with his plagiaristic proclamations, is an imposter and must be dealt with accordingly. Hannibal sets in place a stratagem that results in Gideon being shot by a delusional Will Graham. His message is crystal clear.

From these two usages of bodies we are also given an insight into how Bryan Fuller's Hannibal differs from previous versions of the character. In "Apéritif" Hannibal telephones Garret Jacob Hobbs to warn him that the FBI are coming for him. Hannibal could have done the same and called the FBI to tip them off as to the whereabouts of Gideon in "Rôti" but instead he uses the body of Dr. Carson Nahn, a well-respected psychiatrist, in the same flippant manner as a post-it note.

After analyzing the deaths of Hannibal's victims in the films, Daniel Shaw notes how, "in the course of all three films (with the exception of Mason Verger's flashback) Hannibal kills only when it is necessary for his escape, or in retaliation against his captors of pursuers, and never for the sheer pleasure of it."[49] While Miriam Lass did fall into the category of pursuer, Dr. Nahn did not.

Dr. Nahn's murder is exceptionally brutal, unnecessary, and a vast departure from Shaws' findings. He posed no threat to Hannibal; he was neither his captor nor pursuer. At this point in the series Hannibal is not under any investigative suspicion which makes Dr. Nahn's death even more horrific. The dismissive nature of this death is chilling and a far cry from the sympathetic response, which Charles Gramlich argues we feel after Hannibal kills Sergeants Pembry and Boyle in *The Silence of the Lambs* as a result of his "need to escape his captivity."[50] In those murders, Hannibal had justification for their deaths, but the murder of Dr. Carson Nahn is unjust. We do not feel sympathy for this Hannibal, but rather fear. Hannibal's reasons for killing have surpassed the typical goal of pursuit and evasion: this reveals a version of the character whose motives are less stringent and more indulgent of his needs.

Consumption

> JACK: What am I about to put in my mouth?
> HANNIBAL: Rabbit.
> JACK: He should have hopped faster
> HANNIBAL: Yes, he should have.[51]

In the film *The Silence of the Lambs*, Hannibal tells us that he once ate a census-taker's liver "with some fava beans and a nice chianti," but we do not see it.[52] Hannibal tears the flesh from Officer Pembry's cheek with his teeth during his daring escape from Tennessee but he does not consume the flesh. In the film *Hannibal*, Hannibal skillfully removes the prefrontal cortex from Paul Krendler's brain while he is still alive and then sautés the extracted organ in a pan with caper berries and white wine. Hannibal offers a piece to Krendler, who cannibalizes himself, but Hannibal does not partake. In the five times that we see Hannibal Lecter on film, we do not actually see him eat human flesh; the foundation for his wickedness exists only in hearsay and innuendo. However, this glaring omission of Hannibal Lecter's most prominent characteristic is swiftly rectified in Bryan Fuller's television series.

The first moment we see Hannibal in episode one he is seated at a dining table, eating. The sight of a serving dish with its contents out of focus dares the viewer to question their origin.

But in case we are still uncertain as to what Hannibal is eating, a second sequence in this first episode eliminates any doubts. As Will Graham stands over the impaled corpse of Cassie Boyle in the field, intercuts featuring Hannibal cooking take us back and forth from one horror to another like a twisted "before and after" or "farm-to-table" transition. Forensic Technician Brian Zeller tells Will what was done to Cassie's body: "He took her lungs. Pretty sure she was alive when he cut them out."[53] Standing in his kitchen, Hannibal has his back to us. From the way he moves his body it appears that he is kneading bread. He is not. Over his shoulder we see human lungs, out of which he pushes the last breaths of Cassie Boyle. Hannibal slices the bright pink meat with a knife. Back to Will Graham telling Jack about the person who killed Cassie: "This girl's killer thought that she was a pig."[54] Hannibal flambés the meat in a pan. We visit Will once more in the field as he begins to wrap his head around this new killer. Finally, we return to our gourmand, dressed for dinner and seated at his dining table amidst an organized clutter of carafes and cutlery. Grinning, he eats Cassie Boyle *á la Lung Bourguignonne*. Unequivocally, this Hannibal *is* a cannibal.

Tony Ullyatt, in his essay, "To Amuse the Mouth: Anthropophagy in Thomas Harris's Tetralogy of Hannibal Lecter Novels," writes that Hannibal "may be seen as a blend of exocannibalism and gastronomic cannibalism with a soupçon of sadistic cannibalism."[55] The features of these three arche-types are as follows:

- Exo-cannibalism is the consumption of outsiders as an act to gain strength or demonstrate power over the vanquished, who have usually been murdered.
- Gastronomic cannibalism is non-funerary, non-starvation cannibalism, that is, routine cannibalism for food.
- Sadistic cannibalism is the killing and eating of individuals out of sadistic or psychopathological motives.[56]

Exocannibalism is defined as cannibalizing those individuals outside of a group of people, as opposed to endocannibalism which involves cannibal-izing individuals within a group.[57] The distinction is interesting because Hannibal is not part of any group. He is different from everybody else, therefore everybody else is an outsider and considered fair game. This is reminiscent of Davide Mana's description regarding the novel *Red Dragon,* which can also apply to Bryan Fuller's Hannibal. Mana argues, "In fact, Lecter is a solipsist character, self-centred like a gyroscope and basically unable to relate in any way with other characters, if not by seeking their corruption, destruction or consummation."[58] Throughout the first season we see Hannibal corrupting Jack by feeding him lies about Will and wreaks havoc on Will's state of mind while at the same time attempting to befriend him. He also threatens, albeit playfully, to consume Dr. Chilton's tongue, "Your tongue is very feisty and as this evening has already proven, it's nice to have an old friend for dinner."[59]

Under the moniker of the Chesapeake Ripper, Hannibal is able to demonstrate his power over the vanquished. The removal of organs is a signature feature of the Rippers' murders and the barbaric display of their corpses also sends a message of dominance. While discussing the Ripper with Jack, Will explains the psychological need to enact this kind of behav-ior: "His victims, he wanted to humiliate in death, like a public dissection."[60]

Hannibal is an avid fan of turning his dinner guests into unwitting accomplices with the lure of fine dining. Sonia Allué warns us, "It is easier to fall into the trap of aesthetic pleasures in the face of a serial killer who is cultivated, polished and a gentleman."[61] Hannibal begins his corruption of others in the first episode by serving one of his victims, Cassie Boyle, to Will as an ingredient in a protein scramble for breakfast while Will is inves-tigating the dead girl's murder. This scene is replicated often throughout the first season as Hannibal prepares many dishes for his guests, surreptitiously contaminating their innocence.

We see Ullyatt's gastronomic cannibal and his penchant for haute cui-sine demonstrated in the television series by the multiple award-winning

Chef José Andrés and world-renowned food stylist Janice Poon. The two craft gourmet meals for each episode that become an exemplar of Hannibal's exquisite culinary tastes. The Epicurean facet of Hannibal's character is frequently featured in the television series in a way that marks its limited inclusion in previous films. Now we see that Hannibal exhibits the same level of diligence in the presentation of his meals as he does the artistic presentation of his victims.

Possibly as a result of Hannibal's anthropophagy not being witnessed in the films, Ullyatt says that Hannibal Lecter only possesses a "soupçon of sadistic cannibalism."[62] Daniel Shaw's study of the character also echoes this view, "Lecter is ruthless without being needlessly sadistic…. He doesn't enjoy lording over the weak or innocent."[63] However, the television series frequently demonstrates Hannibal's sadism, and pays particular attention to him lording over the weak and innocent.

In one of the lectures that Will Graham gives on the Chesapeake Ripper he projects images of the Ripper's earlier victims on a screen. Although the murders we see in Will's slide show are not as creatively staged as the others we see during season one (possible due to the production's budgetary restraints), what is apparent in each of them is what Will calls a "distinctive brutality."[64] Despite there being no obvious link in victimology, Will detects a pattern. He says the Rippers' victims are killed in groups of three but he does not use this collective noun; instead he calls them "sounders." He explains his derogatory choice of word: "I use the term sounders because it refers to a small group of pigs. That's how he sees his victims, not as people, not as prey—pigs."[65]

To Hannibal, the people whom he considers to be rude possess more value when they are dead than when they are alive, as do any livestock awaiting slaughter. In the same episode, Will discusses a more recent series of murders committed by the Chesapeake Ripper and achieves great insight into his decorum-driven motives:

> WILL: He's not bothered by cruelty. The reward is for undignified behaviour. These dissections are to disgrace them. It's a public shaming.
> HANNIBAL: Takes their organs away because in his mind they don't deserve them?
> WILL: In some way.[66]

Furthermore, Aaron Taylor tells us how "those whose philistinism affronts [Hannibal's] sensibilities often find their way to his dinner plate."[67] During a conversation in the novel *Hannibal*, Barney, a former orderly at the Baltimore State Hospital for the Criminally Insane, tells Clarice how Hannibal Lecter chose his fare before he was incarcerated: "He told me once that, whenever it was 'feasible,' he preferred to eat the rude. 'Free-range rude,' he called them."[68]

But Hannibal does not just eat the rude, he "eradicates ... social noxiousness" and repurposes them in a bloody process of beautification.[69] Those whom he considers ugly are removed from society and transformed into masterfully prepared meals.

We see this process in a monochrome flashback as Andrew Caldwell, a medical professional, takes a blood sample from Hannibal. Caldwell's abruptness and surly demeanor are enough to warrant Hannibal to ask for his business card for future reference. As Hannibal begins to plan his feast in "Sorbet," Caldwell's name is the first plucked out of the Rolodex. We also learn of what will become of his organs as Hannibal selects from his recipe box: "Crisp Lemon Calf Liver."

The episode "Sorbet" comes to a conclusion with a harpsichord-heavy Aria from Handel. "*Piangerò la sorte mia*" ("I will bemoan my fate") from *Giulio Cesare in Egitto* plays as the camera slowly makes its way down the length of a dinner table sided with eight applauding guests. Janice Poon lists the appetizing fare on her blog: "Galantine pork stuffed with chicken, pistachio, cranberry forcemeat, asparagus in centre. Carpaccio with parmasean, olive oil, capers, fries. Liver pate in peppercorn on wine gelée."[70] At the end of the table stands Hannibal, graciously accepting their praise. He has served the uncivilized, lower-class Caldwell to the civilized, upper-class diners in an extreme form class warfare. As with many of his victims, Hannibal transformed the distasteful Caldwell into a delectable meal.

Conclusion

By analyzing how Hannibal adapts the works of other killers, we learn that this incarnation of Hannibal is a highly artistic individual and often finds inspiration from external sources. He finds faults in the works of others and improves on them, thus displaying his desire for supremacy over his predecessors. Hannibal uses the bodies of his victims and poses them in such beautiful and grotesque formations to prove that his artistry is greater than that of other killers. The rich, visual style of the program, with its color-graded images and lavish set design, reflects how Hannibal views corpses as aesthetic objects that are to be studied and admired.

The convoluted relationship between Hannibal and Will is a focal point for the first season. Hannibal silently grapples with his conflicting desire for greater knowledge in his professional field, which he can achieve by studying Will Graham's unique mental state, and his need for friendship. Throughout the first season we see Hannibal slowly and sadistically manipulate Will into something more like himself, which demonstrates his loneliness and desire to find a companion with similar interests.

Hannibal uses bodies to communicate a message and does so with a savage method. From this action we learn that Hannibal has deviated from previous versions of his character that only killed those who are a threat to him.

Cannibalism is Hannibal Lecter's primary identifying trait, yet the audience had not seen Hannibal consume human flesh on screen until this adaptation. Bryan Fuller rectifies this omission by frequently showing Hannibal preparing, cooking, and eating human organs. The television series employs a culinary consultant and food stylist to heighten this aspect of Hannibal's pathology. We learn that many of Hannibal's victims are killed because they are rude; this is an exemplar of Hannibal's sense of propriety. Hannibal then repurposes these bodies into exquisite cuisine and feeds them to unsuspecting guests.

The production of the television series has performed a similar function to how Hannibal adapts the works of other killers, thus making them more artful and more complete. Bryan Fuller has also improved upon previous representations of the character by giving the audience a closer, more intimate view of this fascinating character.

NOTES

1. John Goodrich, "Hannibal at the Lectern: A Textual Analysis of Dr Hannibal Lecter's Character and Motivation in Thomas Harris' Red Dragon and the Silence of the Lambs," in *Dissecting Hannibal Lecter: Essays on the Novels of Thomas Harris*, ed. Benjamin Szumskyj (Jefferson, NC: McFarland, 2008), 38.
2. *Ibid.*
3. John E. Douglas and Corrine M. Munn, "The Detection of Staging and Personation at the Crime Scene," in *Crime Classification Manual*, ed. Ann W. Burgess John E. Douglas, Allen G. Burgess, and Robert K. Ressler (San Francisco: Jossey-Bass, 1997), 249.
4. James Foley, "Sorbet," in *Hannibal* (Sony Pictures Television, 2013).
5. David Slade, "Potage," *ibid.* (Sony Pictures Television).
6. John E. Douglas and Mark Olshaker, *Mind Hunter: Inside the FBI's Elite Serial Crime Unit* (New York: Pocket Star, 1996), 19.
7. Linda Hutcheon, *A Theory of Adaptation* (New York: Routledge, 2006), 8.
8. Slade, "Apéritif."
9. *Ibid.*
10. Hutcheon, 9.
11. *Ibid.*, 8.
12. *Ibid.*, 20.
13. D. A. Russell, "*De Imitatione*," in *Creative Imitation and Latin Literature*, ed. David West and A.J. Woodman (Cambridge: Cambridge University Press, 1979), 12.
14. Slade, "Potage."
15. Michael Rymer, "Relevés."
16. Russell, 4.
17. Rymer.
18. David Slade, "Potage," *ibid.*
19. "Apéritif."
20. "Potage."

21. Thomas Fahy, "Killer Culture: Classical Music and the Art of Killing in Silence of the Lambs and Se7en," *Journal of Popular Culture* 37, no. 1 (2003): 36.

22. Hutcheon, 31.

23. Boyd H. Hill, "A Medieval German Wound Man: Wellcome Ms 49," *Journal of the History of Medicine and Allied Sciences* XX, no. 4 (1965).334.

24. *Ibid.*

25. Hutcheon, 92.

26. Thomas Harris, *Hannibal* (New York: Delacorte, 1999), 365.

27. Hutcheon, 7.

28. Guillermo Navarro, "Trou Normand," in *Hannibal* (Sony Pictures Television, 2013).

29. Gérard Genette, *Palimpsests: Literature in the Second Degree* (Lincoln: University of Nebraska Press, 1997), 6.

30. Hutcheon, 84.

31. Slade, "Apéritif."

32. Michael Rymer, "Amuse-Bouche," *ibid.*

33. "Relevés."

34. David Slade, "Potage," *ibid.*

35. Michael Rymer, "Amuse-Bouche," *ibid.*

36. John Dahl, "Buffet Froid," *ibid.*

37. Goodrich, 47.

38. *Ibid.*

39. Foley.

40. John Dahl, "Buffet Froid," *ibid.* (Sony Pictures Television).

41. Guillermo Navarro, "Rôti," *ibid.*

42. Phillipa Gates, *Detecting Men: Masculinity and the Hollywood Detective Film* (Albany: University of New York, 2006), 168.

43. *Ibid.*, 169.

44. *Ibid.*, 170.

45. Michael Rymer, "Entrée," in *Hannibal* (Sony Pictures Televison, 2013).

46. *Ibid.*

47. Guillermo Navarro, "Rôti," *ibid.* (Sony Pictures Television).

48. *Ibid.*

49. Daniel Shaw, "The Mastery of Hannibal Lecter," in *Dark Thoughts: Philosophic Reflections on Cinematic Horror*, ed. Steven Jay Schneider and Daniel Shaw (Lanham: Scarecrow, 2003), 16.

50. Charles Gramlich, "Mythmaker," in *Dissecting Hannibal Lecter: Essays on the Novels of Thomas Harris*, ed. Benjamin Szumskyj (Jefferson, NC: McFarland, 2008), 214.

51. Peter Medak, "Œuf," in *Hannibal* (Sony Pictures Television, 2013).

52. Jonathan Demme, *The Silence of the Lambs* (Orion Pictures, 1991).

53. Slade, "Apéritif."

54. *Ibid.*

55. Tony Ullyatt, "To Amuse the Mouth: Anthropophagy in Thomas Harris's Tetralogy of Hannibal Lecter Novels," *Journal of Literary Studies/Tydskrif vir Literatuurwetenskap* 28, no. 1 (2012).

56. *Ibid.*

57. Shirley Lindenbaum, "Thinking About Cannibalism," *Annual Review of Anthropology* 33 (2004): 478.

58. Davide Mana, "This Is the Blind Leading the Blind: Noir, Horror and Reality in Thomas Harris's Red Dragon " in *Dissecting Hannibal Lecter: Essays on the Novels of Thomas Harris*, ed. Benjamin Szumskyj (Jefferson, NC: McFarland, 2008), 92.

59. Rymer, "Entrée."

60. James Foley, "Sorbet," *ibid.* (Sony Pictures Television).

61. Sonia Allué, "The Aesthetics of Serial Killing: Working against Ethics in the Silence of the Lambs (1988) and American Psycho (1991)," *Atlantis* 24, no. 2 (2002): 15.

62. Ullyatt.

63. Shaw, 16.

64. Foley.
65. *Ibid.*
66. *Ibid.*
67. Aaron Taylor, "A Cannibal's Sermon: Hannibal Lecter, Sympathetic Villainy and Moral Revaluation," *Cinema: Journal of Philosophy and the Moving Image*, no. 4 (2013), https://www.uleth.ca/dspace/bitstream/handle/10133/4589/Taylor%20Cinema4.pdf?sequence=1.
68. Harris.
69. Ullyatt.
70. Janice Poon to Janice Poon Art, May 10, 2013, http://janicepoonart.blogspot.com/2013/05/ep-6-sorbet-tarts-barquettes.html.

WORKS CITED

Allué, Sonia. "The Aesthetics of Serial Killing: Working against Ethics in the Silence of the Lambs (1988) and American Psycho (1991)." *Atlantis* 24, no. 2 (2002).
Dahl, John. "Buffet Froid." In *Hannibal*: Sony Pictures Television, 2013.
Demme, Jonathan. *The Silence of the Lambs*. Orion Pictures, 1991.
Douglas, John E., and Corrine M. Munn, "The Detection of Staging and Personation at the Crime Scene." In *Crime Classification Manual*, edited by Ann W. Burgess John E. Douglas, Allen G. Burgess, and Robert K. Ressler, 249–58. San Francisco: Jossey-Bass, 1997.
Douglas, John E., and Mark Olshaker. *Mind Hunter: Inside the FBI's Elite Serial Crime Unit*. New York: Pocket Star, 1996.
Fahy, Thomas. "Killer Culture: Classical Music and the Art of Killing in Silence of the Lambs and Se7en." *Journal of Popular Culture* 37, no. 1 (2003).
Foley, James. "Sorbet." In *Hannibal*. Sony Pictures Television, 2013.
Gates, Phillipa. *Detecting Men: Masculinity and the Hollywood Detective Film*. Albany: University of New York, 2006.
Genette, Gérard. *Palimpsests: Literature in the Second Degree*. Lincoln: University of Nebraska Press, 1997.
Goodrich, John. "Hannibal at the Lectern: A Textual Analysis of Dr Hannibal Lecter's Character and Motivation in Thomas Harris' Red Dragon and the Silence of the Lambs." In *Dissecting Hannibal Lecter: Essays on the Novels of Thomas Harris*, edited by Benjamin Szumskyj, 37–48. Jefferson, NC: McFarland, 2008.
Gramlich, Charles. "Mythmaker." In *Dissecting Hannibal Lecter: Essays on the Novels of Thomas Harris*, edited by Benjamin Szumskyj, 212–16. Jefferson, NC: McFarland, 2008.
Harris, Thomas. *Hannibal*. New York: Delacorte, 1999.
Hill, Boyd H. "A Medieval German Wound Man: Wellcome Ms 49." *Journal of the History of Medicine and Allied Sciences* XX, no. 4 (1965): 334–57. doi:http://dx.doi.org/10.1093/jhmas/XX.4.334.
Hutcheon, Linda. *A Theory of Adaptation*. New York: Routledge, 2006.
Lindenbaum, Shirley. "Thinking About Cannibalism." *Annual Review of Anthropology* 33 (2004): 475–98.
Mana, Davide. "This Is the Blind Leading the Blind: Noir, Horror and Reality in Thomas Harris's Red Dragon ". In *Dissecting Hannibal Lecter: Essays on the Novels of Thomas Harris*, edited by Benjamin Szumskyj, 87–101. Jefferson, NC: McFarland, 2008.
Medak, Peter. "Œuf." In *Hannibal*: Sony Pictures Television, 2013.
Navarro, Guillermo. "Rôti." In *Hannibal*: Sony Pictures Television, 2013.
_____. "Trou Normand." In *Hannibal*: Sony Pictures Television, 2013.
Poon, Janice. "Ep 7: Sorbet: Tarts & Barquettes." In *Janice Poon Art*, 2013.
Russell, D.A. "*De Imitatione*." In *Creative Imitation and Latin Literature*, edited by David West and A.J. Woodman, 1–16. Cambridge: Cambridge University Press, 1979.
Rymer, Michael. "Amuse-Bouche." In *Hannibal*: Sony Pictures Television, 2013.
_____. "Entrée." In *Hannibal*: Sony Pictures Televison, 2013.
_____. "Relevés." In *Hannibal*: Sony Pictures Television, 2013.
Sepinwall, Alan. "Hannibal Producer Bryan Fuller on Cannibal Cuisine, Renewal and More."

HitFix, http://www.hitfix.com/whats-alan-watching/hannibal-producer-bryan-fuller-on-cannibal-cuisine-renewal-and-more.

Shaw, Daniel. "The Mastery of Hannibal Lecter." In *Dark Thoughts: Philosophic Reflections on Cinematic Horror*, edited by Steven Jay Schneider and Daniel Shaw, 10–24. Lanham: Scarecrow, 2003.

Slade, David. "Apéritif." In *Hannibal*: Sony Pictures Television, 2013.

_____. "Potage." In *Hannibal*: Sony Pictures Television, 2013.

Taylor, Aaron. "A Cannibal's Sermon: Hannibal Lecter, Sympathetic Villainy and Moral Revaluation." *Cinema: Journal of Philosophy and the Moving Image*, no. 4 (2013): 184–208. https://www.uleth.ca/dspace/bitstream/handle/10133/4589/Taylor%20Cinema4.pdf?sequence=1.

Ullyatt, Tony. "To Amuse the Mouth: Anthropophagy in Thomas Harris's Tetralogy of Hannibal Lecter Novels." *Journal of Literary Studies/Tydskrif vir Literatuurwetenskap* 28, no. 1 (2012): 4–20. doi:http://dx.doi.org/10.1080/02564718.2012.644464.

VanDerWerff, Todd. "Bryan Fuller Walks Us through the First Three Episodes of Hannibal (1 of 4)." AV Club, http://www.avclub.com/article/bryan-fuller-walks-us-through-the-first-three-epis-100582.

My Darling Cannibal

The Mechanics of Perverse Allegiance in Hannibal

Kirsty Worrow

As Hannibal Lecter steps out into the pouring rain in the final moments of the episode "Mizumono," he pauses on the threshold. Mads Mikkelsen's performance—the gaping of his mouth, the turning of his eyes skywards and the dragging of his hand down over his face—suggest Hannibal is processing the preceding events emotionally. This is accentuated by the use of the rain, employed deliberately as pathetic fallacy connoting the trauma experienced by all at Lecter's townhouse that evening; *all*, including Lecter. Despite his despicable actions and his iconic proclivities, it's easy to feel sympathy with him at this moment. The spectator is given information to understand that for all his willful malevolence, Hannibal's actions are motivated by the hurt he feels after discovering Will Graham's betrayal. The retribution he enacts is certainly extreme, but the motivations are relatable and human. We are positioned to connect with him by the creators here and throughout the series. Given that he is a villain, that connection with him is perhaps best described as a *Perverse Allegiance*: a relationship which draws and compels us to root for this cruel and horrific cannibal.

Throughout this essay, I will explore how Fuller et al. attempt to carefully create a perverse allegiance between spectator and Hannibal Lecter through the use of the macro and micro techniques. I will discuss key moments from the series to exemplify, through textual analysis, the ways in which the spectator is encouraged towards a positive response to the serial killer, and how that response is fluid, with Hannibal's key creatives moving the spectator towards and away from the character to create and release tension in the narrative. I will connect these moments to relevant academic works, narrative theory, interviews with cast and crew and to the critical responses to *Hannibal* provided by pop culture commentators in order to illuminate the context, intention and reception of this incarnation of Lecter. Then, utilizing contributions from fans of *Hannibal*, lovingly known as "Fannibals," who are largely "young, smart, well-read women,"[1] I will examine how these spectators have pledged allegiance to Hannibal, albeit in a way they recognize as problematic. I will also acknowledge how this adaptation of Harris' canon has reframed Lecter increasingly as a Romantic Gothic hero and has been elevated to this through the reflexive interaction of text, producer and spectator.

"God forbid we become friendly"

The notion of Perverse Allegiance is not new, nor is it unconnected to Hannibal Lecter. Murray Smith categorizes how spectators identify with characters, distinguishing between *alignment*, a relationship which is facilitated by "our access to the actions, thoughts, and feelings of characters"[2]; and *allegiance*, "responses of sympathy and antipathy towards characters."[3] Smith suggests that Perverse Allegiance is reliant on a character's "embodiment of socially or morally undesirable traits."[4] In considering *The Silence of the Lambs* (1990), Smith ultimately suggests that the spectator's allegiance to Lecter is unlikely to be truly perverse as we don't find him attractive *because* of his cannibalism, but rather because he possesses appealing traits.[5] Aaron Taylor subsequently contends that viewers might sometimes form perverse allegiances with such characters "*because of*—not in spite of—their abhorrent natures."[6] Taylor's perverse allegiance is "the acceptance of the villain on his own terms"[7] whereby the spectator engages in the revaluation of morality modeled by the character. He notes that this connection is not a pre-requisite for spectatorship of such texts, with viewers being able resist the prioritization of such codes.[8] Taylor concludes that a perverse allegiance with villains is possible when their deeds "can be reconceived as a necessary, and much needed good."[9] In the case of Lecter in *The Silence of the Lambs* and later *Hannibal* (2001), he argues that that Lecter's exuberant criminality is "a cure-all for ignorance, misplaced values, rampant philistinism, and above all unchecked institutional misogyny."[10]

Hannibal creator Bryan Fuller characterizes the initial relationship between Will and Hannibal as "the seduction."[11] That seduction has been mirrored in the seduction of the viewer by the text, which is apparent in online fannish spaces such as Tumblr and Archive of Our Own. The passion for the show, and care for the protagonist Will Graham is not unexpected given the success of television crime drama and the popularity of extra-ordinarily intellectually gifted characters who are also ascribed with Autism Spectrum Disorder–type personal barriers (for example, Dr.

Gregory House in *House* [Fox, 2004–2012], Sherlock Holmes in *Sherlock* [BBC, 2010–] and Dr. Temperance Brennan in *Bones* [Fox, 2005–2017]). Will's status as a usefully neurodiverse character is foregrounded in the second scene of the first episode, as Will explains his abilities to Jack: "My horse is hitched to a post closer to Aspergers and Autistics than narcissists and sociopaths…. I can empathize with anybody. Less to do with personality disorders than an active imagination." *Hannibal* clearly locates the viewer to align with Will by frequently placing sequences inside his head. This fosters alignment with relative ease, as the spectator is given privileged insights into the character's inner-world. However, the potency of allegiance with Lecter is strange, according to geek culture commentator Gavia Baker-Whitelaw.[12] Certainly the spectator isn't given such easy roads into the character. Baker-Whitelaw proposes that our relationship with him is akin to Stockholm syndrome and that "[we] just want him to stay out of jail so that we can keep watching."[13] *Rolling Stone*'s Sean T. Collins expresses a contradictory engagement with the show, drawing a clear comparison between the spectator and protagonist:

> you've got to be like Will Graham voluntarily connecting with the worst humanity has to offer. You must be willing to turn to the work and say "just fuck me up."[14]

Like Will, our allegiance may be *in spite of* or *because of* Hannibal's monstrous acts at different times and the relationship we have with him is an emotional one. This is, in part, created by the artistic identity of *Hannibal*, which can be defined as Expressionist as it is "characterized by exaggeration and distortion in order to create an emotional impact"[15] *Hannibal* deliberately rejects naturalism in favor of an uneasy and oneiric quality which entices the audiences while it engenders fear. Correspondingly, Lecter rationally inspires horror, but is captivating nonetheless.

"Let it be a fairytale, then"

Hannibal may not be the protagonist, but the title—*Hannibal*—suggests his narrative importance. The naming allows a wider audience to be attracted by the existing cultural capital of the Lecter brand and awareness of the character. For a moment, recall the structure of the first episode "Apéritif." It is fashioned to tease the expectant spectator that has previously consumed Harris's texts or adaptations. Half of the episode elapses before Hannibal finally appears on screen. He is introduced playfully; Will's line "He's eating them" precedes a cut to an enigmatic new location. The reveal is delayed to further heighten the audience's anticipation even more. Hannibal is refined and sophisticated, as suggested by the presentation of the food. It is appetizing, reflecting his desire for beauty. His face is only revealed when the camera follows the fork to his mouth. He takes pleasure in the consumption of his meat (which familiar spectators might assume is human). The color palette is luxurious and deep, connoting affluence with a touch of threat. His first close-up is in significant darkness, reflecting his true nature in this moment of solitary pleasure, and his connection with the spectator is immediate; he appears to break the fourth wall, but his eyes are shadowed. The music is Bach's *Goldberg Variations*, which suggests his socio-economic status and appreciation of high culture, but is also an homage to past incarnations.

Of course, the possibility of keeping the audience in the dark about the true nature of the titular character would be almost impossible, so it is not unexpected that Hannibal is introduced in such a deliberate fashion. This gives rise to the first major component of the mechanism for allegiance; dramatic irony. We know he's a serial killing cannibal but initially no one else does. His interactions with other characters are crafted by this knowledge which creates moments of *Loudly Implied Cannibalism,*[16] such as this exchange from "Entrée":

> DR. CHILTON: Romans would kill flamingos just to eat their tongues.
> HANNIBAL: Don't give me ideas. Your tongue is very feisty and as this evening has already proven, it's nice to have an old friend for dinner.

Such moments are frequent and darkly comic. This humor is a crucial device for getting us on board with Lecter. If we find them amusing as he does, then we're complicit in his crimes on some level.

Through his analysis of fairy tales, narratologist Vladimir Propp defined a villain's function as "to cause some form of misfortune, damage, or harm."[17] Hannibal's fulfillment of this is typical in his use of persuasion, deception and coercion.[18] Propp suggests that a villain will conventionally threaten cannibalism,[19] and in this way Hannibal exceeds expectations. However, his narrative functionality is more complex; Hannibal's villain status is muddied somewhat through the actions which help maintain the illusion of his non-criminal identity. Employed initially as a support mechanism for Will, Hannibal functions on the surface as a helper.[20] However, we can also interpret his murder of Cassie Boyle as fulfilling the criteria for a donor—a character who gifts something crucial for the completion of the hero's task[21]—as it's Will's interpretation of this particular crime scene which allows him to draw conclusions about the Minnesota Shrike murders. Will remarks on the distasteful usefulness, "That crime scene was practically gift wrapped."[22] Hannibal's role as a donor is also evidenced in his initial meeting with Will, which fits in with one of Propp's narrative stages—the interrogation which prepares the way for receiving help. The greeting of the donor[23] is an important test; Will's behavior would conventionally mean he would not be rewarded (in fact, such rudeness would normally earn an entirely different intervention), Hannibal decides that he warrants special assistance. His line of dialogue following Will's exit foreshadows exactly what Hannibal will do: "This cannibal you have him getting to know…. I think I can help good Will see his face." Hannibal can also be understood as a False Hero[24] as he leads the FBI to believe that Will is the Chesapeake Ripper and in doing so makes himself look beyond reproach. Hannibal occupies the position of Propp's Princess in the first half season three, as he is Will's "sought-for person."[25]

Propp's ideas are useful in unpacking how Hannibal operates in the narrative, though the application above is predicated on one central assumption: that Will is the hero. However, an alternative is possible, for Hannibal can be decoded as an antihero. If Hannibal occupies the position of protagonist for some spectators, then Will can be seen as the villain at times, reinforced by some of his actions which are also consistent with Propp's descriptions of the villain—he abducts and affects a substitution (Freddie), orders a murder to be committed (Matthew Brown), commits a murder (Randall Tier), and engages in cannibalism.[26] Will also fulfills the function of princess for Hannibal in a more ambiguous fashion. Much of season two is concerned with Hannibal's efforts to help realize Will's killer identity, and thus he is seeking a specific version of him. A spectator who views Hannibal as the hero is perhaps more ready to give their allegiance to him as a character, rather than a spectator who engages with the text in a more morally conventional binary manner.

The "good-bad man"[27] is an archetype who can become the subject of alignment or allegiance for the spectator based on relative morality, since characters can be read as good in relation to the others. While it is quite a stretch to define Hannibal Lecter as morally good in a conventional sense, the other villains are represented as perhaps more dislikable in a number of ways: Abel Gideon targets women; Francis Dolarhyde murders whole families; and Mason Verger psychologically tortures his sister, forcibly removes her developing fetus and subsequently transfers it to a pig surrogate. He is also guilty of the most heinous crime; a lack of respect for Hannibal's furniture. Hannibal is either wholly or in part responsible for the justice that these characters receive. *Hannibal* strongly positions us to believe that they are deserving of their fates. Taylor suggests Lecter's crimes can, at times, be regarded as "perverse altruism."[28] Despite not receiving Lecter's form of justice, the Mother in "Oeuf" highlights what Dolarhyde later reinforces; Hannibal doesn't target children. His victims are larger, less innocent and vulnerable, and in his eyes (and ours), deserving of their fates. In these instances Hannibal can be read, if one squints a little, as an avenging angel.

The selection and inclusion of Hannibal's narrative beats are also of value when it comes to forming an allegiance with him. We are shown much which encourages us to view Hannibal positively: Will finds him asleep holding Abigail's hand in "Apéritif" suggesting his care for her, which is reinforced by his actions in "Potage." He voluntarily intervenes in "Sorbet" to save the life of Devon Silvestri's victim. He appears to have genuine and warm friendships with both Alana and Jack. However, what we *don't* see is just as important as what we *do* see; we don't see many of Hannibal's murders. His first on-screen kills are Franklyn and Tobias in "Fromage," and even then his actions are motivated by the threat posed by Tobias. It's not like we don't *know* what he's doing, it's just that *Hannibal* pointedly doesn't show us Hannibal doing his murderous and defiling deeds. Take, for example, the killing of Andrew Caldwell in "Sorbet," whose actual death and subsequent removal of organs is concealed by a cut to black. This visual ellipsis isn't about meeting the standards of taste and decency for network television because violent crimes and horrific acts are still depicted in this show; just think about everything horrible that happens to Dr. Fredrick Chilton. We don't often see Hannibal as the perpetrator of such acts, particularly in the first season when our connection to him is still forming. The elliptical presentation of his crimes is eroded in the second half of the series. By the time the viewer arrives at "Mizumono" and the first half of season three, which features more explicit crimes committed by Hannibal, our allegiance is already established and his motives are more clearly emotional, as Bedelia helpfully signposts in Florence. The emotional motivation is understood by the viewer and, if our allegiance is strong, we feel his pain too.

Lecter confirms his approach to selecting victims in "Tome-Wan": "When feasible, one should eat the rude." The idea of a code of behavior is an important device in allowing the audience to find some positive connection with serial killer characters. This is perhaps most effectively demonstrated in Jeff Lindsay's Dexter Morgan novels and the Showtime adaptation *Dexter* (2006–2013) where the protagonist is a serial killer who only kills other serial killers who have escaped conventional justice. However, in *Hannibal*, the doctor's code is much less convincing; for example, he kills Marisa Schurr in "Potage" for disrespecting her mother. Her murder is hardly a proportional response to a lack of good manners. Nevertheless, the code allows the audience to connect with Hannibal given the dramatic irony which is created when a bit character is rude in Hannibal's presence. We might even enjoy the justice, if we can relate to Hannibal's emotional experience. Another illustration of Hannibal's code appears when Professor Sogliato insults Hannibal repeatedly by suggesting that he is not up to the task of being the curator of Palazzo Capponi. Hannibal is, of course, more than capable of demonstrating his suitability. The negative feelings which arise out of being challenged are relatable, and so Sogliato's intellectual and physical defeats hold cathartic pleasure for some spectators. The result of such approval on our part is arguably a negotiated adjustment of accepted morality while engaged with the text. Taylor discusses this at length, identifying how Hannibal's own ethos is informed by Nietzsche, prizing as he does self-preservation and actualization at any cost. Taylor describes Lecter as being "a profoundly self-contented individual" who "[t]hrough the revaluation of virtue, he fashions himself into a figure in which the disparate qualities of 'good' and 'evil' are realigned and ultimately reintegrated."[29]

Our allegiance with Hannibal, however, is not total. Arguably the fascination with the character comes from the tension between seeing him as a relatable antihero and seeing him as an abhorrent monster. We're distanced from him in the narrative particularly by the instances when the spectator is positioned to find Hannibal's actions much more problematic; specifically the deaths of Beverly Katz, Abigail Hobbs and Rinaldo Pazzi.

The death of Beverly Katz proved controversial in relation to the debates around intersectional representations in mainstream American media, as noted by actress Hettienne Park.[30] However, her loss reminds the spectator of the cost of crossing Dr. Lecter. Her death is also not unexpected, after all, breaking and entering is not just criminal, it's rude. She is a likable character and is arguably the most three dimensional member of the show's forensics group, termed "Team Sassy Science" by Fannibals.[31] If there isn't loss, or if meaningful consequences aren't a possibility, then the emotional connection with the characters and the story is less potent and the spectator is less likely to engage fully. If, by "Mukozuke," we have forgotten the atrocities of which Hannibal Lecter is capable of or if he has become too endearing to audiences, then a reminder of his capabilities and true nature is necessary to restore suspense. This is exactly what Beverly's death does. However, as unpleasant and spectacular as Beverly's death is, Hannibal is still distanced from the crime as, again, we do not see him commit the act.

In fact, we see her death with Will as Hannibal's surrogate in one of his re-enactments. We witness this well-loved character die at the hands of the hero, which reminds us (and in the diegesis, Will) of his responsibility for her death. This is an important moment which helps reinforce the fluidity of roles within *Hannibal*. Will's constant portrayals of himself as the villain through his visions are a means for the writers to maintain Hannibal's inherent likeability while pushing Will into antihero status. This offers an inversion of the conventional dialectical representation of these characters, given Lecter's liberty and the heightened emphasis on Will's physical and spiritual vulnerability while incarcerated. For familiar viewers, the premise of the show provides a reimagined backstory that furnishes the spectator with the opportunity to get to know Lecter outside of his iconic cage, and the role reversal allows for some postmodern pleasures, illustrated clearly in the final moments of "Savoureux," when Lecter greets Will in a knowing intertextual reference to *Silence of the Lambs*.

Abigail Hobbs' death is played out on screen during the finale of the second season, and is accentuated horrifically in "Primavera." Allison McCracken describes Abigail's story as "the central tragedy of the series"[32] Her death is heightened by the mirroring of her attempted murder and her playful faking of her own death with Hannibal. McCracken observes that "Abigail's social deviance as, at once, a trauma survivor and a killer, has made her a source of identification."[33] Abigail's central drive throughout the series is to gain control of her own destiny, a goal she never achieves. Her death is intentionally cruel and heart-breaking, and just as Will is, the spectator is positioned to be happy in the discovery that she is still alive just minutes before she's cruelly and vindictively finally taken by Hannibal. In a manner which also can be read as deliberately punitive, the confirmation of her death is delayed until "Primavera," but not before we've been led up the garden path about her survival.

We also see Hannibal murder Inspector Pazzi, but his death is quick, dramatic, highly unpleasant, and conventional when compared to the artistic labor the doctor invested into other murders. Pazzi is painted as a likable but weary police officer. He's warm, yet grizzled and jaded by his obsession with the crimes committed by "Il Monstro." Throughout the limited time he occupies in the series, Inspector Pazzi wants to see Hannibal Lecter brought to justice; an entirely honorable goal. However, when he contacts Verger in Contorno, we understand that by deviating from the pursuit of legitimate justice in order to personally profit from the situation, his death is inevitable. The conventional moral code of horror dictates that sin should be punished. By becoming an agent of Mason Verger, Pazzi's death can be read by the spectator as a necessary evil in our cannibal's desire to remain alive and at liberty. What unites the deaths of Beverly, Abigail, and Pazzi is the tension for the spectator between the allegiance which is created by the inclusion of more dislikable characters, their more explicitly horrible actions, and the antipathetic retreat when Hannibal's less acceptable or understandable actions are revealed.

"A very well-tailored person suit"

The casting of Mads Mikkelsen was certainly a departure from previous mature versions of the character; both of whom were played by British actors with British accents. For an American audience, villains with British accents are ubiquitous; the RP accent connotes historic and institutional power. The Lecter of Harris's novels is Lithuanian and the casting of an actor with a distinctly European accent allows for a more authentic portrayal. Lecter sounds different and is othered by his voice. Fuller has commented on how Mikkelsen's nationality might have alienated more mainstream viewers, conceding that he might have been; "a little bit hard to understand with his accent."[34]

Why did this casting work so well for the Fannibal audience, then? Mikkelsen's acting career began in his native Denmark in 1996. His raw and bullish performance in Nicholas Winding Refn's *Pusher* set him on a course to becoming one of the most recognizable and well-regarded stars of European cinema. He has often played complex and troubled characters in dramas such as *Exit* (2012) and *Flammen & Citronen* (2008). Sometimes his disturbed characters are portrayed with humor as in *Adams æbler* (2005) or *De grønne slagtere* (2003). He's been a relatable family man in tough situations like in *Jagten* (2012) and *Die Tür* (2009) as well as taking the romantic lead in films like *En kongelig affære* (2012) and *Coco Chanel & Igor Stravinsky* (2009). He is a well-established leading man for European audiences, and has garnered much critical recognition. In Hollywood, he has frequently played villainous characters such as Le Chiffre in *Casino Royale* (2006) and Kaecilius in *Doctor Strange* (2016). Occasionally he has played doomed warriors as in *King Arthur* (2004) and *The Clash of the Titans* (2010). Moreover, Mikkelsen proved to be a "reliable character actor with an intriguing mug" to American entertainment studios.[35]

For the target audience intended by NBC, Mikkelsen must have seemed a good choice; an actor who already had a sinister associations from his big budget English language work. But, for the culturally aware young women who became part of the *Hannibal* fandom, Mikkelsen's image was often broadened through consumption of his wider body of work. He could be sinister and violent, of course, but also heroic, flawed, lost, romantic, brooding, righteous and goofy. These associations, once bought to bear on Mikkelsen's Lecter, gave rise to readings of the character which were different from the dominant readings of previous incarnations. Smith highlights how the spectator's seemingly perverse allegiance might be more readily formed when the performer is known to the viewer; "when a star plays a role, our awareness of the fictional status of the character she plays may be heightened, and this may license our imaginative play with morally undesirable acts to an even greater extent."[36] If we're a Fannibal and/or a fan of Mikkelsen, it becomes possible to characterize Hannibal as a "little shit"[37] or as a love-sick puppy.

There's a pleasing dissonance in acknowledging that by performing the character as closed-off and aloof—thus creating distance between the viewer and the character—the proximity can be increased for some. Mikkelsen's Lecter is supremely controlled at all times. Through his very reserved execution both in his physicality and in his voice, Mikkelsen creates an enigmatic gap which spectators can fill in a way which best fits their own reading of the character. Mikkelsen's use of micro-expressions is a key feature of his performance, as Fuller has commented; "he doesn't over-perform anything. It's all insular and vibrations on the surface."[38] The micro-expressions are small moments that through the use of close-ups, the viewer is forced to register and which signpost the spectator towards Hannibal's well hidden emotional experience, like the flicker of pleasure in his face as he hears Will's analysis of the Cassie Boyle murder in "Potage." The function of such instances is in part to create an emotional and empathetic connection between spectator and character, according to Carl Plantinga:

> we see a character's face, typically in closeup, either for a single shot of long duration or as an element of a point-of-view structure alternating between shots of the character's face and shots of what he or she sees. The prolonged concentration on the character's face is not warranted by the simple communication about character emotion. Such scenes are also elicit empathetic emotions in the spectator.[39]

Mikkelsen doesn't gesticulate, his voice is even and his facial expressions are measured. Even in moments of violence, his control of his body is absolute, as in the fight sequences in "Fromage" and "Kaiseki" and the moment before he attacks Beverly Katz in "Takiawase." His disciplined performance others the character further; his physicality makes him less human. The conceptualization of the character is evident in such moments. Both Fuller and Mikkelsen have commented on the deliberate otherworldliness of their version of the character; Mikkelsen describes Lecter as "the fallen angel"[40] while Fuller acknowledges Mikkelsen has interpreted the character as The Devil.[41] This representation is made more specific in episodes like "Antipasto," when Hannibal's head is seemingly replaced by a medieval image of Lucifer during a lecture. In thinking about the associations such a likening conjures, the attractiveness of Hannibal becomes evident as an integral facet of the construction as Judeo-Christian mythology connects Satan with temptation, corruption and carnal appetites. The Devil is a seducer, a fallen angel who is both monstrous and beautiful.

Metaphors also effectively influence our understanding of his nature. In the very first dialogue scene that Hannibal has, he says to Franklyn "[y]ou have to convince yourself the lion is not in the room. When it is, I assure you, you will know." This is one of the first moments of dramatic irony for the audience. The lion *is* in the room, and immediately through this use of metaphor the spectator is set up to understand that Hannibal is not just a top predator, he's the king of the jungle. This status is reinforced by the images of big game in his office. The stag becomes a key symbol for Hannibal. Although not a predator, a stag connotes grace, beauty, and powerful masculinity. Conversely, there is an associated vulnerability as stags are prize quarry for the right hunter; reinforcing the one of the facets of the Hannibal/Will relationship. These connotations are undoubtedly useful in creating an attractive, powerful but not invincible killer. The attention to detail in his costuming is also important; the beautifully tailored and expensive suits make Lecter look luxurious. Depending on your point of spectatorship, he can become a figure of aspiration and/or an object of desire. In her Tumblr analysis on Hannibal Lecter and the subversion of the male gaze, Tenebrica points out that "there is literally nothing about him that isn't considered desirable—except, you know, the whole eating people thing."[42] Frederick Chilton, Tobias Budge and Mason Verger share qualities or interests which reflect Hannibal, but are presented as more vulgar; they lack his refinement. Through the juxtaposition of these characters against Dr. Lecter, the audience can fully appreciate how much more desirable he is.

"Fancy Allusions and Fussy Aesthetics"

> HANNIBAL: See. This is all I ever wanted for you, Will. For both of us.
> WILL GRAHAM: It's beautiful.—*The Wrath of the Lamb*

Will's final line illuminates one of the principles behind the style of *Hannibal*, as Bryan Fuller explains: "[B]ecause we're telling the story of an aesthete, an erudite dandy, a sophisticate, it was important—even though we do have some graphic imagery—for it to be beautiful in the way it was presented."[43] Aesthetics are of greater importance in *Hannibal* than in other American network television shows. Anne Sheppard states that "[a]esthetic appreciation may be directed at a variety of natural and man-made objects, perceived by any of the five senses."[44] Jason Holt explains an appreciation of Hannibal's desire for aesthetic pleasure is "the very key to unlocking the mystery of his character, elaborated as it is into such an alien, such a grotesque extreme."[45] The spectator is presented with repeated examples of Hannibal's aesthetics in the show; his plates of food, his taste in interior design, art and music, his drawings, his music, his handwriting, his fashion and, of course, his crime scenes. The baroque murder tableaux created by Hannibal are "aesthetic objects, on par with the artistic production of fine artists."[46] While the inclusion of and references to artworks are widely discernible in the series, the construction of the murder tableaux themselves have precedence in art history. Broadly speaking, they belong to the Abject Art movement, which sees artists create works "based on the image of the human body, but specifically the body fragmented and decayed or represented by one of its socially less presentable functions…."[47] *Hannibal's* body horror art echoes the works of Joel Peter Witkin, Honore Fragonard and Dr. Gunther von Hagens, the works of whom feature genuine cadavers and body parts. In *Powers of Horror*, philosopher Julia Kristeva explores the potency of such art. She notes that the corpse is a very powerful reminder of mortality:

> The corpse, seen without God and outside of science, is the utmost of abjection. It is death infecting life. Abject. It is something rejected from which one does not part, from which one does not protect oneself as from an object. Imaginary uncanniness and real threat, it beckons to us and ends up engulfing us.[48]

Undoubtedly, the spectator in *Hannibal* is positioned to feel revulsion, disgust and fear in response to the grim tableaux. Even so, *Hannibal* is informed by classical notions of beauty, employing accepted rules of use of light, color, form, balance and rhythm in order to create visual pleasure. The spectator may experience a type of cognitive dissonance engendered by the tension created between the horror of the content of the images and the pleasure elicited by their construction. These images simultaneously produce responses of attraction and repulsion. Arguably, in these moments the spectator may enter an inertia, unwilling to move towards the image to enjoy the beauty and yet unable to look away to avoid the horror.

There is profound beauty to be enjoyed in both the banal and the horrific constituents of *Hannibal*. Everything is elevated to art, often and unapologetically at the expense of the type of verisimilitude commonly expected in such genre texts. In waiving this convention, the show takes on a much more fluid, liminal quality which may engender responses less reliant on rationality and more informed by the Expressionist qualities. Will experiences explicitly and beautifully staged nightmares which fetishize his suffering, embedded within a world which is implicitly constructed to reflect Hannibal's gaze. The increased visual excess in season three supports this idea, as Hannibal is finally more exposed, more emotional and, as a result, more impetuous. Will's last line becomes more potent if we accept that the stylistic approach to the whole series has been an exercise in encouraging the spectator to see reality as Hannibal does. This structure subtly implies the power dynamic between Will and Hannibal and suggests that Will's own reality, whether internal or external, will always be subject to Hannibal's influence. Again, a pleasing mirroring of intra- and extra-diegetic factors can be proposed; *Hannibal* is manipulating the spectator in a manner similar to Hannibal's manipulation of Will, with the intention to get us all to the same place; the recognition of beauty in the horrific and violent. Plain-Flavored-English sums up this parallel effectively in her meta on *Hannibal*: "Lecter's pleasure is no longer a sign of incomprehensible monstrosity; it has become our pleasure as well."[49]

"You will always have niche appeal"

Hannibal is a rare creature; a mainstream network show with the sensibilities of quality cable fare. The unusual identity of the show arguably contributed to the fact that it never became the success that NBC executives hoped. However, the show did garner critical recognition[50] and an "intensely invested fan base, led primarily by young women utilizing social media."[51] To understand the fannibal's passion it's helpful to examine the identity and heritage of the show more broadly and to shine a light on their reflections on their relationship with this iconic cannibal.

Aside from the conventional generic labels *Hannibal* is also a gothic text. Helen Wheatley identifies the tropes of gothic television, suggesting that gothic shows will likely feature, among other common features; a mood of dread; plots derived from gothic fiction; non-linear narrative structures and "a proclivity towards structures and images of the uncanny."[52] The gothic label is also useful in relation to the audience because, as McCracken outlines,

> the subgenre of gothic horror has always had particular appeal for women, in part because its romanticism privileges emotional intensity over rationality, which in turn has the potential to de-naturalize the "rational" institutions and oppressive structures of patriarchy.[53]

Hannibal can also be read as a gothic romance, as demonstrated in Lori Morimoto's video essay,[54] which juxtaposes text from *Things as They Are; Or, The Adventures of Caleb Williams* (William Goodwin, 1794) and *Jane Eyre* (Charlotte Bronte, 1847) with moments from the series. In looking at *Hannibal* as part of the traditions established by gothic romance and horror which focus emotional conflict, mounting dread, doomed love and monstrous masculinity, it's not hard to identify why *Hannibal* played well for a broadly female audience. Given the romantic element, the absence of central female character to act as a more conventional figure of identification for these spectators is perhaps noteworthy. In the context of debates around gendered spectatorship, the lack of a female protagonist is not usually a huge barrier to engagement with the text for female spectators as Gerard Jones suggests that female spectators learn how to identify with male heroes from a young age, especially when there is an absence of sufficiently complex or central female characters.[55]

It's worth bearing in mind that externally this audience appears female from a binary, traditional understanding of sex and gender. Inwardly, the picture is more fluid and complex. Although many fannibals define their sex as female, they are more likely to define their gender in less binary terms. The impact of their own gender identity on their spectatorship experience is multifaceted and perhaps facilitates a greater level of acceptance of non-heteronormative relationships.

Will is the spectator's primary figure for identification as the Tumblr Fannibal going by the handle of Soundingonlyatnightasyousleep observes; he is "one of the most identifiable, transparent characters."[56] If it is a gothic romance then it follows that Hannibal is the brooding and dangerous Byronic hero to Will's tragic heroine. Pop culture commentator La Donna Pietra notes how well this version of Hannibal Lecter meets the criteria of the Byronic hero:

> Arrogant? Yep. Sophisticated and educated? Intelligent and perceptive? Cunning and able to adapt? Yes indeedy. Cynical? With that coin toss to decide Bella's life, more so than any character on TV since Rustin Cohle, which is saying something. Mysterious, magnetic, and charismatic? He makes plaid suits look good. And sexually dominant? Well, this is network TV, so there's only so much information we're going to get in this category. Self-critical and introspective? So long as Dr. Bedelia Du Maurier is listening[…]. Having a troubled past or suffering from an unnamed crime? Oh, listmaker, you have no idea.[57]

The majority of the female Fannibal respondents I have examined suggested that they find Hannibal attractive. As Tenbrica points out, female spectators often find villains attractive because it's "about defying societal expectations of who you should want to be (or sleep) with."[58] Mikkelsen has been a multiple recipient of Denmark's sexiest man award,[59] and while that might seem fatuous, it does demonstrate that he's considered attractive by many. By casting an attractive actor in the role, the creators are encouraging an attraction to the character, and by extension, fostering a tension between the magnetism of the actor and the actions of the character.

Fan devotion to *Hannibal* has manifested itself in the creation and sharing of transformative works—gifs, memes, art, fic, vids as well as analytic discourse known as "meta." The fandom of this oppressive and dark show has been defined by a lightness of tone, demonstrated by the now iconic meme of Photoshopping of flower crowns onto screen captures. The subversion of the serious tone of the text is further evident in Tumblr user Lecterling's corny joke series[60] and Hannibal Crack vids.[61] This levity provides a context for fan interaction where Hannibal can be defined in less serious terms and where fans can express their desires more playfully.[62] In describing Hannibal, fannibals acknowledge the dichotomous nature of the character and their relationship to him. Tumblr fannibal Damnslippyplanet describes Lecter as "[a] terrible, beautiful, murderous emotional idiot," and summarizes her response thusly: "I alternately want to yell at him, and feel protective of how much of an emotional trash fire he is. It's complicated."[63] This reconciliation between his crimes and the emotional connection the show engenders is evident in some transformative fan responses to the character and is especially apparent in the creation of Chibi fan art. However, this is influenced by Japanese fan culture that has been appropriated into Western fan practice and isn't specific to *Hannibal*.

Nevertheless, this vision of Hannibal does somewhat defang him. This is broadly connected to the concept of woobification, an "audience-driven phenomenon, sometimes divorced from the character's canonical morality"[64] characterized by a heightened sympathetic response to characters. Some Fannibals accept that they are complicit in this practice; "I mean when you have a character that messed up [...] it's kind of natural to want to give him soft blankets and cuddles..."[65] (Vespertineflora). Others acknowledge that "as a fandom we like to make jokes about him ... making him squishier and more fluff-inclined. But I don't think for a second that any of the woobification means that the fandom excuses his actions."[66] (Littlethingwithfeathers). The-winnowing-wind defines herself as a "Hannipologist," explaining that "Hannipologism is about seeing his monstrosity as a part of a bigger picture, a picture that has more aspects to it than simply, Hannibal is a murderer, he's bad[...]. It's about trying to understand who he is and what he does on his own terms, about seeing his perspectives and not judging him solely on acts that appear, on a normal scale, atrocious."[67] Such an approach seems to employ Nietzsche's *moral revaluation*, which Taylor indicates is intrinsic to the forming of perverse allegiance.[68]

Many Fannibals have read Will and Hannibal's relationship as romantic, albeit problematic, and Fannibals understand this. Nightlover62 explains; "we are all fully aware that this [is] unhealthy, that nothing on this show is to be desired or romanticized to be a good thing. [...] None of us advocates that these things are okay in real life and that it's something we only like because it's fictional."[69] While slash shipping is not unique to the *Hannibal* fandom, the "Hannigram" pairing has become a defining characteristic of the interaction between text, spectator and producer. As with other slash pairings on television (e.g., Johnlock and Destiel) "Hannigram" originated in the subtext, with much fan activity focused around the "shipping" of Hannibal and Will together in a manner which to those outside of the fandom will likely have seen as entirely at odds with both the narrative and the genre of the text. Through the interaction between the fans with Bryan Fuller and the official NBC *Hannibal* social media team, this reading gained some legitimacy. Arguably, fan discourse around this relationship influenced the development of the Hannigram arc throughout the series. This is perhaps most clearly evidenced when Freddie Lounds uses the phrase "Murder Husbands" in "…And the Woman Clothed in the Sun" to describe the pair. This reflexive employment of a Fannibal term demonstrates an affectionate and accepting attitude towards the ship by the creators. *Hannibal* went further though, elevating the subtext into text by making Hannigram arguably canon by the end of season 3. Will and Hannibal's final embrace represents a union long wished for by desiring spectators. This moment calls to mind Richard Allen's analysis of iconic tragic romance *Vertigo* (1958) when the longed-for physical union produces a moment when the "gap between self and other has been transcended."[70] Framing this moment in terms of self and other allows an appreciation that both Will and Hannibal have become both self and other for the spectator too. In this moment, we might forget all of the manipulations that have occurred to this point. Will's constant mantra throughout the series, "this is my design" belies the truth: the design was always Hannibal's, and as such Will's allegiance to him was inevitable, as was ours.

NOTES

1. Wieselman, Jarrett. "Bryan Fuller Reflects on 'Hannibal' S1 & Teases S2." *Entertainment Tonight*. Last modified September 23, 2013. http://www.etonline.com/tv/138735_Bryan_Fuller_Hannibal_Interview_Season_Two_Spoilers_Season_One_DVD/.

2. Smith, Murray. "Gangsters, Cannibals, Aesthetes, or Apparently Perverse Allegiances." In *Passionate Views: Film, Cognition, and Emotion*, edited by Carl R. Plantinga and Greg M. Smith, 217–238. Baltimore: Johns Hopkins University Press, 1999. 220.

3. *Ibid*.

4. *Ibid.*, 221.

5. *Ibid.*, 227.

6. Taylor, Aaron. "A Cannibal's Sermon: Hannibal Lecter, Sympathetic Villainy and Moral Revaluation." *Cinema: Journal of Philosophy and the Moving Image* 4 (2014). 184–208. 184.

7. *Ibid.*, 186.

8. *Ibid*.

9. *Ibid.*, 207.

10. *Ibid.*, 206.

11. Sorozatplanet. "Bryan Fuller Interview—Hannibal." *YouTube*. March 2013. https://www.youtube.com/watch?v=TzU7O7Q0R5U.

12. Baker-Whitelaw, Gavia. "What Makes This TV Fandom Sympathetic to a Man Who Eats Human Flesh?" *The Daily Dot*. Last modified July 1, 2013. http://www.dailydot.com/opinion/dunn-hannibal-lecter-fandom-woobiefying/.

13. *Ibid*.

14. Collins, Sean T. "'Hannibal': The Sick Genius of TV's Darkest Show" *Rolling Stone*. Last modified June 4, 2015. http://www.rollingstone.com/tv/features/hannibal-the-sick-genius-of-tvs-darkest-show-20150604.

15. "Expressionism Definition—Creative Glossary." *Home—Creative Glossary*. Accessed July 5, 2016. http://www.creativeglossary.com/art-stylesmovements/expressionism.html.

16. [loudly Implied Cannibalism]. Accessed July 7, 2016. http://fuckyeahhannibalpuns.tumblr.com/.

17. Propp, V. IA. *Morphology of the Folktale*, 2nd ed. Austin: University of Texas Press, 1968. 27.

18. *Ibid.*, 29–30.

19. *Ibid.*, 34.
20. *Ibid.*, 45.
21. *Ibid.*, 43–44.
22. Hannibal. "Apéritif." Episode 101. Directed by David Slade. Written by Bryan Fuller. NBC, May 7th, 2013.
23. *Ibid.*, 40.
24. *Ibid.*, 60–62.
25. *Ibid.*, 79.
26. *Ibid.*, 33–34.
27. Wolfenstein, Martha, and Nathan Leites. *Movies: A Psychological Study*. Glencoe, IL: Free, 1950, quoted in Smith, Murray. "Gangsters, Cannibals, Aesthetes, or Apparently Perverse Allegiances." In *Passionate Views: Film, Cognition, and Emotion,* edited by Carl R. Plantinga and Greg M. Smith, 217–238. Baltimore: Johns Hopkins University Press, 1999.
28. Taylor, 196.
29. *Ibid.*, 188–189.
30. Park, Hettienne. "Racism, Sexism, and Hannibal: Eat The Rude." *Eat This.* Last modified March 25, 2014. https://yellowbird66.wordpress.com/2014/03/25/racism-sexism-and-hannibal-eat-the-rude/.
31. "Team Sassy Science." Fannibal Family. Accessed June 5, 2017. http://fannibalfamily.wikia.com/wiki/Team_Sassy_Science.
32. McCracken, Allison. ""Long Live Abigail Hobbs": The Significance of Hannibal's Deviant "Daughter" | Antenna." *Antenna | Responses to Media and Culture.* Last modified August 25, 2015. http://blog.commarts.wisc.edu/2015/08/26/long-live-abigail-hobbs/.
33. *Ibid.*
34. Pappademus, Alex. "Q&A: Bryan Fuller on the End (for Now) of 'Hannibal,' the Future of Broadcast TV, and His Plans for Clarice Starling." *Grantland.* Last modified August 31, 2015. http://grantland.com/hollywood-prospectus/qa-bryan-fuller-on-the-end-for-now-of-hannibal-the-future-of-broadcast-tv-and-his-plans-for-clarice-starling/.
35. Scott, A. O. "Great Dane." *T Magazine.* Last modified August 16, 2012. http://tmagazine.blogs.nytimes.com/2012/08/16/great-dane/.
36. Smith, "Gangsters, Cannibals, Aesthetes, or Apparently Perverse Allegiances," 227.
37. Angrylamb. "Dear Lovely Fannibals." *Cannibal Aesthetics.* Last modified July 1, 2016. http://angrylamb.tumblr.com/post/146772088957/dear-lovely-fannibals.
38. Gordon, Diane. "Emmy Spotlight—Showrunner: Bryan Fuller, Hannibal." *SSN Insider.* Last modified June 27, 2013. http://www.ssninsider.com/emmy-spotlight-showrunner-bryan-fuller-hannibal/.
39. Plantinga, Carl R. "The Scene of Empathy and the Human Face on Film." In *Passionate Views: Film, Cognition, and Emotion*, edited by Carl R. Plantinga and Greg M. Smith, 239–255, Baltimore: Johns Hopkins University Press, 1999. 239.
40. Labrecque, Jeff. "Hannibal: Mads Makkelsen on Playing Hannibal Lecter | EW.com." *Entertainment Weekly's EW.com.* Last modified April 4, 2013. http://www.ew.com/article/2013/04/04/hannibal-mads-mikkelsen.
41. Gordon, "Emmy Spotlight."
42. Tenebrica. "Hannibal Lecter and the Subversion of the Male Gaze." *Shapeless in the Dark.* Last modified May 23, 2013. http://tenebrica.tumblr.com/post/51139619771.
43. Mellor, Louisa. "Bryan Fuller Interview: Hannibal, Elegant Horror, Gillian Anderson, & More…." *Den of Geek.* Last modified May 1, 2013. http://www.denofgeek.com/tv/hannibal/25439/bryan-fuller-interview-hannibal-elegant-horror-gillian-anderson-more%E2%80%A6.
44. Sheppard, Anne D. R. *Aesthetics: An Introduction to the Philosophy of Art.* Oxford: Oxford University Press, 1987. 57.
45. Holt, Jason. "An Aesthete par Excellence." In *Hannibal Lecter and Philosophy: The Heart of the Matter,* edited by Joseph Westfall, 161–169. Chicago: Open Court Books, 2016. 162

46. Clark, Rowena. "Consuming Television's Golden Age with Hannibal Lecter." *Alluvium*. Last modified March 31, 2016. https://www.alluvium-journal.org/author/rowena-clarke/.

47. Cotter, Holland. "Review/Art—At the Whitney, Provocation and Theory Meet Head-On—NYTimes.com." *The New York Times—Breaking News, World News & Multimedia*. Last modified July/August 13, 1993. http://www.nytimes.com/1993/08/13/arts/review-art-at-the-whitney-provocation-and-theory-meet-head-on.html.

48. Kristeva, Julia. *Powers of Horror: An Essay on Abjection*. Translated by Leon S. Roudiez. New York: Columbia University Press, 1982. 3.

49. Plain-flavoured-english. "'This is My Design': Transgression and Possession by Hannibal's Cannibals." *No Prehensilizing*. Accessed July 5, 2016. http://plain-flavoured-english.tumblr.com/post/121442173244/this-is-my-design-transgression-and-possession.

50. Cain, Sian. "Hannibal: Farewell to the Best Bloody Show on TV | Television & Radio | The Guardian." The Guardian. Last modified August 27, 2015. https://www.theguardian.com/tv-and-radio/2015/aug/27/hannibal-finale-bryan-fuller-best-show-on-tv.

51. McCracken, Allison, and Brian Faucette. "Branding Hannibal: When Quality TV Viewers and Social Media Fans Converge | Antenna." *Antenna | Responses to Media and Culture*. Last modified August 24, 2015. http://blog.commarts.wisc.edu/2015/08/24/branding-hannibal-when-quality-tv-viewers-and-social-media-fans-converge/.

52. Wheatley, Helen. *Gothic Television*. Manchester, UK: Manchester University Press, 2006. 3.

53. Allison McCracken, "'Long Live Abigail Hobbs.'"

54. Morimoto, Lori. "Empathy for the Devil on Vimeo." *Vimeo*. May 2016. https://vimeo.com/165388440.

55. Jones, Gerard. *Killing Monsters: Why Children Need Fantasy, Super Heroes, and Make-Believe Violence*. New York: Basic Books, 2002. 82.

56. Soundingonlyatnightasyousleep. "Dear Lovely Fannibals." *None Fucks, Left "beef"*. Last modified June 29, 2016. http://soundingonlyatnightasyousleep.tumblr.com/post/146660690826/dear-lovely-fannibals.

57. Pietra, La Donna. "Mama, I'm in Love with a Cannibal: How 'Hannibal' Got Romantic." *Complex UK*. Last modified May 29, 2014. http://uk.complex.com/pop-culture/2014/05/hannibal-and-literary-romanticism.

58. Tenebrica, "Hannibal Lecter and the Subversion of the Male Gaze."

59. Hornaday, Ann. "Mads Mikkelsen, Sexiest Man in Denmark, Stars in 'A Royal Affair' and 'Hannibal'—The Washington Post." *Washington Post*. Last modified November 9, 2012. https://www.washingtonpost.com/entertainment/tv/mads-mikkelsen-sexiest-man-in-denmark-stars-in-a-royal-affair-and-hannibal/2012/11/08/65460496-282b-11e2-bab2-eda299503684_story.html.

60. Lecterlings. "That Dog Just Ain't Gonna Hunt." *That Dog Just Ain't Gonna Hunt*. Accessed July 5, 2016. http://lecterings.tumblr.com/tagged/jokeseries.

61. Stowle16. "Hannibal Crackvid #1." *YouTube*. May 2013. https://www.youtube.com/watch?v=7Lwr4X4_DCY.

62. Hall, Ellie. "Meet The "Hannibal" Fannibals, TV's Newest And Most Intense Fandom." *BuzzFeed*. Last modified May 31, 2013. https://www.buzzfeed.com/ellievhall/meet-the-fannibals-tvs-newest-and-most-intense-fandom?utm_term=.uuDLe07GM#.elpx56Ew7.

63. Damnslippyplanet. "Damn Slippy Planet—Dear Lovely Fannibals." *Damn Slippy Planet*. Last modified June 29, 2016. http://damnslippyplanet.tumblr.com/post/146650325081/dear-lovely-fannibals.

64. "The Woobie." *TV Tropes*, n.d. Accessed July 5, 2016. tvtropes.org/pmwiki/pmwiki.php/Main/TheWoobie.

65. Vespertineflora. "Dear Lovely Fannibals." *What is Going on*. Last modified June 28, 2016. http://vespertineflora.tumblr.com/post/146609173204/dear-lovely-fannibals.

66. Littlethingwithfeathers. "Dear Lovely Fannibals." *Just a Little Thing with Feathers…* Last modified June 28, 2016. http://littlethingwithfeathers.tumblr.com/post/146725130979/dear-lovely-fannibals.

67. The-winnowing-wind. "Dear Lovely Fannibals." *Ramblings and Other Things*. Last modified June 30, 2016. http://the-winnowing-wind.tumblr.com/post/146731112039/dear-lovely-fannibals.
68. Taylor, 185.
69. Nightlover62, Tumblr message to Kirsty Worrow, June 28, 2016.
70. Allen, Richard. *Hitchcock's Romantic Irony*. New York: Columbia University Press, 2007. 159.

Works Cited

Allen, Richard. *Hitchcock's Romantic Irony*. New York: Columbia University Press, 2007.

Angrylamb. "Dear Lovely Fannibals." *Cannibal Aesthetics*. Last modified July 1, 2016. http://angrylamb.tumblr.com/post/146772088957/dear-lovely-fannibals.

Baker-Whitelaw, Gavia. "What Makes This TV Fandom Sympathetic to a Man Who Eats Human Flesh?" The Daily Dot. Last modified July 1, 2013. http://www.dailydot.com/opinion/dunn-hannibal-lecter-fandom-woobiefying/.

Cain, Sian. "Hannibal: Farewell to the Best Bloody Show on TV | Television & Radio | The Guardian." The Guardian. Last modified August 27, 2015. https://www.theguardian.com/tv-and-radio/2015/aug/27/hannibal-finale-bryan-fuller-best-show-on-tv.

Clark, Rowena. "Consuming Television's Golden Age with Hannibal Lecter." *Alluvium*. Last modified March 31, 2016. https://www.alluvium-journal.org/author/rowena-clarke/.

Collins, Sean T. "'Hannibal': The Sick Genius of TV's Darkest Show." *Rolling Stone*. Last modified June 4, 2015. http://www.rollingstone.com/tv/features/hannibal-the-sick-genius-of-tvs-darkest-show-20150604.

Cotter, Holland. "Review/Art—At the Whitney, Provocation and Theory Meet Head-On—NYTimes.com." *The New York Times—Breaking News, World News & Multimedia*. Last modified July/August 13, 1993. http://www.nytimes.com/1993/08/13/arts/review-art-at-the-whitney-provocation-and-theory-meet-head-on.html.

Damnslippyplanet. "Damn Slippy Planet—Dear Lovely Fannibals." *Damn Slippy Planet*. Last modified June 29, 2016. http://damnslippyplanet.tumblr.com/post/146650325081/dear-lovely-fannibals.

"Expressionism Definition—Creative Glossary." *Home—Creative Glossary*. Accessed July 5, 2016. http://www.creativeglossary.com/art-stylesmovements/expressionism.html.

Gordon, Diane. "Emmy Spotlight—Showrunner: Bryan Fuller, Hannibal." *SSN Insider*. Last modified June 27, 2013. http://www.ssninsider.com/emmy-spotlight-showrunner-bryan-fuller-hannibal/.

Hall, Ellie. "Meet The "Hannibal" Fannibals, TV's Newest And Most Intense Fandom." *BuzzFeed*. Last modified May 31, 2013. https://www.buzzfeed.com/ellievhall/meet-the-fannibals-tvs-newest-and-most-intense-fandom?utm_term=.uuDLe07GM#.elpx56Ew7.

Hannibal. "Apéritif." Episode 101. Directed by David Slade. Written by Bryan Fuller. NBC, May 7th, 2013.

Holt, Jason. "An Aesthete par Excellence." In *Hannibal Lecter and Philosophy: The Heart of the Matter*, edited by Joseph Westfall, 161–169. Chicago: Open Court Books, 2016.

Hornaday, Ann. "Mads Mikkelsen, Sexiest Man in Denmark, Stars in 'A Royal Affair' and 'Hannibal'—The Washington Post." Washington Post. Last modified November 9, 2012. https://www.washingtonpost.com/entertainment/tv/mads-mikkelsen-sexiest-man-in-denmark-stars-in-a-royal-affair-and-hannibal/2012/11/08/65460496-282b-11e2-bab2-eda299503684_story.html.

Jones, Gerard. *Killing Monsters: Why Children Need Fantasy, Super Heroes, and Make-Believe Violence*. New York: Basic Books, 2002.

Kristeva, Julia. *Powers of Horror: An Essay on Abjection*. Translated by Leon S. Roudiez. New York: Columbia University Press, 1982.

Labrecque, Jeff. "Hannibal: Mads Makkelsen on Playing Hannibal Lecter | EW.com." *Entertainment Weekly's EW.com*. Last modified April 4, 2013. http://www.ew.com/article/2013/04/04/hannibal-mads-mikkelsen.

Lecterlings. "That Dog Just Ain't Gonna Hunt." *That Dog Just Ain't Gonna Hunt.* Accessed July 5, 2016. http://lecterings.tumblr.com/tagged/jokeseries.

Littlethingwithfeathers. "Dear Lovely Fannibals." *Just a Little Thing with Feathers…* Last modified June 28, 2016. http://littlethingwithfeathers.tumblr.com/post/146725130979/dear-lovely-fannibals.

[loudly Implied Cannibalism]. Accessed July 7, 2016. http://fuckyeahhannibalpuns.tumblr.com/.

McCracken, Allison. "'Long Live Abigail Hobbs': The Significance of Hannibal's Deviant 'Daughter.'" *Antenna | Responses to Media and Culture.* Last modified August 25, 2015. http://blog.commarts.wisc.edu/2015/08/26/long-live-abigail-hobbs/.

McCracken, Allison, and Brian Faucette. "Branding Hannibal: When Quality TV Viewers and Social Media Fans Converge | Antenna." *Antenna | Responses to Media and Culture.* Last modified August 24, 2015. http://blog.commarts.wisc.edu/2015/08/24/branding-hannibal-when-quality-tv-viewers-and-social-media-fans-converge/.

Mellor, Louisa. "Bryan Fuller Interview: Hannibal, Elegant Horror, Gillian Anderson, & More…." *Den of Geek.* Last modified May 1, 2013. http://www.denofgeek.com/tv/hannibal/25439/bryan-fuller-interview-hannibal-elegant-horror-gillian-anderson-more%E2%80%A6.

Morimoto, Lori. "Empathy for the Devil on Vimeo." *Vimeo.* May 2016. https://vimeo.com/165388440.

Pappademus, Alex. "Q&A: Bryan Fuller on the End (for Now) of 'Hannibal,' the Future of Broadcast TV, and His Plans for Clarice Starling." *Grantland.* Last modified August 31, 2015. http://grantland.com/hollywood-prospectus/qa-bryan-fuller-on-the-end-for-now-of-hannibal-the-future-of-broadcast-tv-and-his-plans-for-clarice-starling/.

Park, Hettienne. "Racism, Sexism, and Hannibal: Eat The Rude." *Eat This.* Last modified March 25, 2014. https://yellowbird66.wordpress.com/2014/03/25/racism-sexism-and-hannibal-eat-the-rude/.

Pietra, La Donna. "Mama, I'm in Love with a Cannibal: How 'Hannibal' Got Romantic." *Complex UK.* Last modified May 29, 2014. http://uk.complex.com/pop-culture/2014/05/hannibal-and-literary-romanticism.

Plain-flavoured-english. "'This is My Design': Transgression and Possession by Hannibal's Cannibals." *No Prehensilizing.* Accessed July 5, 2016. http://plain-flavoured-english.tumblr.com/post/121442173244/this-is-my-design-transgression-and-possession.

Plantinga, Carl R. "The Scene of Empathy and the Human Face on Film." In *Passionate Views: Film, Cognition, and Emotion,* edited by Carl R. Plantinga and Greg M. Smith, 239–255, Baltimore: Johns Hopkins University Press, 1999.

Propp, V. ÍÀ. *Morphology of the Folktale,* 2nd ed. Austin: University of Texas Press, 1968.

Scott, A. O. "Great Dane." *T Magazine.* Last modified August 16, 2012. http://tmagazine.blogs.nytimes.com/2012/08/16/great-dane/.

Sheppard, Anne D. R. *Aesthetics: An Introduction to the Philosophy of Art.* Oxford: Oxford University Press, 1987. 57.

Smith, Murray. "Gangsters, Cannibals, Aesthetes, or Apparently Perverse Allegiances." In *Passionate Views: Film, Cognition, and Emotion,* edited by Carl R. Plantinga and Greg M. Smith, 217–238. Baltimore: Johns Hopkins University Press, 1999.

Sorozatplanet. "Bryan Fuller Interview—Hannibal." YouTube. March 2013. https://www.youtube.com/watch?v=TzU7O7Q0R5U.

Soundingonlyatnightasyousleep. "Dear Lovely Fannibals." *None Fucks, Left "beef."* Last modified June 29, 2016. http://soundingonlyatnightasyousleep.tumblr.com/post/146660690826/dear-lovely-fannibals.

Stowle16. "Hannibal Crackvid #1." *YouTube.* May 2013. https://www.youtube.com/watch?v=7Lwr4X4_DCY.

Taylor, Aaron. "A Cannibal's Sermon: Hannibal Lecter, Sympathetic Villainy and Moral Revaluation." Cinema: Journal of Philosophy and the Moving Image 4 (2014). 184–208.

"Team Sassy Science." Fannibal Family. Accessed June 5, 2017. http://fannibalfamily.wikia.com/wiki/Team_Sassy_Science.

Tenebrica. "Hannibal Lecter and the Subversion of the Male Gaze." *Shapeless in the Dark*. Last modified May 23, 2013. http://tenebrica.tumblr.com/post/51139619771.

Vespertineflora. "Dear Lovely Fannibals." *What is Going on*. Last modified June 28, 2016. http://vespertineflora.tumblr.com/post/146609173204/dear-lovely-fannibals.

Wheatley, Helen. *Gothic Television*. Manchester, UK: Manchester University Press, 2006.

The-winnowing-wind. "Dear Lovely Fannibals." *Ramblings and Other Things*. Last modified June 30, 2016. http://the-winnowing-wind.tumblr.com/post/146731112039/dear-lovely-fannibals.

"The Woobie." *TV Tropes*, n.d. Accessed July 5, 2016. tvtropes.org/pmwiki/pmwiki.php/Main/TheWoobie.

Wieselman, Jarrett. "Bryan Fuller Reflects on 'Hannibal' S1 & Teases S2." *Entertainment Tonight*. Last modified September 23, 2013. http://www.etonline.com/tv/138735_Bryan_Fuller_Hannibal_Interview_Season_Two_Spoilers_Season_One_DVD/.

Wolfenstein, Martha, and Nathan Leites. *Movies: A Psychological Study*. Glencoe, IL: Free, 1950, quoted in Smith, Murray. "Gangsters, Cannibals, Aesthetes, or Apparently Perverse Allegiances." In *Passionate Views: Film, Cognition, and Emotion,* edited by Carl R. Plantinga and Greg M. Smith, 217–238. Baltimore: Johns Hopkins University Press, 1999.

Empathy for the Audience

Hannibal, *the Fannibals and What Happens When a Show Takes Its Fandom Seriously*

Nicole Michaud Wild

Contemporary audiences now actively engage on social media with show creators with regards to media criticism. Various aspects of media, like violence and representation, become points of contention in this conversation. The unique relationship that emerged between the *Hannibal* fandom (called "Fannibals") and the show's creator Bryan Fuller provides a substantive opportunity to demonstrate what can happen when a show takes its fandom seriously, especially in comparison to other television programs. This essay takes a cultural sociology approach,[1] where culture carries agency and is relatively autonomous. Using conversations from the "Avid Fannibals" documentary on the season three DVD extras, interviews with Fuller and actor Mads Mikkelsen, and posts on the social media site Tumblr, this analysis looks at how individuals and the show's producers used discourse on fan participation to speak about larger social issues. This has included topics such as rape culture, the double standard regarding women being enthusiastic fans of media as compared to men's enthusiasm about sports, and representation of non-heteronormative sexuality.

Beginnings

There is a rich and diverse relationship between the creators (writers, producers, show runner, and actors) of *Hannibal* and its audience. Studies of audiences have not generally situated them as part of a conversational relationship with the culture that they consume. Fandom studies have usually put them in the position of responding back to media, and discussed how they are not just passive consumers, but have transformed the products with which they engage.[2] Although some of "the current tradition of screen studies within film studies in relation to queer representations primarily concentrates on the text and mostly ignores the audience,"[3] more recent studies have focused on how producers see their fans.[4] However, the relationship has often been a negative one, especially regarding how creators perceive fanworks like art and fiction.

Creators once made and disseminated fanworks in relatively protected enclaves, through the mail via fan clubs or distributed through conventions:

> An offshoot of organized science-fiction fandom, media fandom formed around (mostly female) creative engagements with *Star Trek* in the late 1960s. Through conventions and fanzines, a distinct community was built around the creation of stories, art, and later videos featuring favorite characters. Within this community, slash fans focused primarily on male-male relationships and their homoerotic subtext: the term slash derives from the separation of character names with a virgule to denote homosexual content (Kirk/Spock). Often ostracized and ridiculed for their seemingly aggressive interpretations, slash fans developed their own communities.[5]

Even after creators began to distribute fanworks on the internet, the larger non-fan culture was usually not aware of these websites. Eventually, these activities were discovered by non-fans. Talk show hosts and journalists began to ask show writers and actors what they thought of them, and responses were often negative. *Hannibal* (2013–2015) was produced at a time when fanworks were no longer secret, and social media had made sharing them a regular activity for the most devoted fans. Shows now can either embrace or reject their creative fans, or selectively encourage and discourage the content of those works. This essay looks at what media audiences requested for many years through the lens of how the creators of *Hannibal* related to its audience; these include queer representation, not relying on sexual violence against women as a plot point, and a positive relationship between those who create fan art and fiction and the show creators themselves. The result is a kind of community that emerges based upon mutual respect between the Fannibals, writers, actors, and each other.

Representation

People have asked for more female, POC, and queer representation in media texts for decades.[6] One of the most striking things about *Hannibal* is that it specifically "gender-swapped" and "race swapped" several characters from the books by Thomas Harris. Because of the time in which Harris wrote the original material, there were not many female characters in them, other than Clarice Starling, who had to navigate a male-centric profession.

In 2013 when *Hannibal* debuted, such a gender imbalance would have seemed out of place. Bryan Fuller made this change intentionally:

> It's a pretty male world. You have William Graham, Hannibal Lecter and Jack Crawford, as your three leads. And then, there's Alan Bloom and Freddy Lounds…. So, I just thought that we need more female energy because I love writing for women and it was just too male. The piece needed women.[7]

So from its inception, *Hannibal* highlighted diversity. Steve Lightfoot, executive producer and writer, said Fuller did this deliberately, and that he "wanted to empower women within the show." He went on to say that "there are people out there … who are hungry to see themselves represented, I know I have been all my life, looked for myself through movies and television…."[8] Fuller's awareness of this need inspired him to make *Hannibal* more representative than the source material.

But later, it became clear that women, women of color, and queer people, specifically younger ones, made up the bulk of the audience: "I think our fanbase is … the statistics were women between the ages of 15 and 35."[9] The show nudged it in the direction of even greater diversity, arguably as a result of this awareness. It was a virtuous cycle: viewers became fans because of the representation: "That was one of the first things I absolutely loved about *Hannibal* … seeing Jack Crawford talking to this cool female character, and I was like, who is she? … *she's Doctor Alan Bloom! What!*"[10]; and then the writers and Fuller made the show even more diverse when they realized who was watching.

Diverse sexuality is also present. In *Hannibal*, it is arguable whether or not the main characters could be considered a queer couple. Although they never explicitly engaged in romance on the show, it is a depiction of gay subtext, and not "queerbaiting."[11] However, it is clear that Hannibal and Will's relationship is textually romantic, if not sexual. Yet there is an explicitly queer couple on the show, Margot Verger and Alana Bloom. In this way, *Hannibal* achieved a type of queer representation that is almost unprecedented on network television: "audiences who depend on major networks are excluded from certain gay and lesbian articulations on cable television … the larger population of queer characters [is] on cable channels."[12] They marry and eventually have a child, yet the story of how they got to that point is not in the typical heteronormative (but just swapped out for a lesbian relationship) fashion. This is important because

> from a queer theory perspective, subverting heteronormativity is seen as an act or strategy aimed at destabilizing fixed notions of gender and sexuality and questioning their hegemonic positions from within dominant social and cultural systems…. Mimicking heteronormative practices does not suffice as resistance as it keeps the heteronormal centre intact and unharmed.[13]

About the show *The Wire*,[14] Sean Collins writes that, although queer relationships were not the main point, "the series' queer characters are main and recurring characters. Queerness thus becomes continuously articulated through the bodies, actions and expressions of the queer characters" (703). In *Hannibal*, queerness is central to the story. There are two primary queer relationships in the show. Margot Verger and Alana Bloom, where Margot is lesbian and Alana is bisexual, is a textual story. The relationship between Hannibal and Will, which the fans call "Hannigram/Hannigraham," is first a subtextual plotline, and then a textual one. Though they do not have sex, their relationship evolves into a romantic one where multiple characters use the word "love" to describe it. Why is this important to audiences? First and foremost, it is the kind of representation that is almost entirely lacking in popular culture. Speaking about Margot and Alana in the "Avid Fannibals" documentary:

> It is quite rare to just show a proper loving lesbian relationship on television without overly sexualizing it. You'll see TV shows, here's a bisexual character, they're [depicted as] greedy … oh, hey, here's a lesbian, and she's [depicted as] a slut. You see more of that than you do two people actually loving each other and caring for each other.[15]

It causes the viewer who can identify with the character to feel that their experience is not theirs alone, and others to realize that there are people in their lives who may be the same. Speaking about the television show *Glee*, Meyer and Wood (2013) heard from a study participant that "one young woman explained the presence of gay characters as important to queer youth, because, 'for instance, let's say a kid has a hard time coming out because they're gay. That's a real situation, that happens and people have a real difficulty with that.'"[16] When a story shows a person whose experience or identity that is different from your own, and you get to see things through their eyes a little, it increases the potential for empathy, "particularly for young people who need to 'build [their] own thoughts' on controversial identity issues, often before an individual has dealt with them in his/her own life."[17]

The Alana/Margot relationship simultaneously normalizes queer life because of its depiction of domesticity (having a child together) as well as subverts it. While some scholars "reproach contemporary queer representation for having been 'normalized,' especially when what is considered normal comes from the invisible but prevailing discourse of heteronormativity,"[18] Margot and Alana represent a middle ground, where they had to struggle and overcome to reach the place they found themselves in at the end of season three. Alana is clearly bisexual, but this is merely a fact of her character, as it would be for any normal human being, as stated above by Carla Woodson. When she was having an affair with Hannibal in season two, then goes on to later have a relationship with Margot, with no textual explanation, her bisexuality is thus normalized. It is an example of "strategies of subversion [defined as] destabilizing fixed notions of gender and sexuality and questioning their hegemonic positions from within dominant social and cultural systems."[19] Fans of the show recognized this as both extraordinary and helpful to themselves specifically. They depicted "both traditional and transgressive interpretations of homemaking."[20] Margot and Alana go further, because of specific acts of resistance. The central facet of their characters is not domesticity, but their heroism, at both conquering Mason Verger, as well as surviving and escaping Hannibal. As Dhaenens (2013) writes: "the representation of gay, lesbian, and bisexual characters in the fantastic has been complicated. The genre generally omits representations of characters who are explicitly marked as gay and those few characters who are ostensibly gay are either victims or villains."[21] The show portrays their act of killing Mason as heroic; that they do it together demonstrates that they are stronger as a unified force. Hannibal victimizes Margot and Alana, in the way that all characters on the show are victims in one way or another, but unlike many others, they survive. Importantly, the canon relationship between Margot and Alana does not end in one of the characters dying. Known as the "Bury Your Gays" trope in media, LGBT+ characters are disproportionately killed off, often following a positive development in their relationship. When a show introduces a non-heterosexual character, audiences eager for representation celebrate this, and are often let down by how the character's arc ends in violent death. Clearly, the *Hannibal* creators were aware of this pitfall.

Additionally, seeing one's perspective or experience reflected back to the audience is normatively positive in and of itself:

> With Alana and Margot, I thought that was fantastic. Like, as a queer person, to see a bisexual woman and a lesbian together where it's not … sexuality isn't even mentioned. Like it's not an external facet where they have to say, oh, this is what Hannibal is, this is what Will is, this is what Alana is, it's there and it's for you to take as you want it to be … that's something that's incredibly absent in a lot of media that we have today and for women especially, young women especially, when they see that. *It feels very safe* [emphasis added].[22]

The show includes women in such a way as to increase diversity, but they are not one-dimensional. "The way he writes women … he treats them very equally and he never goes an extra step to say…. I'm specifically doing this to appeal to this person … it's very much universal" (Tony Coronado, Natali et al. 2015). When there are multiple female characters, people of color, and queer people, all with different and intersecting identities, tokenism is avoided, which is what the speaker is discussing in this quote. In particular, the intersection of race and gender—along with sexuality and gender—is a factor that researchers have pointed out as lacking in various fictional genres.

> Even though black representation has increased, the recurrent and persistent representation of black men and women as the other only consolidates hegemonic white supremacy ... even though black female audiences have been able to adopt an oppositional gaze to assess patriarchal representations of white womanhood critically, there remains a necessity of providing transgressive representations of blackness.[23]

Hannibal provides just this, and the Fannibals have noticed: "As a woman, as a woman of color, as a queer woman of color ... not a lot of these things are out here for me ... [in *Hannibal*] there's more women ... there are people of color ... there are queer characters, and ... this speaks to me!"[24]

Not Telling Rape Stories

Despite the fact that the source material Fuller drew upon from Thomas Harris had the character Francis Dolarhyde committing rape as a plot device, Fuller changed the story to purposefully leave that element out. In particular, shows about serial killers like *Criminal Minds*, and shows in the detective genre like *Law and Order: SVU*, as well as programs in other genres like *Game of Thrones* or *Outlander*, continually use rape of women in their stories.[25] Serial killers have both male and female victims in the real world. But not all serial killers in reality also rape, and the narrative of *Hannibal* does not suffer by omitting this. As the show's audience grew, it became clear that its core members were young women. Once it got closer to the Dolarhyde storyline, there was a general question in *Hannibal*'s fandom how close the show would stick to the original plot. Fuller specifically recognized this fact: "That was one of the big challenges in terms of how do we keep our promise [to not tell rape stories] to our audience—which is largely female—and also service the novel."[26] There were numerous social media interactions between the show writers and the audience where it became clear that fans were worried what would happen when they got to this story arc. Although the *Game of Thrones* producers responded to fans saying there were too many rape scenes on their show, it was said of them that they "did not want to be too overly influenced by that (criticism) but they did absorb and take it in and it did influence them in a way."[27] *Hannibal* stands out as unique in that the show producers proactively listened to fan concerns before they crossed that line. Other media, including *Ms. Magazine*, took note of this as well: "Fuller's refusal to enter the fray is refreshing. Neither sexual assault nor its survivors are props to be thrown on-screen to make a scene more 'dramatic.' When shows treat them as such, they perpetuate rape culture."[28]

In the book *Red Dragon*, Dolarhyde's sexual violation of dying women and women's corpses was text; in the show, it was subtext. As Fuller said, "You will have to read between the lines" in order to pick up on the fact that is what he was doing. Fuller puts himself in the position of audience member, and asks, what do I want to see? What do I want to avoid?

> There are frequent examples of exploiting rape as low-hanging fruit to have a canvas of upset for the audience. The reason the rape well is so frequently used is because it's a horrible thing that is real and that it happens. But because it's so overexploited, it becomes callous. That's something I can't derive entertainment from as an audience member—and I'm the first person in the audience for *Hannibal.*[29]

Even when programs try to contend with rape in a more nuanced way, they wind up, on balance, on the side of misogyny. Cuklanz and Moorti[30] conducted a study of *Law and Order: SVU* that demonstrated, while the show's depiction of rape as something survivable was an advance compared to the past, it still included many themes of "misogynist feminism [which] includes false claims of rape; negative portrayals of feminine characteristics such as intuition, emotion, and manipulation…" (318). They went on to say that the genre is "traditionally associated with masculinity," and as such "counterbalances the feminist perspective presented in many episode narratives in relation to rape and rape reform" (318). *Hannibal* does the opposite. When Will Graham is seeing himself commit horrific acts through the eyes of killers, he suffers. His extreme empathic abilities are the lens through which the audience is forced to see the crime. This device elevates emotion, stereotypically a vilified feminine quality, to the status of essentially the cure for violence; being made to confront it from a first person perspective is not something common in other shows.

In the "Avid Fannibals" documentary, speakers emphasized that the audience was grateful that this is the direction that the show took. It highlighted two people asking questions at San Diego Comic Con at the *Hannibal* panel in 2014, and this is a particularly emotional section of the short documentary. One person asked Fuller: "How did you go about making Francis Dolarhyde just as sadistic and menacing in the show without including sexual deviancy from the book?" He answered: "There was some omission … but I wanted to keep the promise that we were not going to tell rape stories [wild applause from the audience]. I think they're ubiquitous."[31] Later, another person asks a different question, and prefaces it with saying to him, "Thank you for not telling rape stories, that always needs to be said," and the audience once again applauds loudly.

What effect does rape depiction, or lack thereof have on audiences? For women in particular, there is "a positive relationship between television use and rape myth acceptance [that rape victims are personally to blame for their victimization] … [and] a positive relationship between television use and perceptions that rape accusations are false."[32] Although rape narratives on television have evolved to include the more accurate depiction of the trauma on victims,[33] the continued effect is this myth perpetuation: "Content analyses of television programs that depict rape scenarios confirm such systematic distortions; for example, prime-time depictions of rape have … been shown consistently to perpetuate rape myths."[34] Contrast this to *Hannibal* where the relationship between Margot and Mason Verger, which is based in rape and incest in the Harris novel *Hannibal*, is purged of all but a suggestion of these elements in the show. There was a discussion in the fandom about whether or not Mason removing Margot's reproductive organs constituted sexual assault, but the show did not include the explicit depiction of rape between them that exists in the book. Additionally, it is almost impossible to imagine another show not making the relationship between Garret Jacob and Abigail Hobbs sexually abusive as a plot device.

Hannibal as Fanfiction

The relationship between audiences, show creators, actors, and fanfiction and fanart creators has usually been a contentious one. In the 1980s, Richard Carpenter, the creator of the ITV show *Robin of Sherwood*, directly requested that fans refrain from writing any fanfiction that placed his main characters in a non-heterosexual relationship,[35] and a similar controversy occurred in the fandom for the BBC show *Blake's 7*,[36] as well as other shows and fiction genres. Fanfiction.net, the largest online archive of fanfiction at that time, removed works at the request of Anne Rice who objected to use of her characters.[37] More recently, shows with large fandoms including *Supernatural*, *Sherlock*, and *Teen Wolf* have endured controversies about actors and show creators disparaging fans who want main male characters to develop a relationship, and in the absence of that, write or draw about it themselves. "I guess I had been aware of this 'fan fiction' for a while and I felt like maybe if I ignored it, it would eventually go away," said Jensen Ackles from *Supernatural* in 2014.[38] Besides being insulting to the most invested audience members, this comment shows that he is uneducated about the practice, considering the fact that fanfiction, in the way that it is understood in contemporary usage, dates back to at least *Star Trek* in the 1960s.

Benedict Cumberbatch also expressed his ignorance about why people write it in an interview in *Out Magazine:* "I think it's about burgeoning sexuality in adolescence, because you don't necessarily know how to operate that. And I think it's a way of neutralising the threat…"[39] His words received this response from a blogger for the *New Statesman:*

As far as "neutralising the threat" … a swing and a miss there. Because that's not the least bit patronising, particularly to his youngest fans. I'd put money on the idea that Benedict Cumberbatch and the editors of *Out* are unaware of most, if not all of this … if you don't know about something, and your interview subject sure as hell doesn't know about something, why are you asking about it? I'd like to give them the benefit of the doubt, but these comments, on their own or taken in the context of the whole article, serve to do little more than gawk at Cumberbatch's female fans and their funny ways, and, in turn, to belittle them.[40]

We can contrast these stances to how the people who made *Hannibal* reacted to their fans. They did not take it as an intrusion, mock it, or regard it as a nuisance, but rather spoke of it as an exciting way to engage with the audience.

It's great to see them take ownership of these characters and join with us in this creative process.[41]

The fan art which is just spectacular … the amount of creativity and beautiful artwork that they have made really centering on … Will Graham and Hannibal Lecter … it's just been such a creative force…[42]

Fanfiction is important because it "transforms assumptions mainstream culture routinely makes about gender, sexuality, desire, and to what degree we match them up."[43] Specifically, at the heart of the show is the relationship between Hannibal and Will. Although this is true for the main male characters in above mentioned shows, those who produce them seem to vehemently reject the fans engaging with those relationships in a way that they deem "wrong." The opposite thing happened with *Hannibal*. "Two factors that have been identified as potentially underlying this activity are an intense emotional investment in the original story and resistance toward or a desire to subvert or reinterpret the source material."[44] In the *Hannibal* fandom, other factors emerged which are extensions of this process—the engagement of the creators of the show with the fanworks that the show has produced, and the fans' response back to this engagement. The show creators, especially Fuller, regarded Fannibals as part of the process of production—reception—interpretation and made this circular, not just one way:

What is wonderful about this show for me is that it is fanfiction. And I've been a fan of Thomas Harris' literature for decades. And so the opportunity to tell my version of the story that was rooted in my own selfish interests of what I wanted to see, yet was eclipsed by sharing that fanfiction with others who were creating their own … [who] were taking my interpretation of characters and then expanding on them for their own purposes and sharing that online.[45]

How did fans react back to these comments? Several commentators in the "Avid Fannibals" documentary drew specific attention to Fuller's different sort of attitude:

With Bryan, there's this genuineness you can instantly sense the way he talks to his fans on social media or in person, he's one of us, you can see right away he appreciates us, he shares our art and sometimes the things we write and I've never seen a showrunner have so much communication with the fans.[46]

Actor Caroline Dhavernas pointed to the fact that Fuller had been a fan of television, and worked his way into it, without forgetting where he came from:

I think he remembers when he was a little boy, loving *Star Trek* … so he knows what it feels like to be noticed by the creators…. It's really beautiful to see someone who cares deeply about people who take the time to watch what he's doing.[47]

Even actors who had not been specifically involved in fandom in the past recognized its unique importance:

"Making the show happen to some extent in a little bubble and the feeling that out there, there are people who have tapped into this twisted thing and can appreciate the poetry."[48]

Me not being on Facebook or Twitter I always get extremely surprised when I meet them at conventions … they are so dedicated…. I've seen it before when people dress up, things like *Star Wars* … it's really interesting … and there's a lot of them! It must be fun to be them.[49]

The *Hannibal* creators may set a standard for others to follow, or they may remain the exception. Even the fans themselves do not always want this level of engagement. "There is a shared commitment in the fan community to maintain the underground status of slash … in particular the anxiety among these fans that slash material will be taken to fan conventions and shown to cast and crew."[50] This fear, in part, stems from the negative comments that writers and actors have made when bloggers, journalists, and talk show hosts have brought fanworks to their attention, in an attempt to mock. Often, the person shown it has a negative reaction. But in the age of the internet and social media, and the fact that creators share most fan works this way now instead of printing them, the cat is out of the bag.

The bottom line of convergence culture is that participation has become something media industries must engage with since consumers are already using existing technologies to break up and reformulate media texts for reasons of their own. The industries that survive will be the ones that can best channel such practices.[51]

Despite the difficulties of the past, fanworks occasionally receive praise. The *Hannibal* cast and creators are a prime example of this different attitude, and thus we can examine what happens within the fandom as a result.

In an interview in *Empire Magazine* in April 2015, the interviewer asked Mads Mikkelsen: "Have you read any fan fiction? Besides the inevitable erotic tales, there's one story in which Will and Hannibal team up to fight vampires, and another where they go line dancing together…" and he responded: "I've not seen those. I've only read the erotic stuff … and I enjoyed it tremendously."[52] Later that year, at the "Behold the Red Dragon" Convention in London, several attendees posted on Tumblr that he talked about reading fanfiction again, and heavily implied that his co-star, Hugh Dancy, had been the one to show them to him.

> Right so I asked Mads which fanfics he'd read and he at first asked me to explain what fanfic was … and he caught on pretty quick and said "oh right right right, those stories! Well as I said yesterday I'm a novice in that respect apart from the ones that Hugh has shown me."[53]

It is entirely possible that he was exaggerating, but also equally possible that he was being completely serious. This detail is not particularly important. The point is that he does not denigrate it or distance himself from it. Other actors, when confronted with the same type of question, have usually reacted differently. Some have been polite but disinterested, but others have been hostile, and including a co-star is downright unusual. Even if he was kidding, it shows he considers fanfiction a completely normal aspect of the fandom. He displays this attitude in his reaction to the interviewer in the In the *Empire* article. When the interviewer calls Hannibal/Will ("Hannigram") fanfiction "the inevitable erotic tales," he is subtly putting it down. This occurs yet again in another online piece where the interviewer asks Mikkelsen: "Was there a particular interesting moment, or a piece of fan art that made you cock your eyebrow? There have been so many weird things out there." He responds similarly, refusing to be critical of fanworks:

> So many weird things, but also so many beautiful things. First of all, you'll get surprised at the amount of talent out there when it comes to drawing or painting, whatever. That is like, this is crazy. You should be a millionaire doing this. But they're not. They're just in school doing something else, right? But it's the passion of the fan art that is really impressive, I think. That so many people are doing it but also that they find each other and it becomes an identity for some of these people, who may not … some of them may not have a big social life, and now they have an enormous social life with all the other people. That's a fantastic situation, I think.[54]

He has taken the idea that fan creators do not "have a life," and engage in "weird" socially unacceptable behavior, and turns it on its head. He consistently demonstrates his appreciation for the fans: "The Fannibals are, the sole, one of the reasons for us to be able to continue for three years."[55]

Fans specifically recognize these statements as a departure from how actors usually respond to fanworks. A post on Tumblr that stated "MADS MIKKELSEN HAS PROBABLY READ YOUR DIRTY FANFIC 2K15"[56] caused the exclamation: "GOOD THEN HE APPRECIATES HOW MUCH CHARACTER ANALYSIS WE'VE DONE ON HIS PORTRAYAL OF HANNIBAL."[57] The old fears about actors reading fanfiction emerged when one writer tagged their post: "those poor writers, his reading the porn you wrote about him, and liked it apparently."[58] But another blogger wrote "I am sorry but … ohmygod i'm DYING. This is precious."[59] Tumblr users specifically recognize that Mikkelsen refuses to speak ill of their works. In reference to the interview where he was asked about the "weird" things out there, one blogger commented: "gotta love how the interviewer plainly tried to make mads talk about nsfw fanart here but mads took the opportunity to once again prove that he's the nicest and the sweetest celeb ever, god bless."[60] Two others agree, reblogging this post and tagging it "everyone on this show is so gr8 about fandom it's nice"[61] and "now THIS is how you handle the fanworks question!"[62] demarcating his kind of responses from other actors'.

In particular, Fannibals noted that the actors' appreciation for them came through in the fact that they were open to reading these fan interpretations of the characters.

> Mads and Hugh seemed so comfortable talking about the romantic relationship between Will and Hannibal, it is touching and refreshing. They admitted making it more sexual and intimate; the almost kiss, the touches and the deep love they felt for each other. Mads ships it so hard and it isn't mocking. He is so serious about it, treats it with so much respect and I admire him even more for that.[63]
>
> Comment from another blogger: What a time to be alive indeed![64]
>
> …i'm kind of losing my mind over how deeply this cast not only appreciates but respects the works of its fan community, to the point of that respect seeping into how major players express their interpretations of characters and i just[65]
>
> You know what the best part of the whole "Mads and Hugh read *Hannibal* fanfic together" thing is? That someone, somewhere, has almost certainly gotten anonymous kudos [on fanfiction website AO3.org] from Mads … and Hugh…[66]

The transformation of fanworks from a disparaged part of audience reception and interpretation to one that the actors themselves accept even redeemed the prior expressions of fear about the cast and writers being exposed to them. This is important because it subverted the creator/audience relationship dynamic, incorporating the feelings of the fans about the material in new ways:

> the act of writing is itself a profession in which only a select group of people are allowed to publish, and these are again chosen by a cultural elite as artists or by publishing corporations as hypnotists whose work will create a profit on the open market. In sum, not only are most individuals not allowed to express their own versions of actual events, but they are also restricted from sharing their dreams, fantasies, and desires. Fan fiction may be interpreted as a direct response to these problematic circumstances.[67]

The actors and show creators recognize that this is in fact why their audience is engaging in these practices, and appreciate them back. As such, the "elite" status of art is subverted, and once again returns to its true nature, that of something capable of elevating receivers, rather than just profiting from them. Cultural products become more independent, and more "relatively autonomous," as they move further away from the constraints of the purely capitalist environment in which they are produced.[68] Beyond the separation between those who commercial forces consecrate and grant the status of "legitimate" or "illegitimate" writer or artist, there is also the issue of how people appreciate that cultural product. Fandom theorists often make the comparison between how men vehemently consume culture, such as spending ample time with fantasy sports or displaying emotion when their team wins or loses for example, versus how women often engage with fandom.

> Adult men crying and engaging in acts of physical violence over sports is expected; people crying over a TV show is weird; women writing stories where Kirk and Spock are more than just friends is not only weird but disgusting and dangerous too. Of course, sports fandom is masculine…. (This designation erases the many very real women who are into sports, but it remains our cultural image of sports fandom.) Media fandom's image is, if not feminine, at the very least a hell of a lot less masculine than sports fandom—and that makes it weird. And fanfiction is not only "unmasculine" but actively feminine, designed for women rather than men—and that makes it gross and dangerous.[69]

This is the crux of why the creators and actors of *Hannibal* praising their largely female audience is so important. Clearly, it is normatively valuable to be treated with dignity and respect. Further, this attitude normalizes Fannibals' "dangerous" appreciation for the show.

Conclusion: Community

The show creators also benefited from the positive relationship, which created a virtuous cycle of attention. Producer Martha De Laurentiis compared fan communication on social media to having the same kind of feedback normally reserved for a live performance: "It's just always so gratifying that you get that … like you're on a stage, you get the audience's response … you get that when you're doing a livetweet."[70] Bryan Fuller spoke of the emotional toll that writing a character like Will Graham had, and how the fans' enthusiasm helped him: "It was a very difficult time to be in the Will Graham headspace … but the joy that the Fannibals brought to the series and their interpretation and their participation … was the bright light that kept me going through all the dark places."[71]

> I've never been involved in anything that has had this kind of impact on people … something about this thing which has been so interactive in terms of people creating theory own art, responding to the show, but not just saying that they like it but actually by creating a fandom and making a community and self-identifying in that way.[72]

"The body of queer film studies is a diverse package of possible readings of queer and non-queer films in which the spectator is a mere construction in the mind of the author."[73] It is possible to excuse this state of affairs in the past because of the lack of two-way communication between audience and creators. However, in the age of interconnectedness between these parties, avoidance of the effects upon the audience must be deliberate. The actors and creators now must purposefully isolate themselves so as not to have their interpretation, or "pure artistic vision" tainted by the impact that it is having on people "out there." Television is just like any other cultural product—people invest emotion and gain meaning from it. Audiences demanding representation, questioning the portrayal of sexual violence against women, and to not have their fanworks put down are doing so because people do not appreciate cultural products just to fill time. When creators are sympathetic to these things, community becomes easier, richer, and more fulfilling. Having producers and actors that realize this has helped create a mutual bond.

Fandoms in general are a kind of gathering space, but they usually don't include feedback, approval, and participation from the things they are based on in the way that the *Hannibal* fandom has. As noted above, many fandoms have an oppositional or downright adversarial relationship with creators and actors. What did the fans get out of this difference? "I heard a lot of people saying how the show helped them make friendships when they didn't understand how to have friendships, because of feeling out of place or disconnected as a human being because of whatever circumstances they were in."[74] The narrative of *Hannibal* itself is similar; Hannibal Lecter trying to forge a friendship with Will Graham, who finds it equally difficult to connect with others. The end result of the more positive and empathetic relationship between the audience and the show creators of *Hannibal*, and the respect for what the audience does and does not want to see, is not just a more complete and respectful conversation, but the forging of a community.

Notes

1. Jeffrey C. Alexander and Philip Smith, *The Meanings of Social Life: A Cultural Sociology* (New York, NY: Oxford University Press, 2005).

2. Henry Jenkins, *Fans, Bloggers, and Gamers: Exploring Participatory Culture* (New York, NY: NYU Press, 2006); Henry Jenkins, *Textual Poachers: Television Fans and Participatory Culture* (New York, NY: Routledge, 1992); Henry Jenkins, *Convergence Culture: Where Old and New Media Collide*, Revised (New York, NY: NYU Press, 2008); Anne Jamison, *Fic: Why Fanfiction Is Taking Over the World* (Dallas, TX: Bella Books, 2013).

3. F. Dhaenens, S. Van Bauwel, and D. Biltereyst, "Slashing the Fiction of Queer Theory: Slash Fiction, Queer Reading, and Transgressing the Boundaries of Screen Studies, Representations, and Audiences," *Journal of Communication Inquiry* 32, no. 4 (June 13, 2008): 2.

4. Lucy Bennett and Paul Booth, eds., *Seeing Fans: Representations of Fandom in Media and Popular Culture* (New York: Bloomsbury Academic, 2016).

5. Alexis Lothian, Kristina Busse, and Robin Anne Reid, "'Yearning Void and Infinite Potential': Online Slash Fandom as Queer Female Space," *English Language Notes* 45, no. 2 (Fall/Winter 2007): 105–6.

6. Jenkins, *Fans, Bloggers, and Gamers: Exploring Participatory Culture*, 91.

7. Christina Radish, "Bryan Fuller Talks HANNIBAL, the Overall Series Plan, the RED DRAGON Storyline, and More," *Collider*, May 13, 2013, http://collider.com/bryan-fuller-hannibal-interview/.

8. Ashley Beyer, Vincenzo Natali, et al., "Avid Fannibals," *Hannibal—Season 3* (LIONS-GATE, 2015).

9. Lara Jean Chorostecki, *ibid.*

10. Ashley Beyer, *ibid.*

11. Gavia Baker-Whitelaw, "No, 'Hannibal' Isn't Queerbaiting—that's Just Gay Sub-text," *Daily Dot Geek*, May 8, 2014, http://www.dailydot.com/geek/hannibal-queerbaiting-gay-subtext/.

12. F. Dhaenens and S. Van Bauwel, "The Good, the Bad or the Queer: Articulations of Queer Resistance in The Wire," *Sexualities* 15, no. 5–6 (September 1, 2012): 703–4.

13. *Ibid.*

14. *Ibid.*

15. Carla Woodson, Natali et al., "Avid Fannibals," *Hannibal—Season 3*.

16. Michaela D. E. Meyer and Megan M. Wood, "Sexuality and Teen Television: Emerging Adults Respond to Representations of Queer Identity on Glee," *Sexuality & Culture* 17, no. 3 (September 2013): 442.

17. *Ibid.*

18. Dhaenens and Van Bauwel, "The Good, the Bad or the Queer," 703–4.

19. Frederik Dhaenens, "Gay Male Domesticity on the Small Screen: Queer Representations of Gay Homemaking in *Six Feet Under* and *Brothers & Sisters*," *Popular Communication* 10, no. 3 (2012): 218–19.

20. *Ibid.*

21. Frederik Dhaenens, "The Fantastic Queer: Reading Gay Representations in *Torchwood* and *True Blood* as Articulations of Queer Resistance," *Critical Studies in Media Communication* 30, no. 2 (June 2013): 103.

22. Tony Coronado, Natali et al., "Avid Fannibals," *Hannibal—Season 3*.

23. Dhaenens, "The Fantastic Queer," 104–5.

24. Carla Woodson, Natali et al., "Avid Fannibals," *Hannibal—Season 3*.

25. Debra Ferreday, "Game of Thrones, Rape Culture and Feminist Fandom," *Australian Feminist Studies* 30, no. 83 (January 2, 2015): 21–36.

26. James Hibberd, "'Hannibal' Showrunner Criticizes TV's Rape Scene Epidemic," *Entertainment Weekly's EW.Com*, May 29, 2015, http://www.ew.com/article/2015/05/28/hannibal-rape-thrones.

27. Don Groves, "'Game of Thrones' Rape Scene Repercussions Play Out In New Season," *Forbes*, December 18, 2015, http://www.forbes.com/sites/dongroves/2015/12/18/game-of-thrones-rape-scene-repercussions-play-out-in-new-season/.

28. Carter Sherman, "We Heart: Hannibal's Stance on Sexual Assault," *Ms. Magazine Blog*, August 3, 2015, http://msmagazine.com/blog/2015/08/03/we-heart-hannibals-stance-on-sexual-assault/.

29. Hibberd, "'Hannibal' Showrunner Criticizes TV's Rape Scene Epidemic."

30. "Television's 'New' Feminism: Prime-Time Representations of Women and Victimization," *Critical Studies in Media Communication* 23, no. 4 (October 2006): 318.

31. Natali et al., "Avid Fannibals," *Hannibal—Season 3*.

32. LeeAnn Kahlor and Dan Morrison, "Television Viewing and Rape Myth Acceptance among College Women," *Sex Roles* 56, no. 11–12 (June 26, 2007): 734.

33. Lisa M. Cuklanz, *Rape on Prime Time: Television, Masculinity, and Sexual Violence* (Philadelphia, PA: University of Pennsylvania Press, 1999).

34. LeeAnn Kahlor and Dan Morrison, "Television Viewing and Rape Myth Acceptance among College Women," *Sex Roles* 56, no. 11–12 (June 26, 2007): 735.

35. "Robin of Sherwood—Fanlore," accessed August 5, 2016, http://fanlore.org/wiki/Robin_of_Sherwood#RoS_Fandom_and_Slash.

36. Jenkins, *Textual Poachers*, 201.

37. "Professional Author Fanfic Policies—Fanlore," accessed August 5, 2016, http://fanlore.org/wiki/Professional_Author_Fanfic_Policies#cite_note-rice-139.

38. Sydney Bucksbaum, "Why Jensen and Jared Had an Issue With Supernatural's 200th," *E! Online*, November 11, 2014, http://www.eonline.com/news/596672/why-didn-t-jensen-ackles-and-jared-padalecki-have-a-positive-reaction-to-supernatural-s-200th-episode.

39. Aaron Hicklin, "Poised to Make Alan Turing His Own, 'Sherlock' Star Benedict Cumberbatch Is No Stranger to Sexual Politics and Bullying," *Out Magazine*, October 14, 2014, http://www.out.com/entertainment/movies/2014/10/14/sherlock-star-benedict-cumberbatch-poised-make-alan-turing-his-own-imitation-game?page=0,2.

40. Elizabeth Minkel, "Why It Doesn't Matter What Benedict Cumberbatch Thinks of Sherlock Fan Fiction," *New Statesman*, October 17, 2014, http://www.newstatesman.com/culture/2014/10/why-it-doesn-t-matter-what-benedict-cumberbatch-thinks-sherlock-fan-fiction.

41. Lara Jean Chorostecki, Natali et al., "Avid Fannibals," *Hannibal—Season 3*.

42. Martha De Laurentiis, *ibid.*

43. Jamison, *Fic: Why Fanfiction Is Taking Over the World*, 19.

44. Jennifer L. Barnes, "Fanfiction as Imaginary Play: What Fan-Written Stories Can Tell Us about the Cognitive Science of Fiction," *Poetics* 48 (February 2015): 75.

45. Bryan Fuller, Natali et al., "Avid Fannibals," *Hannibal—Season 3*.

46. Roxanna Paz, *ibid.*

47. Caroline Dhavernas, *ibid.*

48. Hugh Dancy, *ibid.*

49. Mads Mikkelsen, *ibid.*

50. J. Brennan, "'Fandom Is Full of Pearl Clutching Old Ladies': Nonnies in the Online Slash Closet," *International Journal of Cultural Studies* 17, no. 4 (July 1, 2014): 373.

51. Catherine Driscoll and Melissa Gregg, "Convergence Culture and the Legacy of Feminist Cultural Studies," *Cultural Studies* 25, no. 4/5 (July 2011): 574.

52. Nick De Semlyen, "Blood Brothers: In Conversation with the Stars and Creator of the Sumptuous, Nightmarish Hannibal," *Empireonline.Com*, accessed August 14, 2015, http://www.empireonline.com/features/empire-classic-blood-brothers.

53. bu0nanotte, "GUYS OMG OMG," *Cast Iron Bitch*, October 18, 2015, http://bu0nanotte.tumblr.com/post/131408778824.

54. William Bibbiani, "Interview | Mads Mikkelsen on Hannibal, Cannibals and Star Wars," *CraveOnline*, December 8, 2015, http://www.craveonline.com/entertainment/931531-interview-mads-mikkelsen-hannibal-cannibals-star-wars.

55. Mads Mikkelsen, Natali et al., "Avid Fannibals," *Hannibal—Season 3*.

56. idontfindyouthatinteresting, "MADS MIKKELSEN HAS…," *The Cannibal Concierge*, February 26, 2015, http://idontfindyouthatinteresting.co.uk/post/112130864765/mads-mikkelsen-has-probably-read-your-dirty-fanfic.

57. a-kent, "MADS MIKKELSEN HAS…," *The Quiet Sense*, February 26, 2015, http://a-kent.tumblr.com/post/112131092523/idontfindyouthatinteresting-mads-mikkelsen-has.

58. ma-vhenan, "MADS MIKKELSEN HAS…," *Shipping like a Fiend*, February 28, 2015, http://ma-vhenan-is-sky-blue-siha.tumblr.com/post/112294484357/suntosirius-drinkbloodlikewine.

59. bayobayo, "MADS MIKKELSEN HAS…," *Artons-Y!*, February 27, 2015, http://bayobayo.tumblr.com/post/112171382566/memorypalaceofwillgraham-ohshutupitsquick.

60. weareunderthesameskies, "Was There a Particular Interesting Moment…," *It's Not That Kind of a Movie*, March 29, 2016, http://weareunderthesameskies.tumblr.com/post/141887517336/was-there-a-particular-interesting-moment-or-a.

61. marley-manson, "Was There a Particular Interesting Moment…," *Cellar like a Church*, December 8, 2015, http://marley-manson.tumblr.com/post/134811635858/was-there-a-particular-interesting-moment-or-a.

62. allfinehere, "Was There a Particular Interesting Moment…," *Little King*

Trashmouth, March 15, 2016, http://allfinehere.tumblr.com/post/141164211788/was-there-a-particular-interesting-moment-or-a.

63. destiel-is-cockles-fault, "What a Time to Be Alive Fellow Hannigram Shippers~," *Destiel /Cockles & Misha Collins*, October 17, 2015, http://destiel-is-cockles-fault.tumblr.com/post/131363133004/what-a-time-to-be-alive-fellow-hannigram-shippers.

64. sarren1, "What a Time to Be Alive Fellow Hannigram Shippers~," *Bugger That for a Joke*, February 14, 2016, http://sarren1.tumblr.com/post/139334114998/what-a-time-to-be-alive-fellow-hannigram-shippers.

65. momwife, "I Can't Stop Thinking about…," *Sarah Lynn Did Nothing Wrong*, October 18, 2015, http://momwife.co.vu/post/131445078427.

66. faedreamer, "You Know What the Best Part of The…," *No, Eggsy. Yes, Harry.*, October 18, 2015, http://faedreamer.tumblr.com/post/131426632285/you-know-what-the-best-part-of-the-whole-mads-and.

67. Anne Kustritz, "Slashing the Romance Narrative," *Journal of American Culture* 26, no. 3 (September 2003): 373.

68. Jeffrey C. Alexander and Steven Seidman, eds., *Culture and Society: Contemporary Debates* (Cambridge, England; New York: Cambridge University Press, 1990).

69. Constance Grady, "Why We're Terrified of Fanfiction," *Vox*, June 2, 2016, http://www.vox.com/2016/6/2/11531406/why-were-terrified-fanfiction-teen-girls.

70. Martha De Laurentiis, Natali et al., "Avid Fannibals," *Hannibal—Season 3*.

71. Bryan Fuller, *ibid.*

72. Hugh Dancy, *ibid.*

73. Dhaenens, Van Bauwel, and Biltereyst, "Slashing the Fiction of Queer Theory," 2.

74. Natali et al., "Avid Fannibals," *Hannibal—Season 3*.

WORKS CITED

a-kent. 2015. "MADS MIKKELSEN HAS…" *The Quiet Sense*. February 26. http://a-kent.tumblr.com/post/112131092523/idontfindyouthatinteresting-mads-mikkelsen-has.

Alexander, Jeffrey C., and Steven Seidman, eds. 1990. *Culture and Society: Contemporary Debates*. Cambridge, UK: Cambridge University Press.

Alexander, Jeffrey C., and Philip Smith. 2005. *The Meanings of Social Life: A Cultural Sociology*. New York, NY: Oxford University Press.

allfinehere. 2016. "Was There a Particular Interesting Moment…" *Little King Trashmouth*. March 15. http://allfinehere.tumblr.com/post/141164211788/was-there-a-particular-interesting-moment-or-a.

Baker-Whitelaw, Gavia. 2014. "No, 'Hannibal' Isn't Queerbaiting—that's Just Gay Subtext." *Daily Dot Geek*. May 8. http://www.dailydot.com/geek/hannibal-queerbaiting-gay-subtext/.

Barnes, Jennifer L. 2015. "Fanfiction as Imaginary Play: What Fan-Written Stories Can Tell Us about the Cognitive Science of Fiction." *Poetics* 48 (February): 69–82. doi:10.1016/j.poetic.2014.12.004.

bayobayo. 2015. "MADS MIKKELSEN HAS…" *Artons-Y!* February 27. http://bayobayo.tumblr.com/post/112171382566/memorypalaceofwillgraham-ohshutupitsquick.

Bennett, Lucy, and Paul Booth, eds. 2016. *Seeing Fans: Representations of Fandom in Media and Popular Culture*. New York: Bloomsbury Academic.

Bibbiani, William. 2015. "Interview | Mads Mikkelsen on Hannibal, Cannibals and Star Wars." *CraveOnline*, December 8. http://www.craveonline.com/entertainment/931531-interview-mads-mikkelsen-hannibal-cannibals-star-wars.

Brennan, J. 2014. "'Fandom Is Full of Pearl Clutching Old Ladies': Nonnies in the Online Slash Closet." *International Journal of Cultural Studies* 17 (4): 363–80.

bu0nanotte. 2015. "GUYS OMG OMG." *Cast Iron Bitch*. October 18. http://bu0nanotte.tumblr.com/post/131408778824.

Bucksbaum, Sydney. 2014. "Why Jensen and Jared Had an Issue with Supernatural's 200th." *E! Online*, November 11. http://www.eonline.com/news/596672/why-didn-t-jensen-ackles-and-jared-padalecki-have-a-positive-reaction-to-supernatural-s-200th-episode.

Butler, Bethonie. 2016. "TV Keeps Killing off Lesbian Characters. The Fans of One Show Have Revolted." *The Washington Post*, April 4. https://www.washingtonpost.com/news/arts-and-entertainment/wp/2016/04/04/tv-keeps-killing-off-lesbian-characters-the-fans-of-one-show-have-revolted/.

Cuklanz, Lisa M. 1999. *Rape on Prime Time: Television, Masculinity, and Sexual Violence.* Philadelphia: University of Pennsylvania Press.

Cuklanz, Lisa M., and Sujata Moorti. 2006. "Television's 'New' Feminism: Prime-Time Representations of Women and Victimization." *Critical Studies in Media Communication* 23 (4): 302–21. doi:10.1080/07393180600933121.

De Semlyen, Nick. 2015. "Blood Brothers: In Conversation with the Stars and Creator of the Sumptuous, Nightmarish Hannibal." *Empireonline.com.* Accessed August 14. http://www.empireonline.com/features/empire-classic-blood-brothers.

destiel-is-cockles-fault. 2015. "What a Time to Be Alive Fellow Hannigram Shippers~." *Destiel /Cockles & Misha Collins.* October 17. http://destiel-is-cockles-fault.tumblr.com/post/131363133004/what-a-time-to-be-alive-fellow-hannigram-shippers.

Dhaenens, F., and S. Van Bauwel. 2012. "The Good, the Bad or the Queer: Articulations of Queer Resistance in The Wire." *Sexualities* 15 (5–6): 702–17. doi:10.1177/1363460712446280.

Dhaenens, F., S. Van Bauwel, and D. Biltereyst. 2008. "Slashing the Fiction of Queer Theory: Slash Fiction, Queer Reading, and Transgressing the Boundaries of Screen Studies, Representations, and Audiences." *Journal of Communication Inquiry* 32 (4): 335–47. doi:10.1177/0196859908321508.

Dhaenens, Frederik. 2012. "Gay Male Domesticity on the Small Screen: Queer Representations of Gay Homemaking in *Six Feet Under* and *Brothers & Sisters*." *Popular Communication* 10 (3): 217–30. doi:10.1080/15405702.2012.682936.

_____. 2013. "The Fantastic Queer: Reading Gay Representations in *Torchwood* and *True Blood* as Articulations of Queer Resistance." *Critical Studies in Media Communication* 30 (2): 102–16. doi:10.1080/15295036.2012.755055.

Driscoll, Catherine, and Melissa Gregg. 2011. "CONVERGENCE CULTURE AND THE LEGACY OF FEMINIST CULTURAL STUDIES." *Cultural Studies* 25 (4–5): 566–84. doi:10.1080/09502386.2011.600549.

faedreamer. 2015. "You Know What the Best Part of The..." *No, Eggsy. Yes, Harry.* October 18. http://faedreamer.tumblr.com/post/131426632285/you-know-what-the-best-part-of-the-whole-mads-and.

Ferreday, Debra. 2015. "Game of Thrones, Rape Culture and Feminist Fandom." *Australian Feminist Studies* 30 (83): 21–36. doi:10.1080/08164649.2014.998453.

Grady, Constance. 2016. "Why We're Terrified of Fanfiction." *Vox.* June 2. http://www.vox.com/2016/6/2/11531406/why-were-terrified-fanfiction-teen-girls.

Groves, Don. 2015. "'Game of Thrones' Rape Scene Repercussions Play Out In New Season." *Forbes*, December 18. http://www.forbes.com/sites/dongroves/2015/12/18/game-of-thrones-rape-scene-repercussions-play-out-in-new-season/.

Hibberd, James. 2015. "'Hannibal' Showrunner Criticizes TV's Rape Scene Epidemic." *Entertainment Weekly's EW.com.* May 29. http://www.ew.com/article/2015/05/28/hannibal-rape-thrones.

Hicklin, Aaron. 2014. "Poised to Make Alan Turing His Own, 'Sherlock' Star Benedict Cumberbatch Is No Stranger to Sexual Politics and Bullying." *Out Magazine*, October 14. http://www.out.com/entertainment/movies/2014/10/14/sherlock-star-benedict-cumberbatch-poised-make-alan-turing-his-own-imitation-game?page=0,2.

idontfindyouthatinteresting. 2015. "MADS MIKKELSEN HAS..." *The Cannibal Concierge.* February 26. http://idontfindyouthatinteresting.co.uk/post/112130864765/mads-mikkelsen-has-probably-read-your-dirty-fanfic.

Jamison, Anne. 2013. *Fic: Why Fanfiction Is Taking Over the World.* Dallas, TX: Bella Books.

Jenkins, Henry. 1992. *Textual Poachers: Television Fans and Participatory Culture.* New York, NY: Routledge.

_____. 2006. *Fans, Bloggers, and Gamers: Exploring Participatory Culture.* NYU Press.

_____. 2008. *Convergence Culture: Where Old and New Media Collide.* Revised. New York, NY: NYU Press.

Kahlor, LeeAnn, and Dan Morrison. 2007. "Television Viewing and Rape Myth Acceptance among College Women." *Sex Roles* 56 (11–12): 729–39. doi:10.1007/s11199-007-9232-2.

Kustritz, Anne. 2003. "Slashing the Romance Narrative." *The Journal of American Culture* 26 (3): 371–84. doi:10.1111/1542-734X.00098.

Lothian, Alexis, Kristina Busse, and Robin Anne Reid. 2007. "'Yearning Void and Infinite Potential': Online Slash Fandom as Queer Female Space." *English Language Notes* 45 (2): 103–11.

marley-manson. 2015. "Was There a Particular Interesting Moment..." *Cellar like a Church*. December 8. http://marley-manson.tumblr.com/post/134811635858/was-there-a-particular-interesting-moment-or-a.

ma-vhenan. 2015. "MADS MIKKELSEN HAS..." *Shipping like a Fiend*. February 28. http://ma-vhenan-is-sky-blue-siha.tumblr.com/post/112294484357/suntosirius-drinkbloodlikewine.

Meyer, Michaela D. E., and Megan M. Wood. 2013. "Sexuality and Teen Television: Emerging Adults Respond to Representations of Queer Identity on Glee." *Sexuality & Culture* 17 (3): 434–48. doi:10.1007/s12119-013-9185-2.

Minkel, Elizabeth. 2014. "Why It Doesn't Matter What Benedict Cumberbatch Thinks of Sherlock Fan Fiction." *New Statesman*. October 17. http://www.newstatesman.com/culture/2014/10/why-it-doesn-t-matter-what-benedict-cumberbatch-thinks-sherlock-fan-fiction.

momwife. 2015. "I Can't Stop Thinking About..." *Sarah Lynn Did Nothing Wrong*. October 18. http://momwife.co.vu/post/131445078427.

Natali, Vincenzo, Marc Jobst, Guillermo Navarro, and Adam Kane. 2015. *"Avid Fannibals," Hannibal—Season 3*. LIONSGATE.

"Professional Author Fanfic Policies—Fanlore." 2016. Accessed August 5. http://fanlore.org/wiki/Professional_Author_Fanfic_Policies#cite_note-rice-139.

Radish, Christina. 2013. "Bryan Fuller Talks HANNIBAL, the Overall Series Plan, the RED DRAGON Storyline, and More." *Collider*. May 13. http://collider.com/bryan-fuller-hannibal-interview/.

"Robin of Sherwood—Fanlore." 2016. Accessed August 5. http://fanlore.org/wiki/Robin_of_Sherwood#RoS_Fandom_and_Slash.

sarren1. 2016. "What a Time to Be Alive Fellow Hannigram Shippers~." *Bugger That for a Joke*. February 14. http://sarren1.tumblr.com/post/139334114998/what-a-time-to-be-alive-fellow-hannigram-shippers.

Sherman, Carter. 2015. "We Heart: Hannibal's Stance on Sexual Assault." *Ms. Magazine Blog*. August 3. http://msmagazine.com/blog/2015/08/03/we-heart-hannibals-stance-on-sexual-assault/.

weareunderthesameskies. 2016. "Was There a Particular Interesting Moment..." *It's Not That Kind of a Movie*. March 29. http://weareunderthesameskies.tumblr.com/post/141887517336/was-there-a-particular-interesting-moment-or-a.

Interview

Tom de Ville

Nicholas A. Yanes

Tom de Ville has been a film and television writer since working on *Urban Gothic* in 2000. De Ville has since gone on to write for *Lexx: The Dark Zone Stories* and *Stan Lee's Lucky Man*. In 2015 he wrote the *Hannibal* episode "Contorno." Wanting to gain a better insight into how a writer approached this version of *Hannibal*, Nicholas A. Yanes was able to interview De Ville.

Nicholas A. Yanes: Dr. Hannibal Lecter has been a popular culture icon since 1981. Prior to the creation of Hannibal what was your first interaction with Dr. Lecter and Thomas Harris's writings?

Tom de Ville: Like many people, I first became aware of the good Dr. Lecter when *The Silence of the Lambs* became a worldwide box office smash back in 1991. I was a little too young to see the movie at a theater, so I caught it on VHS a year or so later and then discovered Michael Mann's *Manhunter* on television around the same time. I remember loving the idea that two different distinguished British actors (Anthony Hopkins and Brian Cox) had played Lecter onscreen. He was like the James Bond of serial killers.

A few years after that, it was announced that Thomas Harris was writing *Hannibal*, a sequel to *The Silence of the Lambs* and that Ridley Scott would be directing the film adaptation of it. I picked up a copy of the book out of raw curiosity and quickly fell in love with the dry intelligence and grotesque flourishes of Harris's prose. Since then I've gone back to all of his Lecter books several times, particularly when working on the TV show.

Yanes: Prior to joining *Hannibal* what did you think of the franchise?

De Ville: If you're talking about the franchise as a whole—films, books, etc.—I thought it was a vital evolution of the police procedural. Harris brought an intelligent, detailed approach to his FBI investigators and their processes, in particular the developing field of forensic psychology. Importantly, Harris was also one of the first writers to take his readers inside the mind of his killers and help them see that there was method in their madness. Lecter's acts may have been unutterably evil, but they spoke to perverse sense of artistry and justice. He was inflicting his own form of beauty on the world.

   If you're talking specifically about the TV show, then I remember being initially skeptical about it, largely because network television tends to make rather bland police procedurals. That changed when I heard that Bryan Fuller and Mads Mikkelsen were involved—these aren't people that tend to involve themselves in bland work. As soon as I saw the first episode, I was smitten. Yes, it was a police procedural, but it didn't shy away from the raw savagery and codified beauty of Harris's writing. Bryan had turned a few paragraphs from *Red Dragon* on Will Graham's first encounter with Hannibal into a fascinating, nightmarish psychodrama. By the beginning of the second season, the show had mutated into a fully-fledged arthouse horror story, and I was a devout fan. It was possibly the most thrilling show I could think of to be offered a job on.

With so many crime procedural shows on television, why did you think Hannibal stood out?

   De Ville: Several thoughts come to mind.

   Bryan Fuller approached the show as an auteur show-runner. Every detail of the show, every visual flourish, every performance, was filtered through Bryan's highly cinematic sensibilities. Working in this way he brought a level of nuance and design to television that hadn't really been seen before.

   The actual content of the show is in itself quite extraordinary. It is never just a police procedural. It is an operatic, grande guignole horror story, which fuses cold brutality with an almost spiritual beauty and revolves around the love between two men who are literally trying to fuck each other in the brain. That's quite an achievement for a piece of network television.

   Finally—and this should never be underestimated—the show had an irreverent wit about itself. It was never afraid to step aside from the horror and perversion and say "Aren't we all just a little bit strange? Isn't this all a bit funny?" The *Hannibal* writers' room was an exceptionally focused space, but we were also always laughing, always seeing the lighter side of murder.

Yanes: *Hannibal* was critically acclaimed but struggled to find a large viewership. Why do you think that is?

   De Ville: I'm not sure I can give a direct answer to this, because unfortunately I'm not a TV scheduling guru. A few thoughts spring to mind:

Some of Thomas Harris's fan base may have stayed away from the show, assuming that it would be a watered down, made-for-TV imitation of his work (many of my friends told me that was their natural assumption about the show before they watched it). How wrong they were!

The show's more grotesque elements and arthouse flourishes may have scared away a more mainstream, conservative audience, used to shows like CSI, particularly when it stepped away from its police procedural routes in the second half of season one.

As brave and brilliant as NBC were for airing the show, I wonder if a network station was the right home for it. Being aired on a content provider like HBO or Netflix might have given the show a chance to flourish to a more niche audience.

Yanes: One of the unique aspects of *Hannibal* was how it visually depicted murders, fashion and food. What are your thoughts on these potentially disparate elements of the show?

De Ville: Right from the beginning of season one, Bryan Fuller and director David Slade brought a distinct tone to the show that made it clear that none of these elements was really disparate. Hannibal Lecter is a man of great aestheticism, so every element of the show, from the wardrobe department, to Janice Poon's extraordinary food designs was contrived to draw you into his world.

In the writers' room we were constantly talking about that visual design and artistry and how to bring it into the storytelling of the program. For instance, one idea we toyed with is that as Will got closer to Hannibal in season three, he would start to dress like him, quoting visual elements like Lecter's infamous squared suit. Writer Jeff Staranchuk would occasionally illustrate these ideas with brilliant little thumbnail sketches. The key was to construct a sharp, compelling story from heady, visually literate sensibilities. Of course, all of this was filtered through Bryan's immaculate taste.

Yanes: You wrote the episode of *Hannibal* titled "Contorno." How did you prepare for this episode?

De Ville: I spent about a month in the *Hannibal* writers' room in LA, working with Bryan and Steve and the brilliant writing team, breaking three episodes of the show—episodes 4, 5 and 6. During that process, I was assigned episode 5 to write up into a detailed outline.

I spent about a week, working on the outline. There was a lot of material from Thomas Harris's *Hannibal* in my episode (Pazzi's death, the hunt for Hannibal using his purchases of fine goods) and Bryan was always very keen on staying as close to the original text as possible, so I devoured the book, mining it for as much information on Pazzi and Hannibal's Florence as possible. Then, when I came back to the UK to write my episode, I also did separate pieces of research into the history of Florence and the museums and galleries that Lecter might frequent to build as clear a picture of that part of the world as possible.

Yanes: Were there any elements that you included that were removed for being thematically divergent from the overarching series?

De Ville: I added one fun idea to Pazzi's death that didn't make the grade. In the episode, Lecter is curating an exhibit on medieval torture devices, so I thought it might be fun to have him put Pazzi in a scold's bridle (a horrifying mask with a barbed bit that is inserted into the victim's mouth) before he hangs and disembowels him.

I wouldn't say that it was thematically divergent from the overarching series, but Bryan was very keen on staying as true to Thomas Harris's most iconic scenes as possible, so the scold's bridle was most likely removed for being an unnecessary embellishment to an already very grisly scene.

Yanes: Looking back on the episode, what aspect of it makes you proud?

De Ville: I wish I could claim it was the "spitters are quitters" line, but that was Bryan's.

The sequence I was actually proudest of working on was Jack Crawford and Hannibal going another round. Their confrontation in the second season was a stunning piece of television, so it was an exhilarating challenge to find new ways to have them knock heads, even more so when it was decided that this was going to be a fight that Hannibal would barely be able to walk away from.

Yanes: Your episode features the death of Rinaldo Pazzi. What are your thoughts on this character?

De Ville: Pazzi is really the centerpiece of the first half of Harris's book of "Hannibal"—a police detective who stumbles across Lecter in Florence and then damns himself in his attempts to sell him to Mason Verger, before Lecter kills him in a spectacularly gruesome fashion.

I always loved that portion of the book and film. The shadowy sequences stalking Hannibal through the piazzas of Florence, Lecter's magnificent lecture on the fate of traitors, and then finally Pazzi's grande guignole demise.

In the show, we set up Pazzi as more of a companion for Jack Crawford, who would bring a little warmth and humanity back into his life (after losing Bella), before Lecter kills him. Central to this was the dinner that Jack has with Pazzi and his wife, that leads to him finally being able to finally lay Bella to rest in Florence.

Yanes: On this note, how much of the episode was directly taken from the book, versus crafted by you and the show-runners?

De Ville: As mentioned above, we tried to take as much from the book *Hannibal* as possible. Pazzi, and his unfortunate demise were obvious examples, as were the way that Alana hunted Hannibal through his tastes (in the book, the same thing is done by Clarice). I also mined details from the other books as well. In the Jack–Hannibal confrontation, I originally took a beat from *Hannibal Rising* in which Lecter sneaks up on an opponent by slipping his shoes off. On the show we thought it would be more fun to give that beat to Jack, particularly as it's such an unlikely move for him to use.

Yanes: An element of the show that fans continue to discuss is the relationship between Hannibal Lecter and Will Graham. What do you think of their relationship? Specifically, do you see it as romantic or something else?

De Ville: In the writers' room we were pretty certain that Will and Hannibal's relationship was a romantic affair, and I certainly think that by the end of season three, Bryan had made that very clear.

I suppose what interests me is the nature of that romance. Would they be lovers? Yes, I think so. But their love for one another is bigger than that—romance in the grand, classical sense. They recognize the capacity for horror and passion in each other and the way they inspire each other to greater heights of both humanity and inhumanity.

Yanes: Few fan bases are as passionate as the Fannibals. How do you think Hannibal fans differ from other fan groups?

De Ville: I met some Fannibals when I attended the Pannibal at San Diego Comic-Con a couple of years ago and since then I've got to know many more on Twitter, and I think they're a delightful, creative and very intelligent group of people.

I've not really interacted closely enough with any other fandoms to see how they differ. I would guess that Fannibals are more attuned with the particular kind of artistry, taste and delightful perversion that the show offered.

Yanes: Though *Hannibal* was only around for three seasons, what do you hope its legacy will be?

De Ville: I hope it will be remembered as a rare thing in the television schedules: a lavish, cinematic thriller with an unflinching eye. If that inspires more show-runners to be bolder and more beautiful about the choices they make when putting a show together, then television will continue to flourish as a dramatic medium.

Bodies That Change

Transformation, Body Dysmorphia and the Malleability of Identity in Bryan Fuller's Hannibal

Samantha McLaren

In the final moments before the pair plunge from the edge of a steep cliff, potentially to their deaths, Dr. Hannibal Lecter looks at Will Graham and tells him, "See. This is all I ever wanted for you, Will. For both of us." Both men are gravely injured and drenched in the blood of the man that they have just killed together. The music swells, a song composed specifically for the scene by Siouxsie Sioux and Brian Rietzell, titled "Love Crime." Graham, the investigator previously responsible for catching Lecter, looks the man in the eye and whispers, "It's beautiful," before pulling him into a tighter embrace, his head resting on Lecter's chest. The camera lingers on this moment of intimacy, before Graham pulls them both from the edge, and out of sight. It is the last we see of them as the episode, and the series, draw to a close.

The scene described above appears in "The Wrath of the Lamb" (2015), the final episode of the television series *Hannibal* (2013–2015) developed by Bryan Fuller for NBC. Both characters, particularly Lecter, were well-known long before the series aired, yet for anyone familiar with them only as they appear in Thomas Harris's 1981 novel *Red Dragon* (or its film adaptations, 1986's *Manhunter* and 2002's *Red Dragon*), the scene would likely cause confusion. In these previous incarnations, Graham and Lecter's relationship is deeply antagonistic. Yet in the context of Fuller's adaptation, the scene marks the culmination of a relationship which turns on violence and tenderness in equal measure, and which forces both men to the very precipice of their own separate identities as the two begin to irreversibly overlap.

The final image that we see of the men—bodies pressed together and blood mingling—represents a moment of conjoining that the series has built towards since the beginning. A distance has been bridged. It is both physical—now that Lecter's straightjacket, muzzle, and other methods of

71

restraint have been stripped away—and ideological; Graham, who once described murder (even in self-defense) as "the ugliest thing in the world" ("Potage," 2013) now admits it to be beautiful. The roles of murderer and detective, predator and prey, have become meaningless; the men, who were "identically different" ("Digestivo," 2015), have begun to move in tandem. Yet, as Sioux's lyrics indicate, the conjoining of the pair also represents a change that is both "anatomical and metaphysical." The very moment after the bodies vanish from the frame, Sioux sings "rushing through my veins, burning up my skin; I will survive." These lyrics, couched in the language of the body, recall countless allusions to physical transformation throughout the series, and mark the culmination of both Graham's "Becoming" ("Naka-Choko," 2014) and, ultimately, of Lecter's.

The aim of this essay is to explore the ways in which the body functions in *Hannibal* as both a site for transformation, and as a material that is susceptible to being transformed. In Part I, *Breaking Apart*, we will consider how the human subject is dismantled and repurposed, and examine the resemblances between Lecter's view of ethics and aesthetics and that displayed in Gothic texts of the fin-de-siècle period. These texts, like *Hannibal*, are often deeply preoccupied with the threats and possibilities inherent in transgressing the realm of the unified human subject.

Through images of corpses deconstructed and transformed, *Hannibal* challenges the notion of the body as a stable and contained entity. Boundaries between interior and exterior are breached and perverted as torsos are sliced open and organs removed to be consumed into the body of another. The line between devourer and devoured becomes blurred as cannibalism and auto-cannibalism are practiced; the cannibal may himself be cannibalized, and humans are compared to pigs when eaten, while pigs are encouraged to eat humans.

In Part II, *Coming Together*, we'll move on to explore the ways in which mental changes are played out upon the body in *Hannibal*, as well as the desire to transcend the human form. Just as the physical boundaries of the body are breached, so too is the distinction between body and mind. Mental changes are coded visually through images of bodily trauma and transformation, while violence against the bodies of others becomes the necessary fuel to effect change in the identities of various killers. Both body and mind become sites of slippage; one is not immune to the changes of the other, nor is it impermeable to influence from those outside of itself. By virtue of his empathy, Graham essentially becomes the killers he is hunting as he adopts their points of view to analyze their crimes. Having internalized these killers' and cannibals' mindsets so completely, it seems fitting that his physical body seems to echo this change as it regurgitates a human ear he has no memory of ingesting ("Savoureux," 2013).

This slippage is epitomized in the figure of the series' eponymous antagonist. As psychiatrist and cannibal, Lecter "makes little of the classic body/mind split as he eats bodies and sucks minds dry" (Halberstam 1995, 164). Yet Lecter's own identity is not impervious to slippage. In his quest to manipulate Graham into becoming more like himself, Lecter allows his own identity to become blurred with Graham's. Throughout the series, he increasingly appears to welcome this conjunction, despite his initial ploy to frame Graham for his own murders in the first season, and his admission in "The Wrath of the Lamb" that his "compassion for [Graham] is inconvenient." This mental conjunction is also played out upon the body, as both try to remove the other through acts of physical violence. Unable (or perhaps unwilling) to force a separation, the two men must inevitably sacrifice their individual bodies to a mutual fate.

Breaking Apart

At its core, *Hannibal* is focused on the mind. As a psychological thriller, its central concern is what makes serial murderers tick; equally, it explores the mental toll that investigations into serial murder may take on law enforcement officers and agents. Large portions of the series take place entirely in the minds of its characters, whether in the nightmares and mental re-enactments of Will Graham, or the lavish spaces of Lecter's memory palace.

But at its most material level, *Hannibal* is all about bodies. While an abundance of slain and mutilated corpses is to be expected from a series of its nature, *Hannibal* is less interested in showing its audience the fragility of human life than it is in testing the boundaries of what constitutes the human subject. As flesh is dismantled and repurposed as raw material, viewers are forced to view the bodies on screen (and, by extension, our own bodies) as intensely malleable, a canvas of possibilities upon which killers can create their art. It is, to quote Lecter as he imagines his own death and transformation at the hands of Francis Dolarhyde, both "a glorious and rather discomforting idea" ("The Wrath of the Lamb").

As an audience, we experience these conflicting emotions through the eyes of Will Graham, whose "pure empathy" makes it impossible for him not to "see too much" ("Apéritif," 2013). In "Apéritif," Graham is haunted by nightmares of the bodies he has seen, including one lying in bed with him. Later, in "Coquilles" (2013), he tells Jack that "it's getting harder and harder to make myself look." But as he continues to look, and to allow Hannibal Lecter deeper into his mind during their psychiatry sessions, his appreciation for the artistry grows and horror gives way increasingly to fascination.

In the latter half of the third season, as Graham tries to seclude himself from both Lecter's influence and the FBI, his return to murder investigations in "The Great Red Dragon" (2015) leaves him initially deeply shaken. But by the end of this scene, immersed in the killer's artistry, this hesitance and terror is forgotten. By the final episode, Graham's perspective on murder (and his personality) have been transformed. The fear and horror have been replaced; what remains is a calm, accepting sense of awe.

The transformation of Will Graham is central to Hannibal's story. Transformation is also the preoccupation of two of the novels' most famous serial killers: Francis Dolarhyde in *Red Dragon* (1981) and Jame Gumb in *The Silence of the Lambs* (1988). These men use serial murder as a means to effect a desired change in themselves and, in doing so, also transform the bodies of their victims, turning them into the necessary raw material that they require. We will examine Francis Dolarhyde and the body dysmorphia he suffers in greater depth in Part II, but for now it should be noted that, in the novels, neither Dolarhyde nor Gumb is successful in completing the transformation they desire—nor, I believe, does the reader expect them to. Part of the fear generated by these texts comes from the horror of conceiving what would happen if these men *did* succeed—if Gumb finally climbed inside his completed woman-suit and adopted the "posthuman gender" (Halberstam 1995, 164) it represents, or if Dolarhyde physically became the Dragon he imagines is inside of him—yet we enjoy this fear from a comfortable distance, knowing that our protagonists, representatives of law and order, will prevail in destroying these monsters and thus return us safely to the realm of the contained human subject.

Hannibal the television series does not operate in the same way. Our belief in the law enforcement of this universe falters as we witness its chief representative, Will Graham, murder a man (Randall Tier) and mutilate his body. How can we trust the law to maintain the sanctity of the human body, we think, when even their own bodies are susceptible to violation, to being opened up and put on display? Such is the case with Special Agent Beverly Katz in "Mukōzuke" (2014), whose body is sliced down the middle, one half further sliced into thin strips, all of which are displayed in glass cases as if in a museum, becoming less recognizably human with each cut. In fact, how can we trust any body at all, when a monster has already infiltrated the ranks of the human, wearing its skin like a suit? This, we are told, is what Hannibal Lecter has done, and done profoundly well. He is "wearing a very well-tailored person suit," Lecter's therapist Bedelia du Maurier enlightens us in Sorbet (2013), later referring to it further as his "human veil." In the same episode, unaware that it is Lecter he is describing, Graham refers to the killer he is hunting in similar terms, stating that "he looks normal. Nobody can tell what he is."

When the monster is indistinguishable from the human subjects that surround it, we realize with horror that they are no longer confined to distant Gothic castles, recognizable immediately by disfiguring marks; the modern monster may be the man next door. Lecter performs the role of confidant and friend for Jack Crawford; for Alana Bloom, he is the lover. The repercussions of this ghastly realization are played out in "Mizumono" (2014) as Lecter reveals his true predatory nature to them both, with Bloom recognizing that she was "blind" and Crawford understanding that his friendship with Lecter was a lie, stating "this is the clearest moment of our friendship."

What is beneath Lecter's person suit? Daryl Jones notes that our fear of the masked killer in slasher films comes not only from their actions, but because beneath the mask "there may be no face at all, for the killer may have no identity other than as an embodiment of unmotivated destructiveness" (Jones 2002, 115). In many ways, *Hannibal* reflects many of the tropes of slasher killer franchises—elaborate murder tableaux, constructed by a killer with seemingly preternatural abilities at avoiding death or capture—yet it constantly upends our expectations of both the appearance and actions of its masked killer. Lecter has no physical deformities, a change from the source material, in which he has an extra finger on his left hand. As a handsome, wealthy, and cultured socialite, he is the embodiment of desirable upper-class values.

Yet as the series progresses, Lecter is shown to have what appear to be genuine human emotions alongside the many he feigns. He cries at beautiful music in "Sorbet," and as his relationship with Will Graham develops, he displays feelings ranging from loneliness and betrayal, to affection and even love. The lines of monster and man are frequently blurred, and for Will Graham, the answer to what lies beneath Lecter's human veil seems increasingly to be a mirror.

To understand how the breakdown of the boundaries of the human subject open up new possibilities for transformation in *Hannibal*, it will be useful to examine the series' relation to Gothic literature—specifically, that produced during the fin-de-siècle Gothic period (circ. 1880–1900). The following exchange between Lecter and Bedelia du Maurier in the first episode of the third season, "Antipasto" (2015), calls to mind late Victorian anxiety about aestheticism and decadence leading to moral decline:

> DU MAURIER: You no longer have ethical concerns, Hannibal. You have aesthetical ones.
> LECTER: Ethics become aesthetics.

This exchange takes place in Lecter's lush apartment in Florence as the man looks down upon the city, having fled America to avoid incarceration. The rich aestheticism of the spaces Lecter occupies in Italy is far removed from the brutalist architecture—emphasizing function and uniformity—that characterizes law enforcement spaces in the series; Hannibal's Florentine apartment, filled with art, music, wine, and food, is a cornucopia of sensual pleasures, free from the moralizing eye of the law. No bodily pleasure is denied, including murder.

Gothic literature of the fin-de-siècle period often used the human body as the site upon which to play out contemporary fears. In the wake of Darwin's *On the Origin of the Species* (1859) and *The Descent of Man* (1871) which challenged an anthropocentric worldview, texts exploring the human body and mind suffering strange mutations and corruption emerged, many of which find echoes in *Hannibal*. The monstrous true nature which Dr. Lecter obscures behind the person-suit of his exterior recalls the murderous subhuman Hyde who lurks inside the outwardly respectable Jekyll in Stevenson's *Strange Case of Dr. Jekyll and Mr. Hyde* (1886). Like the titular character of Wilde's *The Picture of Dorian Gray* (1890), Lecter remains impeccably attractive and well-groomed, regardless of the heinous acts he commits. The shadow of Bram Stoker's *Dracula* (1897) is never far away as Lecter feasts on the bodies of his victims for sustenance—including a reference in the episode "The Great Red Dragon" to making a blood-based dessert, sanguinaccio dolce, using human blood. Indeed, the great crumbling edifice of Castle Lecter glimpsed in season three's "Secondo" (2015) might as well be a substitute for Castle Dracula, transplanted from Transylvania to Lithuania, the place from which the foreign threat has escaped to spread its corruption in the world.

With the threat of the monstrous Other becoming indistinguishable from one's own body, we see the horror that both *Hannibal* and texts of the fin-de-siècle address: if the monsters look like us now, then the borders of the human body have already been breached. If one body has been invaded and changed, then all bodies may be susceptible:

> "In place of a human body stable and integral … the *fin-de-siècle* Gothic offers the spectacle of a body metamorphic and undifferentiated; in place of the possibility of human transcendence, the prospect of an existence circumscribed within the realities of gross corporeality; in place of a unitary and securely bounded human subjectivity, one that is both fragmented and permeable" [Hurley 1996, 3].

In this tradition, *Hannibal* is obsessed with the dismantling of the human body and subjectivity.

In fact, the dismantling and transformation of bodies becomes part of Lecter's aestheticism in and of itself. Discussing a scene from *The Silence of the Lambs* (1991) in which, accompanied by the strains of Bach's Goldberg Variations, Lecter bludgeons a man to death as if conducting an orchestra,

Thomas Hibbs notes that "Lecter should be understood as turning evil into a form of aesthetic self-creation" (Hibbs 2007, 92). Self-creation through artistry was a key theme of Nietzsche's philosophy in *The Gay Science* (1882); Nietzsche believed that, in the absence of a designer God, meaning and logic are found in the artistic creations of man. Martha C. Nussbaum writes that Nietzsche's artist is "filled with Dionysian joy and pride at his own artistry," for the arts "enable us to take pride in ourselves and the work of our bodies" (Nussbaum 1998, 58; 59).

Lecter as we find him in *Hannibal* the series takes great pride in the work of bodies. Perhaps too much pride, for as Bedelia points out in "Tome-Wan" (2014), "Hannibal can get lost in self-congratulation at his own exquisite taste and cunning." It is his taste for the fine arts in particular that inspires his particular brand of creation, for Lecter takes the bodies of those he considers rude or tasteless and transforms them into works of art. In season three's "Primavera" (2015), Inspector Rinaldo Pazzi tells us that, as a young man, Lecter would "arrange his victims like a beautiful painting." One such tableau features a couple laid out to resemble a section of Botticelli's *Primavera* (1482), the painting's details flawlessly recreated in flesh. What the audience knows, having witnessed Lecter's contemporary murders in previous episodes, is that an older Lecter has moved on from recreating the art of others to creating elaborate pieces of his own design.

Lecter is not the only killer in the series for whom murder becomes an art form. In an essay which traces fascination with real American serial killers through contemporary American serial killer film and television, Sorcha Ní Fhlainn writes:

> "The artistry of murder in the series, where corpses are violently rendered for extravagant exhibition, demonstrates that serial murder is here completely reconfigured and stylized into an inventive creative industry—victims' bodies are recast as raw materials to be transformed and commodified for our visual pleasure" [Ní Fhlainn 2016, 200].

This is most evident in "Sakizuke" (2014) in the work of James Gray, a killer of over forty people who, after injecting his victims with an overdose of heroin, preserves the bodies and arranges them in an empty silo to form the shape of an eye. Graham alludes to the comparison between murder and artistry when he says of Gray "Every body is a brushstroke. He's making a human mural." Bodies of varying skin color are here transformed into the raw material with which the artist/killer may create his masterpiece.

Finding the killer's unfinished work, Lecter—whom the series presents as the most accomplished and skilled of these artists—takes it upon himself not only to finish the piece, but to improve upon it. Stitching Gray into his own mural, Lecter references Piero della Francesca's *The Resurrection* (1468), noting that the artist depicted himself within the painting. The concern with aesthetic self-creation and the imposition of order through art in the absence of a designer God becomes the focus of their discussion:

> GRAY: There is no God.
> LECTER: Certainly not with that attitude. God gave you purpose. Not only to create art, but to become it.

It is difficult to imagine that the traditional Judeo-Christian interpretation of God would approve of serial murder and the butchery of human bodies as a means of artistic creation. Yet in Lecter's eyes, a God who would drop a church roof on his followers during Mass could hardly object; in fact, Lecter believes he would love it. As Graham expresses in "Primavera," "God can't save any of us because it's inelegant. ... Elegance is more important than suffering. That's His design." This leads Abigail Hobbs to question "You talking about God or Hannibal?" (2014) Graham recognizes that the "elegance" that Lecter and other killers in the series create through murder, at the expense of those who suffer, is a form of creation akin to God himself. This transcendence necessarily involves the dehumanization of the bodies that are used as raw material.

It is notable that, in this scene, Abigail is already dead—the version of her which talks to Graham is one he has constructed in his mind after her body was deconstructed by Lecter for his own purposes. Both Abigail's corporeal and spiritual bodies, ultimately, are recast and used freely by the two men; Lecter removes her ear and a jar of her blood to frame Graham, then slices her throat to punish him, while Graham uses a construct of her first as a symbol for a family he craves and later to cope with his guilt over betraying Lecter.

But the most significant recasting of bodies occurs in Lecter's kitchen. While all iterations of the character have at least referenced his cannibalism, it is in *Hannibal* the series that viewers are presented with the starkest images of the act in question. We witness organs and even whole limbs sliced, minced, cooked, and eaten, though not before being arranged and presented with great care on the plate. Cannibalism, too, becomes an act of artistic creation—Lecter tells Jack Crawford that he practices "Kaiseki. A Japanese art form that honors the taste and aesthetic of what we eat" ("Kaiseki," 2014).

The meat in question comes from the bodies of those whom Lecter considers rude. In "Futamono" (2014), Graham realizes that Lecter "eats his victims because they're no better to him than pigs." Again, we see the body being dehumanized and, in this case, recast as an animal body; since pigs represent baseness and boorishness, the rudeness Lecter perceives in his victims lowers them to this stratum in his eyes, and he treats them accordingly.

In *The Descent of Man*, Darwin argues—having already shown that man and ape descended from a common ancestor—that the fundamental difference between human and animal minds is a matter of degree rather than type, and that no huge gulf exists between the two. While he believed all animals experience some mental states comparable to those felt by man (such as pleasure and pain), Darwin felt that only higher animals like primates are capable of more complex emotions, further demonstrating the very slight degree of difference. He goes on to compare the degree of difference between the minds of humans and lower animals to that which exists between civilized, intellectual men (giving the examples of Newton and Shakespeare) and savages.

In *Hannibal*, this distinction plays out at the level of the plate. If there is no fundamental difference between human and animal minds, and if the degree of difference is comparable to that of civilized men (as Lecter considers himself) and savages (the rude), then in Lecter's eyes, there is no real difference between eating lower animals (as pigs are typically considered, despite their intelligence) and lower men. To paraphrase Graham, Lecter's victims are no better or worse to him than pigs, and their bodies can be treated as he would treat a pig's.

But in one of many acts of mirroring in the show, this goes both ways, with pigs encouraged to eat humans by a man who is himself boorish and rude, Mason Verger. Mason's intention is to eat Lecter slowly, while he is still alive, and finally feed Lecter's face to his pigs. After having Lecter and Graham kidnapped in "Digestivo," Mason transports them to his pig farm strung upside down in the back of a truck like animal carcasses, before branding Lecter and tying him up in a pigpen. Lecter notes "it's very important to Mason that I have the pig's experience," an inversion of Lecter's treatment of his own victims.

The border between human and animal bodies having been crossed, slippage starts to occur. The corporeal form, *Hannibal* demonstrates, is not as stable as we believe; in fact, it is immensely fluid. If a body considered to be a pig is sliced, cooked, and consumed as "pork," then for all intents and purposes, it might as well have been a pig all along. The difference exists in the mind of the onlooker, but with the unreliable perspective of Graham as proxy for the audience, this too becomes fluid.

As the border between human and animal bodies breaks down, so too do the borders between interior and exterior, and between self and other. Skin, the ultimate boundary between our interior and our exterior, is subject to all manner of violations in *Hannibal* as it is pierced and flayed. Though we will come back to the loss of individual identities in Part II, a version of this takes place at the level of skin as faces are removed, destroyed, or worn by others. As the primary signifier by which we recognize each other in a visual society, the face is also an important factor in how we self-identify; recognition of one's own face in a mirror, Lacan tells us in "The Mirror Stage" (1949), is a crucial moment in the childhood development of subjectivity and narcissism. Mason's violent removal of his own face in "Tome-Wan," and his desire to wear Graham's face as a replacement in "Digestivo" elicits a different horror in us than we might feel about any other area of skin receiving the same treatment, because by removing the face, one's identity is (wholly or partially) removed as well.[1] Wearing the face of another, then, is an ungovernable breach of the self/other distinction, a case of physical identity theft.

Cannibalism is the most blatant act of border-crossing in the series, the moment at which the body of one because incorporated into the body of another. In his book *Coming to Our Senses*, Morris Berman describes the way in which the eating of a body, human or animal, was seen as an act of respect in some early cultures:

> "By eating the animal, you absorbed its power, its characteristics. (The same is true of cannibalism.) Eating is the most fundamental form of Self/Other relationship, the incorporation of another into your own body" [Berman 1989, 69].

In the case of the first cannibal we encounter in *Hannibal*, this description is very telling. Garratt Jacob Hobbs, introduced in "Apéritif," is afraid of losing his teenage daughter Abigail as she approaches the age at which a child typically leaves home. In response to this fear, he murders girls who look like his daughter, ingesting their organs as a way to absorb them into himself (with their bodies as representative of his daughter's, this ritual prevents her from every leaving him). Hobbs uses every part of their bodies for something, like stuffing pillows with human hair. In his mind, this is a way to "honor" them. His actions, though morally repugnant, stem from a place of intense love.

The irony for Hobbs is that, by turning their bodies into food and furniture, into *things*, he is also responsible for dehumanizing them. In her seminal writing on abjection, Julia Kristeva describes the corpse as being the ultimate abjection, the complete breakdown of exclusionary borders:

> "the corpse, the most sickening of wastes, is a border that has encroached upon everything. … The corpse, seen without God and outside of science, is the utmost of abjection. It is death infecting life. Abject. It is something rejected from which one does not part, from which one does not protect oneself as from an object" [Kristeva 1982, 3–4].

We can see by this description why the ingestion of a human corpse is so disruptive in *Hannibal*; by eating it, the cannibal is putting the very thing which threatens all borders into their own body, an act of border-crossing in and of itself. Interior and exterior, mind and body, self and other—all are threatened with becoming undifferentiated. This slippage occurs to such an extreme degree that even acts of auto-cannibalism start to occur—as is the case with Abel Gideon, forced to eat his own legs in "Futamono," thus becoming his "own last supper." With all exclusionary borders in a state of collapse, it seems inevitable that bodies will start to digest themselves.

Coming Together

Having examined the susceptibility of bodies to undergo change against one's will in *Hannibal*, we move on to look at bodies which transform voluntarily. *Hannibal* introduces two killers with bodily transformation on their minds. The first is Randall Tier in "Shiizakana" (2014), a man "suffering from a kind of 'humanity dysphoria'" (McLean 2015, 46). Lecter describes Tier as suffering an identity disorder which makes him feel as though he is "an animal born in the body of a man." Building a hydraulic suit which fuses the skull of a cave bear with his own body, Tier eviscerates his victims in a manner which is initially mistaken by law enforcement for an animal attack.

Tier provides the series a means of exploring the notion of a body which does not fit without straying into the potentially problematic territory of gender or sexual dysphoria, while also furthering its dismantling of what constitutes the human. Randall's surname, Tier, is the German translation of the word *animal*, an indicator to the audience that the body dysmorphia he suffers does correspond with who (or what) he really is.

Francis Dolarhyde, the second killer obsessed with transformation, appears in *Hannibal*'s third season. In the novel *Red Dragon* (1981), Dolarhyde is a man who was traumatized during his childhood both by threats of castration by his grandmother, who would place his penis between the blades of scissors, and by the abuse which he was subjected to as a result of being born with a cleft palate. As an adult, he becomes obsessed with the William Blake painting *The Great Red Dragon and the Woman Clothed in Sun* (1803); believing the Dragon of the painting to be inside of him, he murders families in order to "Become" it. Part of this process involves the necrophilic rape of the mothers' corpses, and it is implied that, prior to developing a relationship with Reba McClane, he is unable to perform sexually without committing or witnessing acts of violence.

These elements of psychosexual disturbance in Dolarhyde's character are given a backseat in *Hannibal*. Instead, the series focuses on Dolarhyde's physical engagement with his alternate personality, which he envisions as a creature literally tearing out from beneath his skin. His skin and the canvas of the painting become one and the same; in "The Number of the Beast is 666" (2015), as Dolarhyde imagines clawing at the paper and watching it rupture and bleed like living flesh, we see he is actually dragging his nails down his back, which has been inked to resemble the painting.

Unlike either film adaptation of the novel, in which Dolarhyde's psychosis is entirely confined within his own head, the series presents audiences with a physical manifestation of the Dragon on screen. In the episode "…And the Woman Clothed in Sun" (2015) we see Dolarhyde as the Dragon, his massive wings outspread, roaring and surrounded by flames. This occurs during a phone conversation between Dolarhyde and Lecter while the latter is incarcerated. Dolarhyde makes the call from inside Lecter's former office, and during the call he imagines watching himself and Lecter talking to one another as patient and therapist in the room. While the scene would appear to take place entirely from Dolarhyde's point of view, this is complicated by the fact that the office doubles as a room inside Lecter's memory palace, which the audience has seen him inside of, dressed similarly, in earlier episodes. When Lecter says, "See how magnificent you are," looking on in contemplative fascination at the Dragon rampant, the audience is left with the impression that Lecter has indeed witnessed the same thing that we and Dolarhyde have seen. With the physical body of the Dragon on screen before us, and Lecter seeming to see it too, it is all too easy to believe that the Dragon of Dolarhyde's psychosis may in fact be real.

But is bodily metamorphosis possible? In the case of Randall Tier, Lecter confirms that it is not—and that Tier knows this—stating: "He didn't believe metamorphosis could physically take place, but that wouldn't stop him from trying to achieve it" ("Shiizakana," 2014). The most complete transformation Tier can achieve (at least in life) is a compromise or symbiosis between his own body, unchanged, and the animal suit he encases himself in. In the case of Dolarhyde, the character seems closer to achieving metamorphosis as the audience witnesses his notion of it through his own eyes, but it is ultimately all in his head. When Dolarhyde dies in "The Wrath of the Lamb," the scene intercuts Dolarhyde's perspective with what is really happening; from his perspective, the Dragon's wings sprout from his back, but we see this is only in his mind.

It is only in death that both killers achieve a physical embodiment of their "Becoming." For Dolarhyde, it comes as he lies dead beneath the moon, his pooling blood spreading across the ground on either side of him and forming the shape of the Dragon's wings. For Tier, this occurs when Graham mutilates his corpse and displays it, fusing his flesh with the bones of a saber-toothed cat in the museum where he worked, a grotesquely beautiful hybrid of man and animal ("Naka-choko"). To put it another way, neither man is able to complete their bodily transformation into something other than human without first sacrificing their human body.

Discussing the duality of meaning found in the motif of the death'-s-head moth stuffed into the mouths of Jame Gumb's victims in the film *The Silence of the Lambs* (1991), Karren B. Mann asks "is death the meaning of bodies, or does the desire to transcend/transform bodies mean only death? Stuck at the very place between in and out, standing for life and death, the moth reinforces the paradox of being in a body" (Mann 1996, 600). In *Hannibal*, as we have seen, bodily transformation (whether willing or unwilling) always involves a sacrifice of the human body. This sacrifice should be understood as both literal and symbolic. The murders committed by Tier and Dolarhyde (the transformation of human bodies into raw material, into fuel) are symbolically necessary to complete the transformation in their minds, and the physical sacrifice of their own bodies is required in order for them to escape and transcend the confines of that form.

The parallels between Tier and Dolarhyde (and, as we will see, Graham himself) are significant. Both Tier and Dolarhyde strive for physical transformation, are encouraged by Lecter to commit murderous acts to fuel their transformations, and both ultimately meet their deaths at Graham's hands. It is through their deaths that Graham himself is able to transform.

In Graham, Lecter sees a kindred spirit. After shooting Garratt Jacob Hobbs' to death to prevent the man from murdering his daughter, Graham struggles to cope with the knowledge that he enjoyed the act. Lecter tries to push Graham into killing again, believing he would be so much happier if he embraced his murderous urges (after all, he himself is very happy with his lifestyle). "If you followed the urges you kept down for so long, cultivated them as the inspirations they are, you would have become someone other than yourself" he tells Graham in "Savoureux." As Graham begins to follow his advice in the second season, the changes he undergoes are played out upon his body. After sending a man to kill Lecter in "Mukōzuke," Graham imagines a pair of enormous antlers piercing through the skin of his back. He is at first distressed and confused as the sharp points protrude, before dropping to his hands and knees as the antlers extend, huge and magnificent; the look on his face is akin to one experiencing the throes of religious of sexual ecstasy, caught between pain and rapture. Antlers have great symbolic significance to Graham—his first kill, Hobbs, impaled the bodies of his victims upon antlers, and it was through killing Hobbs that Graham's transformation found its first kindling.

After murdering Tier and pretending to murder and eat Freddie Lounds, Graham undergoes a symbolic rebirth in "Kō No Mono" (2014). Throughout the series, he has imagined Lecter's monstrous true form as an antlered humanlike creature with black skin, white eyes, protruding ribs, and elongated fingers—the Wendigo. Here, birthed from the body of a stag, Graham emerges as an antlered wendigo-like himself, gasping and screaming, still recognizably "human" but different, changed. To return to a comparison with the fin-de-siècle Gothic, this scene is entirely characteristic of the transformations Gothic bodies often undergo:

> The abhuman subject is a not-quite human subject, characterized by its morphic variability, continually in danger of becoming not-itself, becoming other.... But a movement away is also a movement towards—towards a site or condition as yet unspecified—and thus entails both a threat and a promise. ... The fin-de-siècle Gothic is ... convulsed by nostalgia for the "fully-human" subject whose undoing it accomplishes so resolutely, and yet aroused by the prospect of a monstrous becoming [Hurley 1996, 3–4].

As Graham struggles to remain himself while also reveling in what he is becoming, the audience experiences this horror and fascination alongside him. We root for Graham to do the "right" thing, yet we are also drawn down the darkly seductive path that Lecter is beckoning from. Throughout the series, Lecter is positioned as both a threat and a friend to Graham and his other patients, for though the doctor advocates monstrous courses of action in encouraging his patients to kill, it appears he also wants what is best for them. For Tier and Dolarhyde, unable to live inside their own bodies, Lecter's advice leads them to understand who they are inside, before helping them shed the bodies which do not fit them. For Graham, the tool Lecter uses to shed Tier and Dolarhyde from their bodies by manipulating Graham into killing them, Lecter helps Graham live with his own mind.

Graham has "pure empathy" ("Apéritif"). He is able to assume the point of view of anyone, but this is not something he can control; Graham *cannot help* but assume the point of the view of anyone he encounters. Given his work in law enforcement, forced to get inside the minds of violent and disturbed killers and allow them into his own mind perforce, this disorder is extremely distressing for him. As noted earlier, Graham's mental reenactments of crimes are coded in bodily terms—we hear the organic hum of his body's circulatory system as he opens his mind up to accept theirs into him, and see his body in place of the killer in question; when he describes the killer's actions, he does so in the first person. The boundary between self and other collapses; Graham and the killer become one and the same.

However, once exclusionary boundaries erode or approach a state of complete collapse, the self and other are at risk of become irreversibly undifferentiated. In the pilot episode, while Hannibal and Graham are hunting Garratt Jacob Hobbs, a secretary asks them, "What did you say your names were?" to which Graham replies, "Garratt Jacob Hobbs." On a literal level, he is referring to a name he has just read on a file and ignoring the woman's question. Yet, on a symbolic level, he is also answering truthfully—he can empathize completely with Hobbs; he might as well be Hobbs.

This is the first hint the series gives that Graham is unable to extricate his own identity from falling irrevocably into an amalgam of other identities he has assumed. As Lecter expounds in "Savoureux," "You catch these killers, Will, by getting into their heads, but you also let them into yours." As a result of the collapsing boundaries between mind and body, however, Graham has also let Hobbs into his body, resulting in a physical reenactment of Hobbs' being shot down in his kitchen, Will's body in Hobbs' place, repeating the same dialogue: "See? See?"

The mind/body distinction breaking down, the proximity between minds becomes figured in terms of bodily distance. "Don't let him [Graham] get too close," Alana Bloom warns Jack Crawford in the very first episode, a warning which is entirely ignored; Graham is put close enough to be in danger of both bodily harm and mental breakdown, and the two are not always mutually exclusive. Lecter's penetrative mind is comparable to the feeling of "a fly flitting around" inside Graham's head ("…And the Woman Clothed with the Sun," 2015). The cannibal's quest to get inside Graham's head involves a number of physical penetrations as well. This begins at the level of Graham's immediate environment as Lecter invades Graham's home to plant evidence which will incriminate him ("Œuf," 2013). When we realize that Graham's home is figured as an expression of his psyche, the full of impact of this invasion becomes clear—Graham's home, like his mind, is "a sanctuary with the thinnest possible membrane between interior and exterior…. The main floor of the house had long and wide windows that allowed an undisturbed flow from the interior to the lush, green world outdoors" (McLean 2015, 114). This border crossed, Lecter moves on to penetrating Graham's body; in a flashback in "Kaiseki," we witness him forcing a tube down Graham's throat in order to plant an ear in his stomach. Both actions are performed in order to frame Graham for murder, an effort which mirrors Lecter's attempts to penetrate his mind and convince him to kill. What Lecter does not expect, however, is that by getting inside Graham's head, his own identity will become so subsumed by Graham's permeable mind that neither is able to separate.

The collapse of Lecter's identity into Graham's is first signaled to the audience by images of the men's faces becoming combined or blurred into one (the face, we remember, is a visual signifier of identity). Examples of this occur in the episodes "Naka-choko" and "Dolce" (2015). In "…And the Woman Clothed in Sun," Graham's image is overlaid on Lecter as the pair face each other on opposite sides of Lecter's glass prison cell. From this we may interpret three things: firstly, that Graham looks at Lecter, a killer, and sees himself reflected back at him; secondly, that Graham believes that he himself belongs on Lecter's side of the glass, incarcerated, as he too is a killer (he has already murdered and mutilated Tier, and will soon kill again); and thirdly, that part of Graham's identity now inhabits Lecter, as the shot shows Graham's image contained within Lecter's own body.

Both men conceive the body of the other as a means by which they can untangle their identities. Given how entirely the mind/body distinction collapses in *Hannibal*, this does not seem an illogical conclusion to come to. In "Mizumono," Lecter attempts to eviscerate Graham with a linoleum knife. It is made clear that he is trying to gut out the part of himself that has been changed by Graham: Lecter asks, "Did you believe you could change me the way I've changed you?" to which Graham replies, "I already did." Graham attempts the act in reverse in "Dolce," drawing a similar knife on Lecter. In the same episode, Lecter then attempts to eat Graham's brain, a blatant attempt at absorbing Graham into himself while preserving the oneness of his own body. Recall Hobbs, who ate women who resembled his daughter because he loved her/them and wanted to absorb her/them into himself. Unsuccessful in this venture, and irreversibly changed, by "The Wrath of the Lamb" Lecter is willing to deliberately sacrifice his own body to protect Graham's, placing himself between Graham and Dolarhyde, taking a bullet from the latter, telling Will, "No greater love hath man than to lay down his life for a friend."

Again, the physical distance of bodies comes into play as a means by which to convey the erosion of the self/other distinction. For the majority of the first season, Graham and Lecter are on the opposite sides of a room, a professional and clinical divide between them as they engage in therapy. More intimate physical contact occurs in the second season after Graham has killed Tier and, in doing so, allowed himself to become more like Lecter. Graham attempts to force distance between them in the third season by telling Lecter to run and that he doesn't want to know where he goes; when Lecter refuses him this request, Graham retires from the FBI and gets married, leaving Lecter safely confined inside a prison cell. Inevitably, though, he is drawn back in; as the season progresses, we see various shots of Graham and Lecter walking towards each other on opposite sides of the glass until, by "The Wrath of the Lamb," they are not only on the same side of the glass, but stand together in Lecter's memory palace, intimately cohabiting a shared mental space. As the episode continues, Lecter escapes his cage and is stripped of his straightjacket, muzzle, and prison clothing, until the two stand as equals far away from the grasp of law enforcement, sharing a bottle of wine. Finally, as they kill Dolarhyde together, their bodies working in complete synchronicity, the last modicum of distance has been bridged; they hold each other close, Graham's head resting on Lecter's chest.

And so we return to where we began, to the final image of Lecter and Graham holding one another atop the cliff. The scene is filmed in a manner which is immensely sensual, lingering on shots of blood dripping, on close-ups of the men's faces as they lose themselves in each other; the sound of their heavy breathing compliments the stirring swells of Siouxsie Sioux and Brian Reitzell's "Love Crime." The breakdown of the self/other distinction, Berman tells us, occurs during such moments of closeness:

> "Situations of intense relatedness—romantic love, psychosis, mystical experience—involve a "regression" to syncretic sociability, wherein it is impossible to distinguish where Self ends and Other begins…. We long for this, but it is the ultimate horror as well, the collapse back into the abyss" [Berman 1989, 38].

Is the scene an expression of romantic love? Psychosis? Mystical experience? Perhaps it is a combination of the three, and more besides. Throughout the series, we have witnessed the complete collapse of exclusionary boundaries—between self and other, body and mind, interior and exterior—and here we witness the final movement towards the abyss. Unable to "survive separation" ("Dolce"), the pair sacrifice individual existence and disappear from the frame, presumably into the ocean below. As we have seen microcosms of in the transformations of Tier and Dolarhyde, the sacrifice of their bodies is required for metamorphosis. As the post-credits scene of the episode reveals, at least one of the pair has survived—Bedelia du Maurier has not cut off and cooked her own leg, and there are *two* places besides hers at the dinner table.

The audience is not privy to who, or what, survived the fall—at least not yet. But having witnessed the complete coming together of minds, the complete breaking apart of bodies, the transcendent possibilities of this Becoming fascinate us.

NOTE

1. It is interesting to note that Mason Verger's actor switches between seasons two and three, from Michael Pitt to Joe Anderson. Though it was allegedly Pitt's decision not to reprise the role, it seems almost natural that this change should happen. With his face hacked to pieces, part of Mason's identity has been altered, and the change of actor unintentionally mirrors this change.

WORKS CITED

Berman, Morris. *Coming to Our Senses: Body and Spirit in the Hidden History of the West.* New York: Simon & Schuster, 1989.

Darwin, Charles. *The Descent of Man.* Hertfordshire, UK: Wordsworth Editions Limited, 2013.

_____. *The Origin of Species.* Hertfordshire, UK: Wordsworth Editions Limited, 1998.

Halberstam, Judith. *Skin Shows: Gothic Horror and the Technology of Monsters.* London, UK: Duke University Press, 1995.

Harris, Thomas. *Hannibal.* London, UK: Arrow Books, 2009.

_____. *Red Dragon.* London, UK: Arrow Books, 2009.

_____. *The Silence of the Lambs*. London, UK: Arrow Books, 2013.

Hibbs, Thomas. "Virtue, Vice, and the Harry Potter Universe." In *The Changing Face of Evil in Film and Television*, edited by Martin F. Nordon, 89–100. New York, NY: Rodopi, 2007.

Hurley, Kelly. *The Gothic Body: Sexuality, Materialism, and Degeneration in the Fin de Siècle*. Cambridge, UK: Cambridge University Press, 1996.

Jones, Darryl. Horror: A Thematic History in Fiction and Film. London, UK: Arnold, 2002.

Kristeva, Julia. *Powers of Horror: An Essay on Abjection*. Trans. Leon. S. Roudiez. New York, NY: Columbia University Press, 1982.

Lacan, Jacques. "The Mirror Stage as Formative of the Function of the I as Revealed in Psychoanalytic Experience." In *The Norton Anthology of Theory and Criticism*, Second Edition, edited by Vincent B, 1163–1169. Leitch. New York, NY: W. W. Norton & Company, Inc., 2010.

Mann, Karen B. "The Matter With Mind: Violence and "The Silence of the Lambs"" *Criticism* 38, no. 4 (1996): 583–605. http://www.jstor.org/stable/23118159.

McLean, Jesse. *The Art and Making of Hannibal: The Television Series*. London, UK: Titan Books, 2015.

Ní Fhlainn, Sorcha. "Screening the American Gothic: Celluloid Serial Killers in American Popular Culture." In *American Gothic Culture: An Edinburgh Companion*, edited by Joel Faflak and Jason Haslam, 187–202. Edinburgh, UK: Edinburgh University Press, 2016.

Nietzsche, Friedrich. *The Gay Science*. Trans. Walter Kaufmann. New York, NY: Vintage, 1974.

Nussbaum, Martha C. "The Transfigurations of Intoxication." In *Nietzsche, Philosophy and the Arts*, edited by Salim Kemal, Ivan Gaskell, and Daniel W. Conway, 36–69. Cambridge, UK: Cambridge University Press, 1998.

Stevenson, Robert Louis. *Strange Case of Dr Jekyll and Mr Hyde*. Hertfordshire, UK: Wordsworth Editions Limited, 1999.

Stoker, Bram. *Dracula*. London, UK: Penguin Group, 2003.

Wilde, Oscar. *The Picture of Dorian Gray*. Hertfordshire, UK: Wordsworth Editions Limited, 2001.

Filmography

Hannibal: The Complete First, Second and Third Seasons. 2013–2015. Created by Bryan Fuller. Issy-les-Moulineaux, France: Studiocanal, 2015. DVD.

Manhunter. Directed by Michael Mann. 1986. Santa Monica, CA: MGM, 2004. DVD.

Red Dragon. Directed by Brett Ratner. 2002. London, UK: Universal Pictures, 2003. DVD.

The Silence of the Lambs. Directed by Jonathan Demme. 1991. London, UK: 20th Century Fox, 2006. DVD.

Cannibalizing *Hannibal*

The Horrific and Appetizing Rewriting of Hannibal *Mythology*

Naja Later

When NBC adapted *Hannibal* for television, one of the changes it made to the franchise was the sumptuous scenes of food preparation.[1] Fans are invited to Hannibal Lecter's kitchen to watch him take bodies and masterfully transform them into succulent dishes. The cooking scenes in *Hannibal* are a channel through which the process of transformative adaptation is explored and encouraged. These scenes encode *Hannibal* as a multi-authored, cross-media, and trans-textual mythology through their dense allusion, portraying cooking as a transformative, reproducible process. The adaptation of a cooking show aesthetic takes advantage of the genre's didacticism to suggest that fans "try this at home," creating transformative fanworks that perpetuate *Hannibal*'s mythology. In this sense, while other *Hannibal* scenes may provide content for fanworks, the adaptation of the cooking genre cryptically endorses transformative processes of fandom.

The sequences of food in *Hannibal* are richly synesthetic, evoking a sensorium of pleasures exceeding the capacity of television to show. By densely layering allusive codes in the cooking sequences, the implicit product of transformative works is not only food but other transferences of touch, taste, and smell for *Hannibal*. I am concerned particularly with the show's romance between Lecter and his pursuer, Will Graham, an affair conspicuously lacking in diegetic intimacy. The show's coded dialectic with fandom means queer intimacy is substantiated through slash fanworks such as fanfiction, fanart, and videos. This may be understood through Lecter's key ingredient being bodies—both human bodies and bodies of work—highlighting a complex fusion between food, eroticism, and the grotesque. Food demonstrates the transformative process in the diegesis; eroticism the subject matter of slash works; and the grotesque implies the cultural context of transformative fandom as cannibalistic. In this context, I wish to reexamine the metaphor of fans as textual poachers, reading "poaching" as an act of both hunting and cooking which Lecter suggestively performs for fans. When Lecter cooks, he demonstrates the significance of the transformative process to the narrative drive and very survival of *Hannibal*.

The Fandom Dialectic

This essay considers the relationship between cooking sequences and fandom as fascinating and convoluted, while recognizing that the relationship's existence and convolution depend on problematic cultural attitudes toward queer content in television and fandom. When discussing the dialectic relationship between NBC's *Hannibal* and transformative fanworks, the show itself may be considered as a transformative work of the novels and movies. Showrunner Bryan Fuller has referred to the show as his own "fanfiction" to which fanworks are "parallel":

> […] this fanbase […] has taken this show, made it their own and created parallel worlds of fanfiction to this work of fanfiction—because that's very much what this show is. I feel like it was a unique experience of myself as a fannibal [the nickname *Hannibal* fans appoint themselves], writing the show as I imagined it—it was my fan fiction—and then sharing it with other fanfiction writers who then elaborated on it in their own ways.[2]

Here Fuller alludes to how the boundary between adaptation and fanwork is upheld only by licensing laws and cultural capital—though considerable privileges are attached to both. Where once acknowledgment of—let alone dialogue with—fandom, particularly transformative slash fandom, has been taboo, Fuller is among a growing trend of official creators engaging with fandom.[3] In the above statement, Fuller approaches fandom not as an elephant in the room but the underwater mass that keeps a textual iceberg afloat. This suggests that a dialogue between show and fandom is viable to be read as deliberately coded and significantly symbiotic.

There are many ways in which NBC's *Hannibal* creates a dialectic relationship with fandom that invites transformative works, particularly slash. The homo-romantic story arc between Graham and Lecter is the most obvious: many suggestions of sexuality are clearly signposted in the show for fans to fill with slash works. The show is not coy about the symbiotic relationship with transformative fandom: the fandom nickname "Murder Husbands" appears re-incorporated in the third season's script. This acknowledgment is still backhanded: journalist Freddie Lounds coins the term as the invasive and provocative young woman whose excessive online writings aggravate the lead characters: Graham spits the phrase at her with contempt. The "Murder Husbands" nod is indicative of how the show-fandom relationship exists in the context of deep cultural inequalities between creators and transformative fandom, whose most active members are often women.[4] Graham and Lecter's onscreen romance remained obtusely chaste for a show whose success depended desperately on a hyper-engaged fandom—and permitted scenes such as live humans being used as mushroom crops in its second episode.

In describing *Hannibal* as the tip of an iceberg, I am acknowledging how transformative fandom is relegated to culturally "beneath" and "below" the surface of the "official" texts. Understanding transformative fandom's continuing suppression is key in researching why the dialogue with fandom suffuses the show, but is communicated through codes and ciphers. *Hannibal*'s cooking sequences are a coded invitation for transformative work, and in arguing such I suggest that these sequences are another of the show's proxies for representation of same-sex affection beyond longing looks and violent embraces. This strategy perpetuates a common and regressive deferral of actual same-sex intimacy to transformative works, and the context for why *Hannibal* favors cannibalistic cooking sequences over queer intimacy must frame this discussion.

Rather than speculate on the real author of this strategy—likely a combination of Fuller; various directors; NBC executives; and a broader culture of queer chastity in "quality" television—I suggest that diegetically, Lecter is often the author of his mythology. Lecter acts so often as the agent of his cultural context, threatening the boundaries of diegesis into a monstrous inter-textuality. Fuller's candid engagement with fandom highlights *Hannibal* mythology as a multi-authored, multi-media network of texts anchored not by canon but by Hannibal Lecter himself. Adaptation and transformation are fundamental to the storytelling of *Hannibal* texts. From fans who misquote "Hello, Clarice" to those writing novel-length fanfiction, the mythic proportions of AFI's "greatest screen villain of all time" are sustained by transformative works great and small.[5] Lecter grows his legend through quotability, his captivating presence, and an uncanny talent for bending both characters and fans to his will. There is no small significance in the cooking sequences of the show being chiefly Lecter's. Lucy Scholes argues that the celebrity chef's "towering persona" is—as we may read Lecter's—buoyed by media synergy of television, books, and home-made creations.[6] In the scenes that mimic cooking shows, Lecter "feeds" both guests and fans; he adapts bodies of humans and texts; and he leads by example in transforming creations of his cannibalistic legend. As the chef, Lecter "authorises" these scenes as intertextually dialectical, demonstrating the necessity of monstrous adaptation—and, of course, cannibalism— to his mythology.

Fancy Allusions and Fussy Aesthetics

The adaptation of the *Hannibal* mythology for television opened up new opportunities for intertextual allusions. It allowed a recognizable aesthetic of the edutainment cooking show to infuse the narrative week to week. The addition of frequent cooking scenes complement a typical habit in *Hannibal* texts of omnivorous allusion and quotation. The cultural impact of *Hannibal* owes in no small part to a complex and dynamic interplay between "high" and "low" aesthetics, and how fans read these allusions in relation to *Hannibal*. As both a monstrous cannibal and a Renaissance man, Lecter is often the source of these paradoxical conflicts. His taste (metaphorical, not literal) is recognizable through his frequent allusions to—and reproductions of—works with high cultural capital. Each medium must adapt these allusions carefully: they must not be so obscure to fans of the novels, movies, or television that they are unrecognizably "fancy." Carlo Cenciarelli researches this process in depth, analyzing Glenn Gould's performance of the "Goldberg Variations" of Bach's work in the novel and film *The Silence of the Lambs*, and the *Hannibal* movie.[7] The "Goldberg Variations" must be accessibly recognizable as "high" taste, without being alienating to those with "middlebrow" taste in crime fiction and horror movies.[8] The careful game of cultural literacy creates a strange harmony with the many coded allusions to such "low" cultural works as crime procedurals; body horror; and, of course, transformative fanworks. Allusion is used not only to orient Hannibal mythology as tasteful: the perpetual momentum of the crime procedural's formula; the envelope-pushing bodily extremes of horror; and the transformative fanwork are as vital to sustaining the cultural relevance of *Hannibal* as his fancier allusions.

This mélange of high and low aesthetics is endemic to "quality" television. Sudeep Dasgupta's deconstruction of the label identifies the problems with assuming the tastes of "quality" audiences and their capacity to recognize intertextuality:

> In the hybrid, cross-medial, and multi-textual landscape within which contemporary television (over)flows [...] is not the equation of taste with one group too simple a picture to characterise the reality of both television and its audiences in a cross-medial landscape?[9]

Dasgupta compellingly argues that despite many attempts, "quality television" cannot be aesthetically or demographically separated from "popular television."[10] Dasgupta's argument seeks to destabilize our conceptualization of high/low boundaries between aesthetics and audiences of quality television: in *Hannibal*, this transgression is characteristically monstrous. *Hannibal* alludes to high art and cooking shows, and in its own transmedia extensions, to independent cinema and to fanworks. This reflects a similar crossover between the two vital demographics whom NBC and Fuller identified as essential to *Hannibal*'s two season renewals: reviewers and women-dominated fandom.[11] Dasgupta argues against scholarship's unnecessary privileging of reviewers' categorization of quality television, instead emphasizing marginalized groups such as women as having an under-recognized capacity for cultural literacy and critical enjoyment of quality television.[12] Dasgupta claims of fans:

> They are not just elitist snobs or mindless emotional addicts—they seem to be both, possibly even more. The dislocations produced by so-called "Quality TV" engender complex and unclassifiable responses from audiences who themselves become hard to categorise within the rigid protocols of high/low distinctions.[13]

The underestimation of women fans is compounded by the gendered marginalization of the largely female demographic of transformative fandom, as Kristina Busse argues.[14] The dislocation of "quality" television from traditional generic boundaries extends in Dasgupta's argument of the dislocation of audiences from specific genres. In turn, I would argue that *Hannibal*'s dialogue with transformative works is similarly dislocated from traditional diegetic fan-allusion through the code of cooking. By appealing and alluding to fandom, *Hannibal* uses quality television's omnivorous approach as a form of transgressive monstrosity. Monstrosity defies category, classification, and limitation: it is dislocative. Omnivorous quotation and appropriation across boundaries of taste is, in the context of *Hannibal*, a transgression of the ostensible "quality" marker that would associate television only with "high" tastes. To take liberally from texts often restricted, whether by cultural capital or licensing, is a practice *Hannibal* has in common with transformative fanworks. This transgressive monstrosity speaks to the transformative fandom's characterization as transgressive and monstrous; and is spoken through the cooking show aesthetic.

The cultural status of the cooking genre being alluded to makes it a complex conduit between *Hannibal* and fandom. The cooking genre has its own gendered issues: male celebrity chefs often outnumber women as the most popular masters of the kitchen.[15] It is worth considering whether this appropriation and subsequent celebration of a traditionally female art is comparable to Fuller's description of *Hannibal* as his "fanfiction."[16] Transformative fandom, like cooking, is implicitly women's work, as Isabelle de Solier argues in her analysis of cooking television.[17] Dasgupta argues that melodrama's perceived demographic of women lowers its cultural capital: the practice of cooking, and de Solier describes how the lifestyle edutainment genre has similar associations.[18] Dasgupta's study emphasizes how these associations between a female demographic and genre are not quantified but stereotyped, and how the *perception* of this association is what creates the broader cultural assumptions about what makes "quality."[19] As Dasgupta asserts, the perceived female interest does not preclude "quality" television from appropriating these genres; nor can one easily isolate aesthetic intertextuality as an elevation or denigration of relative cultural capital in either the quoted or quoting text.[20] Rather, I suggest that the culturally contested ground of cooking television demonstrates how queer narratives and transformative fandom are in similar states of contestation.

Sensing Taste

Hannibal's allusion to cookery provokes intertextuality through one's cultural literacy and one's senses. Cenciarelli discusses a similar sensory allusion, noting that the adaptation from the novel to film medium transforms the function of the allusions to Bach due to a sensory shift. The medium of the novel requires Harris' clear description of the piece and complicates the immediacy of Lecter's refinement in the diegesis, as Cenciarelli describes:

> Harris marks Lecter's sociocultural difference by citing a performer whose name would have stood a good chance of being familiar to the 1989 reader: precisely thanks to his popularity, [Glenn] Gould can mediate a representation of Bach's exclusiveness and refinement. In this sense, [Hannibal] asking for Gould of Lecter's origins in middle-brow fiction—it betrays the novel's middlebrow perception of what constitutes the highest refinement in music. In providing a shared code for constructing Lecter's high taste, the choice of Gould thus speaks of the dual nature of Lecter as a cultural aristocrat and a character in popular fiction[…].[21]

The allusion to a past text—Bach's music—also alludes to the potential for a future sound-enabled medium to adapt *Silence of the Lambs*. This suggests a way of understanding the show's allusion to potential transformative fanworks in more queer-welcoming media such as fanfiction and fanart.

Cenciarelli subsequently notes how *Silence of the Lambs* alludes to Bach with relative subtlety: in the diegesis Lecter plays an unidentified tape that a musically educated movie fan must recognize by ear.[22] This double-coding for both novel fans and Bach enthusiasts capitalizes upon cross-media adaptation for a more sensorially rewarding form of allusion. The show takes up the motif of Bach by suffusing it the extradiegetic musical score, where snatches may be heard in food sequences. Without Harris' narration to canonize Bach, the show's music becomes a cipher for the perpetual momentum of cross-media *Hannibal* adaptations. As with the embedded prompt to fandom in the cooking sequences, the fragments of unattributed Bach are only recognizable to those with the appropriate cultural literacy.

Cenciarelli's comparison of the novel and the movies highlights how *Hannibal* mythology itself is monstrous, identifying Lecter-the-character as an exemplary monster because, through his selection of music and food, he is the agent of intertextual and (culturally) omnivorous transgression.[23] Lecter's media-transgressive monstrosity in the case of Bach and the cooking show also provokes a synesthesia that transgresses the technical and cultural limitations of the medium and the sensorium. Ndalianis notes that: "The tastes synaesthetically evoked by the spectacle of Hannibal's decadent feasts [… works] to absorb the 'viewer' on the level of the sensorium."[24] The book vividly describes music which it cannot play; the show vividly describes a taste it cannot convey. Even the synesthetic taste of food substitutes another sensory code for the physical intimacy which it will not portray. These prompt a transformation of the text into a different medium to fully explore the synesthetic potential: screen adaptations of *Hannibal* allow Bach to be actualized in sound; fandom adaptations explore a queer sensorium of touch, smell, and taste between Graham and Lecter that television does not show.

Hannibal imitates the cooking show's masterful stimulation of the sensorium not simply by shooting delicious-looking food: when quoting from the cooking show, *Hannibal* retains the educational element of edutainment. This education is as much in cooking as it is in transforming *Hannibal* texts: Isabelle de Solier explains that cooking television has always been educational in more than just food preparation; in the case of *Hannibal*, there is a trans-textual education taking place.[25] There is a palpable encoding of didacticism in the cinematography of the cooking show: point-of-view overhead shots; close-ups of manual techniques; quick cuts between steps of cooking; medium shots to showcase the chef's stunts; and a final presentation of the full dish served on a table to a hungry diner. An example in *Hannibal* may be seen in the episode "Shiizakana," where Lecter prepares an omelette for Jack Crawford.

This simulation is a stimulation: the viewer is implicitly invited to enact Lecter's work. The cooking show cinematography creates a questionable prompt not only to imagine the food, but to imagine *making* the food. The popularity of fan/food blogs dedicated to *Hannibal*-inspired recipes demonstrates how fandom heeds the call for emulation encoded in the cooking sequence.[26] The synesthesia of Lecter's lessons presses creativity and transformation, transferring onto fans the compulsion of all cooking shows to cook like the television chef cooks. This is echoed in the show's repeated invitation by its cannibals for others to "*see*": to "see" in *Hannibal* is an invitation to *do*. As Lecter's diegetic action so often carries an extradiegetic context, the fan is drawn into Graham's growing affinity with Lecter; to "adapt; evolve; *become*." Jeff Casey describes how "*Hannibal* specifically sends singles to its queer fan base, peppering episodes with thinly veiled queer references."[27] Casey's reading blurs queer-identified fans with slash fans, who "take genuine pleasure in the homoerotic courtship between the two handsome leading men."[28] Casey describes food scenes such as the ortolan bunting scene in "Ko No Mono" as "fodder for slash fans, while providing plausible deniability to fans who may be uncomfortable with its homoerotic possibilities."[29] Casey's compelling reading of Graham as queer is linked to his uncanny insight and his malleability; his capacity to "see" and then "become."[30] The synesthetic temptation of the food begs not only to see a meal; not to cook a meal; but to further Lecter's mythology. Cooking adapts the legend of *Hannibal*, and the fan is taught by a cannibal of bodies and a cannibal of texts.

Food, Porn and Food Porn

In *Hannibal*, food is never just food. Lecter's meals lavish in sensorial, textual, and representational excess, blending the sublime and grotesque in the rituals of food preparation. These scenes are naturally rich in suggestion due to the inherent sensorial excess of food on screen: its taste, among many other qualities, may only be suggested. *Hannibal*'s cooking sequences suggest the taste, smell, and texture of a meal; the cooking show genre; a didactic imperative to create new works; an intertextual knowledge of Lecter's legendary diet; an erotic potential in the temptation of the forbidden; a relationship to fandom; and the grotesque excess found in both cannibalism and the density of meaning. In the following I wish to outline the transferal of romantic, intimate, and erotic queerness onto food in *Hannibal*, and in doing so, identify how this models the necessity of queerness' reconstitution from the show into fanworks.

The cipher between food and queer love is decoded in the diegesis by Bedelia Du Maurier and Lecter in the episode "Secondo." Du Maurier obliquely introduces "forgiveness" as a code word for "love," following which she asks Lecter how he will "forgive" Graham. Lecter declares: "I have to eat him." Graham later translates this love as romantic in "The Number of the Beast is 666," when he asks Du Maurier: "Is Hannibal *in love* with me?"—to which she affirms the connection between food, violence, and romance: "Could he daily feel a stab of hunger for you, and find nourishment at the very sight of you? Yes." The outing of the titular character is submerged in dense verbosity, necessitating a translation by fans of all preceding implications both romantic and culinary. The confirmation that this romance has been deferred and dislocated onto food imbues food with the power to interpret further dislocations of intimacy, namely into the realms of fandom.

Du Maurier's metaphors are rooted in a long-standing symbolic relationship between food and sexuality, particularly taboo sexualities such as—unfortunately—Lecter's queer sensuality. In her essay on the intersections between "body genres," Linda Williams describes how her young son finds the romantic intimacy of kissing onscreen excessively "gross."[31] By upholding the taboo of queer intimacy on TV, *Hannibal*'s use of food as a substitute follows a similarly childish logic Marina Warner describes: "In myth and fairy tale, the metaphor of devouring often stands in for sex."[32] Williams identifies a fluidity of pleasure between physical excesses of violence, emotion, and sexuality in "body genres"—horror, melodrama, and pornography.[33] Being made from human bodies, food in *Hannibal* similarly samples the horrific and pornographic. Warner compares cannibalism to "sexual union, by which a form of reciprocal devouring takes place."[34] The cooking sequences of *Hannibal* may link these more explicitly in a sumptuousness that earns the nickname "food porn."

The aesthetic of the cooking show builds upon and exaggerates the relationship between food and eroticism. De Solier emphasizes this by linking the concepts synaesthetically, claiming: "Culinary television aestheticises food in terms of both stylisation and simulation, as it transforms material food into a delectable image, a form of 'gastro-porn' (see Smart, 1994), designed to be consumed with the eyes."[35] Andrew Chan performs a pornographic reading of the cooking genre, claiming:

> TV cooking shows today are, in a word, pornography. As in the contemporary pornographic film industry, the modern TV cooking programs appeal to our hidden or perverse side. They seduce us to desire the virtual, while complicating our relationship with what is real (or desired).[36]

Chan's argument is effective for the categorization of the cooking show as an extension of Williams' "body genres." His characterization of celebrity chefs' sensuality fits Lecter's process aptly: "The chef starts building the viewer's expectations and hunger by his cleaving, stirring, and whisking—every gesture, raised eyebrow, and licked lip a sign of what is to come."[37] The genre's didactic cinematography is described by Chan as having sexual overtones: "Food preparation is a form of foreplay in which the ritual of cooking is announced with sensory cues: the sizzle of oil in the frying pan, pots bubbling away, the crescendo of chopping, dicing, and slicing."[38] To Chan, the sensory cues precede an ultimately unfulfilling experience: "We are physically unable to taste the meal the host presents to us; thus, for us, the relationship between the chef's exertions on the program and

the resulting by-product is never consummated."[39] This lack of consummation in *Hannibal* may be worth comparing to queer characters in popular
television, who remain relatively chaste.[40] However, Chan's dissatisfac-
tion lies in the illusion of synesthesia; that screen representations of food
and sex are more glamorous than tangible food and sex.[41] I suggest that
the un-fulfillment Chan describes is contextualized through the didactic
nature of cooking shows as an invitation for fans to fulfill a missing sensuality. The process of substitution is a familiar genre trope in the cooking
show, and is appropriated by *Hannibal*'s implication: *if you can't find any
queer intimacy in the show, you can make your own at home.* This depen-
dency on transformative works demonstrates how *Hannibal* lore has always
been a sum of textual parts, exceeding through the senses into further
adaptations.

A reading of Lecter's cooking as an erotic and grotesque "body genre"
is supported by Lecter's larder including the human bodies of characters.
The grotesque secret that the meat is human does not detract from the
romantic and erotic potential in these scenes: as Angela Ndalianis argues,
"fluid sensory shifts" between disgust and pleasure are allowed through
the hybridity of horror and romance in the Gothic.[42] Ndalianis discusses
how, in this confluence; "the sensorium [...] takes illicit delight in the horror, darkness, and chaos that can lie in the core of eroticism."[43] The slippage between darkness and eroticism accompanies the sensory shift when
watching Lecter's handling of meat. Chan claims of the standard celebrity
chef: "Sexual scenarios become manifest with every gesture."[44] The typical
extensive close-ups of the cooking show follow Lecter's graceful handling
of the human body, stripped beyond its skin to the organs. The recognition of bodies as Lecter's favorite ingredient depends upon a fan's intertextual knowledge of *Hannibal*. The first season creates beautiful scenes of
food preparation while staggering the growing certainty—a certainty that
originates not in the show but allusions to earlier *Hannibal* texts—that the
dish is likely of human origin. Lecter's preceding acts of butchery are sel-
dom shown: from the first episode, one must know through suggestive editing and transmedia literacy that Lecter is a cannibal. Consequentially, one
must know of future potential adaptations in transformative fanworks to
appreciate the erotic potential in Lecter's handling of human bodies.

The other indication that Lecter's cookery is more than it seems
comes from his excessive capacity to pun, and in this context, the "body"
is an exceedingly useful term. A pleasure and horror tied to the knowledge of these bodies' origin is compounded by the knowledge of other
"bodies of work" in the *Hannibal* canon. Lecter does what *Hannibal* does:
he takes bodies (of work) and transforms them into grotesquely appetizing, sometimes unrecognizable creations. The grotesque taboos around

transformative fandom inform this process deeply: Lecter is butchering the sanctity, autonomy, and cohesion of bodies when he cooks them, much as a fan-creator may be accused of doing with their subject matter. The show is instructional in this respect, using lines, characters, and story arcs from earlier bodies of *Hannibal* work as ingredients to be mixed up in the show's canon. Lecter's cooking is analogous to the slash fan's process, transforming both bodies of work and the bodies of characters—the two becoming inextricable—in unorthodox and erotic ways.

While this self-reflexive process characterizes the transformative work as butchery, in the context of the pivotal character being a charming cannibal, butchery is both grotesque and deeply pleasurable. Like the splendid meals the celebrity chef presents to diegetic admiration, the transformative work is a synaesthetically rich, tantalizing piece of cannibalism. De Solier summarizes the significance of the meal's progression from ingredient to presentation in cooking television:

> [the process] thus operates through what I call a "transformative aesthetic," which displays the transmutation of food not merely from raw ingredients into a cooked dish (see Levi-Strauss, 1969), but importantly, from raw ingredients into a stylised dish.[45]

This description of cooking as transformative crystallizes the parallel between the production of dishes and transformative fanworks, and the inviting context of both in *Hannibal*. Lecter's kitchen demonstrates and endorses cannibalism of humans and of works, encoding in its highly aestheticized foods a wicked delight in the production of transformative works.

Poached to Perfection

In the context of cooking and cannibalism, Henry Jenkins' popularization of fans as "textual poachers" becomes another productive metaphor.[46] My reading of bodies as both works and living beings demands a reexamination of "poacher" for literal and homonymous meaning. Jenkins' work borrows Michel de Certeau's analogy of active readers in general; where texts are the territory of official storytellers, and a negotiated reading is the vulnerable prey hunted by poachers.[47] Both Jenkins and de Certeau valorize the poacher's counter-hegemonic process, while using the popular condemnation of wildlife poachers to characterize "[…] the relationship between readers and writers as an ongoing struggle for possession of the text and control over its meanings."[48] Despite the wider cultural connotations of wildlife poachers as evil, Jenkins uses the term as a reclamation that acknowledges the marginalized and controversial position of fandom. However, for this discussion it is worth considering the connotations of metaphors like poaching, butchery, and cannibalism as an emphasis of transformative slash fandom as grotesquely carnivorous.

Once more we return to Lecter himself, this time as the poacher. Various acts of poaching signify Lecter as the author-agent of dialogue with transformative fandom. Beyond the kitchen, Lecter is a textual poacher of classical fandoms. He draws what could be called fanart of Botticelli's *La Primavera* with Graham and du Maurier's faces in the episode "Dolce." In "Tome-Wan," he tells a tale in which he is Achilles and Graham is Patroclus—his *Iliad*-real-person-slash crossover fanfic. He takes poaching more literally as he prowls the South for the highly prized remains of humans, a free-ranging, protected species. Finally, the kitchen becomes the locus of his transformative process when he poaches meat by simmering it: Lecter is a poacher, a poacher, and a poacher.

These examples suggest that Lecter—like Fuller and Jenkins—strongly endorses poaching, despite its questionable position in popular culture. The centrality of the kitchen offers an interpretation of "poaching" not exclusively as destructive hunting, but a method of tenderly cooking food. It suggests the ease through which the canon work may be transformed into a fandom creation. Hunter-poaching suggests that *Hannibal* lore has always been adapted through predatory appropriation; cook-poaching suggests it is simply a matter of taking something raw and preparing it for consumption. Considered in a queer context, the show contains the raw ingredients for intimacy, but requires some poaching to be palpable. Often very little preparation is needed: the time-saver meals of *Hannibal* fandom are the fanvids or graphics that juxtapose canonical scenes in an order that emphasizes their romantic and erotic context. This textual rearrangement is often done by the show itself, where quotations from the books and movies are, when compared, infused with considerably greater meaning. Consider the exchange beginning with "You would take my life?" between Clarice Starling and Lecter in the *Hannibal* movie, presented as a pretext to their romantic consummation in the movie but quoted opaquely by Graham and Lecter in "Mizumono." The onus is on fans to recognize the allusion and contextualize it through transformative works. The opacity obfuscates the romantic overtones to those who do not wish to recognize *Hannibal* as trans-textual: the transformative process may be decontextualized as simply a pan of simmering stock and some chopped meat with no regard to their origins or intentions.

Poaching in *Hannibal* cannot be isolated to singular meanings: humans are hunted to be cooked, and the ingredients of cooking are human. In embracing poaching as a keystone in *Hannibal*'s continuing mythology, the show does not shy away from the grotesqueness of physical or textual cannibalism. Instead, the grotesque is shown as inextricable from the process of transformation, and symbiotically linked with the pleasures of productions like food and fandom. Ndalianis suggests this is endemic to *Hannibal*:

> The savage and the cultured, the rotting and the cooked, the disgusting and the beautiful are no longer binary opposites but instead the extremes of both are thrust together in an experiment that is about testing the limits of human experience[...].[49]

This grotesqueness is fundamental to these processes because it characterizes the excess of monstrous textuality and transformative works. Fandom as grotesque is a gendered connotation: the perceived excess of transformative works by fangirls is, as Elizabeth Grosz says of the female body, "leaking, uncontrollable [...] secreting."[50] This vivid evocation is a useful allegory for the condemnation of transformative works as over-productive results of what Busse calls the "excessive affect" of a fangirl.[51] The abject elements of poaching and fandom are present in the show, which Ndalianis notes is masterful in being powerfully affective.[52] The grotesque is essential to fandom as an excess of textuality, and thus cannot be divorced from the show's cooking procedures. When Lecter spoons oozing sauce over human meat, abjection and attraction are harmoniously alluding to other transformations of *Hannibal*'s body (of work). Thus, while Jenkins is overwhelmingly positive and figurative in discussion of poachers, *Hannibal* relishes in the affective potential of textual poaching as grotesque, pleasurable, and necessary.

Poaching is demonstrated through these sequences to be essential to the legacy of *Hannibal*. Fandom simmers below the surface of the text, infusing its bodies with richer and more complex flavors. Fuller's own remediations, acknowledged as a transformative fan practice, only further encourage *Hannibal* to be read as open to poaching. *Hannibal* lore has never been static: hunting, transforming, and consuming are essential to its growth. This process is localized to Lecter's kitchen in the show, where the cooking show aesthetic uniquely promotes the pleasures of poaching. Fans may take inspiration from the emotionally charged scenes between characters for their transformative works, but Lecter's kitchen is where the act of transformation takes place—with equally affective power. Without reading the coded endorsement of fandom in the show's cooking sequences, poaching could be interpreted as superfluous, indulgent, or unwelcome. It is therefore essential to consider how the dialectic, didactic, generically unique, and synaesthetically stimulating aspects of cooking influence fans as textual poachers.

Conclusion

To consider Lecter without considering his food would be as fruitless an endeavor as considering *Hannibal* without transformative fandom, and I argue that all are fundamentally linked. The cooking sequences of *Hannibal* suggest a complex and coded dialectic with transformative fandom. While the coding process may be problematized as a substitute for conspicuous omissions of queer representation by the show, a fascinating synesthetic and textual transference takes place because of it. This process always returns to Lecter himself, the monstrous chef. He adapts the didactic and synesthetic aspects of the cooking show to invite transformations of his texts that explore a sensorially rich trans-textuality across media. These scenes highlight the intertextuality that situates *Hannibal* as belonging in a network of texts that span media and tastes. The synesthetic aspect of this intertextuality functions as an invitation to imagine that which could be part of *Hannibal*; particularly, its excessively sensory pleasures. The complex relationships woven between food and sexuality—particularly the sexuality between Lecter and Graham—signifies the cooking sequences as significant to slash fandom, and how textual and physical bodies may be transformed through adaptation allegorized as cooking.

The show's adaptation of a distinctly televisual aesthetic signifies how transformations of *Hannibal* into new media will be productive and complementary. I have suggested that representations of queer intimacy are the particular advantages of typical fanworks such as fanart, fanfiction, and fanvids over network television; further specialties may be discovered through close analyzes of these media. Now that Lecter's cooking sequences have concluded with the show's cancellation, it is textual poachers who will take up the demonstration in these media that *Hannibal* is a highly adaptable work. Fans' sustained enthusiasm may see the show transformed post-cancellation into a streaming series with its own medium-specific advantages. In the meantime, fans are the prolific and accomplished "chefs" of *Hannibal* media, and custodians of the *Hannibal* legacy.

Notes

1. *Hannibal.* NBC. 2013–2015.
2. Fuller, Bryan, interviewed by Prudom, Laura."'Hannibal' Finale Postmortem: Bryan Fuller Breaks Down That Bloody Ending and Talks Revival Chances." *Variety*. 29th August, 2015. Accessed 9th September, 2016. <http://variety.com/2015/tv/news/hannibal-finale-season-4-movie-revival-ending-spoilers-1201581424/>.
3. Busse, Kristina. "Geek hierarchies, boundary policing, and the gendering of the good fan." *Participations: Journal of Audience & Reception Studies* 10:1 (May 2013): 77.
4. This inequality has been very recently discussed by fandom bloggers in relation to *Harry Potter and the Cursed Child* being referred to derisively as "fanfiction." See: Schick, Michal. "On 'The Cursed Child' as fanfiction, and where the problem really lies." *Hypable*. 2nd August, 2016. Accessed 9th September, 2016. <http://www.hypable.com/the-cursed-child-fanfiction-or-canon/>.
5. "AFI's 100 years… 100 Heroes & Villains." *American Film Institute*. Accessed 9th September, 2016. <http://www.afi.com/100Years/handv.aspx>.

6. Scholes, Lucy. "A slave to the stove? The TV celebrity chef abandons the kitchen: lifestyle TV domesticity and gender." *Critical Quarterly* 53:3 (October 2011): 2.

7. Cenciarelli, Carlo. "Dr Lecter's Taste for 'Goldberg,' or: The Horror of Bach in the Hannibal Franchise." *Journal of the Royal Music Association* 137:1 (2012): 107–134; Harris, Thomas. *The Silence of the Lambs*. London: Arrow Books, 1988/1989; *Silence of the Lambs*. Dir. Demme, Jonathan. Orion Pictures. 1991; *Hannibal*. Dir. Scott, Ridley. Dino Di Laurentis Company. 2001.

8. Cenciarelli, Carlo. "Dr Lecter's Taste for "Goldberg."" 112.

9. Dasgupta, Sudeep. "Policing the people: Television studies and the problem of 'quality.'" *NECSUS: European Journal of Media Studies* 1:1 (2011): 35–53.

10. Dasgupta. "Policing the people." 36.

11. Dibdin, Emma. "Exclusive: Hannibal season 3: Bryan Fuller 'very confident' about renewal chances." *Digital Spy*. 30th April, 2014. Accessed 9th September, 2016. <http://www.digitalspy.com/tv/hannibal/news/a567981/hannibal-season-3-bryan-fuller-very-confident-about-renewal-chances/>.

12. Dasgupta. "Policing the people." 46.

13. Dasgupta. "Policing the people." 45–46.

14. Busse. "Geek hierarchies, boundary policing, and the gendering of the good fan." 85.

15. Scholes, "A slave to the stove?." 48–50.

16. de Solier, Isabelle. "TV Dinners: Culinary Television, Education and Distinction." *Continuum: Journal of Media & Cultural Studies* 19:4 (December 2005): 469.

17. de Solier. "TV Dinners." 469.

18. Dasgupta. "Policing the people." 41.

19. Dasgupta. "Policing the people." 41.

20. Dasgupta. "Policing the people." 41.

21. Cenciarelli. "Dr Lecter's Taste for 'Goldberg.'" 112.

22. Cenciarelli. "Dr Lecter's Taste for 'Goldberg.'" 113.

23. Cenciarelli. "Dr Lecter's Taste for 'Goldberg.'" 108.

24. Ndalianis, Angela. "Hannibal: A Disturbing Feast for the Senses." *Journal of Visual Culture* 3 (2015): 1.

25. De Solier. "TV Dinners." 470.

26. The best example of a *Hannibal* recipe blog is run by Janice Poon, the show's food stylist herself. See: Poon, Janice. *Feeding Hannibal*. 2013–2015. Accessed 9th September, 2016. <http://janicepoonart.blogspot.com.au/>.

27. Casey, Jeff. "Queer Cannibals and Deviant Detectives: Subversion and Homosocial Desire in NBC's Hannibal." *Quarterly Review of Film and Video* 32:6 (2015): 560.

28. Casey. "Queer Cannibals and Deviant Detectives." 559.

29. Casey. "Queer Cannibals and Deviant Detectives." 560.

30. Casey. "Queer Cannibals and Deviant Detectives." 558.

31. Williams, Linda. "Film Bodies: Gender, Genre, and Excess." *Film Quarterly* 44:4 (1991): 2.

32. Warner, Marina. *From the Beast to the Blonde: on Fairy Tales and their Tellers*. London: Vintage, 1994/1995. 259.

33. Williams. "Film Bodies." 3.

34. Warner. *From the Beast to the Blonde*. 260.

35. De Solier. "TV Dinners." 467.

36. Chan, Andrew. "'La grande bouffe': Cooking Shows as Pornography." *Gastronomica* 3:4 (Fall 2003): 47.

37. Chan. "'La grande bouffe.'" 47.

38. Chan. "'La grande bouffe.'" 47.

39. Chan. "'La grande bouffe.'" 47.

40. Kathleen Battles and Wendy Hilton-Morrow discuss this issue in the context of sitcoms, and unfortunately similar issues have carried over to quality TV such as *Hannibal*. See: Battles, Kathleen, and Hilton-Morrow, Wendy. 'Gay Characters in Conventional Spaces: *Will and Grace* and the Situation Comedy Genre.' *Critical Studies in Media Communication* 19:1 (March 2002): 87–105.

41. Chan. "'La grande bouffe." 48.
42. Ndalianis, Angela. *The Horror Sensorium: Media and the Senses.* Jefferson, NC: McFarland, 2012. 75.
43. Ndalianis, Angela. *The Horror Sensorium.* 76.
44. Chan. "'Le grande bouffe.'" 49.
45. De Solier. "TV Dinners." 467.
46. Jenkins, Henry. *Textual Poachers: Television Fans and Participatory Culture.* 2nd Edition. Hoboken: Taylor and Francis, 2015. xii.
47. Jenkins. *Textual Poachers.* 23.
48. Jenkins. *Textual Poachers.* 24
49. Ndalianis. "Hannibal." 2.
50. Grosz, Elizabeth. *Volatile Bodies: Toward a Corporeal Feminism.* Bloomington and Indianapolis: Indiana University Press, 1994. 203.
51. Busse. "Geek hierarchies, boundary policing, and the gendering of the good fan." 86.
52. Ndalianis. "Hannibal." 3.

Works Cited

"AFI's 100 years… 100 Heroes & Villains." *American Film Institute.* Accessed 9th September, 2016. <http://www.afi.com/100Years/handv.aspx>.
Battles, Kathleen, and Hilton-Morrow, Wendy. 'Gay Characters in Conventional Spaces: *Will and Grace* and the Situation Comedy Genre.' *Critical Studies in Media Communication* 19:1 (March 2002): 87–105.
Busse, Kristina. "Geek hierarchies, boundary policing, and the gendering of the good fan." *Participations: Journal of Audience & Reception Studies* 10:1 (May 2013): 73–91.
Casey, Jeff. "Queer Cannibals and Deviant Detectives: Subversion and Homosocial Desire in NBC's Hannibal." *Quarterly Review of Film and Video* 32:6 (2015): 550–567.
Cenciarelli, Carlo. "Dr Lecter's Taste for 'Goldberg,' or: The Horror of Bach in the Hannibal Franchise." *Journal of the Royal Music Association* 137:1 (2012): 107–134.
Chan, Andrew. "'La grande bouffe': Cooking Shows as Pornography." *Gastronomica* 3:4 (Fall 2003): 46–53.
Dasgupta, Sudeep. "Policing the people: Television studies and the problem of 'quality.'" *NECSUS: European Journal of Media Studies* 1:1 (2011): 35–53.
De Solier, Isabelle. "TV Dinners: Culinary Television, Education and Distinction." *Continuum: Journal of Media & Cultural Studies* 19:4 (December 2005): 465–481.
Dibdin, Emma. "Exclusive: Hannibal season 3: Bryan Fuller 'very confident' about renewal chances." *Digital Spy.* 30th April, 2014. Accessed 9th September, 2016. <http://www.digitalspy.com/tv/hannibal/news/a567981/hannibal-season-3-bryan-fuller-very-confident-about-renewal-chances/>.
Grosz, Elizabeth. *Volatile Bodies: Toward a Corporeal Feminism.* Bloomington and Indianapolis: Indiana University Press, 1994.
Fuller, Bryan, interviewed by Prudom, Laura."Hannibal' Finale Postmortem: Bryan Fuller Breaks Down That Bloody Ending and Talks Revival Chances." *Variety.* 29th August, 2015. Accessed 9th September, 2016. <http://variety.com/2015/tv/news/hannibal-finale-season-4-movie-revival-ending-spoilers-1201581424/>.
Harris, Thomas. *The Silence of the Lambs.* London: Arrow Books, 1988/1989.
Jenkins, Henry. *Textual Poachers: Television Fans and Participatory Culture.* 2nd Edition. Hoboken: Taylor and Francis, 2015.
Ndalianis, Angela. *The Horror Sensorium: Media and the Senses.* Jefferson, NC: McFarland, 2012.
Ndalianis, Angela. "Hannibal: A Disturbing Feast for the Senses." *Journal of Visual Culture* 3 (2015): 279–284.
Poon, Janice. *Feeding Hannibal.* 2013–2015. Accessed 9th September, 2016. <http://janicepoonart.blogspot.com.au/>.
Schick, Michal. "On 'The Cursed Child' as fanfiction, and where the problem really lies." *Hypable.* 2nd August, 2016. Accessed 9th September, 2016. <http://www.hypable.com/the-cursed-child-fanfiction-or-canon/>.

Scholes, Lucy. "A slave to the stove? The TV celebrity chef abandons the kitchen: lifestyle TV domesticity and gender." *Critical Quarterly* 53:3 (October 2011): 44–59.

Warner, Marina. *From the Beast to the Blonde: on Fairy Tales and their Tellers*. London: Vintage, 1994/1995.

Williams, Linda. "Film Bodies: Gender, Genre, and Excess." *Film Quarterly* 44:4 (1991): 2–13.

"If I saw you every day, forever, I'd remember this time"

Deconstructing Gender Performance and Heteronormativity Through Adaptation

Megan Fowler

This essay analyzes the ways in which the *Hannibal* TV series as an adaptation "queers" the original Hannibal film and book franchise by reproducing dialogue and re-framing Hannibal Lecter's heterosexual love interest Clarice Starling with male lead Will Graham in her position. By drawing parallels between Clarice and Will, the show "gender-bends" Clarice's feminist protagonist into the male Will. This gendered adaptation carries the potentially troubling ramifications of appropriating a feminist narrative for a male character. However, *Hannibal*'s frequent replication of scenes of Clarice throughout the franchise with Will in her place highlights some of the more conservative expressions of Clarice's gender in the original franchise. This reproduction also complicates the strict boundaries of binary gender in Will's character. *Hannibal* frequently alludes to the romantic relationship between Clarice and Hannibal in Will and Hannibal's relationship. These allusions imbue Will and Hannibal's dynamic with romantic desire, using the previous heterosexual constructions in the series as a framework for depicting an explicit romantic but asexual relationship between two men. In this way, *Hannibal* creates new queer meanings from the original franchise.

In order to understand *Hannibal* as a transformative adaptation, it is important to consider its position in relationship to the Hannibal franchise as well as the characters of Clarice Starling and Will Graham in the original franchise. Although I have referred to the TV series as an "adaptation," the show functions more complexly. In its relationship to the original franchise, *Hannibal* shares similarities with various transmedia modes including adaptation, remake, prequel, and even remix. Although presented as a prequel to and adaptation of the first novel *Red Dragon*, chronologically set before the events of *Silence of the Lambs* and its sequel, the show often shifts the chronological order of events from the original series. For instance, the show works much of the plot of the final book in the series into the first half of its third season, while adapting the plot of the first novel *Red Dragon* in the second half of its third and final season. The show often utilizes this shifting chronology to unfold more gradual arcs for its characters and complicate its place in the larger mythology of the franchise. *Hannibal*'s showrunner Bryan Fuller has himself said, "The poetry of the show really does hinge on going right back to the source material, finding quotes, and re-appropriating them…. It is, on one hand, our interpretation of the novels, but in another sense, it's very, very true to his spirit and his purple poetry" (VanDerWerff 2016). This approach is extremely similar to Robert P. Arnett's interpretation of Daniel Craig's first James Bond film *Casino Royale*, which he considers a remix of the Bond franchise due to its "sampling" of the transmediated Bond mythos (2009, 1). Therefore, I consider the TV series a reworking of the original Hannibal franchise, liberally borrowing various components from the entire series and reimagining them. Subsequently, I draw on a variety of theory including theories of adaptation, remix, and remake to describe the way the show transforms the original franchise.

The creators of *Hannibal* largely construct the show with the assumption that even the casual viewer will have some knowledge of the iconic franchise. For instance, the pilot episode of the series makes very few explicit allusions to Hannibal's cannibalism, instead creating suspense, horror, and morbid humor by taking for granted that the audience is familiar with horror icon Hannibal Lecter and his unusual dining habits. With this assumption of recognizability comes an expectation that viewers will also be familiar with the second most iconic figure to come out of the franchise, Clarice Starling. Given her iconic status, the decision not to utilize her character in the series seems surprising. Clarice's absence in the show is in fact the result of a copyright issue, with MGM holding the rights to all the characters that originated in the book *Silence of the Lambs* and refusing to allow Fuller and NBC to make use of any of these characters in *Hannibal* (Goldman 2016). This copyright issue effectively tied the hands of Fuller and his crew when it came to Clarice, demonstrating that the series may not have been developed with queering the franchise as its primary conception or goal.

However, the *Hannibal* team's decision to borrow extensively from the characterization of the female lead and love interest of the established franchise for its male protagonist rather than making no reference to Clarice at all results, whether originally intended or not, in the queering of the central narrative of their reinterpretation. Will Graham accordingly becomes a composite character, comprised of both the original Will Graham from *Red Dragon* and Clarice Starling. This gender-bending does have some negative ramifications in the show's relationship to the feminism of the original series. For instance, the fluctuating chronology in the show and its status as a "prequel" set before *Silence of the Lambs s* means that within the show's universe Will chronologically becomes Hannibal's original love interest as Hannibal has yet to meet Clarice. In addition, having Will as the primary detective throughout the television show undercuts some of the progressive work of the original franchise, as without Clarice Starling as a lead, this adaptation loses a strong primary female protagonist and no longer focuses on the sexism women face when working in the field of criminology, one of the most praised facets of the *Silence* film adaptation (Phillips 2008, 41). However, by adapting Clarice's narratives with Will in her place, the show inflects Will's gender and sexuality with a complex femininity, thus complicating his gender identity and notions of gender in media. The series thus not only queers the central romantic narrative but critiques hegemonic expectations and assumptions about same-sex relationships and gender.

By having Will usurp Clarice's position, both narratively and romantically, the TV series re-articulates the franchise through a queer lens, subsequently critiquing heteronormativity and revealing the constructed nature of gender through intertextual allusion. I use "queer" here to describe two different types of queerness that appear in the show: "queer" meaning same-sex desire, which manifests in the relationship between Hannibal and Will, and "queer" meaning the critique of binary gender norms, which manifests in the character of Will as an amalgamation of *Red Dragon*'s Will Graham and the franchise's female lead Clarice Starling. This critique is unique to various modes of transforming previous texts, because "we experience adaptations as palimpsests through our memory of other works that resonate through repetition with variation" (Hutcheon 2006, 8). Thus, *Hannibal* relies on allusions to the urtext specific to the mode of transformation to queer narratives and critiques gendered constructions in previous texts of the franchise. In this way, *Hannibal* queers the original franchise, utilizing the potentiality of adaptation as queer mode.

Hannibal references Clarice and Hannibal's relationship to indicate the romantic nature of Will and Hannibal's. There are key differences, however, between the two dynamics. The relationship between Clarice and Hannibal is more sexual than between Will and Hannibal. For instance, Clarice and Hannibal kiss in the novel and the film franchise. By contrast, Will and Hannibal never kiss on screen or engage in any sexual behavior that is not a part of Will's own fantasy. In spite of this lack of sexual consummation, the TV series lifts scenes from previous entries in the franchise to construct Hannibal's relationship with Will as equally romantic to his relationship with Clarice. Hannibal's response is exactly the same upon encountering Clarice in the *Hannibal* novel and Will in the series after an extended period of separation:

> "Dr. Lecter handed one to Clarice Starling. 'If I saw you every day, forever, I'd remember this time'" [Harris 2006, 522].
>
>   Hannibal: If I saw you every day, forever, Will, I would remember this time ["Dolce" 2015].

Both encounters illicit a response of longing and desire from Hannibal, a seeming reunion with his beloved from whom he has been long parted. Both moments indicate the intensity with which Hannibal is enamored with Clarice and Will, singling out the importance of this moment while also hinting at Hannibal's desire for a future together. Although the show's dialogue alone is intensely romantic, the intertextual interplay further emphasizes the queer desire between Will and Hannibal in spite of the absence of a sexual encounter. *Hannibal* uses such allusions, however, to move beyond subtextual hinting at Hannibal's feelings for Will, confirming the romantic nature of his feelings.

In another instance of reproduction, the *Hannibal* series uses allusions to the prior adaptations in the franchise to solidify the romantic nature of Hannibal's desire for Will. In the film *Hannibal*, an adaptation of the novel of the same name, when discussing Dante's first sonnet, Hannibal asks, "Could he daily feel a stab of hunger for her and find nourishment in the very sight of her? I think so. But would she see through the bars of his plight and ache for him?" His words serve as a reaction to and analysis of the sonnet, but more importantly as an obvious metaphor for his own feelings for Clarice, which he fears may be one-sided longing. In "The Number of the Beast is 666...," the penultimate episode of the series, Will asks his psychiatrist Bedelia du Maurier, Hannibal's former lover, about the nature of Hannibal's feelings for him. "Is Hannibal ... in love with me?" the FBI consultant asks hesitantly, to which Bedelia replies, "Could he daily feel a stab of hunger for you, and find nourishment at the very sight of you? Yes. But do you ache for him?" Will's use of the phrase "in love" dispels any notion that the dynamic is purely platonic rather than romantic. This moment not only confirms the nature of Hannibal's feelings for Will, but Bedelia's question and Will's silence in response creates an ellipses that opens up the possibility of this queer longing as reciprocal. Thus, the series appropriates dialogue and moments from Clarice and Hannibal's relationship and reworks them in the show to not only allude to but confirm the romantic nature of Will and Hannibal's relationship.

Hannibal uses the inflections of the established romantic relationship between Clarice and Hannibal to establish the queer dynamic between the two male protagonists. In this way, Fuller's reworking functions similarly to non-mainstream forms of queer remixing. Elisa Kreisinger writes, "Appropriation has always played a key role in the survival of queer communities … creators … deconstruct appropriated pop culture texts and experiment directly with mainstream images of gender and sexuality, recreating more diverse and affirming narratives of representation" (2012). Fuller's adaptation responds to and transforms a previously established popular mainstream narrative, reworking that narrative to provide more diverse representation just as queer remix does. Although Kreisinger is discussing the production of fan videos in response to mainstream texts, these fan activities have clear similarities with Fuller's Hannibal. Fuller has even spoken about *Hannibal* as being akin to fan production, stating "The show is fanfiction. I'm a huge Thomas Harris fan. It's not a literal adaptation, even though so much of the literature does make it into the show. It is relatable to that community that is fanfiction writers and storytellers" (Fisher 2016). Kreisinger suggests that the remix process may in and of itself be a queer mode, as "If queer act is defined as any act that challenges, questions, or provokes the normal, the acceptable, and the dominant, then remixes' required rejection of the dominant and acceptable notions of copyright challenges the author/reader and owner/user binaries on which these notions are based" (2012). Although Fuller works within the mainstream (as demonstrated in the above copyright issues), the fraught relationship between original franchise and adaptation can be said to have some of the same dynamics, with the question of "originality" causing the urtext to become the dominant in the hierarchy, positioned as being of a higher quality than the adaptation. *Hannibal* as a reinterpretation also challenges the heteronormative and gendered constructions in the original Hannibal franchise. Thus, *Hannibal* operates within the tradition of queer reinterpretation of mainstream texts, but here taking advantage of the potential of adaptation to depict that representation within the mainstream medium of television.

By applying the romantic framework of a heterosexual relationship onto a sexless dynamic, *Hannibal* complicates the correlation between romantic and sexual desire, offering a depiction of a romantic but asexual bond. Portraying Hannibal and Will's dynamic as asexual while still depicting them engaging in sexual relationships with women problematizes queer representation in the show. However, the asexual nature of Will and Hannibal's romantic relationship subverts the hegemonic construction of the romantic as automatically sexual, undermining the traditional romantic-sexual dynamic. By directly lifting scenes and dialogue from a romantic heterosexual relationship for an asexual same-sex one, *Hannibal* also plays with heteronormative expectations. For those who read the relationship between Will and Hannibal as completely "platonic," knowledge of the allusions to Hannibal and Clarice's relationship undermines that reading and exposes the default heteronormative gaze directed at mainstream media. The show uses allusions to the original franchise to not only highlight the romantic nature of Will and Hannibal's relationship, but also critique the heterosexist dynamic between Clarice and Hannibal through imitation.

By exactly reproducing dialogue and visuals that formerly depicted Clarice and Hannibal in the queer dynamic of Will and Hannibal, the series highlights not only the performativity of heterosexuality but also gender as well. There are two scenes in the television series which borrow heavily from visuals of the *Hannibal* film in order to create direct parallels between Will and Clarice, placing Will into a highly feminized position. The first is from the *Hannibal* season two finale, "Mizumono," when Hannibal discovers that Will's season-long pseudo-seduction, in which he misled Hannibal into thinking he planned to run away with him to Florence, Italy and become a cannibal, has been a ploy to betray him to the FBI. This scene draws from a sequence at the end of the *Hannibal* film, in which Clarice attempts to recapture Hannibal to turn him over to the FBI. Both scenes depict the detectives "betraying" Hannibal. While Will's betrayal is much more straightforward, Clarice continues to show her loyalty to the Bureau and her moral code, refusing Hannibal's offer to go with him and holding strong to her conviction to arrest him instead. Both characters visibly show their pain and regret at this betrayal through body language. The acting in this scene demonstrates the way the show visually highlights gender performativity through mimicry and body language, as Hugh Dancy, who plays Will Graham in the show, perfectly replicates Julianne Moore's performance as Clarice Starling.

> HANNIBAL: You would deny me my life, wouldn't you?
> CLARICE: Not your life.
> HANNIBAL: Just my freedom. You'd take that from me [*Hannibal* 2001].

> HANNIBAL: You would deny me my life.
> WILL: No, not your life, no.
> HANNIBAL: My freedom then, you would take that from me ["Mizumono" 2014].

Both scenes are nearly identical. The dialogue repeats. Both scenes are shot with close-ups of Dancy and Moore's faces, emphasizing the strain on their faces and showing that both are quietly crying. Hugh Dancy mimics Julianne Moore's pained expression. The scene from the show is an almost exact replication of the scene from the *Hannibal* film, just with Will in

Clarice's place. The intense similarity between the two scenes demonstrates the deliberate decision by the creative team of the TV series to draw allusions to Clarice through Will's character. Dancy reproduces Moore's gestures, copying her body language to convey Will's emotions. In addition, Dancy employs feminized overtures in his mimicry; he closes his eyes, unable to look at Hannibal in this moment of betrayal, and he is clearly overwrought with emotion that he is trying to contain as Moore's Clarice did. The moment captures the emotion and desire Hannibal elicits from Clarice and Will, even in a moment of betrayal.

By exactly replicating Moore's performance, Dancy imbues the character of Will with gestures that have previously been coded as feminine. These gendered codes have become a visual norm in film and television and thus can be easily read without knowledge of the *Hannibal* film. However, because of the careful replication of the scene from the *Hannibal* film, the act of replication here also serves as a critique which highlights gender performativity through the performance of an actor imitating an actress, functioning similarly to queer acts such as drag which deconstruct performativity through mimicry. By transposing a female body for a male body, the show explores the possibility of the performing acting body and acting itself as "performance," a site for such critiques of hegemonic gender norms. Dancy's mimicry disrupts constructions of hegemonic binary gender, revealing these feminized gestures are not inherent to one particular gender, but rather coded, as "there is no original or primary gender … *but gender is a kind of imitation for which there is no original … a kind of imitation that produces the very notion of the original as an effect and consequence of the imitation itself"* (Butler 2012, 314). This reproduction thus uses the constructions of the original heteronormative framework to blur the boundaries between masculine and feminine gestures, indicating the constructed nature of such binaries of separation.

Through visual reproduction that highlights the gendered construction of Clarice's character, this reworking of the Hannibal franchise essentially talks back to the urtext, critiquing the original and inflecting it with new meanings in a way unique to transformative reimaginings (Brooker; Heinze and Krämer 2015, 12). By replicating the performance of a female romantic lead with a queer male love interest, the series reveals the ways in which adaptations inflect the "original" text they derive from, exposing that the urtext is in fact an intertextual construction as well, since "even the original was influenced, or inspired, by something prior, hence the notion of intertextuality…" (Marazi 2014, 238). This intertextual dialogue rewrites the original franchise in some ways, as the two texts depend on each other (Heinze and Krämer 2015, 12) and the transformative texts opens up the possibility for "revers[ing] the chronology of source text and its adaptation, putting the second before the first. In which case the consequence of reading or viewing back to the source text will inevitably be to resituate and transform the supposedly fixed and authentic original" (Brooker). Through repetition with difference, *Hannibal* uses the mode of adaptation to critique gendered constructions in the other adaptations of the franchise in a way that reflects back upon the original texts, thus offering a critical lens of Clarice's character that can transform readings of the Hannibal franchise.

Along with this scene, the *Hannibal* series reproduces another sequence from the film that even more clearly highlights Will Graham as a feminized figure by borrowing heterosexual cues of romance for Will's relationship to Hannibal. The narrative of this scene in the TV series exactly replicates the *Hannibal* film and plot of the final novel. After having been kidnapped by Hannibal's former patient, sadistic child molester Mason Verger, and antagonist of the film and third season of the show respectively, Hannibal and Clarice/Will attempt to escape from Mason's horrifying Muskrat Farms. Both Clarice and Will are injured and knocked unconscious in the process, requiring Hannibal to save them. In both scenes, Hannibal carries Clarice and Will, the respective objects of his desire, away from a scene of danger in his arms bridal style. The composition reverberates with the gendered and heterosexual visual of the husband carrying the bride over the threshold into marriage. The body language here draws upon long traditions of swooning maidens who must be saved by a strong male hero. By placing Will, the male protagonist of the show, into this ordinarily feminized position, the series critiques the long-standing heterosexist construction of women as the weaker gender that need to be saved by men. By directly lifting this sequence from the *Hannibal* film, the show also demonstrates the ways in which the original franchise constructed Clarice in more traditionally gendered ways in spite of her feminist status as a figure who challenged such roles. In addition, in both scenes, Clarice and Will's necks are exposed, the parallel eroticizing Will's body in a gesture usually reserved for depictions of sensual femininity. These scenes continue to queer Will beyond his same-sex romantic entanglement with Hannibal, feminizing his character and thus complicating his presentation of masculinity. The series thus presents his character as having both masculine and feminine coded characteristics, reflecting the composite nature of his character's gender. Through the inclusion of shades of Clarice's characterization in Will, particularly the more traditional gendered components of her character, *Hannibal* depicts Will's presentation of gender as more fluid, his masculinity co-existing with his femininity.

By eroticizing Will's body in a stereotypically feminine way, *Hannibal* also offers a critique common in the gender inversions of homoerotic horror films, exposing the cultural comfort with the abuse and objectification of the female body (Benshoff 2012, 142). Writing this extraordinarily feminized body language onto male cop Will Graham draws attention to the performative nature of gender in film as well as complicating Will's masculinity. Placing Will into Clarice's position allows *Hannibal* to reveal the ways in which Clarice had been traditionally feminized in previous adaptations and thus expose the heterosexist dynamics of other entries in the franchise. *Hannibal* critiques through replications with difference. By exactly reproducing visuals from the *Hannibal* film but with male Will in female Clarice's place, the show highlights the way gender had been conceived and hegemonically constructed in the previous adaptation. In this way, the intertextual allusions in these scenes operate similarly to visual remix, making its argument "at least in our culture, far more effectively than could words.... It doesn't assert the truth. It shows it. And once it is shown, no one can escape its mimetic effect.... [Remixes'] meaning ... comes from the reference, which is expressible only if it is the original that gets used" (Lessig 2008, 74).

The show's position as a prequel to *Silence of the Lambs* also complicates the relationship between original and reimagining. Due to *Hannibal* being chronologically set before *Silence*, this version of Will is a composite character that not only precedes but frequently replaces Clarice Starling's previous position in the franchise. This supplanting of the original mimics queer performativity and the relationship between queerness and heterosexuality, in that as "heterosexuality only constitutes itself as the original through a convincing act of repetition. The more the 'act' is expropriated, the more the heterosexual claim to originality is exposed as illusory" (Butler 2012, 314). Thus, the supplanting of the original through repetition mimics a queer act of deconstructing heterosexuality. Heinze and Krämer discuss the relationship between transformative works and their urtexts in a similar manners, stating, "There is no remake [or adaption] without a text to remake, and the 'original' is only conceived as one because another text has, if not copied, then transformed it" (2015, 12). Much like the performance of heterosexuality, the "original" status of an urtext for an adaptation is only achieved through the act of transformative repetition. Thus, the reimagined prequel has the potential to act in similar ways to queer performativity. *Hannibal* utilizes this mode to queer a heterosexual romance, replacing a heterosexual love interest with a same-sex love interest, and then supplanting that original heterosexual love interest completely within the chronology of the narrative. As a prequel, the series not only assumes a somewhat queer positionality in relationship to the original franchise but transforms the franchise's primary heterosexual romance into a same-sex one.

Hannibal not only exposes the troubling depiction of Clarice's femininity through visual adaptation, but also through replications of Clarice's narrative in Will's character arc. Nowhere is this more clear than in a comparison between the ending of the TV series and the ending of the *Hannibal* novel, the final book in the franchise. Unlike the film adaptation of the *Hannibal* book, in which Clarice resists Hannibal's attempts to seduce her, at the end of the *Hannibal* novel Clarice ultimately joins Hannibal as his romantic and criminal partner. The ending of the show parallels this resolution of Clarice's narrative arc, with Will giving in to Hannibal's desires by killing with him, the show's final epilogue heavily hinting that Will has joined Hannibal in his cannibalistic lifestyle. However, there are fundamental differences between the resolutions for these two characters. Will's parallel character arc highlights the problems with the ending of the *Hannibal* novel in terms of Clarice's feminist narrative, as Clarice joins Hannibal as the result of brainwashing and coercion, whereas Will chooses to embrace Hannibal's lifestyle of his own free will. By maintaining Will's agency, the show places itself in sharp contrast with the novel, highlighting the troubling undertones of the book's ending.

The ending of the *Hannibal* novel was extraordinarily controversial, leading the team behind the adaptation to write a completely different conclusion for the series and causing actress Jodie Foster, who had played Clarice Starling in *Silence*, to refuse to participate in the sequel, stating that the *Hannibal* novel's ending had "negative attributes" which "betrayed" Clarice's character ("Lambs" 2000). Criticism of the ending often had to do with the likelihood that Clarice would ever join Hannibal, the climax of the book seeming disingenuous to Clarice's prior characterization. The implications of the last section of the *Hannibal* novel are, however, even more insidious and troubling than that, especially in light of the feminist overtones of Clarice's arc in *Silence of the Lambs*.

Throughout the *Hannibal* book, flashbacks are shown of Hannibal's childhood, particularly in regard to the grim fate of his sister Mischa, who was murdered and cannibalized when the pair were children. Over the course of the novel, Hannibal becomes preoccupied with Stephen Hawking's theories about entropy and the idea that the universe will someday contract upon itself, reversing time, an image exemplified by a shattered teacup coming back together in the film *A Brief History of Time*. In the final section of the book, Hannibal attempts to replicate this concept psychologically with Clarice, who has drugged, through a series of hypnotic psychiatric sessions and brainwashing as part of his "desperate wish to make a place for Mischa in the world, perhaps the place now occupied by Clarice Starling" (Harris 2006, 490). As part of his "therapy," Hannibal attempts to sour Clarice toward the patriarchal figures in her life, such as Jack Crawford and her dead father. Although Hannibal's plan ultimately fails—Clarice never becomes a conduit for Mischa—he does ultimately alter Clarice through his brainwashing, who does break with her sentimental loyalty to law enforcement and her father and at the novel *Hannibal*'s end runs away with him as his lover and partner in crime. The alterations to Clarice's personality can be seen in her speech patterns as well as her indulgence in cannibalism. In the scene following several sessions of hypnotism, in which Hannibal and Clarice eat the brain of Clarice's FBI colleague Paul Krendler, who has been horrendously misogynistic to her throughout the novel, Paul even notes the change in Clarice, exclaiming "'*Who are you anyway?*' Krendler said. 'You're not Starling. You've got the spot on your face, but you're not Starling'" (Harris 2006, 530).

In some ways, this final section depicts Clarice finally breaking from a patriarchal system that does not appreciate her, an act with feminist potentiality. However, the fact that Hannibal merely supplants these figures with another patriarchal figurehead, himself, complete with the incestuous undertones of himself as father figure to his sister, and does so under coercion, undermines that subversive potential. The end of the novel makes some attempts to mark Clarice's brainwashed state as ambiguous. In the final chapter, set after Clarice and Hannibal having been living as cannibals and lovers for extended period, the narrator states, "The drugs that held [Clarice] in the first days have had no part in their lives for a long time. Nor the long talks with a single light source in the room.... Someday.... Starling may hear a crossbow string and come to some unwilled awakening, if indeed she even sleeps" (Harris 2006, 544). However, regardless of Clarice's ambiguous state at book's end, the nature of Clarice originally joining Hannibal comes at the cost of her ability to choose for herself, to make her own decision and retain her agency, and thus the strong feminism imbued in her character throughout the rest of the series is ultimately ripped away.

In contrast, the ending of the show seems to attempt to combine the respective endings of the film and book. Having cornered the Red Dragon, the season's serial killer antagonist, on a cliff outside the safe house in which Hannibal and Will have been lying in wait, Will gives into Hannibal's ultimate desire for him: that he will join Hannibal as a killer. He willingly kills the Red Dragon with Hannibal in a manic, animalistic fight which involves unleashing the dark urges Hannibal has sought to cultivate within him throughout the course of the series. This moment signifies Will's ultimate identification with Hannibal; he has essentially become him, the transformation that propels his arc throughout the entire series. Looking upon the bloody scene before them, Hannibal explains to Will, "This is all I ever wanted for you. For us." "It's beautiful," Will replies before tenderly embracing him, his head leaning on Hannibal's chest in an intimate and romantic gesture. He then slowly leans over the edge of the cliff, pulling Hannibal along with him, the pair still locked in a tight embrace as they fall to their presumed death in the waters below. This final act of Will's replicates some of Clarice's resistance to Hannibal in the film; however, although Clarice completely refuses to give in to Hannibal's machinations, Will surrenders, with the understanding that he has been corrupted and can only end Hannibal's crime spree killing them both. The epilogue to the show, however, depicts an ending more akin to the book's resolution.

An after-credits scene reveals Bedelia sitting at a dining room table. A pan to her legs under the table reveals that one has been cut off, the table furnished with her missing leg as the entree. The table is set for three. Thus, the series ends with the implication that Hannibal and Will have survived their fall and Will has joined Hannibal as a cannibal, following the narrative conclusion of the *Hannibal* book for Clarice. Will succumbing to Hannibal's desires comes after a long arc of seduction. The show makes use of its adapted chronology to slowly unfold the narrative of Will falling to darkness. By the series finale, Will has rejected Hannibal two other times throughout the course of the show. He rejects Hannibal during the season two finale in a scene that replicates the ending of the *Hannibal* film, and again in the mid-season three finale, after he and Hannibal have escape from Muskrat Farms. However, unlike Clarice, whose rejection of Hannibal comes at the film's end and thus constitutes the climax of her filmic narrative, Will expresses regret that he did not join Hannibal in the season two finale, telling Jack Crawford that he warned Hannibal of his impending capture "because ... because he was my friend. And because I wanted to run away with him" ("Aperitivo" 2015). The show thus utilizes its mixed chronology as well as the long-form narrative format of television to slowly unfold the narrative of seduction between Hannibal and Will and uses the opportunity to depict Will as much more susceptible to Hannibal's advances than Clarice ever proves to be. This makes the coercion depicted at the end of the *Hannibal* novel unnecessary in Will's case; the audience believes that Will would succumb to Hannibal's desires because his resistance has slowly eroded away after several rejections.

By contrasting the TV show's ending to the novel, the differences between the two become clear: Will is allowed to retain agency, while Clarice is stripped of hers. This contrast between the original and adaptation is where the binary gender of the two protagonists becomes most rigid. While Hannibal's desire for Will and Clarice, to indulge in his cannibalistic lifestyle and become his partner, is the same, his motivations and the barriers that stand in the way of him helping each realize this potential differs. In the case of Clarice, Hannibal wants to break her completely of her moral code and her loyalty to law enforcement, understands that as an ingrained part of her character that must be disposed and overcome, and intends to replace the patriarchal figures in her life, such as his father and Jack

Crawford, with himself. By contrast, with Will, Hannibal both recognizes his intense empathy as an asset that makes Will one of the only people who might truly understand Hannibal, and recognizes a more intense darkness within Will that he intends to help him realize. As with Will's slow succumbing to Hannibal's seduction, the show makes this darkness and Hannibal's recognition of it a slow-building and repeated component of Will's narrative arc. In the Pilot episode, Hannibal states that he and Will "are just alike," a connection he continually draws between them as he becomes obsessed with Will's "becoming" via his own attempts to get Will to realize his potential for darkness and become a cannibal like him. This sharply contrasts with Clarice's depiction in the franchise as a pillar of upstanding morality that can only be shaken through brainwashing and coercion, retaining a certain sense of feminine moral "purity" that Will never has.

By placing Will within Clarice's narrative and effectively "genderbending" her character in the show, *Hannibal* creates a new kinship between Hannibal and his love interest, as they are now the same gender. Within this same-sex dynamic forms a new commonality: a masculine propensity for violence. Although Will's character is imbued with femininity in the series that complicates the strict codes of gender, in the show's constant allusion to the darkness within Will lays a toxic masculinity not present in his female counterpart. The contrast between the original and adaptation still creates some interesting and subversive dialogue around gender. For instance, Clarice is by no means the easily corrupted Eve figure, as she only gives in to temptation when the choice is literally stripped from her, and although Will falls prey to masculine violence, he does so for romantic love, and love of another man no less, a narrative rarely allowed for a male protagonist. Ultimately, when read together, depictions of gender for both Clarice and Will are fraught, containing both subversive and conservative elements. By adapting characteristic of Clarice's character into Will Graham, *Hannibal* acts as a sounding board for the original franchise as offering an original articulation of gender codes for Will's character. In the way that adaptations can open up possibilities, the contrast between Will and Clarice's characters poses a question rather than answers it: if Fuller had had the rights to Clarice's character, would she have been allowed to follow Will's path and succumb to Hannibal with her agency still intact? Although this question ultimately goes unanswered, the unique portrayal of gender through adaptation in *Hannibal* opens a dialogue for complicating and considering femininity and masculinity, creating a space in which to reflect on both the subversive potentials and continued pitfalls of depictions of gender in media.

By drawing parallels between Will Graham and Clarice Starling, *Hannibal* deconstructs gender performance and heteronormativity. By feminizing Will's body, the show draws attention to the eroticization of Clarice in previous adaptations, revealing the gendered associations of sensuality to be a construction. In addition, the series mimics the romantic elements of a heterosexual relationship to create a queer romantic if asexual one. This replication operates in the series in much the same way as queer performativity does: as a means of revealing the constructed nature of heterosexuality. According to Butler, repetition is the means by which heterosexuality claims originality. Thus, when queerness mimics heteronormativity, the act of performance reveals heterosexuality itself to be an imitation and therefore disputes its claims to originality. *Hannibal* uses the slippery sense of "originality" in the modes of adaptation and remake to queer romantic narratives and critique the construction of gender in previous entries of the Hannibal franchise.

WORKS CITED

Filmography

Hannibal. Directed by Ridley Scott. 2001. Beverly Hills, CA: MGM Studios, 2001. DVD.
Hannibal. "Aperitivo." Directed by Marc Jobst. Written by Nick Antosca, Bryan Fuller, and Steve Lightfoot. National Broadcasting Company, June 25 2015.
Hannibal. "Digestivo." Directed by Adam Kane. Written by Steve Lightfoot and Bryan Fuller. National Broadcasting Company, July 18 2015.
Hannibal. "Dolce." Directed by Vincenzo Natali. Written by Don Mancini, Bryan Fuller, and Steve Lightfoot. National Broadcasting Company, July 9 2015.
Hannibal. "Mizumono." Directed by David Slade. Written by Steve Lightfoot and Bryan Fuller. National Broadcasting Company, May 23 2014.
Hannibal. "The Number of the Beast is 666...." Directed by Guillermo Navarro. Written by Jeff Vlaming, Angela LaManna, Bryan Fuller, and Steven Lightfoot. National Broadcasting Company, August 22 2015.
Hannibal. "The Wrath of the Lamb." Directed by Michael Rymer. Written by Bryan Fuller, Steven Lightfoot, and Nick Antosca. National Broadcasting Company, August 29 2015.
The Silence of the Lambs. Directed by Jonathan Demme. 1991. Los Angeles, CA: Orion Pictures, 1991. DVD.

Bibliography

Arnett, Robert P. "Casino Royale and Franchise Remix: James Bond as Superhero." *Film Criticism* 33, no. 3 (2009): 1.
Benshoff, Harry. "'Way Too Gay to be Ignored': The Production and Reception of Queer Horror Cinema in the Twenty-First Century," in *Speaking of Monsters: A Teratological Anthology*, ed. Caroline Joan S. Picart and John Edgar Browning (New York: St. Martin's Press, 2012), 255–265.
Brooker, Peter. "Postmodernism and Adaptation: Pastiche, Intertextuality and Re-functioning," in *The Cambridge Companion to Literature on Screen*, ed. Deborah Cartmell and Imelda Whelehan (New York: Cambridge University Press).
Butler, Judith. "Imitation and Gender Insubordination," in *The Lesbian and Gay Studies Reader*, ed. Henry Abelove, Michèle Aina Barale, and David M. Halperin (New York: Routledge, 2012), 307–321.

Fisher, Natalie. "Bryan Fuller and Hugh Dancy on Ditching the 'Hannibal' Procedural and Will's Quest." *Hypable.* Last modified July 14, 2015. http://www.hypable.com/hannibal-press-conference-sdcc-2015/.

Goldman, Eric. "Hannibal: How Bryan Fuller Approached the Iconic Character." *IGN.* Last modified April 3, 2013. http://www.ign.com/articles/2013/04/04/hannibal-how-bryan-fuller-approached-the-iconic-character-and-why-clarice-starling-cant-appear-red-dragon-the-silence-of-the-lambs?page=4.

Harris, Thomas. *Hannibal.* New York: Bantam Dell, 2006.

Heinze, Rüdiger, and Krämer, Lucia. Introduction to *Remake and Remaking: Concepts—Media—Practices,* Edited by Rüdiger Heinze and Lucia Krämer. Deutsche Nationalbiblotek, 2015.

Hutcheon, Linda. *A Theory of Adaptation.* New York: Routledge, 2006.

Kreisinger, Elisa. "Queer Video Remix and LGBTQ Online Communities." *Transformative Works* 9 (2012).

"Lambs in Doubt without Foster." *BBC News.* Last modified January 6, 2000. http://news.bbc.co.uk/2/hi/entertainment/592904.stm.

Lessig, Lawrence. *Remix: Making Art and Commerce Thrive in the Hybrid Economy.* New York: Penguin, 2008.

Marazi, Katerina. "Brand Identity, Adaptation, and Media Franchise Culture." *Acta Universitatis Sapientiae, Film and Media Studies* 9 no. 1 (2014): 229–242.

Phillips, Kendall R. *Controversial Cinema: The Films That Outraged America.* Westport: Praeger, 2008.

VanDerWerff, Todd. "Bryan Fuller Walks Us through the Second Season Premiere of Hannibal." *A.V. Club.* Last modified March 1, 2014. http://www.avclub.com/article/bryan-fuller-walks-us-through-second-season-premie-201684.

Go with the Flow

Will Graham and Liminality in Bryan Fuller's Hannibal

Lorianne Reuser

Though liminality was first introduced as a concept in 1909 by Arnold van Gennep as the transitional stage in an individual's rite of passage, theorists like Manuel Aguirre and William Veeder have long since established liminality as a concept highly suited to the Gothic genre. Liminality refers to thresholds, the space betwixt-and-between set categories, where the interpenetration and destabilization of definitions and binaries can occur. The Gothic genre, Manuel Aguirre has argued, is a liminal space, a betwixt-and-between genre, caught between the serious and popular, the low and the high. Hearkening back to Horace Walpole's *The Castle of Otranto*, the Gothic is a mediating genre, halfway between fantasy and psychology, romance and the novel.[1] Veeder examines the Gothic as a potential third space, neither the "internal psychological or the external social," but committed to exploring both.[2] The Gothic is about the "blurring of different levels of discourse while it is also concerned with the interpenetration of other opposed conditions—including life/death, natural/supernatural … and unconscious/conscious—along with the abjection of these crossings into haunting and supposedly deviant 'others.'"[3] Peter Messent, in "Liminality and the Gothic in Thomas Harris's Hannibal Lecter Novels," examines Harris's use of the Gothic and liminality with reference to Clarice Starling and Hannibal Lecter in the four Lecter novels, and states: "the boundary crossings that Harris represents in his texts … are tied in symbiotic connection to the Gothic form he uses."[4] Bryan Fuller constructed his television adaptation *Hannibal* around a similar theory, positioning the series as an entity between genres, thus opening it as a space in which binaries of identity, especially with regards to the oft forgotten Will Graham, can be thoroughly interrogated.[5] The liminal spaces Will Graham

121

experiences demonstrate destabilized binaries, particularly those of dream/reality, and inner/outer self, where monstrosity arises from the interstitial mixing between the two, and is projected onto the unstable relationship between Will Graham and his Double, Hannibal Lecter. But the liminality that destabilizes Will's boundaries also provides potentiality, where engagement with his Double leads him to truth and transformation.

Bryan Fuller's *Hannibal* was, from its inception, in between genres. With gruesome murders and a surrealist aesthetic more suited to cable, it aired for three years (2013–2015) on NBC. Like Harris's *Red Dragon* and *Silence of the Lambs*, Fuller's *Hannibal* originally seemed like crime fiction, with a "serial killer of the week" format common to other network crime shows. Like the novels, however, the Gothic and Horror notes quickly overwhelmed the traditional structure, and as the show subverted boundaries, it became much more difficult to define. Bryan Fuller once defined the show as a "pretentious art film from the 80s"[6] and in a later interview he explained how he viewed *Hannibal's* genre:

> [I]t's evolved from a crime procedural into an opera, just because we had done so much with the crime procedural world and it was always an element that I never fully embraced—I was always looking for ways to subvert it or enhance it with the death tableaus. It was an umbrella under which we would tell the metaphor for Will Graham and Hannibal Lecter's relationship. So the context of the show being a crime procedural was always a loose one, and I really always felt the show was a romantic horror, and I feel like this season more than any other fully embraces those elements of romantic horror.[7]

Though Fuller does not use the term "Gothic" here, his concept of romantic horror is remarkably similar. Echoes of the genre are obvious: the sinister yet charming European aristocrat villain; the focus on dark and closed spaces like Hannibal's house or the Baltimore State Hospital for the Criminally Insane (BSCHI); and the monstrous figures that haunt Will's visions. Also, just as the Harris novels "operate within an ominously Gothic environment where the daily practice of morality and justice constantly slide away from idealistic centers, epitomizing a destabilizing strategy common to Gothic fiction,"[8] so too does Fuller's *Hannibal* undermine the moral centers and "solid systems" of society. The FBI, the BSCHI, the courts, and even medical personnel like Dr. Sutcliffe are unworthy of society's trust. In the *Hannibal* universe, no system is solid.

Fuller further destabilizes *Hannibal's* universe through the use of a framing strategy in which the seasons all open and close within a layer of liminal instability. The first season opens with Will imagining himself a participant at a crime scene, and concludes with Will hidden away, buried alive in the BSCHI, a liminal being with "physical but not social reality."[9] The second season begins with the infamous fight scene that occurs twelve weeks into the future, thus playing with the viewer's sense of time, and stops abruptly with Jack's fate uncertain. The season returns to the fight scene in the finale, "Mizumono," and concludes with an abundance of blood and water, both connected to Will and his dreamscape, and with Hannibal and Bedelia in transit (another type of liminal space).[10] The third season begins with Hannibal and Abel Gideon discussing stories over the dinner table, and much like how "the Gothic exaggerates its own extreme fictionality,"[11] Hannibal's words: "Once upon a time" signal the crossing of the threshold into the story, just as the curtain drawing back across the frame and the injection of color into the action suggest a theater play.[12] Fuller takes care to construct the episodes and seasons as spaces of unreality, of destabilization, already between fiction and reality, so as to establish an environment suited to exploring Will's Gothic liminality in all its complexity.

Will Graham is, from his introduction, established as a liminal being who can, with his extremely fluid imagination, identify with anyone, victim or killer, thus placing his own stability of self in a precarious position. "Apéritif" opens with a doorway into a house, a threshold from outside to inside.[13] The next two shots show, in close-ups, a pool of blood on the floor, and a spatter of blood on the wall. The blood, and the body in the next shot, establishes the house as a liminal space of both life and death.[14] Will Graham stands in a medium shot, framed by a window, with police officers crossing by in the foreground. Like the initial doorway shot, the window acts as a threshold symbol, with our focus drawn to Will in the center. The officers do not engage with Will or make eye contact, and as the scene progresses there is no dialogue between them, only Will's narration and a request for a file responded to by a figure outside the frame. Will is here established as both present and not, the window framing him as a figure on a threshold both inside and outside. To the others, he seems invisible, almost a ghost.

Then the pendulum swings, and without explanation the viewer watches time reverse, the blood draw back, the policemen disappear, and the colors saturate. Will walks backward, through the doorway and down the steps into the crowd of police and lights, and still no one reacts. He sees the now living Mrs. Marlow through the window, and the viewer watches in confusion as Will kicks in the door, forcing himself into the home, and proceeds to enact the violence of which we have already seen the aftermath. Will's standing position in the window, and his multiple crossings of the doorway within the space of the pendulum's swing, figure him as a liminal figure who can move between physical and symbolic spaces, through which the boundaries between present and past, and self (Will) and other (the murderer) dissolve. And when the scene shifts to reveal that Will is not even present at the house at all—he is lecturing about the murder in the classroom, through photographs, another threshold layer is added.[15]

The entire scene has perhaps been an imagined reality, a space between the past and present, translated through Will's imagination. Will's natural ability to suspend himself in the area between real and not-real establishes him as someone "endowed with numinous power ... who walk[s] the line—often precariously—between the worlds."[16] The key term here is "precariously," because as the seasons progress, Will's anxiety over the forts in his mind proves well founded, and as those forts collapse and he finds himself increasingly in spaces of the betwixt-and-between, he proves Aguirre's theory that "individuals already predisposed to the Numinous, or endowed with a particular moral constitution, or made receptive by specific circumstances, are liable to become exposed to the dangers (as to the sublimities) of numinous encounters.

Thus, characters already living on a physical or metaphorical threshold or leading a liminal existence are prone to Gothic experiences."[17] It is in those "betwixt and between" spaces whose materiality is increasingly suspect as the dream and the real merge that Will, like classic Gothic protagonists, must confront both the monsters without, and the monstrous within. Will, as Hannibal helpfully explains to Jack, doesn't simply reflect the monstrous that he analyzes and experiences in these liminal spaces back to itself, he absorbs it.[18]

From the first episode to the finale, Will's character is associated with fluidity and liquid, as seen in the blood and waters of his unconscious, which represent both safety and danger to Will's state of mind. Images of water have long been associated with the dream-state, the unconscious. The shower scene in "Apéritif" establishes this connection in the context of the show: in this scene Will is standing in the shower, washing away the horrors of the day in which he analyzed the body of a girl impaled on antlers. As the water flows over him, the camera zooms into the darkness between the gap in the shower curtain, and through the steam, a stag with raven feathers appears.[19] The "Ravenstag," the symbolic manifestation of Will's connection to Hannibal in his subconscious, is a recurring symbol and guide, often appearing in liminal places: in Will's waking dreams, on the road as Will sleepwalks, in the corridors of the BSCHI, in the bloodbath kitchen of "Mizumono" where its death unleashes a sea of blood, and on the train tracks to Florence. The stag also appears in Will's stream, Will's equivalent to Hannibal's mind-palace. The stream is a "between" place in its status as Will's subconscious retreat, but also as a body of flowing water between two banks, often with Will in the middle. Seen in conjunction with Will's past as a fisherman and boat mechanic, the stream functions as a reprieve for Will, a benefit of his ability to slip into liminal spaces. But water is an inherently unstable element, constantly eroding at the banks that contain it. Such spaces, however, are also sites where monstrosity arises, as it does in "Hassun" when the wendigo, Will's subconscious manifestation of Hannibal's monstrosity, rises eerily out of the stream. Here the liminal is again subject to the intrusion of monstrous figures taking advantage of the threshold's permeability, and the interstitial mixing of Will and Hannibal in his mind prefigures the mingling of Inner with Outer that manifests in the body's inability to contain Will's illness.

Will's susceptibility to the numinous places him in a situation common to horror narratives, when the subject becomes impure because the boundaries between what is normally distinct collapse into what Noel Carroll defines as categorical interstitiality.[20] In Will's case, the flimsy border between skin and the mass of fluids within becomes as precarious as the line between dream and reality, and the body becomes grotesque and Other as a result. Barbara Creed, in "Horror and the Carnivalesque," discusses how we can only know the inside of the body through the outside; the inside is essentially an unknowable, mystical mass of which we are always afraid of losing control.[21] A proper body is stable, fixed, and clean, with skin as a guaranteed border against the inner bodily wastes. But "skin as mobile, fluid, and fragile reinforces an image of the grotesque body as constantly in a state of becoming."[22] Will's fever-dream moments of the first season and resulting sweatiness, the manifestation of his inner turmoil, employs Creed's theory of the fluidity of the skin corresponding to the fluidity of the mind, and prefigures the moments of transformation and "becoming" that will occur in the second and third seasons. Creed argues that the "destruction of the physical body is used as a metaphor to point to the possibility that the self is also transitory, fragile, and fragmented."[23]

For Will, the grotesque dissolving of his physical body reaches its peak, visually, in the first season episode most concerned with identity, "Roti." The episode opens with Will removing his glasses, one of the barriers he uses to keep his forts intact, to view a crumbling wall of ice. The ice crashes into the sea, and the nightmarish totem pole from "Trou normand" (interestingly enough situated on a beach, a liminal space between land and sea), appears. The gruesome mass of bodies echoes the moment in that episode when Will somehow traveled from the beach to Hannibal's house with no awareness of the trip. The reminder of this loss of control over his own body occurs now in Will's dream where the totem pole is suddenly overwhelmed with a wave, and in a blink Will is panting in his bed and sweating through his shirt. The clock, a marker of Will's ability to ground himself in reality, distorts and melts into a puddle. A steaming puddle spreads from Will's body onto the bed, and, interspersed with images of an overwhelming wave, his soaking, thrashing body dissolves into a splash of water. Such night-sweats, here at their most extreme, transition to the daytime, and often accompany moments of hallucinations and extreme instability, as when Will imagines himself surrounded by a thicket of antlers, or later in the episode when, at the peak of his illness, he projects the imagined Garrett Jacob Hobbs onto Abel Gideon. Will's inability to control the images in his mind is reflected in his inability to govern his body. Will frequently loses control, both in lost time, where he blinks in one location and opens his eyes in another with no memory of the transition, and in the seizures that wrack his body in Hannibal's dining room. The permeability of his body's boundaries indicates his mind's slippage between sanity and insanity, the boundary of which is dependent on the line between outer and inner. He even states to Hannibal: "I don't know how to gauge who I am, anymore."[24] His greatest fear of not knowing who he is, of being crazy, is realized. His body, like his mind, has lost the security of solid forts and has become interstitial through the mixing of the inner and outer—his nightmare visions projected onto the physical world while awake, and the waves in his mind manifested as sweat, the body's inner fluids now on the other side of his skin. The complete destabilization of boundaries, fundamental to the liminal, not only makes Will's body a site of interstitiality, a characteristic quality of the monstrous according to Carroll, also creates a site of potentiality, much like the Gothic genre itself, where Will's unconscious self, the repressed desires he is so frightened of accepting as part of himself, may rise to the surface. And as the visions in his mind are projected into the waking world, so too is this struggle with the unconscious.

The notion of the inner, irrepressible and dangerous self is a common trope of Gothic and horror, a product of the Enlightenment ideal of the rational self, and finds expression in D.H. Lawrence who, contemptible of this ideal, wrote: "Oh, but I have a strange and fugitive self shut out and howling like a wolf or a coyote…. See his red eyes in the dark? This is a self who is coming into his own."[25] That fugitive self is the same monstrous half that Dr. Jekyll, in his wish to extricate it from the body, projected outward into his own Double, Mr. Hyde. Indeed, the struggle between the protagonist and their Double is a recurring theme in the Gothic genre, in texts like Stevenson's *The Strange Case of Dr. Jekyll and Mr. Hyde* and Thomas De Quincey's *Confessions of a Justified Sinner*. The Monster of Gothic fiction is often the Double of its protagonist, where the self is projected into a space hitherto defined as Other.[26] Fear of the Double, in this reading, is fear of self-knowledge.[27] In *Hannibal*'s Gothic universe, then, it follows that Will project his struggle with his own repressed, fugitive self onto the very man who is already constructed as both monstrous and Other, a cannibal and murderer, and who is aggressively encouraging that very same struggle within Will. Thus, as the seasons progress, Hannibal Lecter is increasingly portrayed as Will's Double against whom Will struggles.

In the first season, Will and Hannibal are linked initially through

Garrett Jacob Hobbs. Hobbs is the killer with whom Will must identify in order to catch, and Will's empathizing is so strong that he begins to exhibit what he fears are Hobbs's traits, including his sense of parental responsibility and affection for Abigail Hobbs. Hannibal aggressively encourages Will's fatherly aspirations, while also positioning himself as a partner father-figure. Concurrently, Hannibal acts as a double for Hobbs when he copies the aesthetics of Hobbs's murders in his own murder tableau. Hannibal is the Copycat killer that Will is later mistaken for. The final moments of "Savoureux," when Hannibal walks down the corridor of the BSCHI and greets Will Graham imprisoned behind bars is a meta-textual moment that evokes similar scenes in *Silence of the Lambs* and *Red Dragon*, but switches their positions across the prison bars. The viewer cannot help but imagine how the narrative is *supposed* to go, and, as a result, place Will in Hannibal's position and Hannibal in Will's.

The Doubling motif returns and intensifies in the second season, especially in the second half. In the effort to seduce Hannibal into custody, Will performs a version of self that takes on traits of Hannibal's personality, but that complement his own darker yearnings. He empathizes with Hannibal in order to imagine what Hannibal will do, and what he would have Will do. The act of imagining himself as Hannibal allows Will the freedom to express his repressed violence, both in the liminal space of Will's guided imaginings and dreams, many of which are partaken under Hannibal's guidance, and in the situations where their relationship is projected onto the secondary characters—like Randall Tier and Clark Ingram, the latter a parallel of Hannibal, the former of Will—that Will enacts violence upon. This doubling reaches its peak of visual expression in "Ko No Mono," where the two, in a highly charged conversation, imagine themselves in the other's place. The effect is uncanny, in the full sense of Freud's meaning, both for the viewer and for the characters, as Hugh Dancy and Mads Mikkelsen adopt the speech patterns and mannerisms of the other. Just as their relationship has becomes difficult to define, as Alana points out,[28] so too do the lines that demark their identities from each other, a theme which follows through into the third season.

The third season sees the most extreme expression of the double motif, and the heightened unreality established through the previously discussed framing techniques establishes this season in particular as a highly liminal space in which Will and Hannibal come to blur, especially in the fluid spaces of their mind-palace. Indeed, if Will's relationship with Hannibal is the projection of his struggle with his unconscious self, then the blurring and merging of Will and Hannibal in these moments is a continuation and reflection of the destabilized boundary between Will's Inner and Outer selves. The first half of the third season involves Will in a traumatic liminal state; he is unable to move on from Hannibal, and repeatedly has flashbacks to "Mizumono" and Abigail, thereby destabilizing the binary between past and present. He also converses with Hannibal in mind, as in "Secondo" when he travels to Hannibal's childhood home, an attempt to bridge the present with the past, so as to unlock Hannibal's mind-palace and understand him. It is Chiyo, however, the witness to Hannibal's childhood, who forces Will to verbalize Hannibal's significance as Will's Double, and Hannibal's role in allowing Will to understand himself. "I have never known myself as well as I know myself when I'm with him."[29] Significantly, Will does not need the pendulum when he imagines Hannibal's crime scenes, such as in the chapel in Palermo. Hannibal and Will are established now as conjoined, a zero-sum game. The blurring between the two achieves visual form in Will's drugged mind as he sits at Hannibal's table in "Dolce." Like inkblots spreading through water, their faces slowly diffuse and merge with the red of blood, until they swirl into each other.

Their conversations within a shared mind-palace return in the second half of the season, when Hannibal and Will, physically in the depths of the BSCHI, are instead shown meeting in the Palermo chapel. As they discuss the Tooth Fairy's crime scene, they are both transported to the site of the murder with no pendulum marking the threshold. They easily transition from indoors to outdoors as their conversation progresses.[30] But the lines separating the two are permeable even in the objective, physical world. Though separated from each other for three years, Hannibal's mirroring of Will's movements in their first conversation is uncanny. Their discussions in the BSCHI are often constructed between two types of shots: in the one, they stand paralleled, in profile to the camera, with the single pane of glass separating them in the middle. These shots are often interspersed with close-ups on their faces beyond the glass, sometimes so close that the conversations feel uncomfortably intimate. Even more significant, however, are the shots when the camera views their conversation over the shoulder of one character, a type of shot usually meant to establish a sense of coherency. That coherent separation is undermined in "...And the Beast from the Sea," when Hannibal's blurred reflection superimposes itself over Will's as they discuss the dragon and his desire for change, a conversation that is really about Will. The intimacy and connection between the two, especially in these conversations isolated from the rest of reality, with the tendency to slip into their shared mind-palace, suggests that here is another boundary subject to destabilization, especially in these intensified liminal spaces. Whether he struggles against it or accepts it, Will cannot escape Hannibal, because he is a second soul dwelling within his breast.

The liminal state, though a site of destabilization and collapse, is also a site of enlightenment and transformation. As the binaries and definitions that construct who we are collapse, previously unrealized truths are exposed when we are forced to confront our unconscious selves. All of Will's revelations tend to occur when he crosses a threshold or is in a liminal space connected to his unconscious. It is in his dream state that Will realizes Abigail is a killer; it is at the peak of his illness when Will, shaking and sweaty, concludes in Hobbs's kitchen that Hannibal is a killer; it is in the strange black and white dream of "Shiizakana" that Will hears Hannibal speak of his love, and realizes he can use their connection to destroy Hannibal; it is in a waking dream that Will sees Anthony Dimmond's corpse, broken and molded into a heart, come alive as a deformed stag-like creature—making Will realize that Hannibal misses him. The unconscious, much like Will's cell in the BSCHI, or the depths of a lake or sea, is figured as a site of descent and heroes often must descend in order to climb. As Carl Jung says in his discussion on dreams and the unconscious, "the descent into the depths always seems to precede the ascent."[31] Will Graham's "descent" into the liminal state of his unconscious and the destabilization he must endure are pivotal to his goal of helping the victims of criminal situations, and to his own quest for the self-knowledge that will empower him to combat Hannibal's machinations. His powers of imagination give him the ability to see the past, to hear the victims' stories, to speak for the dead, even if that victim is himself.

Though imprisoned at the BSCHI in the first half of the second season, Will becomes, as Hannibal confirms: "more in control now than you have ever been."[32] His position as a liminal figure, buried alive in the underworld of the BSCHI, places him outside of society, and gives him the means and opportunity to delve into his unconscious for memories he knows he has been denied access. With the aid of Alana Bloom and Dr. Chilton, Will steps into his own memories at numerous points from the first season, and views moments where he had before been unconscious. The knowledge he gains: that Hannibal force fed him Abigail's ear (another case of violating the boundaries between self/other, not to mention that of food/human), and the conversation between Abel Gideon and Hannibal, empowers him to regain his agency. He may be physically trapped, but he can still affect changes on the outside through the exploration of the inside. Similarly, even his recurring conversations with Hannibal are moments of uncomfortable truths, and most occur in their own sort of "between" space, many in Will's mind, which later merges with Hannibal's to become a shared "mind palace." To engage with his "projective Other means reengagement with [his] own power,"[33] thus for Will, the liminal spaces, because of their instability, are sites of empowerment.

Liminal spaces are, furthermore, sites of transformation. Turner describes this positive aspect of the liminal as: "undoing, dissolution, decomposition are accompanied by processes of growth, transformation, and the reformation of old elements in new patterns."[34] With awareness, one has the ability to change, not just the outer world, but themselves. *Hannibal* exhibits Will Graham, with his definitions destabilized and with his access to hidden truths, as one not only caught in a constant "inbetween" state, but on the cusp of a "Becoming." First introduced with the Angel-Maker of the first season, the theme of transformation, especially Will Graham's, continues through season two and culminates in the latter half of season three. In the second season the viewer watches Will literally transform into a monster, the very monster that Hannibal admonishes him for not admitting exists and is growing inside.[35] In "Mukozuke" after he sends Matthew Brown to kill Hannibal, antlers pierce out from underneath his skin and grow, spreading beyond the confines of Will's cage. The antlers and the blood-water in the sink, both elements of Will's unconscious that overflow their containers, are outer projections of Will's crossing a moral threshold. Scenes of Will as an outwardly monstrous creature appear from this point: when he is birthed from the Ravenstag as a wendigo similar to Hannibal, and echoed in "…And the Woman Clothed with the Sun" when he, imagining himself as the yet unknown Dolarhyde, envisions himself as drenched in blood, black in the moonlight. The show parallels Will's transformation with Dolarhyde's transformation, both visually and through the line Hannibal says to both: "blood and breath are only elements undergoing change to fuel your radiance."[36] The latter half of season three, then, is where the themes of liminality, doubles, monstrosity and transformation will reach their apex.

The *Red Dragon* arc in the third season splits the narrative between Francis Dolarhyde's desire to transform from his flawed, disabled self into William Blake's Great Red Dragon, and Will Graham's return to the FBI and Hannibal. The doubling of the narrative foregrounds the theme of transformation. Though Will has found a family and apparent stability, he quickly becomes embroiled in the familiar struggle of his socially constructed self, now with a family in tow, against the Doubles, Hannibal and Dolarhyde, who would threaten that self. Yet again, as a result of empathizing with a murderer, the violent impulses of the Other, both from within and without, threaten to overwhelm Will's family and his identity. Hannibal sees beneath the placid waters that Will so desperately wishes to project, and in "…And the Beast from the Sea" asks him if, like the Dragon, he doesn't crave change. Aguirre might describe Will as detained in a liminal state, the victim of an incomplete passage.[37] Hannibal uses Dolarhyde as a catalyst to provoke the change that they all crave.

The aforementioned themes and symbols of liminality and doubling culminate in the final scenes in "The Wrath of the Lamb." Will and

Hannibal flee to Hannibal's house that lies on the edge of a cliff, composed of seemingly nothing but windows. As Will and Hannibal observe the ocean waves crashing below, they discuss the erosion of the cliffs, and how soon "all this will be lost to the sea."[38] Dolarhyde's evening attack begins with a bullet that explodes Hannibal's bottle of wine into a shower of liquid, just as the window shatters (reminiscent of Randall Tier), and Dolarhyde literally crosses the threshold. Once the battle begins in earnest, the action moves outside onto the cliffside, underneath the light of the full moon. The moon is an important symbol that ties the themes of liminality, monstrosity, and doubleness together. The moon is associated with the liminal in van Gennep's original study on transitional rites when he connects death to the moon: "among a great many peoples the origin or introduction of death is attributed to the moon."[39] The moon is also fluid, its form changing as it waxes and wanes. The classic horror monster of the werewolf and its transformation from human to monster is associated with the moon. Dolarhyde prefers to perform his brutal murders, equated to rituals in the process of his becoming, his transformation, by the light of the full moon. Furthermore, Carl Jung associates the moon with the unconscious when he says: "In the unconscious, one is unfortunately in the same situation as in a moonlit landscape. All the contents are blurred and merge into one another, and one never knows exactly what or where anything is, or where one thing begins and ends."[40]

How fitting, then, that this final scene occurs beneath the moonlight, on a cliffside, with the three figures drenched in blood, and the final moments of Dolarhyde's death teetering between the dream-state and the literal. Dolarhyde dies in a strange moment of surrealist imagery, full of flames and bloody wings, that suggests the moment is from Will's perspective, the dream-state in which *Hannibal's* monsters exhibit their symbolic forms. Will's next comment, that the blood "really does look black in the moonlight" hearkens back to an earlier moment in the season when Hannibal and Will examined Dolarhyde's crime in their shared mind-palace, suggesting a blurring of past and present. It also draws attention to those two elements, blood and moonlight, both previously discussed as prominent symbols of the threshold and transformation. In this moment, finally, to Hannibal's perspective, Will has achieved his Becoming. The wrath of the lamb has turned him into a lion, a pack hunter that not just tolerates, but enjoys the thrill of killing, a pleasure to share with Hannibal. Will has come to accept the monster now fully grown inside him. Even the blood that flows from Will's face, from Hannibal's stomach, is a connecting force. Blood from wounds links "the inside and the outside of the body ... [and points] ... symbolically to the fragile nature of the self, its lack of secure boundaries, the ease with which it might lose definition."[41] Creed even draws attention to the mouth, the site of Will's stab wound, and how "blood that flows from the mouth links the inside to the outside." In this "between" place, a cliff poised over the sea, where everything is blurred in the moonlight and linked through blood, Will allows for the merging of his repressed desires with his outer self, just as he and Hannibal, the self and the other, embrace. And when Will pulls Hannibal over the cliffs into the waters below, he is, we may conclude, embracing the potential of the liminal, both in the water and the fall. Perhaps he was choosing to die, but the camera does not show their end. The viewer is left, particularly after the post-credits scene, uncertain of their fate. We see them tip, but with no confirmation we are left with the image of them falling in that liminal space between cliff and sea. The fate of Will Graham and Hannibal Lecter is left, just like the fate of the show, in a "betwixt-and-between," finished but not. In that final moment, even the boundary between character and viewer is destabilized, as we all wait for a closure that might never occur.

Hannibal is a highly stylized show that subverts stable definitions of genre in its quest to tell a story worthy of its characters. The liminal state the show achieves through its Gothic narrative and framing devices creates a "betwixt-and-between" space in which the stability of identity, formed through binaries, can be interrogated. With a mind already made fluid through his extreme imagination and empathy, Will Graham's repression of his unconscious self is weakened through Hannibal's machinations, and the blurring between inside/outside, unconscious self/social self, is reflected in the imagery of water and blood that often overwhelms Will physical body. Within a reality made liminal through Will's imaginative perspective, the conflict with the unconscious is projected onto his relationship with his Double, Hannibal Lecter. But *Hannibal* also explores how the liminal can be a site of empowerment through instability. In the end, Will Graham achieves victory through liminality—we leave Hannibal and Will conjoined and at peace, but falling to the sea. However, a fall may precipitate a rise once more and, as Jung might suggest, the plunge into the depths may simply be required for the two to rise again.

Notes

1. Manuel Aguirre, "Narrative structure, Liminality, Self-similarity: The Case of Gothic Fiction," in *Gothic Horror: A Guide for Students and Readers,* ed. Clive Bloom. 2nd ed. (New York: Palgrave Macmillan, 2007), 233.

2. William Veeder, "The Nurture of the Gothic, or How can a Text be Both Popular and Subversive?" in *American Gothic: New Interventions in a Naitonal Narrative,* ed. Robert K. Martin and Eric Savoy. (Iowa City: University of Iowa Press), 21–22.

3. Jerrold E. Hogle, Introduction to *The Cambridge Companion to Gothic Fiction,* ed. Jerold E. Hogle. (Cambridge: Cambridge University Press), 5.

4. Peter Messent, "American Gothic: Liminality and the Gothic in Thomas Harris's Hannibal Lecter Novels," in *Dissecting Hannibal Lecter,* ed. Benjamin Szumskyj. (Jefferson, NC: McFarland), 14.

5. *Hannibal* is full of liminal spaces and characters, but I sacrificed breadth for focus. Many of the other characters either exhibit liminal qualities or pass through liminal stages, and with Abigail and Alana this reflects issues of gender. Hannibal also is an example of interstitiality and Gothic liminality, and his obsession with the present/past binary informs much of his actions. Even the medium of the television show itself is a liminal threshold, and the viewer's relationship to the murder/art binary raises interesting questions of the threshold between participation and observation.

6. Eric Thurm, "Hannibal showrunner: 'We are not making television. We are making a pretentious 80s art film from the 80s,'" *The Guardian,* Last modified June 3, 2015, https://www.theguardian.com/tv-and-radio/2015/jun/03/hannibal-tv-showrunner-bryan-fuller.

7. Laura Prudom, "Hannibal Showrunner Bryan Fuller Says Season 3 is the 'Series I've Always Wanted to Make,'" *Variety,* last modified June 4, 2015, http://variety.com/2015/tv/news/hannibal-season-3-will-relationship-red-dragon-1201512730/.

8. Sian MacArthur. *Crime and the Gothic: Identifying the Gothic Footprint in Modern Crime Fiction* (Oxfordshire: Libri Publishing), 94.

9. Victor Turner, "Betwixt and Between: The Liminal Period in Rites de Passage," in *Magic, Witchcraft and Religion: An Anthropological Study of the Supernatural,* ed. Arthur C. Lehmann and James E. Myers. (California: Mayfield Publishing Co., 2001), 49.

10. *Hannibal,* "Mizumono," directed by David Slade. Written by Bryan Fuller. NBC, May 23, 2014.

11. Hogle, Introduction to *The Cambridge Companion,* 14.

12. *Hannibal.* "Antipasto," directed by Vincenzo Natali. Written by Bryan Fuller. NBC, June 4, 2015.

13. Hannibal Lecter is also associated with thresholds, but uses his charm to invite people to cross over into his space, as opposed to Will's method of crossing into the other's. The breakfast in which Will and he develop their friendship begins in an opposite manner, with Will opening the door and being socially obligated to invite Hannibal inside.

14. Barbara Creed, "Horror and the Carnivalesque: The Body-monstrous," in *Fields of Vision: Essays in Film Studies, Visual Anthropology, and Photography*, ed. Leslie Devereaux and Roger Hillman. (Los Angeles: University of California Press, 1995), 151.

15. *Hannibal,* "Aperitif," directed by David Slade. Written by Bryan Fuller. NBC, April 4, 2013.

16. Aguirre, "Narrative Structure," 237.

17. Aguirre, "Narrative Structure," 236.

18. *Hannibal,* "Buffet Froid," directed by John Dahl. Written by Bryan Fuller. NBC, May 30, 2013.

19. Ravens can also be construed as liminal entities, as many cultures believe them to be messenger birds, and they are often associated with death.

20. Carroll, Noel. The Philosophy of Horror. 32. 1990. Routledge. Abingdon.

21. Creed, "Horror and the Carnivalesque," 128.

22. Creed, "Horror and the Carnivalesque," 151.

23. Creed, "Horror and the Carnivalesque," 143.

24. *Hannibal,* "Roti," directed by Guillermo Navarro. Written by Bryan Fuller. NBC, June 6, 2013.

25. D.H. Lawrence, *Studies in Classic American Literature* (Harmondsworth: Penguin, 1977), ii.

26. Paul Coates, *The Double and the Other: Identity as Ideology in Post-Romantic Fiction.* Macmillan Press. London. 1988. 32.

27. Coates, *The Double and the Other,* 3.

28. *Hannibal,* "Naka Choko." Directed by Vincenzo Natali. Written by Bryan Fuller. NBC, May 2, 2014.

29. *Hannibal,* "Secondo." Directed by Vincenzo Natali. Written by Bryan Fuller. NBC, June 18, 2015.

30. *Hannibal,* "The Great Red Dragon," directed by Neil Marshall. Written by Bryan Fuller, NBC, July 25, 2015; *Hannibal,* "…And the Woman Clothed with the Sun," directed by John Dahl. Written by Bryan Fuller, NBC, August 1, 2015.
31. Carl Jung, *The Archetypes and the Collective Unconscious,* trans. R.F.C. Hull. (New York: Princeton University Press, 1990), 19.
32. *Hannibal,* "Futamono," directed by Tim Hunter. Written by Bryan Fuller. NBC, April 4, 2014.
33. Veeder, "The Nurture of the Gothic," 34.
34. Turner, "Betwixt and Between," 49.
35. *Hannibal,* "Shiizakana," directed by Michael Rymer. Written by Bryan Fuller. NBC, April 25, 2015.
36. *Hannibal,* "The Wrath of the Lamb," directed by Michael Rymer. Written by Bryan Fuller. NBC, August 29, 2015.
37. Manuel Aguirre, "A Grammar of Gothic: Report on a Research Project on the Forms of the Gothic Genre," in *Romantic Textualities: Literature and Print Culture, 1780–1840,* 21 (Winter 2013), http://www.romtext.org.uk/reports/rt21_n07/.
38. *Hannibal,* "The Wrath of the Lamb."
39. Arnold van Gennep, *The Rites of Passage,* trans. Monika B. Vizedom and Gabrielle L. Caffee. (Chicago: University of Chicago Press, 1960), 184.
40. Carl Jung, *Man and His Symbols,* ed. John Freeman. (New York: Dell Publishing, 1964) 183.
41. Creed, "Horror and the Carnivalesque," 144.

Works Cited

Aguirre, Manuel. "A Grammar of Gothic: Report on a Research Project on the Forms of the Gothic Genre." *Romantic Textualities: Literature and Print Culture, 1780–1840,* 21 (Winter 2013): Online. http://www.romtext.org.uk/reports/rt21_n07/.
Aguirre, Manuel. "Narrative Structure, Liminality, Self-similarity: The Case of Gothic Fiction." In *Gothic horror: A Guide for Students and Readers,* edited by Clive Bloom. 2nd ed., 226–247. New York: Palgrave Macmillan, 2007.
Brown, Jennifer. *Cannibalism in Literature and Film.* New York: Palgrave Macmillan, 2013.
Carroll, Noel. *The Philosophy of Horror.* Abingdon: Routledge, 1990.
Coates, Paul. *The Double and the Other: Identity as Ideology in Post-Romantic Fiction.* London: Macmillan Press, 1988.
Creed, Barbara. "Horror and the Carnivalesque: The Body-monstrous." In *Fields of Vision: Essays in Film Studies, Visual Anthropology, and Photography,* edited by Leslie Devereaux and Roger Hillman. 127–159. Los Angeles: University of California Press, 1995.
Hannibal. "Antipasto." Directed by Vincenzo Natali. Written by Bryan Fuller. NBC, June 4, 2015.
Hannibal. "…And the Woman Clothed with the Sun." Directed by John Dahl. Written by Bryan Fuller, NBC, August 1, 2015
Hannibal. "Apéritif." Directed by David Slade. Written by Bryan Fuller. NBC, April 4, 2013.
Hannibal. "Buffet Froid." Directed by John Dahl. Written by Bryan Fuller. NBC, May 30, 2013.
Hannibal. "Futamono." Directed by Tim Hunter. Written by Bryan Fuller. NBC, April 4, 2014.
Hannibal. "The Great Red Dragon." Directed by Neil Marshall. Written by Bryan Fuller, NBC, July 25, 2015.
Hannibal. "Mizumono." Directed by David Slade. Written by Bryan Fuller. NBC, May 23, 2014.
Hannibal. "Roti." Directed by Guillermo Navarro. Written by Bryan Fuller. NBC, June 6, 2013.
Hannibal. "Secondo." Directed by Vincenzo Natali. Written by Bryan Fuller. NBC, June 18, 2015.
Hannibal. "Shiizakana." Directed by Michael Rymer. Written by Bryan Fuller. NBC, April 25, 2015.
Hannibal. "The Wrath of the Lamb." Directed by Michael Rymer. Written by Bryan Fuller. NBC, August 29, 2015.

Hogle, Jerrold E. Introduction to *The Cambridge Companion to Gothic Fiction,* edited by Jerrold E. Hogle. 1–20. Cambridge: Cambridge University Press. 2002.

Jung, Carl. *The Archetypes and the Collective Unconscious.* Translated by R.F.C. Hull. New York: Princeton University Press, 1990.

Jung, Carl. *Man and His Symbols,* edited by John Freeman. New York: Dell Publishing Inc., 1964.

Lawrence, D.H. *Studies in Classic American Literature.* Harmondsworth: Penguin, 1977.

MacArthur, Sian. *Crime and the Gothic: Identifying the Gothic Footprint in Modern Crime Fiction.* Oxfordshire: Libri Publishing, 2011.

Messent, Peter. "American Gothic: Liminality and the Gothic in Thomas Harris's Hannibal Lecter Novels." In *Dissecting Hannibal Lecter,* edited by Benjamin Szumskyj, 13–36. Jefferson, NC: McFarland, 2008.

Prudom, Laura. "'Hannibal Showrunner Bryan Fuller Says Season 3 is the 'Series I've Always Wanted To Make,'" *Variety.* Last modified June 4, 2015. http://variety.com/2015/tv/news/hannibal-season-3-will-relationship-red-dragon-1201512730/

Thurm, Eric. "Hannibal showrunner: 'We are not making television. We are making a pretentious art film from the 80s,'" *The Guardian.* Last modified June 3, 2015. http://www.theguardian.com/tv-and-radio/2015/jun/03/hannibal-tv-showrunner-bryan-fuller.

Turner, Victor W. "Betwixt and Between: The Liminal Period in Rites de Passage." In *Magic, Witchcraft and Religion: An Anthropological Study of the Supernatural,* 5th ed., edited by Arthur C. Lehmann and James E. Myers, 46–55. California: Mayfield Publishing Co., 2001.

Van Gennep, Arnold. *The Rites of Passage,* Translated by Monika B. Vizedom and Gabrielle L. Caffee. Chicago: University of Chicago Press, 1960.

Veeder, William. "The Nurture of the Gothic, or How Can a Text be both Popular and Subversive?" In *American Gothic: New Interventions in a National Narrative,* edited by Robert K. Martin and Eric Savoy, 20–39. Iowa City: University of Iowa Press, 1998.

Interview

Nick Antosca

NICHOLAS A. YANES

Nick Antosca's writing career began as author of novels and novellas such as *Fires, Midnight Picnic, The Hangman's Ritual,* and more. Antosca's writing work expanded to include television when started working on *Teen Wolf* (2011–2017), *Last Resort,* and *Believe.* After writing episodes of *Hannibal* in 2015 Antosca went on to create the shows *Channel Zero* and *The Act.* In regards to *Hannibal,* Antosca wrote the season three episodes "Aperitivo," "The Great Red Dragon," and "The Wrath of the Lamb." Wanting to gain further insight into how episodes of *Hannibal* were made, Nicholas A. Yanes was able to interview Antosca.

Nicholas A. Yanes: Dr. Hannibal Lecter has been a pop icon since 1981. Prior to the creation of Hannibal what was your first interaction with Dr. Lecter and Thomas Harris's writings?

Nick Antosca: I saw the *Silence of the Lambs* movie poster at the video store in the early '90s when I was probably in thirds or fourth grade. It seemed evil. Perverse and sexual. I wasn't allowed to watch it. I became obsessed with it. I'm not sure when I finally saw the movie but in middle school I read the book and *Red Dragon.* When the novel *Hannibal* came out, I faked sick and stayed home from school to read it.

Yanes: Did you read the books or watch the movies? If so, what did you think of these interpretations of Dr. Hannibal Lecter, and did you try to incorporate any particular element from previous interpretations in your episodes of *Hannibal*?

Antosca: I read all the books (except the last one, which I never finished) and watched all the movies (except the Ratner one and the young Hannibal one). I certainly didn't try to incorporate anything from the Hopkins or Cox versions—by the time I was writing on the

136

show, Bryan had already created the Mads Mikkelsen version as fully its own thing.

Yanes: You started writing for *Hannibal* during its 3rd season and final season. Prior to this, what did you think of the first two seasons? Were there aspects of the show that stood out to you?

Antosca: I was a fan of the first seasons. I begged my agents to get me a meeting on the show. In part, because I just wanted to learn how to get something so weird on TV. I couldn't believe it was on NBC. It was like a Matthew Barney video art installation sometimes. I was just amazed and I wanted to learn.

Yanes: Given how uniquely visual *Hannibal* was, did this influence how individual *Hannibal* episodes were written? If so, how?

Antosca: The *Hannibal* scripts are incredibly technical. They describe shots. They're insanely visually specific. Bryan insisted on that. He wanted it to be clear to the episode directors exactly what they were supposed to be shooting. The scripts were visual blueprints in a way that scripts aren't normally supposed to be.

Yanes: *Hannibal* was critically acclaimed but struggled to find a large viewership. Why do you think that is?

Antosca: It was too weird. It's not for everyone.

Yanes: From hunting Hannibal in Italy, to dealing with Mason Verger, to fighting Francis Dolarhyde. Season three can be easily broken up into unique arcs. What do you see as season three's overarching narrative, if there is one?

Antosca: It's actually two mini-seasons. It's one season in name only. But to me, the overarching narrative of the entire show is kind of a perverse "you complete me" story between Will and Hannibal. They're parts of a whole. Will is the human and Hannibal is the divine. If we can let the definition of "divine" include the satanic.

Yanes: You co-wrote the episode, "The Great Red Dragon," which introduces Francis Dolarhyde into the series. What were some of the goals you had when adapting Dolarhyde into the series? Were there elements of the character in the novel that were left out of *Hannibal*?

Antosca: I'm sure there were but I can't remember which ones, honestly. Other than a lot of detail about his history, which there wasn't enough screen time to get into. The goal was to make him human and weirdly sympathetic.

Yanes: You were one of the writers on the final episode of *Hannibal*. How did Bryan Fuller, Steve Lightfoot, and you approach "The Wrath of the

Lamb"? Specifically, what do you think were the treads that this episode tied up?

Antosca: We knew we probably weren't getting a fourth season. Bryan knew the ending he wanted. We were very close to shooting and the script wasn't written yet. I flew up to Toronto to help with it. We worked out the first few acts—the staged escape, the seeming alliance between Will and Dolarhyde—and then we just wrote it as fast as we could. One thing I didn't expect was the beautiful montage at the end to the Siouxsie Sioux song, as Dolarhyde dies. Bryan did that in post. It's one of my favorite things in the show.

Yanes: If there is a fourth season of *Hannibal* in some form, what stories and/or themes would you want it to address?

Antosca: I'm going to resist talking about this, since I know that if a fourth season does happen, Bryan has very specific ideas about what he wants to do, and they're really cool.

Yanes: An element of the show that fans continue to discuss is the relationship between Hannibal Lecter and Will Graham. What do you think of their relationship? Specifically, do you see it as romantic, or as something else?

Antosca: It's not traditionally romantic, but they are complementary psyches. They understand each other. Isn't that what we look for in a life partner?

Yanes: Few fan bases are as passionate as the Fannibals. How do you think *Hannibal* fans differ from other fan groups?

Antosca: *Hannibal* fans have a much higher tolerance than most people do for art installations featuring dismemberment.

Yanes: Do you see your writing and engagement with the fans change as a result of social media? Your new show *Channel Zero* reflects some of these changes by incorporating horror elements that originated on social media into the show. Did your time on *Hannibal* shift as a result of engaging with fans through social media?

Antosca: No, not really. I'm on social media but I wish I wasn't. I'm trying to look at it less. I started the *Hannibal* writers room twitter because one didn't exist when I joined the show. But I don't think of it as a big part of my career. I did hire my assistant on *Channel Zero* off twitter though— she was a fan of *Hannibal* who was already in LA.

Yanes: Though *Hannibal* was only around for three seasons, what do you hope its legacy will be?

Antosca: I hope people remember *Hannibal* as a horrifying and beautiful and sometimes hilarious art installation that somehow got on NBC.

Eating Exquisite Corpses and Drinking New Wine

The Chesapeake Ripper as the Authentic Surreal Murderer

VITTORIA LION

Bryan Fuller's television adaptation is unique among installments in the Hannibal Lecter franchise for blatantly drawing upon the conventions of Surrealism, including bizarre transformations, the juxtaposition of incongruous images, the distortion of bodies, and unorthodox use of religious symbolism, to aestheticize the crimes of its eponymous murderer. *Hannibal* (2013–2015) can thus be interpreted as continuous with the celebration of violent criminals by prominent members of the Paris-centered early twentieth-century Surrealist group, notably Benjamin Péret, René Crevel, Philippe Soupault, and Robert Desnos.[1] In the tradition of the Comte de Lautréamont's *Les Chants de Maldoror*, the archetypal avant-garde glorification of evil, the early twentieth-century Surrealists frequently created lurid visual and literary portrayals of serial murderers and criminals like Jack the Ripper, Edgar Manning, Joseph Vacher, Henri Landru, and the French pulp character Fantômas. This aspect of the movement has been explored at length by Jonathan P. Eburne in *Surrealism and the Art of Crime*, and Virginie Pouzet-Duzer extends his investigation to avant-garde representations of cannibalism, specifically, stating that "*Surréalisme* devours exquisite corpses."[2] This tradition has not yet been examined as a precursor to the figure of Hannibal and the associated novels, films, and television adaptation; however, the visual style of Fuller's *Hannibal* makes these connections explicit. Bearing strong similarities to Lautréamont's antihero, Robert Desnos' Jack the Ripper, Soupault's Edgar Manning, and Surrealist variations on Fantômas, his interpretation of Hannibal (portrayed by Mads Mikkelsen) fits among "those beautiful men, those adorable women"[3] praised by Desnos for disrupting a stagnant, industrialized civilization with dreamlike expressions of desire. Like the aforementioned characters, who represent complete freedom from stultifying social norms to the Surrealists, Hannibal has an uninhibited authenticity that leads Will Graham, Bedelia du Maurier, and viewers of the television series into temptation. Moreover, the position of viewers as dinner guests drawn into a world of visually edible content intensifies this effect. Authenticity carries a risk of disturbing the status quo, making it inherently violent and provocative: in the words of Surrealist revolutionary Louis Aragon, "Absolute liberty offends, disconcerts."[4] Ultimately, this focus on authenticity aligns *Hannibal* with modernism, from which its surreal imagery originates.

In "The Untamed Eye and the Dark Side of Surrealism: Hitchcock, Lynch and Cronenberg," Barbara Creed cursorily proposes that "the figure of Hannibal Lecter epitomises a surreal monster, one both sympathetic and repulsive, a man of learning and refined appetites whose desire to cannibalise representatives of bourgeoise mediocrity and hypocrisy is deliciously surreal.[5] Will (portrayed by Hugh Dancy) immediately recognizes Hannibal's desire to aestheticize violence in the pilot episode, stating that the Copycat Killer wished to "elevate" Garret Jacob Hobbs' preferred method of murder "to art" with his installation of Cassie Boyle's remains.[6] In the series' second season, Hannibal praises patient-turned-serial murderer Randall Tier for creating scenes of terror "like a sculptor bears dust from the beaten stone," adding that Tier's description of his violent desires is "beautiful."[7] In consistence with its goal of undermining bourgeois values, Surrealism revels in the iconography of death and destruction: the drawing and poetry game of "exquisite corpse," for instance, has been used by Surrealists past and present to create images of fantastically contorted and fragmented bodies.[8] For Surrealist writers and artists, making the defilement of the body beautiful is a quintessential example of a contradiction that can give rise to the marvelous, producing a feeling of wonder that pushes the limits of reason.[9]

In the *First Manifesto of Surrealism*, André Breton suggests that "moral concern" curtails possibilities for the expression of the marvelous, and characters in Surrealist fiction are often uncannily amoral.[10] "Violence is ultimately desired because it can be aestheticized," writes Pouzet-Duzer.[11] The most brazen expression of Surrealism's fascination with violent acts is perhaps found in the *Second Manifesto of Surrealism*, in which Breton recommends shooting randomly into a crowd as a way of exploding ordinary life, transforming it into radical performance art.[12] "Anyone who, at least once in his life, has not dreamed of thus putting an end to the petty system of debasement and cretinization in effect has a well-defined place in that crowd," he elaborates.[13] Surrealism directly inherits the tactic of deliberately shocking an audience as an unconventional form of public art from the Dadaists (with whom early Surrealism bears a significant overlap), whose visually assaulting exhibitions and violent writings, including Francis Picabia's *Manifeste Cannibale Dada* (1920), caused widespread outrage. Here, it is useful to reference Antonin Artaud's first manifesto for his "Theater of Cruelty," in which he states that a performance should display the viewer's most scandalous unconscious desires, not excluding "his taste for crime, his erotic obsessions, his savagery ... even his cannibalism."[14] For Eburne, it is relevant that Surrealism's founders were anarchists and Communists who anticipated violent revolution and adored Germaine Berton, a young woman who infiltrated the office of the extreme right-wing organization *Action Française* and shot the editor of its journal.[15] Killings of European men by women and people of color were of particular interest to the early twentieth-century Surrealists, who viewed this as an excellent way of resisting the repressive structures of patriarchy and colonialism: for instance, Soupault deeply admired the African American criminal Edgar Manning, the hero of his novel, *Le Nègre* (1927).[16] Other influences for Surrealist representations of violence include the Gothic aesthetic of *Les Chants de Maldoror*, with its vampirism and tales of Satanic challenge to the divine; Matthew Gregory Lewis' fantastic novel, *The Monk*[17]; and the works of the Marquis de Sade. However, the text that laid the initial groundwork for explicit discussion of the aesthetics of murder is Thomas de Quincey's 1827 essay, "On Murder Considered as One of the Fine Arts," a satire on Immanuel Kant's moral philosophy that plays a pivotal role in the ancestry of Surrealist crime fiction and, ultimately, *Hannibal*.

Hannibal's statement in "Antipasto" that ethics can be replaced with aesthetics could easily be a brief summary of De Quincey's piece: the essay mocks moral condemnation as a poor approach to its subject matter and argues that murder should be recognized as a respectable art form with its own technique, stating that murders should be evaluated for their "design ... grouping, light and shade, poetry, sentiment."[18] As evidenced by his catchphrase, "This is my design," the idea that murders can be interpreted like works of art informs Will's approach to reconstructing crime scenes and imagining the motives of serial murderers.[19] Originally intended to be an absurd declaration in the tradition of Jonathan Swift's *A Modest Proposal*, De Quincey's essay inevitably attracted interest from members of the Surrealist movement. For instance, Eburne references Péret's musings on the case of Rolande Leprieux, a six-year-old girl from Versailles who was raped, murdered, and subsequently butchered into fifty-five pieces by her attacker in 1920. Reflecting on the sensational documentation of the crime by tabloids, Péret condemns the killer's act as an uninspired outburst of sexual aggression, but additionally offers advice for improvement to murderers.[20] If the killer had only used "some imagination," Péret enthusiastically claims, his act could easily have been perceived as ingenious rather than abominable: "If the girl's pieces had been received under the rubric 'confectionery' by some outstanding personality ... what wouldn't our admiration be for such a gesture!!!!"[21] Such imagination is something that

Hannibal has no shortage of, especially when it comes to aestheticizing bodily mutilation with the tools of the culinary arts, his defining trait and primary method of defying social convention.

Accustomed to playfully blending art and its audience through the use of games and performance pieces, the early twentieth-century Surrealists appreciated that the wild claims, graphic detail, and wide dissemination of true crime writing could intimately involve audiences in the events described, making them active participants.[22] After she witnesses him dispatching a young victim with a bust of Aristotle, Hannibal tells his psychiatrist, Bedelia (portrayed by Gillian Anderson), that observing murder is a form of participation, simultaneously addressing the audience.[23] In the early twentieth century, this effect was dramatically enhanced by the popularization of crime scene photography, which allowed readers to enter the private spaces where abominable acts took place and stare at the carnage themselves. During this period, Alphonse Bertillon developed techniques for photographing murder victims from above and under dramatic lighting, like shadowy still lifes.[24] Within Surrealism, the influence of this imagery is perhaps most viscerally demonstrated in Hans Bellmer's photographs of gruesomely dismembered mannequins, and the eighth issue of the journal *Minotaure* displayed grisly images of Jack the Ripper's victims like avant-garde artworks.[25] The serialized form of true crime reporting relies upon the regular production of consumable content by the murderer-turned-artist; in *Hannibal*, this is represented by Freddie Lounds, who deliberately provokes serial murderers and investigators in order to obtain dramatic images and lurid details. This is supported by the research of the late former FBI agent Robert K. Ressler, who argues that the behavior patterns of serial murderers imitate the weekly installments of pulp adventure fiction (and, more recently, television programs).[26] Television has largely taken over the role of these media in dramatizing and aestheticizing crime, replacing static photographs and illustrations with the beautiful sets, indulgent slow-motion sequences, and grotesque close-ups seen in series like *Hannibal*. Closely following the format of a weekly police procedural in its first season, *Hannibal* slowly dissolves into a series of fragmented and ornate spectacles of violence: Fuller's series is the penny dreadful ascended to an art form.

Marvelous "Becomings": *The Surreal Visual World of* Hannibal

Hannibal is filled with "exquisite corpses" to the extent that the phrase would make a fitting alternate title for the series. With unusual frequency and creativity, human corpses are deformed, contorted, repurposed as vaguely analogous objects, and juxtaposed with religious symbols that give them an aura of holiness: in the universe of *Hannibal*, every murderer appears to be an artist. Elliot Budish poses bodies as praying angels in "Coquilles," pulling the skin from their backs to create wings of flesh. Violinist Tobias Budge transforms a man's body into a cello, repurposing his victim's vocal cords as its strings, and leaves the completed sculpture on a stage. James Gray uses the skins of his victims as shreds of colored paper for an enormous collage depicting an eye, a common Surrealist motif exemplified by Georges Bataille's pornographic novella, *Story of the Eye* (1928), and the opening scene of Luis Buñuel and Salvador Dalí's *Un Chien Andalou* (1928). Katherine Pimms grows beehives in human craniums, replacing the convolutions of her patients' brains with intricate honeycombs.[27]

However, the most aesthetically remarkable of the series' corpse installations are made by its eponymous character, who is unique for being both a trained artist and anatomist. To a greater extent than those of his rivals, Hannibal's sculptures are intended to be seen by an audience that will comment on his technique, materials, and influences, and reproduce and widely circulate shocking images. This audience is not limited to other characters in the series. The mediums of television and the internet provide platforms for spreading crime stories unimagined by Péret or Desnos, and fans gape at Hannibal's art and disseminate it further in the form of GIFs and memes on social media. Hannibal's installations interrupt the monotony of public places and desecrate sacred spaces: guerrilla sculpture is perhaps the closest non-violent analogy, appearing randomly in public with the intention of provoking passersby, uncommissioned and uninvited. From 2013 to 2015, the celluloid images of Hannibal's art were jarringly broadcast between advertisements on network television, increasing this disruptive effect. The first Lecter sculpture shown in the series is a dark parody of a reclining figure, purposely highlighting the sexual connotations of Hobbs' crimes: a naked young woman lies prostrate across the taxidermy head of an elk, the curve of her back supported and penetrated by the prongs of the animal's antlers. In the second season, the body of Judge Davies is suspended inside a federal courtroom and posed as the classical representation of Justice, blindfolded and holding scales containing his heart and brain. In "Futamono," councilor Sheldon Isley is surgically grafted into the branches of a live cherry blossom tree in a crucifixion pose, adorned with a bird's nest for a crown, and incongruously placed in a parking lot. Like the woman in Dalí's *The Bleeding Roses* (1930), his abdomen has been slit open and his internal organs have been replaced with matching bouquets of flowers. In his youth, Hannibal recreated a detail of Sandro Botticelli's *Primavera* with corpses in the back of a pickup truck, imitating the sublime with the most grotesque of materials. When he returns to Italy decades later, he carves

Anthony Dimmond's body into an enormous human heart and displays the finished sculpture before the sanctuary of the Cappella Palatina, illuminated softly by the basilica's skylights and mounted on swords to evoke the Three of Swords tarot card.[28] It is not coincidental that Hannibal frequently selects individuals tasked with protecting society's order for these transformations, notably law enforcement personnel, judges, and politicians. Will imitates Hannibal's technique in order to better understand his friend, mounting Randall Tier's remains on a prehistoric skeleton in a museum gallery and transforming a prisoner into a giant insect that glitters in the *chiaroscuro* lighting of the third season.[29]

Hannibal's preparation of his victims as food constitutes another way of creating "exquisite corpses," and the transformation and contradiction inherent in his cannibalism perhaps qualifies it as a Surrealist act. Like his installations, his beautiful meals of human flesh are reflections of his desire to exhibit his crimes and have them consumed by an amazed audience. This extends to the visual consumption of the victims served at Hannibal's table by television viewers, who envy his creations even with full knowledge of their ingredients. This tempting allure explains the popularity of food artist Janice Poon's blog, *Feeding Hannibal*. Poon lovingly details all of Hannibal's recipes, and fans praise her work with adoring comments and send her images of their recreations of recipes featured in the series.[30] Pouzet-Duzer provides a precedent for this in Surrealist art, noting that "exquisite corpses" are "produced to be devoured" visually: disassembling and reassembling words, phrases, and images of unusual body parts, a game of "exquisite corpse" is a spectacle of dissection that invests the attention of artists and their amused audience like a fantastic anatomy theater (the latter being another example of the visual consumption of corpses).[31] The phrase that provides the technique's name, "the exquisite corpse will drink the new wine," evokes the imagery of a fine meal.[32] "The ceremonies and sights and exchanges of dinner can be far more engaging than theater," Hannibal philosophizes to a drugged and restrained Will in "Dolce," strongly suggesting that he views preparing and serving food as a form of performance art.[33] Dining scenes are frequently preceded by long, glamorous shots of Hannibal preparing individual ingredients set to classical music, miniature operas hidden from his guests that television viewers alone are privy to. Hannibal's dining room is an inviting and mesmerizing domestic Garden of Eden, a curiosity cabinet replete with rows of herbs growing in delicate containers, François Boucher's *Leda and the Swan*, preserved butterflies, eggs, feathers, flowers, and aurochs and kudu horns. Hannibal's sensibilities bear an affinity to the final lines of Hans Arp's introduction to Max Ernst's *Histoire Naturelle* (1926), itself a fantastic re-envisioning of Edenic prehistory, which depict the primordial murder and consumption of the father hypothesized by Sigmund Freud as a scene of erotic splendor: "and so you see that one's honorable father can be consumed only slice by slice. impossible to finish him in a single luncheon on the grass and even the lemon falls on its knees before the beauty of nature."[34] Within his sanctuary, Hannibal breaks down the divide between spectator and participant in a chillingly visceral way: in all of his incarnations, the greatest of Hannibal's horrors is that he turns his houseguests into unwilling co-conspirators in his crimes.

The contradiction and confusion of subjectivities inherent in the act of eating one's own (or oneself) holds fascination for Surrealists. Naturally, Hannibal plays with this paradox in ways that are disgusting and humorous in their absurdity: in a flashback in "Antipasto," he fattens a colony of snails on Abel Gideon's amputated arm with the intention of feeding them to Gideon later, deliberately confusing the diner with the creatures being eaten.[35] Pouzet-Duzer argues that cannibalism can be read as an analogy for personal transformation, a kind of alchemy from living flesh to food: she references a dream of "cannibalistic becoming" recorded by Crevel, a description heavily reminiscent of Hannibal's poetic commentary on his nurture of Will's aggressive instincts.[36] In Leonora Carrington's novel, *The Hearing Trumpet* (1974), heroine Marian Leatherby simmers herself in an enormous cauldron of soup at the climax of her occultic journey, addressing her fellow ingredients with dark humor.[37] Often described with the metaphor of ruminating on oneself, dreaming and introspection can be viewed as cannibalistic.[38]

For those who cross paths with him, and especially for Will, Hannibal's presence infuses everyday life with the bizarre, disconcerting, and marvelous. A superficial introduction to Hannibal triggers Will's descent into a surreal world of lush and terrifying hallucinations, beginning with the feathered bull elk that greets him behind his shower curtain, in the hospital, and at the door of his house.[39] The series' second season increases the boldness and frequency of this imagery. In "Kaiseki," Will dines at a table reminiscent of the "unholy cannibals' banquet in lieu of the Eucharist" in Carrington's *The Meal of Lord Candlestick* (1938), covered with live animals, bones, human body parts, fruit, and exotic vegetation.[40] The living and dead human bodies, flora, fauna, and inanimate objects of *Hannibal* are in a constant state of "becoming," wriggling, growing into foreign shapes, and melting into each other as if driven by a carnivorous life force. In a drug-induced flashback during his incarceration in the Baltimore State Hospital for the Criminally Insane, Will watches Hannibal's face twist and warp unnervingly until it appears cyclopean. "Futamono" features white blossoms sprouting from the musical notes of a composition written by Hannibal and a tree growing inside Will's prison cell. "I am enchanted and terrified," Mason Verger muses with childlike wonder after being kidnapped and drugged by Hannibal, expressing the contradictory heart of the Surrealist marvelous.[41]

However, the most dramatic of these dream sequences appear in the third season, which frequently mimics Surrealist film by abandoning a linear plot. In one of the series' most nightmarish scenes, the heart made from Dimmond's remains inexplicably writhes to life, sprouts hooves and antlers, and stalks Will across the floor of the Cappella Palatina. In search of insights into Hannibal's origins, Will approaches a brooding Eastern European castle surrounded by thick undergrowth, a Gothic setting that would have delighted Breton. Immersed in the dark woods of his unconscious, Will encounters Hannibal in an imagined therapy session that takes place in the middle of the forest. At the beginning of "Dolce," Mason dreams about tasting Hannibal's succulently-cooked body, picturing it laid out identically to the nude model at the center of Méret Oppenheim's *Cannibal Feast* (1959).[42] Following their reunion, the figures of Will and Hannibal emerge from melting pools of butter and ecstatically "blur," liquefied like the mutually devouring couple in Dalí's *Autumnal Cannibalism* (1936). During her lecture in "…And the Woman Clothed in Sun," Bedelia visually represents her courtship of Hannibal with a monstrous hellscape painted by an imitator of Hieronymus Bosch, whose infernal and Edenic menageries anticipate Surrealist images. The camera lingers on the painting as Bedelia speaks in an airy tone of hallucinatory losses of time, entrapment in hell, and unusual devourings.[43] The tale of the Chesapeake Ripper is "surreal," "a dream," a series of events that took place "once upon a time": showing awareness of *Hannibal*'s visual references, NBC released a promotional video for its third season set to a cover of "Pure Imagination."[44] Hannibal's adversaries and lovers remain unconvinced of his reality; in the words of the *First Manifesto of Surrealism*, he belongs "elsewhere."[45]

Hannibal's existence is incongruous with the mundane world to the extent that his human status is repeatedly called into question. "You have a click in your hoof," Gideon remarks. Most significantly, Hannibal casually breaks the taboo against eating human flesh: this action reveals his placement of himself outside the category of the human, allowing him to cook and devour human beings alongside members of other species. In "Hassun," Hannibal appears at Will's trial as an antlered human silhouette, an archetypal image reminiscent of the 15,000-year-old "Sorcerer" painting discovered in the Cave of the Trois-Frères. Hannibal undergoes a similar transformation in the midst of intercourse with Alana Bloom in "Naka-Choko," evoking a litany of fears surrounding sexual relations with demons and animals.[46] Among Hannibal's talents is an incredible sense of smell, a link to the animal world that Freud argues early humans lost during their transition to bipedalism.[47] In "Antipasto," Hannibal appears to his audience at the Palazzo Capponi as Dante's Satan in a bowtie. The Italian media labels him "Il Mostro," a grotesque inhabitant of medieval visions of hell.[48] Living close to nature and in the company of the demonic, Hannibal represents the intrusion of repressed appetites into the monotonous civilized world.

"Beautiful, Like a Flower of Flesh": Tracing Hannibal's Avant-Garde Genealogy

The most glaring and neglected of Hannibal's literary ancestors is perhaps the antihero of *Les Chants de Maldoror* ("The Songs of Maldoror"), completed by the Uruguayan-born French poet Isidore Ducasse under the pseudonym of the Comte de Lautréamont in 1869. Largely forgotten until its rediscovery by the Surrealists, this loosely-defined "novel" is a major source for their depictions of violent crime. Lacking any coherent plot, *Maldoror* is a collection of lurid and fragmentary prose poems detailing the gruesome and sexually graphic exploits of Maldoror, a Byronic serial murderer motivated by hatred of humanity and Christian morality. Rejecting the values of piety, compassion, and chastity, Maldoror devotes himself to pursuing ecstasy by performing acts of extreme cruelty. Like Hannibal, whose "idea of a good time" is challenging God, Maldoror simultaneously views himself as God's rival and envies the immense destructive potential of the divine.[49] When he encounters God in the Second Canto, Maldoror is overwhelmed with awe upon discovering that the Christian supreme being is a cosmic cannibal who perpetually gnaws the limbs of his human victims in a manner heavily reminiscent of Francisco Goya's *Saturn Devouring His Son*. Women perceive Maldoror to be very charismatic, but he secretly laments that he cannot find any other being who resembles himself: "friendship" and "love" are alien concepts. The first creature in the world who Maldoror deems to be his equal and expresses anything resembling love for is a female shark, a being with a destructive, predatory appetite that matches his own (in a bizarre sequence, they have intercourse in a billow of sea foam).[50] Another point of comparison unique to Fuller's adaptation is Maldoror and Hannibal's shared homosexual predilections. Although Hannibal is comparatively humane in his acceptance of Will as his friend and romantic partner, Maldoror's misanthropy mirrors Hannibal's perception of himself as inhuman that justifies his behavior—as he tells Gideon, "It's only cannibalism if we're equals."[51]

Fuller's interpretation of Hannibal is reminiscent of Maldoror's preference for unusual and grotesque methods of murder, heavily embellished by Lautréamont's use of colorful and sacrilegious language. Maldoror fantasizes about forcing a young girl to eat her own arms, using her brain as an ointment for his eyes, and smearing her body "across the wall like an overripe pear." He breeds an enormous colony of lice in a pit and distributes them to all of the world's major cities in the hope that they will eat the human species to extinction. He advises his audience to chop off their mothers' arms, dice them, and consume them in one day "[f]or an astringent and tonic diet." The novel ends with the death of Mervyn, a young sexual target of Maldoror, flung like "a comet" from an enormous slingshot and slammed against the dome of the Panthéon. The dome becomes Mervyn's final resting place, where he hangs upside down and trails a garland of flowers from his skeletal hands. The knife that Maldoror uses to disembowel a victim is a "steel Hydra" placed on a "sacrificial altar," and "rosettes" of blood and sperm stain God's face after the deity visits a prostitute. Maldoror saves the scalp of his first victim, Falmer, and carries it "like a holy relic."[52] Although Maldoror has not been extensively compared to Hannibal, Thomas Harris' character—and especially Fuller's interpretation of him—would likely have been unimaginable without the forerunner of Lautréamont's dreamlike antichrist.

Maldoror's world is compelling in comparison to the banality of ordinary life, and his reflections are filled with invocations of the sublime that make Lautréamont's outpouring more than a catalogue of obscenities. "Alas, what is good and what is evil?" Maldoror asks in the midst of drinking a child's blood. "Are they both one single thing with which we furiously attest our impotence and passion to attain the infinite by even the maddest means?"[53] Maldoror recognizes that holiness and profanity frequently intersect; Freud, a great source of inspiration for Surrealism, identifies the beginning of religion with an act of bloody cannibalism in *Totem and Taboo*. Scenes of extreme violence and horror can inspire a mixture of wonder, awe, and fear that closely resembles feelings of being in the presence of the divine. Like individuals who dedicate their lives to harrowing attempts to repair a corrupt world or performing selfless acts of compassion, violent criminals live on the margins of social order, acting on desires that most people are discouraged by convention, laws, and institutions from satisfying. In this way, they appear more than human. An anonymous narrator introduces *Maldoror* with a warning to the reader: despite the repulsiveness of the novel's contents to bourgeois sensibilities, Lautréamont believes that the pleasure and temptation that his poetry will give his readers is overwhelming.[54] Although his crimes are appalling to an extreme degree, Maldoror is an alluring character because of his authenticity and drive to live in complete accordance with impulses repressed by civilization. For Lautréamont, conformity with traditional morality and bourgeois society is, frankly, boring: "I shall set down in a few lines how upright Maldoror was during his early years, when he lived happy. There: done," the narrator sarcastically remarks.[55] Like Hannibal, who proudly states, "Nothing happened to me. I happened," Maldoror is not driven by any discernible mental pathology, but acts on a deliberate choice to fulfill his most socially and theologically abhorrent aspirations.[56] Both Maldoror and Hannibal, to quote Eburne, represent "divorce from everyday possibility—whether clinical, legal, or moral."[57] "There is no name for what this man is," reads a line from a *Tattle Crime* article published in the wake of Hannibal's capture by the FBI.[58] Maldoror relishes a dream of metamorphosis into a wild pig, completely shunning civilization at last: "There, no more constraint! When I wanted to kill, I killed…."[59] Hannibal similarly encourages Randall Tier to pursue his murderous fantasy of transformation into an animal, whispering to him, "Revel in what you are."[60] In contrast to the everyday manipulation of the death drive in industrial weapons production and the exploitation of natural resources, the evils committed by Maldoror and Hannibal appear more deserving of Immanuel Kant's label of "radical evil," being powerful, seductive, and shocking expressions of personal free will.[61]

The crimes of Maldoror and Hannibal are also likened to theological understandings of serious acts of evil as having no purpose other than deliberate defiance of God.[62] Fuller claims that his interpretation of Hannibal is intended to be Satan incarnate, making his series ultimately a story about the devil walking among people who do not recognize him.[63] Maldoror possesses supernatural abilities, corrupting an angel with a kiss, changing into animal forms, and holding a conversation with a hair from the head of God. An archangel fears Maldoror to be more powerful than Satan, who has been neutralized by God ever since his imprisonment in hell.[64] Attesting to his demonic nature, Maldoror shares Hannibal's otherworldly ability to evade law enforcement, slipping through the streets of Paris like a phantom.[65] Hannibal even dresses entirely in black and haunts Maldoror's city by the light of its streetlamps in "Antipasto," introduced with a sinister cloud of railway smoke before he skillfully stalks Roman Fell and terrorizes his wife in their beautiful home.[66]

Lautréamont's feverish interplay of the beautiful and macabre directly informed the writings of Robert Desnos, whose fascination with serial murderers—most notably, Jack the Ripper—inspired his true crime serial in the *Paris Matinal* and aspects of his 1924 novel, *Liberty or Love!* Believing in the power of crime film to transport individuals bound by capitalist civilization to "regions where the heart and mind finally free themselves," Desnos frames the Ripper as an artist and magician in a way that strongly prefigures Fuller's treatment of Hannibal.[67] Corsair Sanglot and Louise Lame, the hero and heroine of *Liberty or Love!*, have sex in a hotel room used by Jack the Ripper for one of his "most splendid" murders. The furnishings of the room are "modest props," lending the space a theatrical quality, as if the Ripper's dreadful scene were an installation or piece of performance art intended to be discovered. For Desnos, the Ripper is the maker of a "masterpiece," clarifying his equation of the murderer with an artist. No trace remains of the Ripper's act in the hotel room, but the space has been permanently transformed by "the passage of an extraordinary being."[68] As an agent of the marvelous, Eburne claims, the Ripper passes undetected in a world that his existence is incompatible with; he is a dream, a hallucination, a manifestation of the "terrible desire" brewing in the collective unconscious of Victorian London.[69] Eburne's analysis can be applied to Hannibal's talent for dispatching his victims and planting delicate installations in public places without being noticed by others, even in high-security settings such as hospitals and courtrooms. The inability of the Behavioral Analysis Unit to imagine that Hannibal might be the Ripper terrorizing the Eastern United States speaks to their lack of imagination. Both Hannibal and Desnos' Ripper are invisible to those bound to the routines of industrial society, committing their atrocities when others are sleeping: the apparent absence of security cameras in the world of *Hannibal* is thus perhaps more than an irritating plot inconsistency.[70] It is important for Desnos that the Ripper is never caught and studied. The Ripper cannot be a symbol of unconstrained human creativity and freedom if he is neutralized and reduced to a psychiatric curiosity, the conclusion being that he was never responsible for his actions.[71] A statue of the Ripper stands in a town square in *Liberty or Love!*, commemorating the killer like a monument honoring a great artist: Desnos remarks that such recognition of the Ripper is evidence of a respectable and cultured civilization.[72] Unlike Jack the Ripper, Hannibal is eventually caught, but Frederick Chilton admits that his own psychological evaluation is bogus and the cannibal inevitably escapes, incapable of being defined and contained by the restrictive social and moral codes that he abhors.[73]

Eburne takes particular notice of Desnos' use of culinary analogies to describe methods of murder. This cannibalistic imagery makes Desnos' Ripper stories particularly interesting for *Hannibal* enthusiasts. In his *Paris Matinal* article, Desnos writes that the Ripper slices open his victims' abdomens "with as much facility as one cuts, every Sunday in English households, the traditional plum cake."[74] According to Eburne, a sense of the marvelous is created through the transformation of a mundane bourgeois tradition into a criminal act. Desnos compares the Ripper's dismemberment of a human corpse to a *maître d'hotel*'s preparation of a chicken for the table, likening culinary knowledge to a dissector's familiarity with anatomy: a domestic role is turned into something threatening and out of the ordinary.[75] The kitchen becomes a morgue, and the cook's knife turns into a scalpel. Overnight or within hours, Hannibal transforms the entrails, organs, limbs, and blood of his former adversaries and colleagues into omelets, sausages, veal cutlets, beef *osso buco*, kidney pies, prosciutto roses, chocolate desserts, and beer like a magician, randomly selecting business cards of his victims for inspiration.[76] Making the wild and predatory lurk even in seemingly tame and homely rituals is a striking example of the Surrealist technique of combining opposites to create the marvelous. In *Liberty or Love!*, the image of a pitcher filled with blood rather than water is used to construct the mysterious and erotic backdrop of Corsair Sanglot and Louise Lame's intimacy.[77] Another lurid scene of inextricably mixed violence, eating, and sensuality is crafted in Desnos' short poem, "Verse on the Butcher." The narrator, who is not stated to be Jack the Ripper but resembles him, invites his lover to sleep among the dissected animal bodies of his shop, where his knives will transform by night into "magic mirrors." He coaxes her to curl up "[i]n the open womb of a heifer," an image that inevitably brings to mind the discovery of Sarah Craber's body in a mare's uterus for *Hannibal* enthusiasts.[78] Gazing at his lover "like a hangman," the butcher unsubtly hints at his murderous intentions.[79] Desnos makes the reader wonder if the butcher's view of his lover's body as consumable flesh is not very different from his routine dismemberment of animals: similarly, a meal of human flesh cooked by Hannibal appears identical to any other elaborately crafted meal. Hannibal is particularly astonishing and fascinating because of his choice to hide beneath an impeccably constructed veneer of civilized and domesticated upper-class life, cooking for his colleagues, surrounding himself with art and music, and working in a profession dedicated to the taming of abnormal mental states. Figures like Hannibal and Desnos' Ripper reveal domesticity to be a repressive illusion that can be shattered and inverted all too easily.

For the early twentieth-century Surrealists, the vapidity and artificiality of European sensibilities was most explicitly revealed by the experiences of individuals living under colonial subjugation. Soupault's *Le Nègre*, which centers on Edgar Manning's symbolic killing of a prostitute tellingly named "Europe," exemplifies this. Manning, the elegantly-dressed paragon of Surrealist "absolute liberty," is an inhabitant of a "noble world" who breathes "rarified air" and dwells in "unfathomed waters."[80] Naturally, Soupault reverberates the lionization of the criminal as a free agent and creative force found in the writings of Lautréamont and Desnos: recognizing that the values of the European bourgeoisie have been coercively imposed on him, Manning lives in complete freedom from ideétification with them. Problematically, Soupault interprets Manning's personality and crimes in light of his blackness in order to frame him as an atavistic window into a primordial, more genuine state of being.[81] Most of all, Manning's ability to see through civilized niceties makes him fiercely "alive," echoing how Hannibal is perceived by intimate friends who are aware of his secret life.[82] Hannibal turns Abigail Hobbs, Margot Verger, Randall Tier, Will, and even his own psychiatrist, Bedelia, into murderers, believing that he can introduce them to experiences of pleasure and liberty that they have neglected out of adherence to traditional morals; the latter two characters reluctantly admit that Hannibal is right in this respect.

This idea greatly informs Surrealism's adoration of Fantômas, a Maldoror-esque "Genius of Evil" who uses outlandishly elaborate means to commit serious crimes, trapping a man inside an enormous bell, detonating bombs filled with shreds of human flesh, murdering a woman with poisoned roses, and infesting a ship with plague-carrying rats, all while defying at the last minute even the most foolproof schemes to contain and kill him.[83] Like his predecessors, Fantômas shares significant traits with Hannibal. In *Pulp Surrealism: Insolent Popular Culture in Early Twentieth-Century Paris*, Robin Walz argues that the immensely popular *Fantômas* novels written by Pierre Souvestre and Marcel Allain and their subsequent film adaptations represent one of the twentieth century's first widely accessible and successful examples of the crime serial.[84] Although the writers, editors, and directors of *Fantômas* stories were largely politically conservative artists who would have denounced the Surrealists' radical politics, the forces of good often lose and law enforcement personnel are rarely successful in the *Fantômas* series. In comparison to the killer's nearly magical powers, the values and institutions of capitalism and Christianity appear incompetent and unappealing.[85] Even more horrifying to bourgeois moral sensibilities is the complete lack of explanation given for the killer's behavior. Troubling Victorian psychology's association of criminality with the underclass, Fantômas is an aristocratic character who holds many enviable positions under his impossibly numerous aliases, and Walz points out that the killer himself gives no reason for his incredible feats other than inflicting terror for the sake of it.[86] "Fantômas is conjured up, not motivated," Walz emphasizes.[87] Fantômas and Hannibal are pictures of physical health, able-mindedness, and financial stability, ruling out crises in these respects as motivations for their crimes. In contrast to Harris' *Hannibal Rising* (2006), Fuller's series is careful to avoid providing a clear Freudian explanation for Hannibal's personality and pastimes, ensuring that his behavior remains inexplicable and terrifying. Hannibal frequently echoes Fantômas' theatrical escapes, being rescued by Jack Crawford from Matthew Brown's crucifixion attempt, catching a plane to France following the disastrous failure of Will's plan to capture him, and fleeing from Muskrat Farm across a snowy field with an unconscious Will in his arms. The series finishes with Hannibal breaking free from prison with the aid of Will and Francis Dolarhyde and making his way to the coast, where he falls into the sea with his beloved under the cover of night in a sequence filled with Gothic splendor.[88]

Fantômas was adopted as a symbol of the Surrealist movement and celebrated in paintings, poetry, and films by René Magritte, Yves Tanguy, Man Ray, and Desnos, who juxtapose the killer and his work with lush words and surroundings that Hannibal would likely appreciate. Quoting a poem by Desnos, Man Ray suggests that Fantômas is "[b]eautiful, like a flower of flesh."[89] In *Fantômas* (1925), Tanguy places Fantômas and his bleeding victim in a cryptic, dreamy scene containing shadowy vegetation, childlike figures, and a collection of eggs.[90] Magritte's *The Menaced Assassin* (1926) is a particularly dramatic interpretation, depicting two detectives waiting expectantly before the entrance to the bedroom of a female Fantômas victim. The viewer is invited to enter the chamber, surveying the nude woman sprawled across her bed as if merely resting, the handsome and unsuspecting murderer standing over a phonograph, a suitcase, and clothes draped over a chair, all meaningfully arranged like props. Three faces peer up from behind the iron railing of the house's balcony, over which a mountain peak looms.[91] Desnos' "Ballad of Fantômas," read over French radio in 1933, portrays the character as an almost Godlike specter looming over the globe, capable of masterminding events of historical significance without ever revealing himself.[92] This mirrors Hannibal's uncanny ability to influence the choices and courses of the lives of Will, Bedelia, Alana, and Jack down to minute details without their knowledge. Like emanations from the unconscious, Fantômas and Hannibal are beyond the grasp of those who falsely believe that they are, in the words of Freud, "master in [their] own house."[93]

Anthropophagy and Authenticity: Hannibal's *Deadly Allure*

Fascinated by the hidden dimensions of the self and disregard for social constraints revealed in dreams and hallucinations, Surrealists wish to uncover and nurture a more authentic life with their tactics of shock and subversion. This focus on authenticity positions past and contemporary Surrealist movements as outgrowths of modernism, an early twentieth-century artistic, literary, and philosophical movement contemporaneous with the emergence of psychoanalysis and existentialism. According to Fredric Jameson, the dichotomies of "essence" and "appearance," conscious and unconscious, and "authenticity" versus "inauthenticity" are central to modernism.[94] He argues that these concepts have been abandoned by postmodern theory, which tends to reduce the idea of the authentic self to an antiquated social construct.[95] In its place, he claims, postmodernism celebrates a superficial feeling of euphoria at the pace of the market and unprecedented opportunities for consumption, and individuals are encouraged to view themselves as fragmented and "depthless"; modernist art and literature, exemplified by T.S. Eliot's *The Waste Land* and the novels of James Joyce, delights in fragmentation, but this breakdown of conventional notions of "selfhood" is not intended to erase the existence of an authentic, pre-originary core (or cores) of the personality.[96] Although Surrealism's debt to Freud lends the movement toward particularly deep skepticism of representations of the "self" as a unified whole, questions of personal and collective freedom remain vital for it, and many figures associated with Surrealism have expressed hostility toward postmodernism.[97] No longer concerned with realities underlying appearances, including unconscious impulses buried beneath their civilized disguise, late capitalist culture glorifies simulation, and consumers are taught that they can endlessly enhance or alter themselves superficially by purchasing commodities.[98] *Hannibal* is consistent with modernism because of the series' fixation on the concepts of authenticity and free will, depicting a permanent and often disturbing layer of existence that is largely incompatible with a simplistic view of individuals as consumers or commodities. Bedelia and Will may not genuinely share the appetite of the series' cannibalistic villain, but he provides a tempting taste of authenticity within a cultural context seemingly devoid of it.

Will experiences "irresistible" attraction to Hannibal, while Bedelia is more drawn to the killer than she would like to admit, both feeling that he represents something missing in their lives. Rather than avoiding him whenever possible, Bedelia makes romantic gestures and is shown to be complicit in Hannibal's murders during their sojourn in France and Italy. To use his own words, Hannibal is a character who is deeply invested in "life-enhancing" things. "I've never felt more alive," Will states after killing Randall Tier with Hannibal's encouragement. Hannibal repeats his Darwinian mantra that mirrors Nietzsche's belief in overcoming the stifling values of Christianity: "Adapt, evolve, become." By the end of the third season, Will becomes irreparably enamored with Hannibal and completely sacrifices his moral pretenses in order to join his lover in a life of eroticized crime (appropriately, Bedelia's leg is served at their table). During a revealing conversation with Will in "…And the Woman Clothed in Sun," Bedelia confronts the nightmare of her own free will. After publicly denying her agency in her relationship with Hannibal with a fabricated story, she admits in private to an awareness that nothing prevents her from committing acts of extreme cruelty toward the vulnerable that simultaneously horrifies and intrigues her. Her knowledge that she is capable at any moment of crushing a tiny bird or asphyxiating another human being is evidence of her personal freedom that she perhaps cannot find elsewhere within industrial civilization, and she is drawn to Hannibal for teaching her this.[99]

Forced to wear his "human veil," Hannibal lives with an acute awareness of the dissonance between the expectations of society's institutions and his interior life, between appearance and reality.[100] From behind the plexiglass of his prison cell, Hannibal suggests that truly condemnable evils are committed in an inauthentic and unfree state, referencing the oppressive and limiting conformity with others that existentialist thinker Martin Heidegger refers to as the "they-self": "The essence of the worst in the human spirit is not found in the crazy sons of bitches. Ugliness is found in the faces of the crowd."[101] Although Hannibal does not offer any satisfying ethical theory in place of the degraded values of the masses, he represents the promise of release from stifling bureaucracy and endless repression to his lovers and audience. After realizing that Hannibal murdered and impersonated Roman Fell, Anthony Dimmond refuses to call the police and expresses interest in befriending Hannibal, stating that he desires to "see what still seems wicked" when evil has largely been rendered crude, routine, and uninteresting.[102]

Dimmond, like Will and Bedelia, stands in for the audience. After Hannibal repeatedly indulges their every sensory pleasure and tolerates their violent outbursts, the initial moral revulsion that Will and Bedelia feel becomes complicated by a sense of envy. Sharing Hannibal's feeling of alienation from the human world, individuals like Will, Randall Tier, and Francis Dolarhyde believe that the cannibal psychiatrist can provide affirmation and acceptance of their true selves. However, becoming close to the monster always ends in a brush with death or worse: although *Hannibal* celebrates the neglected world of dreams and nightmares, the complete liberation of unconscious impulses from their repression is ultimately portrayed as traumatic, deeply flawed, and incompatible with any form of psychological and social stability. Even Will and Bedelia, the two individuals who Hannibal appears to genuinely love and perceive to be his equals, are constantly threatened with visceral reminders of their status as potential main courses, ranging from a dinner of oysters to a whirring cranial saw. At the climaxes of the second and third seasons, Will suffers the terrible consequences of his inability to leave Hannibal's vicious embrace, and the series closes with a shot of Bedelia left butchered by her former lover and passively waiting at his dinner table in terror.[103] *Hannibal* was critically successful precisely because it recognized that authenticity is something that individuals desperately desire and will go to extremes to taste in a world that feels stagnant and predetermined by market algorithms. Exercising freedom without moral judgment, however, can be deadly: Hannibal's behavior deprives others of their freedom and brings the tremendous suffering depicted in "Primavera." Fuller's conservative reminders of the need to abstain from evil represent a departure from Lautréamont and pre-war Surrealist fiction. Nevertheless, the cancellation of *Hannibal* after its third season leaves the series without any clear triumph of good over evil, and the events of the finale suggest that even greater horrors may have been unleashed through Will and Hannibal's partnership.

Jameson derides contemporary art films as producing "surrealism without the unconscious": there is no shortage of vaguely "surreal" imagery in popular culture, frequently appearing in television and advertising, but he recognizes that its use within the context of consumerism and capitalism is purely cosmetic, largely divorced from the political and philosophical positions of the movement.[104] *Hannibal* presents a possible exception because of the similarity of its plot to narratives written and enjoyed by Surrealists and its concern with the idea of authenticity. With its blossoming corpses and stories of violent erotic desire, Fuller's reinvention of Harris' character as a quasi-Surrealist aesthete parallels the early twentieth-century movement's adaptations of the stories of Fantômas and Jack the Ripper. Arguably, the success of *Hannibal*'s modernist imagery and invocation of related themes, including radical freedom and the existence of evil, represents growing discontentment with philosophically popular positions that clear ideas of these concepts no longer exist. When authenticity cannot be found in the outside world, viewers can experience a semblance of it by entering Hannibal's kitchen and devouring his marvelous illusions.

Notes

1. Although I will largely be focusing on this particular historical moment for the purposes of this essay, I would like to stress the diversity and ongoing continuity of the global Surrealist movement.

2. Virginie Pouzet-Duzer, "Dada, Surrealism, Anthropofagia: The Consuming Process of the Avant-gardes," *L'Esprit Créateur* 53, no. 3 (Fall 2013): 81.

3. Robert Desnos, "La Morale du cinéma" (1923), in *Œvres*, ed. Marie-Claire Dumas (Paris: Gallimard, 1999), 187, quoted in Jonathan P. Eburne, *Surrealism and the Art of Crime* (Ithaca and London: Cornell University Press, 2008), 128.

4. Louis Aragon, *La Révolution surréaliste* (1924), quoted in Eburne, *Surrealism and the Art of Crime*, 74

5. Barbara Creed, "The Untamed Eye and the Dark Side of Surrealism: Hitchcock, Lynch and Cronenberg," in *The Unsilvered Screen: Surrealism on Film*, ed. Graeme Harper and Rob Stone (London and New York: Wallflower Press, 2007), 117.

6. *Hannibal*, "Apéritif," season 1, ep. 1, dir. David Slade, written by Bryan Fuller, NBC, April 4, 2013.

7. *Hannibal*, "Shiizakana," season 2, ep. 9, dir. Michael Rymer, written by Jeff Vlaming and Bryan Fuller, NBC, April 25, 2014.

8. Virginie Pouzet-Duzer, "Dada, Surrealism, Anthropofagia: The Consuming Process of the Avant-gardes," 81–82.

9. André Breton, "Manifesto of Surrealism" (1924), rpt. in *Manifestoes of Surrealism*, trans. Richard Seaver and Helen R. Lane (Ann Arbor: University of Michigan Press, 1969), 20.

10. Breton, "Manifesto of Surrealism," 26.

11. Pouzet-Duzer, "Dada, Surrealism, Anthropofagia: The Consuming Process of the Avant-gardes," 81–82.

12. André Breton, "Second Manifesto of Surrealism" (1930), rpt. in *Manifestoes of Surrealism*, trans. Richard Seaver and Helen R. Lane (Ann Arbor: University of Michigan Press, 1969), 125.

13. *Ibid.*

14. Antonin Artaud, "Theater of Cruelty (First Manifesto)" (1932), rpt. in *Selected Writings*, trans. Helen Weaver, ed. Susan Sontag (New York: Farrar, Straus and Giroux, 1976), 244.

15. Jonathan P. Eburne, *Surrealism and the Art of Crime* (Ithaca and London: Cornell University Press, 2008), 76.

16. Eburne, *Surrealism and the Art of Crime*, 176–80; 99–108. Arguably, the Surrealists' fascination with murderous young women like Berton, Violette Nozière, and Christine and Léa Papin finds a representative in *Hannibal* in the figure of Abigail Hobbs.

17. Breton, "Manifesto of Surrealism," 14–15.

18. *Hannibal*, "Antipasto," season 3, ep. 1, dir. Vincenzo Natali, written by Bryan Fuller and Steve Lightfoot, NBC, June 4, 2015; Thomas De Quincey, "On Murder, Considered as One of the Fine Arts," in *The Collected Writings of Thomas De Quincey*, ed. David Masson, vol. 13 (1890; rpt. New York: AMS Press, 1968), 13, quoted in Eburne, *Surrealism and the Art of Crime*, 55.

19. *Hannibal*, "Apéritif."

20. Eburne, *Surrealism and the Art of Crime*, 53–54.

21. Benjamin Péret, "Assassiner," *Littérature* 15 (July-August 1920); rpt. in *Œvres complétes*, vol. 7 (Paris: José Corti, 1995), 13, quoted in Eburne, *Surrealism and the Art of Crime*, 53.

22. Eburne, *Surrealism and the Art of Crime*, 8.

23. *Hannibal*, "Antipasto."

24. Eburne, *Surrealism and the Art of Crime*, 36–37.

25. Therese Lichtenstein, "Return to the Enchanted Garden of Childhood," in *Behind Closed Doors: The Art of Hans Bellmer*, exhibit. cat. (Berkeley and New York: University of California Press and International Center of Photography, 2001), 144; Linda Steer, "Surreal Encounters: Science, Surrealism, and the Re-Circulation of a Crime-Scene Photograph," *History of Photography* 32, no. 2 (2008): 110–22.

26. Klaus Bartels, "Serial Killers: Sublimity to Be Continued. Aesthetics and Criminal History," *Amerikastudien / American Studies* 43, no. 3, "The American Sublime" (1998): 497.

27. *Hannibal*, "Coquilles," season 1, ep. 5, dir. Guillermo Navarro, written by Scott Nimerfro and Bryan Fuller, NBC, April 25, 2013; "Fromage," season 1, ep. 8, dir. Tim Hunter, written by Jennifer Schuur and Bryan Fuller, NBC, May 16, 2013; "Kaiseki," season 2, ep. 1, dir. Tim Hunter, written by Bryan Fuller and Steve Lightfoot, NBC, February 28, 2014; "Takiawase," season 2, ep. 4, dir. David Semel, written by Scott Nimerfro and Bryan Fuller, NBC, March 21, 2014.

28. *Hannibal*, "Apéritif"; "Hassun," season 2, ep. 3, dir. Peter Medak, written by Jason Grote and Steve Lightfoot, NBC, March 14, 2014; "Futamono," season 2, ep. 6, dir. Tim Hunter, written by Andy Black, Bryan Fuller, and Scott Nimerfro, NBC, April 4, 2014; "Primavera," season 3, ep. 2, dir. Vincenzo Natali, written by Jeff Vlaming and Bryan Fuller, NBC, June 11, 2015; *Hannibal*, "Antipasto."

29. *Hannibal*, "Naka-Choko," season 2, ep. 10, dir. Vincenzo Natali, written by Steve Lightfoot and Kai Yu Wu, NBC, May 2, 2014; "Secondo," season 3, ep. 3, dir. Vincenzo Natali, written by Angelina Burnett, Bryan Fuller, and Steve Lightfoot, NBC, June 18, 2015.

30. Janice Poon, *Feeding Hannibal* (blog), Blogspot, 2013–2015, http://janicepoonart.blogspot.ca.

31. Pouzet-Duzer, "Dada, Surrealism, Anthropofagia: The Consuming Process of the Avant-gardes," 82.

32. Eburne, *Surrealism and the Art of Crime*, 122.

33. *Hannibal*, "Dolce," season 3, ep. 6, dir. Vincenzo Natali, written by Don Mancini, Bryan Fuller, and Steve Lightfoot, NBC, July 9, 2015.

34. Hans Arp, "Introduction to Max Ernst's 'Natural History'" (1926), trans. Ralph Manheim, rpt. in *Max Ernst: Beyond Painting, and Other Writings by the Artist and His Friends*, vol. 7 of The Documents of Modern Art, edited by Robert Motherwell (New York: Wittenborn, Schultz, Inc., 1948), 125.

35. *Hannibal*, "Antipasto."

36. René Crevel, "Sommeil," *La Révolution surréaliste* 2 (15 January 1925), 26, quoted in Pouzet-Duzer, "Dada, Surrealism, Anthropofagia: The Consuming Process of the Avant-gardes," 83.

37. Leonora Carrington, *The Hearing Trumpet* (1974; rpt. London and Henley: Routledge and Kegan Paul, 1977), 137–38.

38. Pouzet-Duzer, "Dada, Surrealism, Anthropofagia: The Consuming Process of the Avant-gardes," 83.

39. *Hannibal*, "Apéritif"; "Amuse-Bouche," season 1, ep. 2, dir. Michael Rymer, written by Jim Danger Gray, NBC, April 11, 2013; "Relevés," season 1, ep. 12, dir. Michael Rymer, written by Chris Brancato and Bryan Fuller, NBC June 13, 2013.

40. *Hannibal*, "Kaiseki"; Susan L. Aberth, *Leonora Carrington: Surrealism, Alchemy and Art* (Aldershot: Ashgate, 2004), 41.

41. *Hannibal*, "Naka-Choko"; "Takiawase"; "Futamono"; "Tome-wan," season 2, ep. 12, dir. Michael Rymer, written by Chris Brancato, Bryan Fuller, and Scott Nimerfro, NBC, May 16, 2014. Notably, Freud identifies the motif of a primordial, hyper-eroticized nature, a frequent fixture of horror film and television, with the dreams of hysterical patients (Lomas 2000: 79).

42. *Hannibal*, "Primavera"; "Secondo"; "Dolce"; Pouzet-Duzer, "Dada, Surrealism, Anthropofagia: The Consuming Process of the Avant-gardes," 88.

43. *Hannibal*, "...And the Woman Clothed in Sun," season 3, ep. 10, dir. John Dahl, written by Jeff Vlaming et al., NBC, August 1, 2015.

44. *Hannibal*, "Tome-wan"; "Antipasto"; "Hannibal S3 official PROMO / Pure imagination," YouTube video, 2:02, posted by "Snow," June 28, 2015, https://www.youtube.com/watch?v=RLb12Eg4f00.

45. Breton, "Manifesto of Surrealism," 47.

46. *Hannibal*, "Antipasto"; "Hassun"; "Naka-Choko."

47. Sigmund Freud, *Civilization and Its Discontents* (1929), rpt. in *Civilization, Society, and Religion: Group Psychology, Civilization and Its Discontents, and Other Works*, trans. James Strachey, ed. Albert Dickson, vol. 12 of The Pelican Freud Library (Harmondsworth and New York: Penguin, 1985), 289.

48. *Hannibal*, "Antipasto"; "Primavera."

49. Comte de Lautréamont (Isidore Ducasse), *Maldoror* (1868–69), rpt. in *Maldoror and the Complete Works of the Comte de Lautréamont*, trans. Alexis Lykiard (Cambridge: Exact Change, 1994), 29; *Hannibal*, "Primavera"; Lautréamont, *Maldoror*, 91–93.

50. Lautréamont, *Maldoror*, 76–77; 93–94; 32; 98–99.

51. *Hannibal*, "Antipasto."

52. Lautréamont, *Maldoror*, 69; 82–83; 161; 218; 115; 126; 157.

53. Lautréamont, *Maldoror*, 32.

54. Lautréamont, *Maldoror*, 27.

55. Lautréamont, *Maldoror*, 29.

56. *Hannibal*, "Secondo."

57. Eburne, *Surrealism and the Art of Crime*, 132.

58. *Hannibal*, "The Great Red Dragon," season 3, ep. 8, dir. Neil Marshall, written by Nick Antosca, Steve Lightfoot, and Bryan Fuller, NBC, July 25, 2015.

59. Lautréamont, *Maldoror*, 149.

60. *Hannibal*, "Shiizakana."

61. Immanuel Kant, *Religion within the Boundaries of Mere Reason* (1793), rpt. in *Religion within the Boundaries of Mere Reason and Other Writings*, trans. and ed. Allen Wood and George Di Giovanni, in Cambridge Texts in the History of Philosophy (Cambridge: Cambridge University Press, 1998), 45.

62. For a quintessential example, see Book II, "Adolescence," of Augustine's *Confessions*.

63. Laura Prudom, "An interview with *Hannibal* showrunner Bryan Fuller and star Hugh Dancy," *The Week*, February 18, 2014, http://theweek.com/articles/450064/interview-hannibal-showrunner-bryan-fuller-star-hugh-dancy.

64. Lautréamont, *Maldoror*, 89; 103; 123–130; 209.

65. Lautréamont, *Maldoror*, 175.

66. *Hannibal*, "Antipasto."

67. Robert Desnos, film review for *Journal Littérature*, April 18, 1925, rpt. in *Les Rayons et les ombres*, 67, quoted in Eburne, *Surrealism and the Art of Crime*, 128.

68. Robert Desnos, *Liberty or Love!* (1924), trans. Terry Hale and Stanley Chapman (rpt. London: Atlas Press: 1993), 45; 46; 108; 46.

69. Eburne, *Surrealism and the Art of Crime*, 132; 133.

70. Eburne, *Surrealism and the Art of Crime*, 133.

71. Eburne, *Surrealism and the Art of Crime*, 131.

72. Desnos, *Liberty or Love!*, 62–63.

73. *Hannibal*, "The Great Red Dragon"; "The Wrath of the Lamb," season 3, ep. 13, dir. Michael Rymer, written by Bryan Fuller, Steve Lightfoot, and Nick Antosca, NBC, August 29, 2015.

74. "Les Crimes Sadiques: Jack L'Éventreur," in *Robert Desnos*, ed. Marie-Claire Dumas (Paris: Éditions de l'Herne, 1987), 249, quoted in Eburne, *Surrealism and the Art of Crime*, 131.

75. Eburne, *Surrealism and the Art of Crime*, 131.

76. *Hannibal*, "Apéritif," "Savoureux," season 1, ep. 13, dir. David Slade, written by Steve Lightfoot, Bryan Fuller, and Scott Nimerfro, NBC, June 20, 2013; "Sakizuke," season 2, ep. 2, dir. Tim Hunter, written by Jeff Vlaming and Bryan Fuller, NBC, March 7, 2014; "Mukōzuke," season 2, ep. 5, dir. Michael Rymer, written by Ayanna A. Floyd, Steve Lightfoot, and Bryan Fuller, NBC, March 28, 2014; "Futamono"; "The Great Red Dragon."

77. Desnos, *Liberty or Love!*, 45–46.

78. *Hannibal*, "Su-zakana," season 2, ep. 8, dir. Vincenzo Natali, written by Scott Nimerfro, Bryan Fuller, and Steve Lightfoot, NBC, April 18, 2014.

79. Quotes taken from Robert Desnos, "Verse on the Butcher" (1942), rpt. in *The Selected Poems of Robert Desnos*, trans. Carolyn Forché and William Kulik, ed. William Kulik (New York: The Ecco Press, 1991), 143.

80. Philippe Soupault, *Le Nègre* (1927; rpt. Paris: Gallimard, 1997), 24–25, 30, trans. Randall Cherry, quoted in Eburne, *Surrealism and the Art of Crime*, 114–17.

81. Eburne, *Surrealism and the Art of Crime*, 114–21.

82. Soupault, *Le Nègre*, 30, quoted in Eburne, *Surrealism and the Art of Crime*, 117.

83. Robin Walz, "The Lament of Fantômas: The Popular Novel as Modern Mythology," in *Pulp Surrealism: Insolent Popular Culture in Early Twentieth-Century Paris* (Berkeley: University of California Press, 2000), 67; 43; 69; 44; 44; 66.

84. Walz, "The Lament of Fantômas: The Popular Novel as Modern Mythology," 49.

85. Walz, "The Lament of Fantômas: The Popular Novel as Modern Mythology," 57.

86. Walz, "The Lament of Fantômas: The Popular Novel as Modern Mythology," 67; 54.

87. Walz, "The Lament of Fantômas: The Popular Novel as Modern Mythology," 67.

88. *Hannibal*, "Mukōzuke"; "Mizumono," season 2, ep. 13, dir. David Slade, written by Steve Lightfoot and Bryan Fuller, NBC, May 23, 2014; "Digestivo," season 3, ep. 7, dir. Adam Kane, written by Steve Lightfoot and Bryan Fuller, NBC, July 18, 2015; "The Wrath of the Lamb."

89. Man Ray and Robert Desnos, *Étoile de mer* (1928), quoted in Walz, "The Lament of Fantômas: The Popular Novel as Modern Mythology," 73.

90. Yves Tanguy, *Fantômas* (1925), oil on canvas, 50 × 149.5 cm, Pierre Matisse Gallery, New York, reproduced in Eburne, *Surrealism and the Art of Crime*, 39.

91. René Magritte, *The Menaced Assassin* (1926), oil on canvas, 59.25 × 64.88 in, Museum of Modern Art, New York, reproduced in Eburne, *Surrealism and the Art of Crime*, 40.

92. Robert Desnos, "Ballad of Fantômas" (1942), trans. Timothy Adès, *Papers of Surrealism* 9 (rpt. Summer 2011): 4. http://www.surrealismcentre.ac.uk/papersofsurrealism/journal9/acrobat_files/Fantomas%207.09.11.pdf.

93. Sigmund Freud, "A Difficulty in the Path of Psycho-analysis" (1917), rpt. in vol. 17 of *The Standard Edition of the Complete Psychological Works of Sigmund Freud*, trans. James Strachey et al. (London: The Hogarth Press, 1955), 143.

94. Fredric Jameson, *Postmodernism, or, the Cultural Logic of Late Capitalism* (Durham: Duke University Press, 1991), 12.
95. Jameson, *Postmodernism*, 15.
96. Jameson, *Postmodernism*, 16; 6.
97. See Bernard Caburet, "You Will Always Cherish your Failures, Machine-Man" (1976), trans. Michael Richardson and Krzysztof Fijalkowski, rpt. in *The Surrealism Reader: An Anthology of Ideas*, ed. Dawn Ades, Michael Richardson, and Krzysztof Fijalkowski (Chicago: University of Chicago Press, 2015), 83–93. For further reading on subjectivity and "selfhood" in Surrealism, see David Lomas, *The Haunted Self: Surrealism, Psychoanalysis, Subjectivity* (New Haven and London: Yale University Press, 2000).
98. See, for example, Black Hawk Hancock and Roberta Garner, "Erving Goffman: Theorizing the Self in the Age of Advanced Consumer Capitalism," *Journal for the Theory of Social Behaviour* 45, no. 2 (June 2015): 163–187.
99. *Hannibal*, "…And the Woman Clothed in Sun"; "Antipasto"; "Futamono"; "Naka-Choko"; "Shiizakana"; "The Wrath of the Lamb"; "…And the Woman Clothed in Sun."
100. *Hannibal*, "Sorbet," season 1, ep. 7, dir. James Foley, written by Jesse Alexander and Bryan Fuller, NBC, May 9, 2013.
101. Martin Heidegger, *Being and Time* (1927), trans. John Macquarrie and Edward Robinson (rpt. New York: HarperCollins, 2008), 167; *Hannibal*, "…And the Beast from the Sea," season 3, ep. 11, dir. Michael Rymer, written by Steve Lightfoot and Bryan Fuller, NBC, August 15, 2015.
102. *Hannibal*, "Antipasto"; a similar interpretation of the series by a fan referencing Hannah Arendt's thought can be found at https://www.overthinkingit.com/2015/06/01/nbc-hannibal.
103. *Hannibal*, "Antipasto"; "Dolce"; "Mizumono"; "The Wrath of the Lamb."
104. Jameson, *Postmodernism*, 67.

Works Cited

Aberth, Susan L. *Leonora Carrington: Surrealism, Alchemy and Art*. Aldershot: Ashgate, 2004.
Arp, Hans. "Introduction to Max Ernst's 'Natural History.'" 1926. Translated by Ralph Manheim. Reprinted in *Max Ernst: Beyond Painting, and Other Writings by the Artist and His Friends*, vol. 7 of The Documents of Modern Art, edited by Robert Motherwell, 124–25. New York: Wittenborn, Schultz, Inc., 1948.
Artaud, Antonin. "Theater of Cruelty (First Manifesto)." 1932. Reprinted in *Selected Writings*, translated by Helen Weaver and edited by Susan Sontag, 242–51. New York: Farrar, Straus and Giroux, 1976.
Augustine. "Adolescence." Book II of *Confessions*, translated by Henry Chadwick, 24–34. Oxford: Oxford University Press, 1991.
Bartels, Klaus. "Serial Killers: Sublimity to Be Continued. Aesthetics and Criminal History." *Amerikastudien / American Studies* 43, no. 3, "The American Sublime" (1998): 497.
Bataille, Georges. *Story of the Eye by Lord Auch*. 1928. Translated by Joachim Neugroschel. Reprint, New York: Urizen Books, 1977.
Breton, André. *Manifestoes of Surrealism*. 1924–53. Translated by Richard Seaver and Helen R. Lane. Reprint, Ann Arbor: University of Michigan Press, 1969.
Buñuel, Luis, and Salvador Dalí. *Un Chien Andalou*. 1928. 35mm print, black and white, silent, approx. 16 min. Museum of Modern Art, New York.
Caburet, Bernard. "You Will Always Cherish your Failures, Machine-Man." 1976. Translated by Michael Richardson and Krzysztof Fijalkowski. Reprinted in *The Surrealism Reader: An Anthology of Ideas*, edited by Dawn Ades, Michael Richardson, and Krzysztof Fijalkowski, 83–93. Chicago: University of Chicago Press, 2015.
Carrington, Leonora. *The Hearing Trumpet*. 1974. Reprint, London and Henley: Routledge and Kegan Paul, 1977.
Creed, Barbara. "The Untamed Eye and the Dark Side of Surrealism: Hitchcock, Lynch and Cronenberg," in *The Unsilvered Screen: Surrealism on Film*, ed. Graeme Harper and Rob Stone (London and New York: Wallflower Press, 2007), 117.
Dalí, Salvador. *The Bleeding Roses*. 1930. Oil on canvas. 61 × 50 cm. Private collection.

_____. *Autumnal Cannibalism*. 1936. Oil on canvas. 650 × 650 mm. Tate, London.
Desnos, Robert. *Liberty or Love!* 1924. Translated by Terry Hale and Stanley Chapman. Reprint, London: Atlas Press: 1993.
_____. "Verse on the Butcher." 1942. Reprinted in *The Selected Poems of Robert Desnos*, translated by Carolyn Forché and William Kulik and edited by William Kulik, 143. New York: The Ecco Press, 1991.
_____. "Ballad of Fantômas." 1942. Translated by Timothy Adès. *Papers of Surrealism* 9 (reprint, Summer 2011): 1–4. http://www.surrealismcentre.ac.uk/papersofsurrealism/journal9/acrobat_files/Fantomas%207.09.11.pdf.
Eburne, Jonathan P. *Surrealism and the Art of Crime*. Ithaca and London: Cornell University Press, 2008.
Freud, Sigmund. *Totem and Taboo: Resemblances between the psychic lives of savages and neurotics*. 1913. Translated by A. A. Brill. Reprint, New York: Vintage, 1946.
_____. "A Difficulty in the Path of Psycho-analysis." 1917. Reprinted in vol. 17 of The Standard Edition of the Complete Psychological Works of Sigmund Freud, translated by James Strachey, Anna Freud, Alix Strachey, and Alan Tyson, 135–144. London: The Hogarth Press, 1955.
_____. *Civilization and Its Discontents*. 1929. Reprinted in *Civilization, Society, and Religion: Group Psychology, Civilization and Its Discontents, and Other Works*, translated by James Strachey and edited by Albert Dickson, vol. 12 of The Pelican Freud Library, 243–340. Harmondsworth and New York: Penguin, 1985.
Hancock, Black Hawk, and Roberta Garner. "Erving Goffman: Theorizing the Self in the Age of Advanced Consumer Capitalism." *Journal for the Theory of Social Behaviour* 45, no. 2 (June 2015): 163–187.
Hannibal. "Apéritif." Season 1, episode 1. Directed by David Slade. Written by Bryan Fuller. NBC. April 4, 2013.
_____. "Amuse-Bouche." Season 1, episode 2. Directed by Michael Rymer. Written by Jim Danger Gray. NBC. April 11, 2013.
_____. "Coquilles." Season 1, episode 5. Directed by Guillermo Navarro. Written by Scott Nimerfro and Bryan Fuller. NBC. April 25, 2013.
_____. "Sorbet." Season 1, episode 7. Directed by James Foley. Written by Jesse Alexander and Bryan Fuller. NBC. May 9, 2013.
_____. "Fromage." Season 1, episode 8. Directed by Tim Hunter. Written by Jennifer Schuur and Bryan Fuller. NBC. May 16, 2013.
_____. "Relevés." Season 1, episode 12. Directed by Michael Rymer. Written by Chris Brancato and Bryan Fuller. NBC. June 13, 2013.
_____. "Savoureux." Season 1, episode 13. Directed by David Slade. Written by Steve Lightfoot, Bryan Fuller, and Scott Nimerfro. NBC. June 20, 2013.
_____. "Kaiseki." Season 2, episode 1. Directed by Tim Hunter. Written by Bryan Fuller and Steve Lightfoot. NBC. February 28, 2014.
_____. "Sakizuke." Season 2, episode 2. Directed by Tim Hunter. Written by Jeff Vlaming and Bryan Fuller. NBC. March 7, 2014.
_____. "Hassun." Season 2, episode 3. Directed by Peter Medak. Written by Jason Grote and Steve Lightfoot. NBC. March 14, 2014.
_____. "Takiawase." Season 2, episode 4. Directed by David Semel. Written by Scott Nimerfro and Bryan Fuller. NBC. March 21, 2014.
_____. "Mukōzuke." Season 2, episode 5. Directed by Michael Rymer. Written by Ayanna A. Floyd, Steve Lightfoot, and Bryan Fuller. NBC. March 28, 2014.
_____. "Futamono." Season 2, episode 6. Directed by Tim Hunter. Written by Andy Black, Bryan Fuller, and Scott Nimerfro. NBC. April 4, 2014.
_____. "Su-zakana." Season 2, episode 8. Directed by Vincenzo Natali. Written by Scott Nimerfro, Bryan Fuller, and Steve Lightfoot. NBC. April 18, 2014.
_____. "Shiizakana." Season 2, episode 9. Directed by Michael Rymer. Written by Jeff Vlaming and Bryan Fuller. NBC. April 25, 2014.
_____. "Naka-Choko." Season 2, episode 10. Directed by Vincenzo Natali. Written by Steve Lightfoot and Kai Yu Wu. NBC. May 2, 2014.

_____. "Tome-wan." Season 2, episode 12. Directed by Michael Rymer. Written by Chris Brancato, Bryan Fuller, and Scott Nimerfro. NBC. May 16, 2014.

_____. "Mizumono." Season 2, episode 13. Directed by David Slade. Written by Steve Lightfoot and Bryan Fuller. NBC. May 23, 2014.

_____. "Antipasto." Season 3, episode 1. Directed by Vincenzo Natali. Written by Bryan Fuller and Steve Lightfoot. NBC. June 4, 2015.

_____. "Primavera." Season 3, episode 2. Directed by Vincenzo Natali. Written by Jeff Vlaming and Bryan Fuller. NBC. June 11, 2015.

_____. "Secondo." Season 3, episode 3. Directed by Vincenzo Natali. Written by Angelina Burnett, Bryan Fuller, and Steve Lightfoot. NBC. June 18, 2015.

_____. "Dolce." Season 3, episode 6. Directed by Vincenzo Natali. Written by Don Mancini, Bryan Fuller, and Steve Lightfoot. NBC. July 9, 2015.

_____. "Digestivo." Season 3, episode 7. Directed by Adam Kane. Written by Steve Lightfoot and Bryan Fuller. NBC. July 18, 2015.

_____. "The Great Red Dragon." Season 3, episode 8. Directed by Neil Marshall. Written by Nick Antosca, Steve Lightfoot, and Bryan Fuller. NBC. July 25, 2015.

_____. "…And the Woman Clothed in Sun." Season 3, episode 10. Directed by John Dahl. Written by Jeff Vlaming, Helen Shang, Bryan Fuller, and Steve Lightfoot. NBC. August 1, 2015.

_____. "…And the Beast from the Sea." Season 3, episode 11. Directed by Michael Rymer. Written by Steve Lightfoot and Bryan Fuller. NBC. August 15, 2015.

_____. "The Wrath of the Lamb." Season 3, episode 13. Directed by Michael Rymer. Written by Bryan Fuller, Steve Lightfoot, and Nick Antosca. NBC. August 29, 2015.

"Hannibal S3 official PROMO / Pure imagination." YouTube video. 2:02. Posted by "Snow." June 28, 2015. https://www.youtube.com/watch?v=RLb12Eg4f00.

Harris, Thomas. *Hannibal Rising*. New York: Random House, 2006.

Heidegger, Martin. *Being and Time*. 1927. Translated by John Macquarrie and Edward Robinson. Reprint, New York: HarperCollins, 2008.

Jameson, Fredric. *Postmodernism, or, the Cultural Logic of Late Capitalism*. Durham: Duke University Press, 1991.

Kant, Immanuel. *Religion within the Boundaries of Mere Reason*. 1793. Reprinted in *Religion within the Boundaries of Mere Reason and Other Writings*, translated and edited by Allen Wood and George Di Giovanni, in Cambridge Texts in the History of Philosophy, 31-191. Cambridge: Cambridge University Press, 1998.

Lautréamont, Comte de (Isidore Ducasse). *Maldoror*. 1868–69. Reprinted in *Maldoror and the Complete Works of the Comte de Lautréamont*, translated by Alexis Lykiard, 25–219. Cambridge: Exact Change, 1994.

Lichtenstein, Therese. "Return to the Enchanted Garden of Childhood." In *Behind Closed Doors: The Art of Hans Bellmer*, exhibition catalogue, 143–60. Berkeley and New York: University of California Press and International Center of Photography, 2001.

Lomas, David. *The Haunted Self: Surrealism, Psychoanalysis, Subjectivity*. New Haven and London: Yale University Press, 2000.

Perich, John. "The Three Stigmata of Hannibal Lecter: What makes Hannibal Lecter's brand of evil so uniquely terrifying?" *Overthinking It*. June 1, 2015. https://www.overthinkingit.com/2015/06/01/nbc-hannibal/.

Picabia, Francis. *Manifeste Cannibale Dada*. Dadaphone, no. 7 (1920): 3.

Poon, Janice. *Feeding Hannibal* (blog). Blogspot. 2013–2015. http://janicepoonart.blogspot.ca.

Pouzet-Duzer, Virginie. "Dada, Surrealism, Anthropofagia: The Consuming Process of the Avant-gardes." *L'Esprit Créateur* 53, no. 3 (Fall 2013): 79–90.

Prudom, Laura. "An interview with *Hannibal* showrunner Bryan Fuller and star Hugh Dancy." *The Week*, February 18, 2014. http://theweek.com/articles/450064/interview-hannibal-showrunner-bryan-fuller-star-hugh-dancy.

Steer, Linda. "Surreal Encounters: Science, Surrealism, and the Re-Circulation of a Crime-Scene Photograph." *History of Photography* 32, no. 2 (2008): 110–22.

Walz, Robin. "The Lament of Fantômas: The Popular Novel as Modern Mythology." In *Pulp Surrealism: Insolent Popular Culture in Early Twentieth-Century Paris*, 42–75. Berkeley: University of California Press, 2000.

Food Culture in *Hannibal*

MEGAN MCALLISTER

When we think of the world of *Hannibal*, one automatically has a list set up in their minds over what it entails: murder, cannibalism, and even food. This series challenges our minds and our ability to stomach the information, with metaphoric table meanings and assumptions that will make audience members believe anything Lecter serves is made of people.

When asked what cannibalism means to someone, it commonly is used to describe either skin or flesh as the source of the food. Offal, or organs that are often considered to be inedible by human beings, are something that one would put on their list a few spaces after. Consuming organs like hearts and kidneys is not as popular in America as the practice is compared to other countries. The United States ranks 135th in the consumption of offal worldwide, according to the United Nations (Estabrook, 2011). To this day, people are still turning away from the use of organ meats in American cuisine. Where does this attitude come from? Reasons range from just pure dislike of the textural differences offal has to the historical connections and traditions that are passed down from the generations. Brian Zivkovic wrote:

> "For a very long time, whenever an animal at a farm was slaughtered, the owners got the steaks, and the slaves got the offal. Thus, there is a racial differentiation here as well—the whites do not have a tradition of cooking offal and tend not to have family recipes and cookbooks about it, while the blacks do have such a tradition and the recipes come down through generations, from mothers to daughters" [Zivkovic, 2011].

The history of cannibalism itself extends into early European times and around the world with examples of it being found in eleventh century England and earlier. There is no direct point in history where cannibalism is said to originate from, but its televisual representation has evolved to the point where the world's most famous cannibal received his own program from 2013 to 2015.

Symbolism in Food and the Dinner Table Decor

Symbolism is a major part in Bryan Fuller's food tableaus. Working alongside food stylist Janice Poon and Chef Jose Andres, Fuller used ingredients, decorative plating elements, and designs to go above and beyond typical television programming. One of the major components that *Hannibal* dishes up are flowers. Flowers are shown throughout the series as symbolic decorative additions that creep up on the viewer without being mentioned in the series themselves. Spider Orchids, for example, are used on Hannibal's plate in "Contorno." Janice Poon mentions this symbolizes the clever escape he makes at the end of the episode (Poon, 2015). The dish is accompanied with the Amaryllis flower, symbolizing pride. Another example is when the camera reveals that a Protea flower nestles beside a Kudal dish in the episode "Roti." The Protea flower is named after the Greek god Proteus, who had a tendency to change his form or shape to avoid detection. This is a parallel resemblance with Hannibal using Gideon as a means to avoid his detection from the FBI.

Hannibal has quite the obsession of turning his ingredients into smaller portions and molding them to resemble flowers. The most frequent flower display on Hannibal's platters is a rose. Roses are commonly known as the symbol of love. This is a symbol that does not quite fit with the approach our favorite serial killer uses as he places them alongside meat taken from the rude and the unworthy. However, roses can also be symbolic as carriers of secrets; a meaning that originates from the Latin term *sub rosa*, meaning "under the roses." Roses as messengers of secrets are a more fitting description considering that these flowers are more often formed by prosciutto or some other form of meat. The secret being what the meat is actually contrived from compared to what Hannibal tells his company is used to produce it.

Another inedible item that appears readily on Hannibal's table is the peacock feather. With its All-Seeing Eye decoration, the peacock feather can be found during some of the most important dinners that Hannibal serves. It has a direct tie to the audience, those outside viewers that can look into a scene while knowing all the details and positions each character holds. These dinners help shape Hannibal as a character while providing a story to the audience explaining plot, character development, and moral beliefs.

In the first season we get our initial glimpse of the peacock feathers during a select few dinners that Hannibal shares with important characters in the story. One dinner features Alana and Chilton as they discuss Abel Gideon's act as the Chesapeake Ripper. This dinner is filled with tension because while Alana, Chilton, and Hannibal all know Abel is not the famed serial killer, Hannibal is the only one—besides the audience—that knows the Chesapeake Ripper's true identity. Another example of this "seeing" symbolism appears during a dinner in the episode "Trou Normand" with Freddie Lounds and Abigail Hobbs as they discuss Abigail's future and the prospect of a book deal with Hannibal and Will Graham. In this scene the audience already recognizes the deeper intentions each character has and what each character knows at that time. Hannibal navigates the dinner with the same insight as the audience, knowing Will's intentions and Abigail's realizations during their time together.

The symbolism of the peacock feather endures through the inevitable discovery and questioning of Hannibal being the Chesapeake Ripper in season two. They are present during Will and Hannibal's less than ethical meals, dining on endangered songbirds while talking about morals and the change Will faces as he continues down the path to finding himself in the way Hannibal wants him to. In this scene, the audience perceives that Will is both finding himself and using Hannibal as a means to trick the man into revealing his own true nature. Their final meal together also displays these feathers of insight, the lamb representing sacrifice and judgment as both parties present feel the sting of betrayal that the other inflicts. The bright colors and patterns on the feathers provide an eye-catching display for the audience that draws the attention to the finer details on the dish and provides deeper insight to the mind of Hannibal and the characters surrounding him.

Like the meat roses Hannibal creates, symbolism flows from the main entrees he provides. In "Secondo," Hannibal displays a ham entree in the form of a winged arm protecting a nest of small quail eggs. This is in direct correlation to Chiyoh and her choice of Pheasant for her daily meals, given that this scene is shown right after Chiyoh's preparation of her food. The transition between the two scenes gives the audience a view of a knife that is held by Chiyoh, and then when it is brought down upon the selected protein, the knife is held by Hannibal. This symbolism emphasizes a relationship of some sort between the two characters that was not previously established for viewers. The only clue the audience receives beforehand is that Chiyoh currently resides on Lecter property. It is not until after Will talks with her that the audience finds out that Chiyoh and Hannibal have a deeper relationship that has its origins in the unseen past.

Symbolism in the Meal as a Whole

There is a distinct difference in having a character knowing what everyone orders from their local Chinese restaurant versus Hannibal displaying lamb as a sort of final supper for himself and Will in Baltimore. Will mentions during this time that the lamb is sacrificial. There are many texts relating lamb to sacrifice, yet there is also a different approach that this symbolism can take. Robert Patterson explains this different approach used in the Bible: "In a dramatic contrast, however, the lamb can at times appear in contexts associated with judgment" (Patterson, 2009). If examined in this light, Hannibal could be showing that he is judging Will by what he knows—along with what the audience knows—versus what Will knows. Then there is the fact that Hannibal calls Will the lamb of God in the third season. It is safe to assume that Hannibal has thought of Will this way for a while, making the dinner reference both judging and sacrificing as Will continues fighting with his eventual acceptance of himself and what he sees himself wanting at that moment. There is a direct correlation in the sacrifice of the lamb as entree in the meal and the eventual sacrifice of Will during the final scene of season two.

A side dish in Hannibal's last supper with Will is adorned with Cala Lilies. These lilies symbolize resurrection and rebirth, overcoming challenges and faith. This symbolism represents what Hannibal wants out of Will but will never attain. Though some form of rebirth does happen at the end of the series, Will is now able to forgive and see more clearly into Hannibal's world.

Most of Lecter's meals have deeper meanings to them, even the ones that potentially have no cannibalism added to them. During one of the final meals Jack Crawford shares with Hannibal, they partake in a particularly inventive dish inspired by the Möbius strip. The Möbius strip is a surface that only has one side and one boundary. This one-sided surface was first described by A.F. Möbius (Bogolmy, n.d.) and is normally seen as a strip that is given a half twist then connected together at the ends to form a circle that is continuous. Hannibal gives this meal the story of the never-ending chase and describes it as the fish moving around and around in the circle to the point that one cannot tell who is chasing who. Jack mentions that he does not know who he is chasing, like the fish, revealing that he is unsure as to which side Will is on at that given point.

There is an underhanded play on cannibalism, with a dish that represents a never ending chase. During their discussion, Hannibal mentions "whomever's pursuing whom, in the moment, I intend to eat them" (Brancato & Fuller, 2014), providing foreshadowing into the next episode where Hannibal intends to kill and eat Jack. The chase finally ending just as it had with the cutting of the Möbius strip at the hands of Hannibal.

Notably, the Möbius strip dinner is one of the few on the program where there are no human ingredients in the dish itself. After prolonged exposure to the idea of cannibalism, it feels like anything and everything in the show

Hannibal can be made out of people, tricking one into second guessing themselves. Was there really nothing human about it? How can Hannibal not slip in something to curb his cannibalistic humor and puns? These entrees keep the audience on their toes and stops the show from falling into a mundane repetition of using shock factors that would dwindle in value.

Another dish that can be cleared of anything human in its production is the chicken soup Hannibal serves to Will when Will is in the hospital. Made from Silkie black chicken and other spices, this Chinese herbal soup is just the thing to cure anyone from any ailment. The chicken soup is made only with the purpose of helping Will recover from the fever he develops over the first season. This is a stark difference from the ordinary fare of manipulation and illusionary tactics Hannibal uses to fly under the radar of cannibal suspicion. The same illusionary tactic that can make the audience believe Hannibal is serving one something entirely different than his explicit presentation.

Is It People or Is It Food?

In the first season finale, the audience gets Abigail as a plate of veal. This setup alludes that Abigail Hobbs was killed by Hannibal after she finds out about the numerous murders that he committed. Later on, Hannibal visits his psychiatrist Bedelia with the veal dish in question. Veal consists of meat from a young cow, and is considered to be the most controversial of the red meats because you are killing the cow that has been confined to a small cage its entire life. Hannibal explains this, and goes on to say that we kill pigs younger than the cow when it tragically dies. This statement further emphasizes the idea that the veal is in fact Abigail, who is embracing the adult world fresh out of high school. It also implies to the audience that Hannibal has killed people younger than Abigail. People who he deems are not fit to continue their lives. It shows us that while Abigail's perceived death is a tragic one, age is only a number to the serial killer.

Throughout the first season we get glimpses of the relationship that Hannibal and Abigail have through food and food references. For example, in the fourth episode "Oeuf," Will Graham mentions being a part of the pack and bonding with one's captor unless they want to be breakfast. The immediate shot after is of Hannibal and Abigail, preparing breakfast for dinner. For Abigail, she has to bond with Hannibal, or else she will be killed and eaten. The veal dish is a deeper look into how Hannibal feels about Abigail, being someone he cherishes. She is someone he has already bonded with and thus he sees Abigail as above those he would kill to make a dish—at least during the first season.

Will achieves the same type of illusion Hannibal creates with the veal in season two when he (falsely) serves up Freddie to Hannibal as long pig that is created from pieces of Randall Tier. Not only is the main part of the meal itself misleading, but so are the side dishes presented with the main dish. These side dishes come to us as carrot coleslaw and a platter with snapper with rice. The coleslaw, using shredded carrots to represent Freddie Lounds' hair, is placed directly in between Hannibal and Will while they eat. Underneath the coleslaw lays a bundle of hydrangea stems and spider mums. In European cultures, spider mums are often used to represent death. Hydrangeas meanings extend to vanity and boastfulness; personalities Freddie primarily showcases in abundance. This symbolizes and further emphasizes Will's hint to Hannibal that the meal they are partaking in is indeed Freddie Lounds.

In a comical twist, there is a platter further back in the shot made up of snapper and rice. Janice Poon tells us in her blog that this snapper dish represents the idea of a red herring which in turn symbolizes deception or misleading information (Poon, 2015). Since the snapper dish is located in the background of the meal, it is reasonable to assume that the red herring is the full meal itself and not just the snapper dish in particular. This is not the first time that Freddie Lounds is mentioned or involved in some fashion when it comes to the dinner scenes.

Freddie Lounds' eventual appearance at Hannibal's table in the form of food has been foretold since the very beginning. It starts with the first meeting that Hannibal has with Freddie and her rude behavior recording his previous conversation with Will Graham. There is no coincidence that the first thing the viewer sees, after Hannibal asks what is to be done with Freddie, is a plate with pork loin and Cumberland sauce. Eventually, Freddie Lounds gets invited to Hannibal's dining table herself, with Abigail Hobbs, and reveals that she's a vegetarian. Therefore, a salad will have to be artistically designed to inspire the menacing and dark tones that a meat filled dish would normally provide. On this subject, Janice Poon writes about this ultimately terrifying and meatless dish: "For the salad, I'll use white asparagus that will suggest finger bones when I cut the stalks into thumb and finger lengths" (Poon, 2013). Freddie can only narrowly miss her death so many times before she finds herself on Hannibal's table, whether it be by an illusion or not.

There is a spark of brilliance in Bryan Fuller's work to provide dishes in the series that challenge one's perception of what can be considered morally acceptable to eat and drink. Symbolism, a major component in Fuller's tale, helps bring the story of a serial killer to life behind the small screen. From flowers displayed on dishes to the main protein in an entree, these details help describe personalities, relationships with the characters, and

plot. This kind of mind play is what makes the audience question everything, and it gives a much deeper involvement into the series that keeps
said audience coming back for more.

WORKS CITED

Bogolmy, A. (n.d.). *Moebius Strip.* Cut the knot from interactive mathematics miscellany and
   puzzles. Retrieved August 25, 2016, from http://www.cut-the-knot.org/do_you_know/
   moebius.shtml.
Brancato, C., & Fuller, B. (2014). *Tome-wan.* http://livingdeadguy.com/wp-content/
   uploads/2015/04/H212-Tome-wan-Web.pdf.
Estabrook, R. (2011, October 31). *Chefs say variety meats, or offal, aren't just for Halloween.*
   NPR.Org. https://www.npr.org/sections/thesalt/2011/10/31/141810654/chefs-say-variety-
   meats-or-offal-arent-just-for-halloween.
Patterson, R. D. (2009, April 7). *Lion and lamb as metaphors of divine-human relationships.*
   Bible.org. https://bible.org/article/lion-and-lamb-metaphors-divine-human-relationships.
Poon, J. (2013, May 23). American Gods table, feeding Hannibal: Ep 9 Trou Normand: Ten-
   derloin and Lotus. *American Gods Table, Feeding Hannibal.* http://janicepoonart.blogspot.
   com/2013/05/ep-8-trou-normand-tenderloin-and-lotus.html.
Poon, J. (2015, July 2). American Gods table, feeding Hannibal: Episode 5 Contorno. *American Gods Table, Feeding Hannibal.* http://janicepoonart.blogspot.com/2015/07/episode-5-
   contorno.html.
Zivkovic, B. (2011, August 10). *Offal is good.* Scientific American Blog Network. https://blogs.
   scientificamerican.com/a-blog-around-the-clock/offal-is-good/.

Matchless in His Irony

*Divinity and the Aesthetics of Death
in Bryan Fuller's* Hannibal

ANAMARIJA HORVAT

"I love your work," Hannibal Lecter (Mads Mikkelsen) exclaims glee-fully in an episode of Bryan Fuller's *Hannibal* (2013–2015), looking admir-ingly down at a mural made entirely of human corpses and arranged so as to resemble an eye, with its murderous author standing next to it. "It's not finished," the killer tells him later, as they calmly converse while Hannibal works at stitching him into his own macabre artwork, having placed him in the position of the eye's pupil. "I'm finishing it for you," Hannibal answers, "We'll finish it together. When your great eye looked to the Heavens, what did it see?"[1]

This sequence, apart from serving as a solid introduction to the par-ticular brand of grim humor which often marks the show, also functions so as to highlight two of its most relevant themes; namely, that of the rela-tionship between artistry and divinity, and the ways in which they relate to the show's highly aestheticized presentation of the act of killing as equiv-alent to artistic creation. After all, when a series goes to such lengths so as to present dying bodies as beautiful, not only arranging them in murals but binding them to tree-trunks and transforming them into musical instruments, it is arguable that the connection between death and art stands not only at its surface, but at its core. When commenting on Lecter's murders, FBI profiler Will Graham (Hugh Dancy) calls them "theater"; when explaining his methods, he tells viewers that Lecter wants to "per-form." Thus, it is precisely the logic beneath the theatricality and perfor-mativity of murder in Fuller's adaptation that this essay seeks to explore, particularly with regard to its presentation of the relationship between art and its audience.

How, in other words, are we to interpret its penchant for beautifying that which is deadly, deifying that which is destructive—primarily by attributing traits of the divine to Lecter himself—while, at the same time, the truly terrifying is shown as lying not in the realm of blood and gore but, through the character of Will Graham and his destructive relationship with Lecter, in a trait usually regarded as both benign and beneficial— namely, that of empathy? Or, more simply put, if extreme violence is made to seem so alluring within the show, what does this tell us about the dangers of looking?

Setting the Stage: Murderers, Artists and the Gothic

In equal measure a horror narrative, gothic romance and detective procedural, Fuller's adaptation certainly challenges the preconceptions of devout Thomas Harris fans. The series begins with Lecter and Graham becoming friends at a time when the cannibalistic psychiatrist roamed free, and ends as they fall in a bloody and battered embrace off a cliff after committing murder together. During the course of the series, characters' genders were also altered (psychiatrist Alan Bloom became Alana [Caroline Dhavernas], while journalist Freddy Lounds was remade into Fredricka [Lara Jean Chorostecki]), and key plot points moved puzzle-like to different parts of the narrative, the most notable shifts taking place with regard to the Lecter-Graham relationship which, though not explicitly sexual, develops in ways similar to the cannibal's much-maligned romance with Clarice Starling in Harris's text. What Fuller did not change but merely enhanced, however, was what Philip L. Simpson describes as the "very often dream-like and hallucinatory" nature of "the Gothic narrative space in Harris's work."[2] While the dialogue between characters frequently came directly from Harris's own prose, Fuller's adaptation added installations ranging from totem poles made out of human corpses and girls dangling from stag antlers surrounded its protagonists. Additionally, viewers were privy to Will Graham's almost supernatural ability to inhabit the minds of murderers, and they simultaneously witnessed the hallucinations which walked alongside him. This made it clear to *Hannibal's* viewers that naturalism applied in the series only to a limited extent; in its place, they were being served the atmosphere of a nightmare.

As has been noted by a number of authors, both Thomas Harris's books on Lecter and their subsequent film adaptations draw greatly on the Gothic tradition, which Peter Messent describes as destabilizing "the relationship between hunter and hunted, criminality and law" so as to set the story in a "liminal space" fit to "challenge our fixed preconceptions." Similarly, Maggie Kilgour writes:

[The Gothic] erodes any neat distinctions between formats and modes, combining sentimentality and the grotesque, romance and terror, the heroic and the bathetic, philosophy and nonsense. This promiscuous generic cross-breeding is part of the Gothic's "subverting" of stable norms, collapsing of "binary oppositions," which makes it appropriate for a postmodern sensibility.[3]

On this subject, Kilgour goes on to note that "the gothic offers itself as a means of *expressing* otherwise taboo forces" and that, "by bringing the unspoken to light," it "draws on the modern assumption that it is dangerous to bury things" and "appears to offer both a critique and an alternative to our Enlightenment inheritance."[4] Thus, it is precisely this "bringing to light" which characterizes the genre that has prompted both Elizabeth Young and Messent to note that "Harris's texts, and the Gothic generally, use a strategy of 'transformation of [the] figurative to [the] literal,'"[5] which is an observation of particular relevance when regarding Fuller's own adaptation and the deadly art installations presented within it.

Certainly, the series is not alone in this. "In fact," writes Steven Jay Schneider, "one distinguishing mark of the modern horror film is a shift in the genre's dominant aesthetic metaphor: what used to be 'a presentation of the murderer or "monster" himself "as" a "corrupt or degraded work of art" has transformed into "the *monster as corrupt or degraded artist.*" Multiple films and television programs have addressed this representation, including *Se7en* and *The Bone Collector* (itself turned into a broadcast television program in 2020).

Thus, if we are to accept the view that the Gothic is defined in part by its tendency to "make the figurative literal," then the proliferation of such grisly artistry within the show needs to be regarded in terms of how it comments not only on the role of the artist and of art, but also in terms of how it portrays the function of either dispassionate observation or immersion into what is being seen. Consequently, what separates Fuller's series from similar Gothic representations within the genre is not that it runs contrary to said literalizing of figurative content, but rather that it utilizes this to such an extent that artistry is deemed an almost inherent part of the destruction depicted within it. Therefore, it's important to ask several of the following questions: Why is it that most of the murderers within the series are also artists? What qualities do artistry and the artistic product reflect that makes them relevant to the horror genre in general and *Hannibal* in particular? Ultimately, if we are to find out how Graham's capacity for empathy comments both on the role of the audience in art and on the role of an individual inevitably influenced by others, we must first see how Lecter stands apart from his fellow artists as an author.

Designing Death: Hannibal as Divine Author

In the series, Lecter is often visually and verbally set apart from the show's other murderers through images linking him either to the demonic or the divine. For instance, in the sequence with which this chapter begins, Hannibal is shown sewing another killer into his own design and, as he does so, the two men converse as follows:

> HANNIBAL: You're not alone, you know? In the *Resurrection*, Piero della Francesca placed himself in the fresco. Nothing flattering; he depicted himself as a simple guard asleep at his post. Your placement should be much more meaningful. … God gave you purpose. Not only to create art, but to become it.
> KILLER: Why are you helping me?
> HANNIBAL: Your eye will now see God reflected back. It will see you. If God is looking down at you, don't you want to be looking back at Him?[6]

In the mise-en-scène, however, it is quite clear that the figure the killer is looking up at in this particular moment is none other than Lecter himself, thus reflecting his role as both judge and creator. Similarly, when Lecter comments upon first meeting the killer that "he loves his work," this moment also grants to him the position of art critic, which both David Lehman and Allen comment is a function normally reserved for the profiler. More precisely, Lehman writes in his examination of detective fiction that the genre usually revolves around a central triad, one composed of "the criminal" as "artist, the detective" as "an aesthete and a critic, and the blundering policeman" as "a philistine." As such, it is by granting Lecter a position above the show's other artists that the character is given almost godlike standing, highlighted within the scene by his physical position above the other killer. In the episode, this same position is echoed yet again as Graham imagines himself being stitched into the killer's place, therein mirroring the depth of Lecter's influence on his psyche, and reinforcing Will's own role as art-critic-turned-artwork within the show's narrative by virtue of his incarceration in the Baltimore State Hospital for the Criminally Insane in the second season.

Comparably, in the series' final episode (evocatively titled "The Wrath of the Lamb"), Graham is shown approaching the gilded altar of a church where Lecter awaits him, positioned in its center and visually imposed on Will as a figure he literally has to look up to in order to communicate with in the end. This scene, intercut with the reality of Graham standing inside Lecter's white cell, therefore works both to equate Lecter himself with the divine, and to establish his relationship with Graham as connected to explorations of the sacred and the devotional. Even the episode's title, taken from a Biblical Book of Revelation and quoted by Hannibal himself in the preceding episode when he tells FBI agent Jack Crawford (Laurence

Fishburne) to "hide us from the wrath of the lamb,"[7] alludes at once to Will's position as the proverbial "lamb of God" and to the larger symbolism of lambs within Harris's Lecter-related novels, thus linking him to the innocents Clarice Starling failed to rescue as a child in *The Silence of the Lambs* (1989). In both cases, this phrasing further strengthens the already pronounced association between the Catholic mythos and *Hannibal*'s own narrative.

In parallel to this, the show's second episode depicts the first moment when Graham visits Hannibal's red-walled office, its mise-en-scène making Lecter a figure Will has to descend to from the office balcony in order to reach, therein visually linking his acquiescence to Hannibal's psychiatric care with his fall into a world commanded by Lecter's murderous logic. Only an episode later, this same setup is echoed once again, as the young Abigail Hobbs (Kacey Rohl) descends from Lecter's balcony towards him in precisely the moment when both characters promise not to reveal what they've learned about each other to the police. By being so positioned, this visual parallel thus effectively marks off both the would-be daughter and partner Lecter hopes to make a murderous family with and casts him in the role of Mephistopheles, whispering in their ears from the darkness. As such, it highlights precisely what Robert H. Waugh describes as Lecter's role within the novels as "the man in charge of the new confessional" and draws to mind the link between, for instance, the encephalitis contracted by Graham under Lecter's psychiatric care during the show's first season, and the syphilis willingly contracted by the protagonist of Thomas Mann's *Doctor Faustus* (1947). In both cases, illness enables these characters to better develop their gifts. while the Mephistopheles in Mann's novel allows composer Adrian Leverkühn to achieve artistic greatness in such a manner, Will's encephalitis leads him to even greater immersion into "the designs" of the killers who surround him.

In many ways, these links stand to reinforce what Joseph Grixti describes as Harris's approach to "the task of fictionalising serial killers by compartmentalizing the phenomenon into two distinct types. The first is the psychopathic loner who turns into a vicious beast," while "the second is the serial killer as an enigmatic devil and modern embodiment of evil." These "prototypes," writes Grixti, "are not Harris's invention, but appear to derive from a popular tendency to stereotype murderers as either 'making sense' because they are 'obviously' psychotic and sexually mixed up, or else, when the label doesn't fit, as somehow being associated with the realm of supernatural evil." Moreover, they add to Lecter's already well-documented capacity to simultaneously embody different visions of evil for different readers or viewers, with authors like Barbara Creed describing him as a "self-appointed guardian of the Symbolic order (signified by his insistence that codes of civil society, good manners, should always be observed),"[8] while Grixti himself links him in equal measure to "a witch-doctor, a monster, and a Jungian shadow" reminiscent of both "a vampire" and all manner of villains ranging from "the charm and enigma of Iago as well as the epic grandeur of Milton's Satan."[9] In the context of Fuller's series, however, the emphasis should be put not only on how well it mimics Harris's early approach to Lecter as an evil somehow removed and above his criminal compatriots,[10] but on his capacity for both the authoring of others, performed through his role as their diabolical psychiatrist, and his capacity for self-authorship.

Namely, when Lecter comments to Will that "killing must feel good to God too, and are we not created in His image,"[11] he is advocating not solely the demise of the dichotomy between good and evil, but drawing a link between God as the supreme figure of creation/destruction and himself as a self-proclaimed author. Similarly, in another conversation with Will, Hannibal comments on the interrelationship between creation and destruction by stepping out of Catholic imagery and into that of Hinduism, visually referenced twice within the episode through his installation of corpse-parts positioned so as to resemble the many-handed Shiva (therein celebrating what he believes to be Will's transformation into a fellow killer) and through Lecter and Graham's shared hallucination of this same deity during a psychiatric session. Lecter explains:

> HANNIBAL: Every creative act has its destructive consequence, Will. The Hindu god Shiva is simultaneous destroyer and creator. Who you were yesterday is laid waste to give rise to who you are today....
> WILL: What god do you pray to?
> HANNIBAL: I don't pray. I've not been bothered by any considerations of deity, other than to recognise how my own modest actions pale beside those of God. ... God is beyond measure in wanton malice, and matchless in his irony.[12]

The same notion is once again highlighted in another conversation between the two, when Graham asks Hannibal "what" he thinks about "when" he thinks "about killing," to which he replies:

> HANNIBAL: I think about God.
> WILL: Good and evil?
> HANNIBAL: Good and evil has nothing to do with God. ... Typhoid and swans, it all comes from the same place.[13]

What is important here is precisely the question of origin or, differently put, of authorship. Like the Creator, Lecter himself is described in Fuller's universe as someone who "cannot be reduced to a set of influences," someone who "made" himself[14] and whose particular madness cannot therefore be explained through the childhood trauma commonly invoked with regard to serial killers in general (be they in real-life or fiction), or to Harris's eventual description of Lecter in particular.[15] Contrary to the novels, Fuller leaves the details of Lecter's sister Mischa a mystery, and so viewers of the series are left wondering whether he dined on her flesh after her death,[16] and are thus never granted the knowledge that he himself is an explicable source of evil. As such, he retains what Terry Eagleton terms in *On Evil* (2010) as "an insight which seems central to the idea of evil," which is that "evil rejects the logic of causality."[17]

More precisely, Eagleton writes that evil "is thought to be uncaused, or to be its own cause"[18] and that "in this, it resembles God,"[19] as "only God is said to be the cause of himself"[20] and "is his own reason for being."[21] This is precisely why the divine and the demonic are linked through the character of Lecter within the series, for the divine exists as the supreme *causa sui*, and can thus bear no questions of either ancestry or a source. Similarly, for Lecter to function as the primary instigator of the events happening within the series, the destruction he creates needs to stay one step beyond comprehension if it is to retain its appeal. Like God, Hannibal needs to remain "wanton in his malice and matchless in his irony" if he is not to be "reduced to a set of influences" and therefore diminished as a protagonist. What defines him, then, is not what has influenced him in life, but his actions, his agency. He stands, as Shakespeare's Coriolanus but wishes to, "as if man were author of himself and knew no other kin."[22]

Consequently, he also retains what Mikhail Bakhtin describes in *The Author and Hero in Aesthetic Activity* (1923) as "the divinity of the artist" which "consists in his partaking of" what Bakhtin calls "supreme outsideness."[23] More precisely, while writing on the position of artists in relation to their work, Bakhtin explains that "the artist is, in fact, someone who knows how to be active outside lived life, someone who not only partakes in life from within (practical, social, political, moral, religious life) and understands it from within, but someone who loves it from without."[24] He writes that "to find an essential approach to life from outside—this is the task an artist must accomplish. In doing this, the artist and art as a whole create a completely new vision of the world, a new image of the world, a new reality of the world's mortal flesh, unknown to any of the other culturally creative activities."[25]

Naturally, Bakhtin is not writing here about the morbid artistry presented in *Hannibal* and similar examples of the horror genre, but of the many real writers and artists who use the material of their luckily more mundane lives so as to create new realities for their audience. Nonetheless, the very fact that the figure of the artist carries such weight within the horror genre in general and *Hannibal* in particular speaks volumes as to the fact that the artistic product itself, reimagined within the show as the reshaping of Man's mortal flesh into new images, needs to be regarded as crucial to its narrative. "You must understand that blood and breath are merely elements undergoing change to fuel your radiance," Hannibal tells Will Graham, and thus positions himself both within and outside the spectacle of suffering which he himself creates. Why is it so necessary for our fascination with him that he do so? Why must Hannibal, like God and the Devil, be inexplicable and, like the author, be capable of at once participating in and distancing himself from the pain which he creates?

The answer lies precisely in the way the series problematizes questions of distance and of closeness. By showing us the complex art installations created by Lecter and his fellow killers, it asks of us as viewers to make a choice; to decide whether we shall be enthralled or repelled. At the same time, it is by depicting the horrifying consequences of Graham's immersion in these artworks and in the character of Lecter that the series forces us consider which position is more pleasant; that of the artist or that of the audience? Thus, when Will Graham claims that "elegance is more important" to God "than suffering,"[26] he is commenting at once not only on Hannibal's own philosophy of aestheticism but on the roles we assume as observers of such representations of suffering. Consequently, it is necessary first that we examine the ways in which *Hannibal's* morbid artworks comment on the nature of looking and representing pain if we are to be able to fully grasp how it comments on the concept of authorship.

Elegance and Suffering: Reading Hannibal's *Murder Tableaus*

Clearly, the amount of attention paid by both reviewers and fans to the series' so-called "murder tableaus"[27] should serve as proof that they fascinate viewers in equal measure, if not more than they repel them. Like Lecter's elaborately designed menus, they work so as to provoke a conflicted sort of appreciation, forcing their audience to at once admire the ingenuity that crafted them and to consider the implications of such creativity. Can we do both at once? Or do we, as Elisabeth Bronfen writes in relation to artistic representations of beautiful female corpses, derive our enjoyment from the fact that they let "us repress the knowledge of the reality of death precisely because here death occurs *at* someone else's body and *as* an image"?[28] As Bronfen insightfully points out in *Over Her Dead Body: Death, Femininity and the Aesthetic* (1992):

Representations of death in art are so pleasing, it seems, because they occur in a realm clearly delineated as not life, or not real, even as they refer to the basic fact of life we know but choose not to acknowledge too overtly. They delight because we are confronted with death, yet it is the death of the other. We experience death by proxy. In the aesthetic enactment, we have a situation impossible in life, namely that we die with another and return to the living. Even as we are forced to acknowledge the ubiquitous presence of death in life, our belief in our own immortality is confirmed. There is death, but it is not my own.[29]

Thus, when a disappointing musician in the Baltimore Orchestra is killed by one of the series' minor murderers, it is difficult not to find some measure of irony in the fact that a cello neck is protruding from his throat. Similarly, when Will Graham imagines himself playing this same half-human instrument, the profiler's performance becomes the focus of the scene, therein leaving behind the suffering which led to it.[30] When Hannibal Lecter kills a young man who looks much like Graham, it is not the act of killing itself that we wonder at, but its intricate presentation, the victim's stomach inlaid with poisonous flowers, his naked body bound to a still-blooming and uprooted tree.[31] Upon viewing the scene, we might wonder; is this Lecter's way of sending Graham a bouquet after his release from the asylum? Certainly, if we are regular viewers of the show, this is a far more likely train of thought than marveling on the complexities of how Lecter could have possibly set up such a sight during his short time away from the office. The mechanics of the scene, then, are not what is important. What is relevant, however, is its meaning.

Therefore, Allen is correct in noting that the "crimes" presented within the artistic serial killer subgenre "become texts, decipherable via the language of the controlled body."[32] These texts, he writes, come to be comprehensible because the murderers in question are depicted as "controlled and guided by" the "cultural capital" which makes them "containable"[33] and leads the profiler to discovering their identities as he too possesses the "specialist taste and learning"[34] necessary to do so. Similarly, Alison Young writes in *Imagining Crime* (1996) of the presentation "in detective fiction," of "the detective as positivist,"[35] able to objectively interpret the clues of the crimes as if he were a scientist. Where Fuller's series differs from this principle resides in its grounding of Graham's gifts as a profiler not in his specialist knowledge, but in his extraordinary ability to empathize with others. "I imagine what you see and learn touches everything else in your mind," Hannibal tells him, "your values and decency are present, yet shocked at your associations, appalled at your dreams."[36] In this sense, Graham could not be further from the scientist envisioned by Young, for his gift of what Lecter terms "pure empathy"[37] makes him unable to retain any objective distance from the crimes which he observes. As such, the permeability of his psyche mirrors the permeability of bodies depicted in the series, and brings to mind Barbara Creed's assertion that "images of the bleeding body

point symbolically to the fragile nature of the self, its lack of secure boundaries, the ease with which it might lose definition, fall apart, or bleed into
nothingness."[38]

Consequently, the fascination these representations hold for us can be
found precisely in the ways in which they remind us of our frailty and, by
reminding us, displace this frailty onto the body of another. In her analysis of monstrous representations of the body in horror cinema, Creed
draws amongst others on the work of Pete Boss, who argues that the modern horror film's obsession with the destruction of the human body lies
in its "reduction of identity to its corporeal horizons."[39] Boss also attests
to "a 'peculiarly postmodern sense of dread' that has partly been brought
about by an increasing sense of individual helplessness in relation to growing powers of medical technology and institutionalized bureaucracy, particularly in the area of medicine and problems related to death and dying."[40]

In the same vein, Mark Seltzer describes in *Serial Killers* (1998) what
he terms our contemporary *wound culture* or rather, "the convening of the
public around scenes of violence—the rushing to the scene of the acci-
dent" and "the public fascination with torn and opened bodies and torn
and opened persons, a collective gathering around shock, trauma, and the
wound."[41] Simply put, Seltzer writes here of the convergence of private and
public suffering, psychological trauma and bodily wounds, and notes that
"the contemporary public sphere presents itself to itself, from the art and
culture scenes to tabloid and talk TV, as a culture of suffering, states of
injury, and wounded attachments."[42] Seltzer comments that:

One detects the model of a sociality bound to pathology. In short, the
opening of relation to others (the "sympathetic" social bond) is at the same
time the traumatic collapse of boundaries between self and other (a yield-
ing of identity to identification). In this way, the opening of a possibility of
relation to others also opens the possibility of violence: the mimetic identification *at the expense of* the subject and a violence *in the name of* a violated
singularity and self-difference. The opening towards others is drawn to the
collective spectacle of torn and open bodies and persons: a wounding and
gaping towards others in the pathological public sphere.[43]

Scenes of violence, Seltzer tells us, are mesmerizing precisely because
they symbolize externally the psychological violence perceived as inherent
in human contact; in the necessity that I as an individual should be changed
by coming into contact with another. Wounds capture our attention
because they are visible, while psychological trauma, though it can be told
and reshaped through mediums such as the chat shows Seltzer mentions,
remains inherently problematic because the very concept of it "poses a radical breakdown as to the determination of the subject," for we no longer
know if he or she is created "from within or without: the self-determined

or the event-determined subject; the subject as cause or as caused; the subject as the producer of representations or their product."[44] As such, our singularity as subjects is ever-threatened, ever-traumatized by the fact that, to live, we must be altered, changed in ways that are beyond our control. Much like the killer whom Lecter sews into his own mural, we are both artists and works of art, producers and products, and it is this inherent contradiction between our identities and the effects others can have on them which breeds such fascination with overt representations of suffering.

More to the point, it also makes clear the parallels between the bodily suffering depicted in the show's murder tableaus and the psychological suffering shown through Graham's immersion in the minds of others, Hannibal Lecter in particular. When, for example, Hannibal tells Will that "friendship can sometimes lead to a loss of individual separateness,"[45] he is voicing precisely the view of Seltzer that "the opening of relation to others" or "'the "sympathetic"' social bond" represents at once a "traumatic collapse of boundaries between self and other."[46] Comparably, when Graham confesses to Lecter that he "used to hear" his own "voice in the back of" his "skull in the same tone, timber, accent as if the words were coming out of" his "mouth" but that "now" this voice sounds like Hannibal,[47] it is the "mimetic identification *at the expense of* the subject and a violence *in the name of* a violated singularity and self-difference"[48] described by Seltzer of which he speaks.

Consequently, it is here relevant to note that the grisly artistry within the series serves two simultaneous functions. On the one hand, the pedestal upon which the artistic serial killer subgenre in general and *Hannibal* in particular places its representations of pain at once attests to the desire for suffering to be made visible, to be granted importance and, conversely, to the need to distance ourselves from it, to reshape it into something other than "merely" wounds. Unlike the character of Will Graham, we are granted the opportunity of standing comfortably outside the destruction and suffering presented on-screen, and of ascertaining the value of its design dispassionately, as if we were art critics. Unlike him, we can observe, but we need not feel or experience what we see at a visceral level, and are thus liberated from overtly acknowledging our own frailty.

On the other hand, however, it is by depicting such destruction most closely through Graham's own immersion and reimagining of it that the series not only highlights our own distance from it, but thematizes the notion that we are, as an audience ready to observe such sights, always complicit in their staging. More to the point, it is by granting to the murderer the capacity of making death aesthetically appealing that these scenes attest to the potential willingness of the viewer to identify with the accomplished mastery over what is merely human and thus perishable, rather than with notions of victimhood. In this sense, *Hannibal's* murder tableaus offer at once the feeling of disgust and that of control, therein numbing the effect of the suffering they depict by encouraging gleeful appreciation of Lecter's ingenuity in the viewer. As such, the multiple positions which we are as viewers able to assume point precisely towards the ways in which the series addresses and problematizes the act of seeing in general, and the notion of empathy in particular.

"Are you observing or participating?" Hannibal asks of Bedelia du Maurier (Gillian Anderson) during their murderous trip to Florence,[49] thus making it clear that it is impossible to watch violence without becoming at least in part culpable of it. At the same time, the distinction between observation and participation again raises questions of authorship, for the series continually utilizes the character of Will Graham to remind us that looking has an effect on the observer and that this effect, if it is deep enough, risks negating the observer's own ability to author themselves. As such, Graham serves as an almost hyperbolic representation of the dangers of perceiving and being perceived by another, thus making it no surprise that the true horror seen in *Hannibal* lies not in the cleverly crafted murder tableaus presented within the series, but in the destructive friendship shared by its two protagonists.

The Terror of Empathy: Will, Distance and the Audience

Throughout this essay, I have emphasized the division between the artist, artwork and audience so as to be able to better understand the peculiar aesthetics which drives *Hannibal* as a series. In doing so, the character of Lecter has been read through his link to the divine and the demonic as the show's supreme creator, capable of authoring both himself and others. As Mikhail Bakhtin writes, this means he is positioned at once inside (as a protagonist) and outside (as a narrator/author) the suffering which he creates, and is as a character defined by the level of control which he exhibits. At the same time, his and the other victims depicted within the show have been regarded through their roles as vehicles for the "designs" of the series' many murderers, and have therefore been read alternatively as reflections of what Seltzer terms our "wound culture," as reminders and negations of our own mortality as viewers, and as visual symbols for the permeability of Will Graham's own psyche. As such, it remains now for us to look at the ways in which the series utilizes the character of Graham so as to establish the distinction between watching and immersion, between seeing and experience, and to find out how its own emphasis on empathy relates both to questions of aesthetics and of ethics.

During the course of the series, the profiler is depicted as alternatively stripped of his sanity, freedom, would-be daughter, wife and adopted son, all because he is unable to definitively sever his ties to Lecter. Similarly, even Lecter himself eventually relinquishes part of his own capacity for agency and self-authorship due to his desire for Graham always to be able to return to him, which prompts Hannibal to surrender to the FBI. "I'm not going to miss you. I'm not going to find you," Will tells him, "I don't want to think about you anymore."[50] and so Hannibal makes of himself a permanent fixture within the geography of Graham's mind, ever-waiting for the moment when his conviction falters, as it inevitably does before the show's conclusion. As such, the fact that the series ends with Graham embracing both Lecter and the consequent demise of his own identity points towards the fact that the cause of his paralysis is to be found precisely in his acceptance of their emotional connection. In turn, the source of this emotional connection is located within the series in Graham's inability to properly distinguish between his own identity and that of Lecter's, which is a development visually underscored through scenes of their faces[51] or reflections merging,[52] Graham's own reflection cracking when he observes it in the mirror,[53] and in his confession to Hannibal that "you and I have begun to blur."[54]

As such, Graham's capacity to empathize with Lecter grants to him not the benefits of ethical behavior commonly associated with the quality of empathy, but rather the lack of what Bakhtin describes in his aforementioned essay *The Author and Hero in Aesthetic Activity* as exotopy.[55] So as to explain this concept, Bakhtin writes:

> Let us say that there is a human being before me who is suffering[…]. I must experience—come to see and know—what he experiences; I must put myself in his place and coincide with him, as it were[…]. But in any event my projection of myself into him must be followed by a return into myself, a return to my own place outside the suffering person, for only from this place can the other be rendered meaningful ethically, cognitively or aesthetically. If this return into myself did not actually take place, the pathological phenomenon of experiencing another's suffering as one's own would result [in]—an infection with the other's suffering, and nothing more.[56]

Thus, it is precisely this ability to "return into myself" which Bakhtin terms exotopy, derived from the Greek *exo* or "to move out of," and it is this ability which Will Graham does not possess, consequently making him incapable of ethical action. Similarly, it is the lack of this ability which makes him susceptible not only to what Bakhtin describes as "an infection with the other's suffering," but also to the joy which the other, in this case Lecter, feels in creating suffering. As such, the destructive connection between the two comes in Bakhtin's terms from the presence of empathy without the return into oneself, and it is here important to note that Bakhtin considers such a return an aspect of primary importance not only with regard to ethics, but in one's perception of the aesthetic.

Specifically, Bakhtin distinguishes between three types of perception in art; that of the aforementioned author, capable of existing both within and outside the tale which he or she creates, and that of two different types of readers or viewers. The first type of viewers are the so-called "naive" ones who, while sympathizing with the protagonist and warning him of the dangers he or she is about to encounter, cannot return into themselves after doing so and are therefore unable to perceive the totality of the work they have just seen.[57] In contrast to this, the second type of viewers are regarded by Bakhtin as the more advanced ones, capable of having what he deems the true aesthetic experience. This experience, as Ilya Kliger summarizes, is one defined by "a double operation whereby the reader or viewer aligns themselves with the 'intentional' perspective of the hero and *simultaneously* recoils back into the totalizing outsideness of the author."[58]

With this in mind, we can now look back at Graham's journey as one in which he moves from the role of a more advanced viewer to that of the naive participant, and can view Lecter's own trajectory in similar terms, for he moves from encompassing both the inside and outside of his own narrative to being contained by it. Similarly, it is here possible to view our own distanced position from the macabre artworks depicted within the show as one which can benefit both from immersion and from exotopy, therefore retaining the potential of what Bakhtin terms the true aesthetic experience. Most importantly, however, it is by linking both the ethical and aesthetic aspects of looking that this reading of the series allows for us to disregard the division between how it presents bodies and how it presents minds, and to see in both a reflection of our own insecurities as to the ways in which we are influenced and shaped by others.

"Fear," *Hannibal* tells us in its first episode, "is the price of imagination,"[59] but it is clear from the show's unfolding that it considers the same to be true of seeing and of being seen. As such, it is my contention that the emphasis placed on artistry within the series attests to its wider examination of the relationship between looking and creating, and that it is within this examination that it questions whether we can ever be entirely sure of the distinction. Differently put, it is by continually showing to its audience both controlled bodies and controlled minds that Fuller's *Hannibal* comments on the dangers of being shaped by what we see, and inquires whether it is possible for us as individuals to also be the authors of ourselves. As such, it is of little surprise that it positions Lecter as both the god and the devil looking back at us, for there is little more frightening than not being able to control what we see, and nothing more terrifying than being seen by that which we cannot control.

I end, therefore, with a brief observation regarding the designs of bodies and minds displayed within the series. In themselves, they reflect the fear that we are ourselves not advanced viewers but naive participants in what surrounds us; namely, that we are capable of being seen by others but not of truly perceiving ourselves. In this sense, then, it is constructive to remember Bakhtin's own assertion that "the world of cognition and every constituent in it are capable of being thought, but they are not capable of actually being perceived."[60] So as to elaborate on this notion, Bakhtin returns precisely to the outsideness of the author and of the more advanced viewer, for it is this distance that in itself encapsulates the difference between myself and the other. Bakhtin writes that:

When I contemplate a whole human being who is situated outside and over against me, our concrete, actually experienced horizons do not coincide. For at each given moment, regardless of the position and proximity to me of this other human being that I am contemplating, I shall always see and know something that he, from his place outside and over against me, cannot see himself.... As we gaze at each other, two different worlds are reflected in the pupils of our eyes. It is possible, upon assuming an appropriate position, to reduce this difference of horizons to a minimum, but in order to annihilate this difference completely, it would be necessary to merge into one, to become one and the same person. ... For only I—the one-and-only I—occupy in a given set of circumstances this particular place at this particular time; all other human beings are situated outside me.[61]

As such, this difference of perspectives between myself and the other determines within Bakhtin's aesthetics not only the positions of the artist and the audience, but one's own position with regard to the world. In other words, while it is both impossible for me to annihilate the distinction between myself and the other, and to live in a world free of influence, it is also precisely through the influence of others that I am able to retain my position at once inside this world (by virtue of being seen) and outside it (through experiencing myself and others in my own mind). Consequently, Michael Holquist is correct in pointing out that, for Bakhtin, other people "are neither heaven or hell, but the necessary condition for both,"[62] seeing as they at once allow for the physical and practical reality of my existence through perceiving it, and enable me to retain my outsideness by becoming the material of my perception.

Thus, when we regard *Hannibal* in its totality, it is important to remember not only the ways in which it makes literal our fears that our position outside others or outside an artwork will diminish depending on how deeply inside it we step, but also Lecter's own assertion that, by its very nature, "perception is a tool that's pointed on both ends."[63] As such, all that remains for us as audience members, artworks and authors is to decide, truly, whether this is something to be afraid of.

Notes

1. *Hannibal*, "Sakizuke," March 7, 2014.
2. Philip L. Simpson, "Gothic Romance and Killer Couples in *Black Sunday* and *Hannibal*," in *Dissecting Hannibal Lecter: Essays on the Novels of Thomas Harris*, ed. Benjamin Szumskyj (Jefferson, NC: McFarland, 2008), 52.
3. Maggie Kilgour, "Dr. Frankenstein Meets Dr. Freud," in *American Gothic: New interventions in a national narrative*, ed. Robert K. Martin and Eric Savoy (Iowa City: University of Iowa Press, 1998), 40.
4. Kilgour, 40.
5. Peter Messent, "American Gothic: Liminality and the Gothic in Thomas Harris's Hannibal Lecter Novels," in *Dissecting Hannibal Lecter: Essays on the Novels of Thomas Harris,* ed. Benjamin Szumskyj (Jefferson, NC: McFarland, 2008), p. 29.
6. *Hannibal*, "Sakizuke," March 7, 2014.
7. *Hannibal*, "The Number of the Beast is 666," August 22, 2015.
8. Barbara Creed, "Freud's Worst Nightmare: Dining with Dr. Hannibal Lecter," in *Horror Film and Psychoanalysis: Freud's Worst Nightmare*, 2004, ed. Steven Jay Schneider (Cambridge: Cambridge University Press 2004), 200.
9. Grixti, 94.
10. As Grixti and others have noted, this removal is achieved in the novels by having him speak in the present as opposed to the past tense reserved for other characters, thus lending Lecter an immediacy they do not possess.
11. *Hannibal*, "Amuse-Bouche," April 11, 2013.
12. *Hannibal*, "Ko No Mono," May 9, 2014.
13. *Hannibal*, "Shiizakana," April 25, 2014.
14. As Hannibal himself says in "Secondo" (2015), "Nothing happened to me. I happened." This sentence, taken from a moment when he addresses Starling in *The Silence of the Lambs*, comes from a larger speech in which Lecter elaborates that "Nothing happened to me, Officer Starling. I happened. You can't reduce me to a set of influences. You've given up good and evil for behaviorism" (21). In the series, the last two lines are spoken by Graham in "Naka-Choko" (2014) in an attempt to convince the psychiatrist that he has truly transformed himself into a killer.
15. Harris connects the source of Lecter's cannibalism with the cannibalization of his sister at the hands of looters. See: Thomas Harris, *Hannibal* (London: Arrow, 2000); Thomas Harris, *Hannibal Rising* (New York: Delacorte Press, 2006).
16. *Hannibal*, "Secondo," June 18, 2015.
17. Terry Eagleton, *On Evil* (New Haven and London:Yale University Press, 2010), 84.
18. *Ibid.*, 4.
19. *Ibid.*, 84.
20. *Ibid.*, 4.
21. *Ibid.*, 84.
22. William Shakespeare, *Coriolanus*, in *The Tragedy of Coriolanus*, ed. R. B. Parker, *The Tragedy of Coriolanus*. Oxford: Clarendon Press, 1994), 5.3.36–37.
23. Mikhail Mikhaïlovich Bakhtin, *Art and Answerability: Early Philosophical Essays*, ed. Michael Holquist, and Vadim Liapunov (University of Texas Press, 1990), 191.
24. *Ibid.*, 190–191.
25. *Ibid.*, 191.
26. *Hannibal*, "Primavera," June 11, 2015.
27. See: Emily Nussbaum, "To Serve Man: The Savoury Spectacle of *Hannibal*," *The New Yorker*, June 29 2015. http://www.newyorker.com/magazine/2015/06/29/to-serve-man;

Adam Bellotto, "*Hannibal*'s Most Beautiful Murders," *FILMSCHOOLREJECTS*, September 2 2015. https://filmschoolrejects.com/hannibals-most-beautiful-murders-fa53fb471b49#. e7cf59m6o; Leah Schnelbach, "Ranking the Corpse Art of *Hannibal*!," *Tor.com*, July 30 2015. http://www.tor.com/2015/07/30/ranking-the-corpse-art-of-hannibal/; Mark Rozeman, "The 15 Most Gruesome Moments From *Hannibal*," *Paste*, May 25 2014. https://www.pastemagazine.com/articles/2014/05/the-13-most-gruesome-hannibal-season-two-moments.html?a=1.

    28. Elisabeth Bronfen, *Over Her Dead Body: Death, Femininity and the Aesthetic* (Manchester University Press, 1992), x.

    29. *Ibid.*, x.

    30. *Hannibal*, "Fromage," May 16, 2013.

    31. *Hannibal*, "Futamono," April 4, 2014.

    32. Allen, 114.

    33. *Ibid.*, 113.

    34. *Ibid.*, 114.

    35. Alison Young, *Imagining crime* (London: Sage Publications, 1996), 84.

    36. *Hannibal*, "Apéritif," April 4, 2013.

    37. *Ibid.*

    38. Barbara Creed, "Horror and the Carnivalesque: The body-monstrous," in *Fields of vision: essays in film studies, visual anthropology, and photography* 1995, ed. Devereaux, Leslie and Roger Hillman (Berkeley: University of California Press, 1995, 144.

    39. Pete Boss, qtd. *Ibid.*, 128.

    40. *Ibid.*, 129.

    41. Mark Seltzer, *Serial Killers: Death and Life in America's Wound Culture* (New York and London: Routledge, 1998), 1.

    42. *Ibid.*, 254.

    43. *Ibid.*, 258.

    44. *Ibid.*, 260.

    45. *Hannibal*, "Kaiseki," February 28, 2014.

    46. Seltzer, 258.

    47. *Hannibal*, "Kaiseki," February 28, 2014.

    48. Seltzer, 258.

    49. *Hannibal*, "Secondo," June 18, 2015.

    50. *Hannibal*, "Digestivo," July 18, 2015.

    51. *Hannibal*, "Naka-Choko," May 2, 2014.

    52. *Hannibal*, "…And the Woman Clothed With the Sun…," August 1, 2015.

    53. *Ibid.*

    54. *Hannibal*, "Dolce," July 9, 2015.

    55. The concept of exotopy has been differently translated by a number of authors and so I here use Todorov's translation of Bakhtin's notion of *vnenakhodimost*. For an excellent analysis of the applications of exotopy in representations of traumatic histories, see: Sophie Oliver, "The Aesth-ethics of Empathy: Bakhtin and the Return to Self as Ethical Act," in *Empathy and its Limits* 2016, ed. Aleida Assmann and Ines Detmers (Hampshire and New York: Palgrave Macmillan UK, 2016), 166–186.

    56. Bakhtin, 26.

    57. Bakhtin, 79.

    58. Ilya Kliger, "Heroic Aesthetics and Modernist Critique: Extrapolations from Bakhtin's 'Author and Hero in Aesthetic Activity,'" *Slavic Review* 67, no. 3 (Fall, 2008): 556. Joseph Grixti, "Consuming cannibals: Psychopathic killers as archetypes and cultural icons," *Journal of American Culture* 18, no. 1 (1995): 91.

    59. *Hannibal*, "Apéritif," April 4, 2013.

    60. Bakhtin, 24.

    61. *Ibid.*, 22–23

    62. Michael Holquist, introduction to *Art and Answerability: Early Philosophical Essays*, by Mikhail Mikhaïlovich Bakhtin (University of Texas Press: 1990), xxxviii.

    63. *Hannibal*, "Apéritif," April 4, 2013.

Works Cited

Allen, Steven. *Cinema, Pain and Pleasure: Consent and the Controlled Body.* New York: Palgrave Macmillan, 2013.

"Amuse-Bouche." Rymer, Michael, director. *Hannibal,* season 1, episode 2, 11 April 2013.

"…And the Woman Clothed with the Sun." Dahl, John, director. *Hannibal,* season 3, episode 9, 1 August 2015.

"Apéritif." Slade, David, director. *Hannibal,* season 1, episode 1, 4 April 2013.

Bakhtin, Mikhail Mikhailovich. *Art and Answerability: Early Philosophical Essays.* Edited by Holquist, Michael and Vadim Liapunov. University of Texas Press, 1990.

Bronfen, Elisabeth. *Over Her Dead Body: Death, Femininity and the Aesthetic.* Manchester University Press, 1992.

Creed, Barbara. "Horror and the Carnivalesque: The Body-Monstrous." In *Fields of vision: essays in film studies, visual anthropology, and photography,* ed. Devereaux, Leslie and Roger Hillman, 127–159. Berkeley: University of California Press, 1995.

Creed, Barbara. "Freud's Worst Nightmare: Dining with Dr. Hannibal Lecter." In *Horror film and psychoanalysis: Freud's worst nightmare,* ed. Steven Jay Schneider, 188–204. Cambridge: Cambridge University Press 2004.

"Digestivo." Kane, Adam, director. *Hannibal,* season 3, episode 7, 18 July 2015.

"Dolce." Natali, Vincenzo, director. *Hannibal,* season 3, episode 6, 9 July 2015.

Eagleton, Terry. *On Evil.* New Haven and London: Yale University Press, 2010.

"Fromage." Hunter, Tim, director. *Hannibal,* season 1, episode 8, 16 May 2013.

Fuller, Bryan. *Hannibal.* Television Series. Created by Bryan Fuller. 2013–2015. Sony Pictures Television. 2014–2016. DVD.

"Futamono." Hunter, Tim, director. *Hannibal,* season 2, episode 6, 4 April 2014.

Grixti, Joseph. "Consuming cannibals: Psychopathic killers as archetypes and cultural icons." *Journal of American Culture* 18, no. 1 (1995): 87–96.

Harris, Thomas. *Hannibal.* London: Arrow, 2000.

Harris, Thomas. *Hannibal Rising.* New York: Delacorte Press, 2006.

Harris, Thomas. *Silence of the Lambs.* London: Arrow, 2002.

Holquist, Michael. Introduction to *Art and Answerability: Early Philosophical Essays* by Mikhail Mikhaïlovich Bakhtin, ix–xlix. University of Texas Press: 1990.

"Kaiseki." Hunter, Tim, director. *Hannibal,* season 2, season 1, 28 February 2014.

Kilgour, Maggie. "Dr. Frankenstein Meets Dr. Freud." In *American Gothic: New interventions in a national narrative,* ed. Robert K. Martin and Eric Savoy, 40–53. Iowa City: University of Iowa Press, 1998.

Kliger, Ilya. "Heroic Aesthetics and Modernist Critique: Extrapolations from Bakhtin's 'Author and Hero in Aesthetic Activity.'" *Slavic Review* 67, no.3 (Fall 2008): 551–566.

"Ko No Mono." Slade, David, director. *Hannibal,* season 2, episode 11, 9 May 2014.

Lehman, David. *The Perfect Murder: A Study in Detection.* Ann Arbor: University of Michigan Press, 2000.

Messent, Peter. "American Gothic: Liminality and the Gothic in Thomas Harris's Hannibal Lecter Novels." In *Dissecting Hannibal Lecter: Essays on the Novels of Thomas Harris,* ed. Benjamin Szumskyj, 13–36. Jefferson, NC: McFarland, 2008.

"Naka-Choko." Natali, Vincernzo, director. *Hannibal,* season 2, episode 10, 2 May 2014.

"The Number of the Beast is 666." Navarro, Guillermo, director. *Hannibal,* season 3, episode 12, 22 August 2015.

Oliver, Sophie. "The Aesth-ethics of Empathy: Bakhtin and the Return to Self as Ethical Act." In *Empathy and its Limits,* ed. Assmann, Aleida, and Ines Detmers, 166–186. Hampshire and New York: Palgrave Macmillan UK, 2016.

Prickett, Stephen, and Robert Carroll, eds. *The Bible: Authorized King James Version.* Oxford University Press, 1997.

"Primavera." Natali, Vincenzo, director. *Hannibal,* season 3, episode 2, 11 June 2015.

"Sakizuke." Hunter, Tim, director. *Hannibal,* season 2, episode 2, 7 Mar. 2014.

Schneider, Steven Jay. "Murder as Art/The Art of Murder: Aestheticizing Violence in Modern Cinematic Horror," In *Dark Thoughts: Philosophic Reflections on Cinematic Horror,* ed. Schneider, Steven Jay and Daniel Shaw, 174–197. Oxford: Scarecrow Press, 2003.

"Secondo." Natali, Vincenzo, director. *Hannibal*, season 3, episode 3, 18 June 2015.

Seltzer, Mark. *Serial killers: Death and life in America's wound culture.* New York and London: Routledge, 1998.

Shakespeare, William. *The Tragedy of Coriolanus*, Edited by R. B. Parker. Oxford: Clarendon Press, 1994.

"Shiizakana." Rymer, Michael, director. *Hannibal*, season 2, episode 9, 25 April 2014.

Simpson, Philip L. "Gothic Romance and Killer Couples in *Black Sunday* and *Hannibal*." In *Dissecting Hannibal Lecter: Essays on the Novels of Thomas Harris*, ed. Benjamin Szumskyj, 49–67. Jefferson, NC: McFarland, 2008.

Waugh, Robert H. "The Butterfly and the Beast: The Imprisoned Soul in Thomas Harris's Lecter Trilogy." In *Dissecting Hannibal Lecter: Essays on the Novels of Thomas Harris*, ed. Benjamin Szumskyj, 68–86. Jefferson, NC: McFarland, 2008.

Young, Alison. *Imagining crime.* London: Sage Publications, 1996.

Interview

Martha De Laurentiis

Nicholas A. Yanes

Martha De Laurentiis co-founded The De Laurentiis Company in 1980 with her husband in 1980. Since then, De Laurentiis has gone on to produce dozens of movies including but not limited to *Firestarter, Silver Bullet, The Bedroom Window, Breakdown,* and *U-571.* She has also played a crucial role bringing Dr. Hannibal Lecter to screens via the films *Hannibal* (2001), *Red Dragon,* and *Hannibal Rising.* De Laurentiis also served as one of the Executive Producers who brought the television show *Hannibal* (2013–2015) to life. Wanting to understand the show *Hannibal* and the franchise from a top-down perspective, Nicholas A. Yanes was able to interview De Laurentiis about how she approached this franchise as a producer and executive producer, its legacy, and its future.

Nicholas A. Yanes: As producers, why do you think this character has been able to remain popular and relevant for over three decades?

Martha De Laurentiis: Mainly, the characters have remained relevant because they're defined in the books with such depth and relatability. Hannibal is a conundrum, in that he's profoundly scary and chilling, but also charming and understandable. There's a strong core to his character that these incredibly gifted actors have been able to interpret in different ways, while maintaining an essential Hannibal-ness. I always go back to the books. The plots are clever and satisfying, yet these are essentially powerful relationship stories, with a big thematic underbelly. There are other scary movies and television shows about serial killers out there, but I can't think of any others that root these extreme killers in such relatable personal stories.

Yanes: From Brian Cox's original turn to Sir Anthony Hopkins's iconic portrayal, and now Mads Mikkelsen's acclaimed recent run, there have

been many great performances of Dr. Lecter. What do you think goes into making a great Hannibal performance?

De Laurentiis: All three of the Lecters have been unique, and so different; really masterful pieces of character conception and acting. What all three actors share is they're fundamentally men with serious gravitas and capacity for menace, yet personally also an incredible amount of charm. And of course, huge acting chops, such that all the minor gestures, details, and reactions are conceived in service of a greater whole of a performance.

Yanes: What was the initial inspiration to bring Hannibal to television? On this topic, why television instead of another film?

De Laurentiis: Whenever Dino or I spoke publicly, people always asked what was next for Hannibal. For many years, we had hoped that Thomas Harris would step back in and write a new chapter in the saga, but I knew that Thomas was writing other ideas. I saw that television was opening up, in terms of what was possible. As recently as 2000, before the show *24*, it was very difficult to sell a show that was so serialized it had to be watched in sequence. I think today is truly a "golden age of television," but that has manifested not only in a lot of opportunity for creators, but a loosening of rules.

Yanes: What was your specific vision and intended themes for this show?

De Laurentiis: As I've mentioned above, there's a thematic continuity among these books and movies, and I intended to stay to true to them. In different ways, all the books are about outsiders working in a bureaucratic world of insiders, as well as an exploration of the cost of violence. A t-shirt was printed for the show with the tagline, "Eat the rude." That sounds like a joke, but the principle of evil, the core of morality by which Hannibal Lecter operates, is that rudeness, callousness and hypocrisy are the really unforgiveable sins. I think these themes, the way that both Will and Clarice are incredibly competent, yet misfits in a hierarchical and superficial world—are always relevant. Certainly, Bryan Fuller put his own spin on them, but he intended a faithfulness to the spirit Thomas Harris created.

Yanes: I can't imagine *Hannibal* without Bryan Fuller's unique touch. How did you know he was the right person to help you produce the show?

De Laurentiis: When I first thought of doing a series, Thomas Harris was understandably concerned that someone would screw this up. I really did not want to disappoint him, and was trying to prevent this from getting transformed into something familiar and derivative. In the last few years, there have been some other exploitations of big movie franchises that basically reimagine things to the point that it's just a name added to a very familiar procedural. And, the procedural versions of these stories have already been made very well. The first *CSI*, especially at the beginning, captured a lot of the storytelling and profiling that was so new and arresting in the book *Red Dragon*. They even cast our first Will Graham as the tortured brilliant investigator!

When Katie O'Connell, who was heading Gaumont, first suggested we meet Bryan Fuller, I honestly was a little skeptical. I had liked his work, but I didn't see the carryover of the brilliance of *Dead Like Me* to a *Hannibal* show. But, Bryan came in on the first meeting, and he had gone back to that core relationship between Hannibal and Will. And, he was the ultimate Thomas Harris fan. He knew the books even better than I did, and he knew where the relationship could turn over the course of five seasons, and how the asides and secondary characters in the books could be fleshed out to a big television ensemble and universe. The rest is basically history. With Bryan involved, we got a deal very quickly. He wrote a fantastic pilot, and we got a series order.

Yanes: What did you see as a major production challenge for this version of *Hannibal* and how do you think the show addressed it? Would you have changed anything about it if you could?

De Laurentiis: The show looks fantastic, and I love that so many critics said that we were the only network show at the time making great cinema for the small screen. Coming from a feature world, however, it struck me how intimate it is compared to a film. It was fantastic that Bryan, Hugh, and Mads could make two men talking across from each other in a therapist's office so riveting. We did do a lot of cross-boarding of multiple episodes trying to keep the show more cost-effective. That worked well up until the third season, when we decided to open the show up and bring it to Europe. It was an exciting thing, and I feel like those scenes look spectacular, but some actor availabilities forced us to work around our plan, and that led to some unfortunate budget overages.

Yanes: Sir Anthony Hopkins as Hannibal was so powerful few thought anyone else could take up the mantle. What was it about Mads Mikkelsen that stood out to you as someone who could embody Hannibal for a modern audience?

De Laurentiis: From his start in *Pusher* to his role as Le Chiffre in *Casino Royale*, Mads has always been fantastic and stolen the scenes of everything he's been in. It's rare that someone that handsome can credibly convey that real menace and atavism. We knew that he had the toolbox to pull Hannibal off, and he had the right kind of feature cachet. Still, no one knew for sure whether he could really make it his own in the wake of Sir

Anthony Hopkins' performance. We took the gamble, and once we started seeing footage, it was clear that he had really found his own Hannibal.

Yanes: The relationship between Hannibal Lecter and Will Graham (and subsequently Hannibal and Clarice Starling in *The Silence of the Lambs*) has been portrayed in a variety of ways onscreen. Why did you choose to portray Hannibal and Will's relationship as a potentially gay romance in *Hannibal*?

De Laurentiis: Certainly, in the books, both Will and Hannibal are straight. But, all of the iterations of Hannibal live as two-person character dramas that are essentially more important than any of the other relationships in the story. It's clearly a pseudo-romance between Hannibal and Clarice in *The Silence of the Lambs* and *Hannibal*. In *Red Dragon*, Will's in love with a woman, but the question Hannibal repeatedly prompts—are they like each other—is there something in Will that's capable of the kind of purposeful violence and cruelty as Hannibal, is almost a more profound personal question. The first two seasons were really a mind-game between Will and Hannibal, and Hannibal was literally trying to trick Will, as he did by framing him with the ear. By season three, the question is more about that question of what this relationship means and whether Hannibal can tempt Will to a dark side. We used the term "bromance" a lot, but I know some of the writers played that as more of a gay subtext or actual romance than others.

Yanes: In addition to the quality of the show, an aspect I enjoyed was the fan culture surrounding *Hannibal*. Why do you think Fannibals were so different from other fan groups?

De Laurentiis: I can't speak to other fan communities, other than that ours was so smart, and passionate. There really was a give and take between all of us and the fans that was new to me, and really exciting. I assume it was a combination of the level of execution of the show, and our willingness to engage fans directly, rather than have someone in a marketing department schedule tweets. Nothing in *Hannibal* pandered, and if you invested the time to watch, it felt like you were becoming a part of a unique universe. I feel like we were giving them something that wasn't quite like anything else out there, and their responding loyalty and enthusiasm was really gratifying.

Yanes: Do you think modern Fannibals differ from previous fans of Hannibal Lecter? If so, how?

De Laurentiis: I'm not sure that the fans are all that different from the audiences of the earlier movies, but there certainly was way more fervor, organization, and opportunity for community. When we made the films

Hannibal and *Red Dragon*, there wasn't the kind of fully-formed online fandom we see today, and I wasn't aware of companies like Titan, Mondo, and Funko, who expand the universe with great licensed products. In the early 2000s, you had fan sites like IGN and Aint-it-Cool, but there wasn't the same amount of space for fans to get involved personally. We had a fan put up her own online Tattler Crime newspaper. The outpouring of love with really sophisticated and skilled fan art blew me away. And, I had never personally been involved with social media the way I became on this. Bryan Fuller creates a lot of accessibility for his fans, and that encouraged me to create a company website, start tweeting, contribute to the show's Tumblr, and keep up my own public Instagram. For the season openers and informally throughout the season, a lot of us live-tweeted the episodes, which is an awesome way to interact with fans in real-time, but I think it would have looked insane to me fifteen years ago.

Yanes: One unique aspect of *Hannibal* was that it frequently re-imagined characters with different genders and races. What do you think other show runners and creative leaders can learn from *Hannibal* when it comes to changing a pre-existing character's gender or race?

De Laurentiis: The American viewing audience is certainly more multicultural than ever, and as a creative community, we need to do better at reflecting it. Honestly, I haven't ever really discussed this with Bryan, so I don't know the extent to which he was purposefully trying to create diversity, or just trying to create a more interesting ensemble and cast the most gifted people he could. I feel like the tabloid culture when *Red Dragon* was written feels a bit old fashioned today, and Lara Jean's brash female Freddie Lounds certainly plays fresher as a running character over three seasons than a conniving white man we didn't wholly mind seeing lit on fire. I feel like Jack Crawford really came into his own a few episodes in, and I don't know whether he was always going to be such a major counterweight to Will and Hannibal, or whether Bryan started creating more for that character once we cast a really brilliant actor in Laurence Fishburne.

Some television is set in more specific culture that dictates specific race and sex choices, but I think, for example, ABC right now is doing a fantastic job of creating on-screen diversity. I hope we're approaching a time when we're more open to race-blind choices—when actresses like Rutina Wesley widely become cast in Reba McClane roles just because they're available and would do a fantastic job in the role. Some of this is a chicken and egg issue—the richer and more interesting roles for women and people of color are—the more we'll have actors who have already risen to the occasion and have established name value for themselves. Foreign markets, especially in film, still lag on this front, so hopefully television will continue to move forward and push the envelope.

Yanes: *Hannibal* was always critically acclaimed but seemed to struggle with ratings. What are some of the reasons why you think it didn't get the audience numbers it deserved?

De Laurentiis: The show was owned by Gaumont International Television rather than NBC, and while we had some real fans and champions within NBC, I've heard that the darkness, violence, and boundary-pushing made for a real challenge for a broadcast network's ad sales department. Because of that, institutionally, I'm not sure we ever had as much support as we would have hoped, and the way it moved around the schedule didn't help.

To be fair, though, what people love—that it's a smart, challenging show on a major network—may have also limited its audience a bit. It's so much a character story, to fully appreciate it, you pretty much need to have seen how the history of Hannibal and Will has evolved. If you're a fan from the beginning, there's richness to the writing and character story that rewards you and even deserves rewatching. I'm not sure if you come into it flipping channels mid-season, that it's easy enough to get sucked in, or even fully follow.

Yanes: On this note, do you think it would have done better on networks like HBO and Showtime, or on a streaming service like Netflix or Hulu?

De Laurentiis: It might have done better elsewhere. It looks more like a cable show than a broadcast one. Certainly, HBO has a reputation for keeping full-bore marketing on a show that's well-made and getting good reviews but hasn't fully found its audience. And, generally, in the cable space, the repeated broadcasting of an episode and the wider availability of in-season on-demand might have helped it find a larger audience. In terms of a streaming service, we started right before Netflix and Hulu had fully come into their own as original content producers. In fact, in the first season, Hulu was still more closely controlled by the broadcast networks, and you could stream current episodes of Hannibal within Hulu as a non-subscriber. Saying that, the show does very much feel something for today's Netflix audience. We did have an off-season streaming deal with Amazon, but again it was a little bit before it became the powerhouse and content destination it is today.

Yanes: While other adaptations of Thomas Harris's novels may be produced, what are you hoping the specific legacy of TV's *Hannibal* will be?

De Laurentiis: I think we did something very modern—and perhaps even a little unprecedented for a thriller series—in taking the cinematic universe of the books and movies, expanding and fleshing it out, and making it live as a thing unto itself, without preempting other movies or interpretations. A critic described *Hannibal* as "fanfic" and I don't think that's a fully fair characterization, because what we made was so consummately professional. However, there *is* something in the way drama organically grew from the nooks and crannies of the underlying material that is related to fan fiction. I'm thinking about the way it was both obsessive in its love for Thomas Harris' universe and characters, yet felt fully free to depart from it, as with Will being on the autism spectrum, the Wendigo, or the way elements from the book *Hannibal* were repurposed much earlier in the timeline.

For me, we succeeded in taking well-loved material and turning it into something fresh and compelling while honoring what has been done before. I was amazed—I've made the *Red Dragon* book three times now—and you can imagine the number of times you read and watch something in a script and editing stage—and as I watched it on the air every week, I still found the third season's telling of the story to be utterly riveting.

Yanes: As new entertainment technologies—VR for instance—become normalized to consumers and traditional media continues to evolve, what are possible future directions for Thomas Harris's characters outside of books?

De Laurentiis: We've had some meetings with VR companies, and Hannibal always comes up. I still haven't come up with or heard a take that makes me want to move on it yet, because I wouldn't want to put anything out there that disappointed the fans or sullied the legacy. And, in truth, even if we heard the perfect idea for how to structure a Hannibal VR experience, there still would be the major question of who is going to write it. Thomas Harris spends at least seven years on each of his books. Bryan Fuller is one of the great show-running writers working in television today, and he's running the new *Star Trek* show and *American Gods*. On the TV show, I saw how much talent and work goes into making this character work on the page. I'm sure those talents are out there, but at this point I don't know the world of game creator-writers enough to feel confident.

It's a Matter of Taste

Bourdieu and the Impeccably Mannered Anthropophagite

Sarah Cleary

Aesthetics and ethics are one.—Ludwig Wittgenstein (1929)

The body here transgresses its own limits: it swallows, devours, rends the world apart, is enriched and grows at the world's expense[…]. Man's encounters with the world in the act of eating is joyful, triumphant; he triumphs over the world, devours it without being devoured himself. The limits between man and the world are erased, to man's advantage.—Mikhail Bakhtin (1965)

From the darkness a silver cloche is wheeled into the room, reflecting the features of a dinner guests as it comes into focus. At the table sits Abel Gideon (Eddie Izzard) in rather glum expectation of his meal. While surveying the lavishly decorated tableaux before him of edible and inedible dishes, the camera pans momentarily below the table to the tightly bandaged stumps revealing a recent amputation to both legs just below the groin. With a smile and a flourish from the host, the cloche is removed and from underneath an extravagantly adorned roast is revealed. Smoked to perfection, glazed and served on a sugar cane claw, the meat of Dr. Abel Gideon is simply, "falling off the bone" (*Hannibal*, "Antipasto," S3E1).

This opening shoot for the third series of *Hannibal*, framed within flashback sequence in muted colors features quite an interesting exchange between host and guest, captor and captive, eater and eaten, as Hannibal Lecter (Mads Mikkelsen) encourages Abel to eat his own flesh. Picking up and toying with the meat, Abel announces quite nonchalantly "Cannibalism was standard practice among our ancestors. The missing link is only missing because we ate him." Smirking gently, Hannibal, simply rebuts, "It's not cannibalism, Abel. It's only cannibalism if we are equals" (S3E1). And in the world of Hannibal Lecter he is yet to meet his. But if he considers himself superior to mankind, *who* or should I say *what* is Dr Hannibal Lecter? Man or monster? Cannibal or connoisseur? Beast or *bon vivant*? Is it possible he is all of these? Or perhaps none? Locating my exploration of the cannibalistic practices of Hannibal Lecter at an intersection between the work of sociologist Pierre Bourdieu's treatise on taste, *Distinction. A Social Critique of the Judgement of Taste* (1979) and some of the most dominant theories on philosophical conceptions of cannibalism, I seek to explore the manner in which Hannibal, through his all-encompassing preference for superlative tastes, has attempted to use cannibalism as a means to distinguish himself from the majority of society and simultaneously transform that which is distasteful to him into the appropriation of something beautiful. Recalling Bourdieu's ultimate thesis that taste and class are inextricably linked, in *Locating Bourdieu* (2005), Deborah Reed Danahay notes that "taste operates [...] in the boundary maintenance between social classes, and acts as a system of classification" (Reed Danahay 2005, 111). When such a notion is applied to Hannibal, his empyreal taste preferences in food, music, art and literature are, by his own provocation of such a culturally superior and refined kind, they essentially remove Hannibal out of any system of classification, leaving him to inhabit a liminal space essentially surpassing mankind.

Manners Maketh the Man

Anthropologically speaking, there has been a wealth of research on the cannibal in its various guises. To that end, various taxonomies have sought to define the motivations for cannibalism in manifold ways. Citing the *Encyclopedia of Food and Culture* (2003) Tony Ullyatt writes how

the practice of human cannibalism is highly variable and can be defined in a number of ways: (1) Endocannibalism is the key consumption of deceased individuals who live within the group, such as kin and friends. (This pattern was common in New Guinea as an act of veneration.) (2) Exo-cannibalism is the consumption of outsiders as an act to gain strength or demonstrate power over the vanquished, who had usually been murdered. (3) Starvation or survival cannibalism is the consumption during actual or perceived starvation. (This is well documented in numerous historical sources.)(4) Gastronomic cannibalism is non-funerary, non-starvation cannibalism, that is, routine cannibalism for food. (This is not well documented). (5) Medicinal cannibalism is the consumption of human tissue such as blood, powered bone, or dried tissue for medicinal purposes. (6) Sadistic cannibalism is the killing and eating of individuals out of sadistic or psychopathological motives. (There is considerable evidence for this pattern of cannibalism.) [Ullyatt 2012, 13].

Seeking to define Hannibal "as a blend of excocannibalism and gastro-nomic cannibalism with a soupcon of sadistic cannibalism" (Ullyatt 2012, 13) in his paper "To Amuse the Mouth: Anthropophagy in Thomas Harris's Tetralogy of Hannibal Lecter Novels" (2012) heavy emphasis is placed on the psychological origins of Hannibal's pathological desire for flesh. A war-torn orphan of a murdered count, in *Hannibal Rising* (2006), a prequel to the trilogy, Hannibal as a young boy witnesses the murder and subsequent consumption of his sister Mischa, inevitably leaving quite an indelible mark upon him. Traumatised by his sister's death and emotionally "blunted" by the ravages of war (Harris 2006, 120) the young Lecter sets upon a "road to monstrous vengeance as he tracks down the Lithuanian cannibals one by one" (Ullyatt 2012, 11). In con-trast to this prequel, the *Hannibal* (2013–2015) series puts much more emphasis on Hannibal's present lifestyle as indicative of his behaviours. While his childhood is at least in the first two seasons inconsequential, the series instead places great import around his clothing, décor, deport-ment and ultimately and most significantly what and how he consumes. As this essay will argue, Hannibal's taste for human flesh is not so much the defining attribute of his pathology but rather a symptom of his sys-tematic classification of humanity as beneath him, with those who trans-gress his strict codes of propriety and comportment eligible for the label of esculent.

As a consummate and indeed cultured aesthete, who prides himself on impeccable manners and taste, Hannibal's lifestyle seeks to oppose notions of being an "antithesis to civilised humanity" and instead preconfigures him as its apex (Daniel 2006, 139). Such a perspective may be viewed in multiple ways however, and while this essay advocates a taste-based read-ing of Hannibal, other similar readings have promoted a view that Hanni-bal considers humanity as nothing short of livestock, to be culled by him at his discretion. In "What is so Bad about Eating People" (2016) Benjamin McCraw remarks how Hannibal treats humans as pieces of meat, reducible to parts necessary for the completion of recipes, a theory which is under-scored by Will Graham's comment that, "the Chesapeake Ripper," who we know to be Hannibal, sees his victims "not as people, not as prey. Pigs" ("Sorbet" S1 E7). Furthermore, such a point is compounded by the visual *mise en scene* of the Verger family farm and the inter-changeability between animals and humans underscored by the feeding of humans to pigs who are in turn ate by humans. Musing upon the famous dinner in "Sorbet," McCraw emphasises Hannibal's use of "Free Range Rude" in that individ-uals who have proven themselves impolite to the good doctor are in seri-ous danger of losing a heart, brain, or even a spleen. Subsequently, McCraw muses, Hannibal's view of humanity is thus:

Humans are social animals. But what of those animals among us who aren't social? The ones that either can't or won't abide the merest of social rules? Well, they just can't be all that human now, can they? The obstinately rude animals around us lack the social community needed to distinguish man from beast. By rejecting communal or social rules in their rudeness, they are rejecting *us* and rejecting the part that makes them like us. In the end, they just aren't human in any meaningful sense [McCraw 2016, 36].

Be that as it may, such a view is overly simplistic as it fails on two points.

In Hannibal's world there is no "us." There is only "him" and "others." Moreover, here exists no one simple justification for his killing. Often it is for food, but in certain cases it's to toy with the people. But unlike the cruel child who plays with insects, pinching their wings and quashing them under thumb, Hannibal's kills are never indiscriminate, no matter how random they may appear. One example is the murder of Sheldon Isley, the Baltimore city councilman who is gutted and "planted" in the very spot that he sold to develop for a car park having destroyed the flora and fauna of the area ("Futamono" S2E6). Cannibalising most of the organs, Hannibal choose to replace them with flowers, thus drawing attention to the ecological nature of his death while also reprimanding Isley post mortem. Consequently I would argue that in opposition to Will's assessment of people as pigs, in the eyes of Hannibal humanity is inextricably flawed and must be reproved by superiors who are in a position to dispense such punishments. In a similar vein against Will's assessment, Joseph Westfall (2016) observes how Hannibal's pathology is at its core motivated by something more than a desire to cannibalise or render human beings as swine. "Unlike an 'ordinary' psychopath, however," Westfall continues,

a vampire isn't motivated by traumas and psychotic urges. A vampire is motivated by hunger. And his hunger is coupled with an understanding of himself as inherently superior to the human beings upon whom he feeds. It is not quite that he thinks of people as pigs—contrary to Will Graham's assessment [...]—but, rather, that he thinks of himself as being as far above ordinary human beings as pigs are below them. [...] He kills and eats because he wants to, because he likes to, and because no objections anyone could provide—in the form or ordinary human law, or ordinary human morality—apply to one a great as he is [Westfall 2016, xvii].

However, while it is abundantly clear that Hannibal sees himself, to use the philosopher Fredric Nietzsche's term, as an *Übermensch* or overman, who deems himself to be intellectually and morally superior to the average human, it's not as clear why or where such motivations stem from. That is until notions of taste are invoked as determinants which dictate both his intellectual and moral perspective, especially in respect to the killing and eating of human beings. However apropos of any further investigation into the ties that bind cannibalism and taste together, if such a line of thought is to be explored, it's important to understand how taste can be perceived as a determinate within the context of social stratification, class distinction and subsequently, though rather controversially, cannibalism.

No Accounting for Taste

"Taste," mused Clarice in Thomas Harris' novel *Hannibal*, "Taste in all things was a constant between Dr. Lecter's lives in America and in Europe, between his life as a successful medical practitioner and fugitive monster. His face may have changed but his tastes did not, and he was not a man who denied himself" (Harris 1999, 225). Similarly invoking Hannibal's penchant for good taste as a method of tracking him in the series Alanna informs Mason Verger, "His taste is how you'll find him" ("Aperitivo" S3E4). But what exactly constitutes good taste? And why is it that Hannibal risks his freedom to enjoy such pleasures?

Seeking to explain taste empirically, the philosopher David Hume stated in his milestone essay "Of the Standard of Taste" (1775) that an individual who appreciates taste has a "strong sense, united to delicate sentiment, improved by practice, perfected by comparison and cleared of all prejudice, can alone entitle critics to this valuable character; and the joint verdict as such wherever they are to be found is the true standard of taste and beauty" (Cited in Taylor 2011, 287). Though describing Hannibal perfectly, such a summation only seeks to define the tasteful individual and doesn't seem to expand any knowledge as to why that individual is referenced this way. Deemed by Carl Wilson as the "aesthetic philosophy's other great-granddaddy" (Wilson 2014, 82) Immanuel Kant in *The Critique of Judgement* (1790) defined taste as the facility through which beauty was judged and as such is considered a "capacity for aesthetic consideration" (Allison 2001, 73). While the pursuit of aesthetic idealism will feature later in this essay as a major trait of Hannibal, problems arise when we consider the claims that for Kant, taste, the facility which judges that which is beautiful operates with a "*sensus communis*" or a common sense agreement with the populous, and is *a priori* in principle, or in other words "comes before" any experience of it.[1]

Firstly, applying common sense to matters of taste is not only "unconvincing from a contemporary, diversity oriented viewpoint" and as Wilson continues, doesn't sound at all "desirable" (Wilson 2014, 83). Moreover if there was *a priori* "*sensus communis,*" the entire debate would essentially be rendered moot due to the fact that we would all know in advance what constitutes good taste. Furthermore, as Lorne Falkenstein notes, "our concepts of sensible qualities cannot be formulated in advance of having the appropriate experience" (Falkenstein 2004, *158*). However we are still no closer to comprehending why a cannibal would strive towards such good taste. That is until we consider the claim put forward by anthropologist David Lewis-Williams regarding the use of cave-paintings by the Homo Sapiens.

In *The Mind in the Cave* (2002) Lewis Williams submits that cave-paintings, the primitive origins of Western Art forms, were a method of "social distinction" practiced by Homo Sapiens who he believed could think symbolically, and as a result produced carvings, etchings and paintings. The Neanderthals, on the other hand, were not advanced intellectually enough to render such images. Thus, he argues, "the development of higher-order consciousness made image-making possible though not inevitable" (Lewis Williams 2002). Moreover he adds this development of image-making (art), religion and social distinctions appeared in Western Europe: at that particular time and in that place, [...] image-making, religion and social discriminations were a "package deal." Accordingly "the people of the Upper Palaeolithic harnessed [...] altered states of consciousness to fashion their society," maintains Lewis-Williams "and used imagery in order to establish and 'define social relationships'" (Lewis Williams 2002) Thus cave paintings were used, John Carey (2006) furthers, to "register superiority to the Neanderthals" (Carey 2006, 117). And having registered their superiority as a species, "the new men could exterminate the Neanderthals with a clear conscience, as it seems probable they did" (Carey 2006, 117).

While Carey does concede that Lewis Williams' theories are not necessarily an empirical fact amongst the anthropological community (Carey 2006, 117) they do seek to compliment contemporary theories regarding modern social distinctions, namely those of French sociologist Pierre Bourdieu. Based on a survey of some 1200 French people taken in the 60's, Bourdieu submits that taste is essentially used to distinguish between the various social classes and "register one's distinction from those lower in the social order" (Carey, 2006, 118). As a result

> taste classifies, and it classifies the classifier. Social subjects, classified by their classifications, distinguish themselves by the distinctions they make, between the beautiful and the ugly, the distinguished and the vulgar, in which their position in the objective classifications is exposed or betrayed [Bourdieu 2007 (1979), 6].

In other words, the choices an individual makes essentially seek to define his or her class, and the class you belong to dictates your taste. "Choosing according to one's tastes," states Bourdieu, "is a matter of identifying goods that are objectively attuned to one's position and which 'go together' because they are situated in roughly equivalent positions in their respective spaces [...]" [Bourdieu 2007, 232].

While Bourdieu has been criticised in the past for his theories on taste being too static (Lupton 1996, 126), it's this very consistency with Hannibal's tastes that define him above all else. With so much emphasis placed on the more refined details of his expensive and upscale lifestyle, from the cut of his bespoke three piece plaid suits to the fact he brews his own beer in Cabernet Sauvignon barrels ("Oeuf," S1E4), Hannibal really is the sum of his parts carefully organised by a complex structure known within Bourdieu's language as the "habitus." Clarifying his point, Bourdieu continues that the habitus is

> a system of lasting, transposable dispositions, which integrating past experiences, functions at every moment as matrix of perceptions, appreciations and actions and makes possible the achievement of infinitely diversified tasks, thanks to analogical transformations of schemes permitting the solution of similarly shaped problems [Bourdieu 2007, 83].

Consequently, this essay argues that the habitus in which Hannibal exists determines his most unique of food choices. If good taste is, as Jennifer Tsien argues in *The Bad Taste of Others* (2012), "proof that [...] society has successfully emerged from the chaos, even if it is in danger of plunging back into it at any moment," the pursuit of good taste and eradication of bad becomes both a moral and social endeavour in order to put forward a presentation of social equanimity (Tsien 2012, 74). Moreover, utilising Bourdieu's interpretation of taste as "strategic tools" used as Wilson notes "to set ourselves apart from those whose social ranking is beneath us, and to take aim at the status we think we deserve. Taste is a means of distinguishing ourselves from others, the pursuit of *distinction*. And its end product is to perpetuate and reproduce the class structure" (Wilson 2014, 90/91). While Wilson perceives Bourdieu's use of taste as a "strategic tool," it's interesting to note Douglas E. Allens and Paul F. Aderson's more potent interpretation of taste, in the context on Bourdieu, as a "social weapon," that "defines and marks off the high from the low, the scared from the profane, and the 'legitimate' from the 'illegitimate' [...]" (Allen and Aderson 1994, 70). And it's precisely this notion of taste as a weapon, rather than a tool that seeks to advance any exploration Hannibal's cannibalism as a feature of his good taste.

Tea for Two and Two for Tea

Cannibalistic tendencies aside, Hannibal is the perfect host. At the dinner table he is flawless in both his presentation and execution of complicated recipes, and his knowledge of proper etiquette seems infinite. While at first glance it appears that Hannibal's actions are simply the product of a cultured individual elucidating on *haute cuisine* for the benefit of his less well-educated guests, a more insidious view perceives Hannibal's ameliorating himself socially while using these "social weapons" to predominate. For example, with each and every meal, Hannibal insists in not only informing his guests of what they are about to eat but he seeks to add tit bits of information regarding the origins of the recipe, often emphasising the unique procurement and cooking methods (while never explicitly mentioning its cost, as that would be a step too vulgar for the gourmand).

In one of the most telling exchanges between Hannibal and a dinner guest, he serves the delicacy of *Jamon Ibérico*. While being served by Hannibal, his guest Dr Sutcliffe comments upon how Hannibal still loves his "little rare treats," adding, "The more expensive and difficult they are to obtain, the better." To which Hannibal retorts, "It's a distinction that adds an expectation of quality" ("Buffet Froid" S1E10). While Hannibal does question the actual superiority in flavour of an Ibérico pig over any other "once fattened and slaughtered and air-cured," he does question whether "it simply [is] a matter of reputation preceding product?" To which Dr. Sutcliffe responds—"It's irrelevant. If the meat-eater thinks it's superior, then belief determines value." An agreeable response in the eyes of Hannibal he replies, "A case of psychology overriding neurology" ("Buffet Froid" S1E10). In a similar scene, Hannibal introduces Will to the "ortolan bunting." Amongst gourmands, Hannibal claims, "the ortolan bunting is considered a rare but debauched delicacy. A rite of passage, if you will. Preparation calls for the songbird to be drowned alive in Armagnac. It is then roasted and consumed whole in a single mouthful" ("Rôti" S2E11). Before taking the dish from Hannibal, Will is careful to point out that the ortolans are endangered. To which Hannibal quips, "Who amongst us is not?" ("Rôti" S2E11). In these scenes it is clear that Hannibal seeks to draw a marked distinction between himself and his guests by not only presenting such rarefied foods to his guest but most importantly knowing the correct procedure for their ingestion. From carving the *Jamon Ibérico* to drowning the bird in its inebriating cask, Hannibal's social weapons are poised and sharpened.

Pointing to the civilizing nature of table manners as representing "a desire to avoid animalistic nature of humanity," Deborah Lupton claims that the employment of such manners emphasized and asserted "the importance of culture over nature" (Lupton 1996, 22). Originating within the higher echelons of society, these rules of table manner and etiquette sought to re-affirm "class boundaries and maintain that hierarchy of power" (Bradley 2016, 17). "The *haute cuisine* that developed in France," continues Lupton, "during the seventeenth and eighteenth centuries was characterized by refined dishes and a complicated hierarchy of tastes as the apogee of 'good taste.' Constraints over eating were slowly internalized as practices of self-control and moderation, but were based on a concern about the appearance of delicacy and the avoidance of vulgarity rather than concerns about bodily size or physical health. Restraint was phrased as the ability to select and discriminate among foodstuffs and dishes guided by social proprieties" (Lupton 1996, 21).

As a result, "Only an expert on etiquette and a real gourmet could always infallibly decide what was good or bad, what was valuable and what was valueless" (Gronow 1993, 280). Reflecting a marked return to the ideals of etiquette implemented in seventeenth and eighteenth-century court life, Hannibal similarly reaches levels of aristocratic suavity in his crusade to distinguish himself from others through his cooking. Thus knowledge in this area quiet literally signified power as it contributed to a form of "cultural capital" which bestowed upon an individual "the knowledge and familiarity with cultural products which enabled a person to know how they work, what to say about them and how to appreciate them and elevate them." Thus showing them how to "how to consume" (Seymour 2004, 4). And if there is one thing that Hannibal is an expert on, it's eating.

More nuanced than perhaps his outward carriage, a further display of both Hannibal's high-class stature and dark wit, is his employment of an "ethical butcher" which of course is implied that Hannibal is one and the same. In "Oeuf" Hannibal serves Dr. Chilton lamb's tongue, or "Langue d'agneau en papillotes," "inspired by Auguste Escoffier" and "served with a sauce of duxelles and oyster mushrooms. Picked myself" ("Oeuf" S1E4). While this meal symbolically represents Hannibal's penchant for playing with his food and reminding those in his presence the consequences of loose tongues, the more literal reading here that Hannibal choose to tell his guest that he handpicked the oyster mushrooms is just as telling. In the same episode, Hannibal serves Jack Crawford, "a modified *boundin nour* from Ali-Bab's *Gastronomie Practique*." Upon being told the meat being served is rabbit, Jack quips, "He should've hopped faster" ("Oeuf" S1E4). While both men laugh, the scene is juxtaposed with another of a man running through a forest and falling before some unknown threat swoops. As Michael Fuchs (2015) notes, the inference here of course is that the "rabbit" in this case was the man we see stumbling in the forest (Fuchs 2015). Similar to the instance with the mushrooms, both these scenes point to the fact that Hannibal not only cooked the product, but personally gathered and hunted it, thus having the leisure time to dedicate to such a pursuit. While I would disagree with Fuch's claim that economic class plays a subordinate role in the series, especially considering how Hannibal uses class in order to distinguish himself from others, Fuchs does emphasize the issue of *choice* in either hunting or buying. "Lecter's desire to leisurely procure food communicates an important message: namely that as a member of the (upper) middle class, he may *decide* to procure food from the butcher or a farmers' market, but he may also *choose* to spend several hours hunting, as he has the economic power to do so" (Fuchs, 2015). Food becomes less and less about biological necessity and more about exercising his vast cultural capital, thus complimenting the habitus of which Hannibal's actions are essentially informed, though not dictated by. Furthermore, as Bourdieu states,

> the style of meal that people like to offer is in no doubt a very good indicator of the image they wish to give or avoid giving to others and, as such, it is the systematic expression of a system of factors including, in addition to the indicators of the position occupied in the economic and cultural hierarchies, economic trajectory, social trajectory and cultural trajectory [Bourdieu 2007, 79].

Thus, in presenting such foods to his guests, Hannibal is not only reveling in the glory of such (often tabooed) product, he is also "showing off a lifestyle" (Bourdieu, 79) which has been carefully crafted. Similarly advocating such sentiments, Erin Metz McDonnel (2016) writes how "there exists a demarcation between those who eat for sustenance, and those who eat for something more—whose class position put them beyond the exigencies of calories for cost-, thereby enabling expressions of alternative logics imbricated with cultural tastes" (Metz McDonnel 2016, 264). With Hannibal positioned quite literally within a class of his own, if we are to follow the edicts of Bourdieu concerning habitus and taste, Metz McDonnel's idea that the consumption of food for non-nutritional gain, as Hannibal does with such élan throughout the series, capacitates "alternative logics," we are left in a position to ponder the cogency of whether the consumption of human flesh is simply a matter of taste? Though such a statement may seem initially troubling, having utilized Bourdieu's taste-based structure in order to investigate whether it is possible to explore Hannibal's actions from the perspective of class stratification, this essay now attempts to expand its sociological remit and explore Hannibal's cannibalism philosophically as well as anthropologically.

No Accounting for Taste

Having offered quite an extensive account of the various theories pertaining to taste which developed throughout the seventeenth and eighteenth centuries, Cătălin Avramescu (2011) remarks that such theories equally marked a turning point in rhetoric concerning cannibalism during the same period. "The Theory of Taste," claims Avramescu,

> signals one of the most important transformations in the debate about cannibalism. Within its framework, the consumption of human flesh is explained not as a product of necessity or of the primary passions, but as a question of education, custom, preference, and in the last instance, "taste." Thus it connects with what was, during the eighteenth

century, the great ascension of "aesthetics." This term initially denotes the science of human sensory perception and only afterward comes to be understood as the study of the more elevated human pleasures. The truth revealed by aesthetics is one of limited validity, a certainty that is born at the surface of contact between the individual and the surrounding world. Considerations of "taste," a concept that designates a capacity for choice relatively independent of external criteria and based on immediate sensations, are therefore inseparable from the new attention towards the specific circumstances of the subject. The replacement of the explanations of natural philosophy with those extracted from the theory of subjective sensations made it possible to reinterpret anthropophagy from the perspective of the aesthetic categories [Avramescu 2011, 174].

Exploring cannibalism from such a perspective leads one to the conclusion that, in order to reassess cannibalism from the "perspective of aesthetic categories," typical moral responses of disgust and horror must make way for a move towards "moral relativism," which claims that all morality is essentially subjective at its core and no more than a certain perspective upon the world. "In the modern age," Avramescu continues, "moral relativism is the primary lens through which the custom of cannibalism is viewed" (Avramescu 2011, 175). However, such a view is in direct opposition to Benjamin McCraw's view that Lecter's morality subscribes to a form of *lex talionis*— or a "natural law" in which retributive justice seems to settle most scores (McCraw 2016, 36) For example in explaining the concept of how *lex talionis* works in the episode "Sorbet" where Hannibal is gathering his ingredients for a dinner party, we return to the scene where Hannibal's doctor Andrew Caldwell implies he may be lying about his health for insurance purposes. Of course taking this slight upon his credibility as exceptionally rude, Hannibal rules that Caldwell deserves nothing other than the chopping block. (McCraw 2016, 34). Having earlier in the essay referred to McCraw's argument that Hannibal sees the rude as pigs, "[a]nd there is nothing immoral, on Lecter's view [...] about killing pigs" (McCraw 2016, 37), this essay argues that such an argument offers a too simplistic reduction of Hannibal's social interactions and relationships. For example, how does that rationalize Hannibal's initial interest in consuming Will's heart and Bedelia's legs? Consequently, as argued earlier, it's not that Hannibal sees the rude as pigs, but having distinguished himself through his exceptional taste choices, the good doctor has positioned himself above humanity and as such practices a form of moral relativism which compliments his lifestyle.

In *Let's Talk About Love* (2014), Wilson maintains "[f]or Bourdieu, taste is always interested—In fact, self-interested—and those interests are *social*. His theories press the point that aesthetics are social all the way down, just a set of euphemisms for a starker system of inequality and competition [...]" (Wilson 2014, 89). If one advocates the view that morality is relative, individuals are then not obliged to ask whether an "act is good or evil in itself, but to what extent it is the result of norms accepted in a given society, a normal result of education" (Avramescu 2011, 175). While Hannibal is wholly aware that in normal society the killing, dismemberment and eating of human beings is considered taboo, if morality is indeed relative—as we are claiming for the sake of argument here—then according to Hannibal, those who transgress his specific code of aesthetics must be dealt with according to his own principles. For this reason, Bedelia is correct in her summation when she claims, "You no longer have ethical concerns, Hannibal. You have aesthetical ones." To which Hannibal retorts, "Ethics become aesthetics" ("Antipasto" E3S1). According to such principles, Hannibal perceives something to be good by virtue of the aesthetic pleasure he derives from it. Thus, the imposition of aesthetic judgment upon it replaces Hannibal's ethical concerns. From such a perspective, "We are urged [...] not to take aesthetic judgments for granted. We should understand them instead as forms of 'cultural capital,' both exertions of social power and exercise in self-description" (Hunter and Kaye 1997, 3).

Returning once again to Bourdieu, he posits the idea that taste is "first and foremost distastes, disgust provoked by horror or visceral intolerance of the tastes of others." Moreover, when one is faced with a scenario which is deemed distasteful, "[a]esthetic intolerance can be terribly violent. Aversion to different life-styles is perhaps one of the strongest barriers between the classes; class endogamy is evidence of this" (Bourdieu 2007, 56). Invoking quite a literal reading of violence to articulate the murdering of an individual transgressing the barriers of taste, may seem slightly exaggerated, yet it is the very basis of Hannibal's taste-based morality which essentially "allows" him to kill and dismember. Hence his claim in reference to Mason Verger; "Discourtesy is unspeakable ugly" ("Tome-wan" E2S12). The world is then experienced through his tastes. And as such when Hannibal does encounter something unspeakable ugly, he believes it to be his aesthetic duty to rectify such ugliness, rendering it beautiful.

For example in "Fromage" S1E8, while it's quite clear that Hannibal is uncomfortable with the level of intimacy between himself and his patient Franklin, one of the defining moments of their brief relationship is Franklin's vocalization of his Michael Jackson fantasy. Though subtle to the point of indiscernible, the moment Franklin mentions his adoration for such a pop icon of mass culture, a slight grimace creeps across Hannibal's face as if Franklin had physically produced a foul smell. Though under different circumstances, a further example of Hannibal's visible rebuke for that which is distaste is illustrated during the scene where Mason Verger stabs Hannibal's chair with his "pig knife" numerous times throughout a zealous diatribe. Though retaining his sangfroid, as evidenced by the slight twitches and grimaces, Hannibal is visibly perturbed by this action, thus compounding his distaste for humanity, especially that of the rude variety. However, instead of tolerating such aversions, Hannibal instead seeks to transform and refine both literally and figuratively that which he deems ugly into something palatable, through the art of cooking. In defense of such a claim, invoking the work of anthropologist Claude Levi-Strauss, Lupton argues how "cooked food is a cultural transformation of the raw, in which nature is transformed and delimited" (Lupton, 1996, 9). Lupton continues, "Cooking is a moral process, transforming raw matter from 'nature' into the state of 'culture,' and thereby taming and domesticating it" (Lupton, 1996, 2). However, in the case of Hannibal, while there are strong transformative motivations at play in the process of cooking human flesh, I would argue that the aspiration here isn't moral but aesthetic. While Hannibal has quite an ambivalent attitude to the humans around him when alive, once civilized through the transformative art of his cooking, inert flesh becomes imbued with beauty, and is thus absolved of past violations.

A perfect illustration is presented during the dinner scene between Hannibal and his fellow murdering enthusiast Tobias Budge. Having confessed their mutual intentions to kill one another, Tobias cagily looks down at his plate, to which Hannibal counters, "I didn't poison you Tobias. I wouldn't do that to the food" ("Fromage" S1E8). While Westfall (2016) suggests this is quite a humorous jest on the part of Hannibal, who is here inferring on the one hand that as potential food, Hannibal wouldn't poison Tobias and risk spoiling the meat. On the other hand, there is as Westfall remarks a comedic "incongruity" in that Hannibal is capable of murdering Tobias yet, stops short at defiling food he was prepared (Westfall 2016, 182). Though this is perhaps one of the many times throughout the series where Hannibal shares a joke with himself at the expense of his companions, there is also an argument to be made here that such a reaction from Hannibal is perfectly reasonable from somebody who considers the lives of others in terms of aesthetic and not ethical judgments.

Is It Still Cannibalism?

While reflecting upon the work of Bourdieu, this essay has explored the manner in which Hannibal has distinguished himself from a society that he considers superior through the execution of superlative tastes. However, in the pursuit of exploring the figure of Hannibal by virtue of his tastes, there remains one last important question. If he perceives himself to be so far removed from the majority of humanity, is the consummation of human flesh still cannibalism? Or from another perspective, if we consider the claim that Hannibal's efforts to transform and ultimately refine vulgar and "rude" members of society into what he considers beautiful art in the guise of exceptionally well executed food and if beauty is the highest attainable ideal, then is it possible to appraise his "monstrosity" as "as nothing less than sublime?" (Kovin 2012, 215).

Pausing for a moment to qualify Alexander V. Kovin's reflections upon the nature of the sublime in *Hannibal*, though the constant barrage of murder and death has the potential to repulse and horrify because of the hyperbolic manner in which they are mediated and ultimately rendered as works of art, one cannot help but be in awe of his actions, especially when one considers the manner in which he renders human flesh into works of art.[2] "Whatever is fitted in any sort to excite the ideas of pain and danger," stated the eighteenth century philosopher Edmund Burke, "that is to say, whatever is in any sort of terrible, or is conversant about terrible objects, or operates in a manner analogous to terror, is a source of the sublime, that is, it is productive of the strongest emotion which the mind is capable of feeling" (Burke 1757). Thus these overwhelming emotional states which Hannibal's actions provoke, allow a loftiness and depth to his art which runs parallel to reality. And while such actions are not meant to replicate reality nor adhere to its rubric, he nonetheless seeks to toy with reality as his muse, a sentiment which is profoundly visible in the first half of series three. So again we ask: Is it cannibalism? Well, perhaps the question is better explored with another question: Is it cannibalism or art? And if within Hannibal's universe the two are not mutually exclusive, has the question therefore become moot?

In the Image of God

Having spent a large part of this essay examining the manner in which Hannibal choose to distinguish himself, the question we now must return to is this; if he is superior to humanity, in what image does this superiority present itself as? "In Thomas Harris' model of cannibalism," Kozin claims,

> the terms that uphold the "monster-human" distinction are not "God" and "no-God," but "good" and "evil." An evil cannibal differs from the savage cannibal not because of his lack of control over the primordial pleasure drives but by his excess, hence, the superhuman abilities of Hannibal Lecter (strength, intellect, sense). Evil does not need to contain itself; it is the nature of evil to spill out [...] [Kozin 2012, 219].

Such a deduction becomes problematic when we reconsider how moral relativism works in place of an objective morality. Moreover, when notions of "good" become bound up in Kantian philosophy with the pursuit of beauty, the issue of whether Hannibal's cannibalism is "good or not," "evil or not evil," becomes much more complex. Therefore, in trying to situate Hannibal actions within moral aestheticism, perhaps it's best to dispense with binaries and towards a more omnipotent interpretation.

Throughout the course of the series and indeed throughout the books, many allusions are made concerning Hannibal's "godlike" presence. Indeed, at one point Alanna defines cannibalism as "act of dominance" ("Futamono" S2E6). Fitting the profile of the "Chesapeake Ripper" Alanna exclaims that Hannibal, "is attracted to medical and psychological fields because they offer power over man" ("Futamono" S2E6). And perhaps Alanna is correct in her summation. Hannibal indeed pulls the string as it were, continually manipulating those around him. However Hannibal is no God. He is above God. "He kills and eats because he wants to," continues Westfall, "because he likes to, and because no objections anyone could provide—in the form of ordinary human law or ordinary human morality—apply to one as great as he is" (Westfall 2016, xvii). However, such a statement could also be expanded outside the remit of "ordinary human morality." Never completely denying the presence of an omnipotent God, Hannibal instead draws attention to his ambivalence, an ambivalence which is on a par, if not more aloof, than his own. For example, in one session with Will, Hannibal broaches the subject of God's indiscriminate use of his powers against mankind. "Killing must feel good to God too," Hannibal explains. "He does it all the time. And are we not created in his image?" Essentially what Hannibal is claiming here is that God, or the theological possibility of an omnipotent deity, is no less bound to objective morality than he is. "God's terrific," Hannibal playfully adds, "He dropped a church roof on 34 of his followers last Wednesday night in Texas, while they sang a hymn." To which Will responds, "Did God feel good about that?" After a brief pause Hannibal answers, "He felt powerful" (Amuse-Bouche S1E2). In another session with Hannibal, Will asks Hannibal what god he prays to. Hannibal, without hesitation declares that he doesn't prey nor is he "bothered by any considerations of deity other than to recognise how my own modest actions pale beside those of God" ("Ko No Mono" S2E11). For Hannibal "God is beyond measure in wanton malice and matchless in his irony." So why should he behave any differently? Whatever acts Hannibal has committed in the pursuit of beauty or brutality, God has done worse. And consequently why should he then agonize or indeed repent over his actions?

Once again returning to the ortolan scene, Hannibal explains that so debauched is this meal, in an act of penitence for such a wanton display of sybaritism shrouds are worn over the diner's heads hiding their faces in shame from God. However neither fearful nor in awe of a deity whose ambivalence towards humanity pars with sadism, Hannibal shirks such customs, in defiance of this God and eats the ortolan whole, "bones and all" in a "stimulating reminder of our power over life and death" ("Ko No Mono" S2E11). Hence from a philosophical perspective, Hannibal is neither monstrous nor deiform in his actions. Having distinguished himself from the rest of humanity, Hannibal is not going to start looking upwards towards a higher power. While not a God, Hannibal is indifferent to Its moral authority and as such is redolent of the philosopher Fredric Nietzsche concept of *Übermensch,* or overman/superman, as pointed to earlier in the essay. "The overmen do not wait for God to approve their actions," explains Andrew Pavlich, "they act as they wish, without the regard for what the masses call morality" (Pavelich 2016, 126). And as a result, as Pavelich states, echoing the dominant thrust of this essay, "Hannibal's transgression is buried in this beauty. His cannibalism has transcended the taboo" (Pavelich, 139).

Conclusion

Throughout the course of this essay, the notion that Hannibal's quest to distinguish himself from the rest of humanity through his exceptional taste facilitates a wider reading of cannibalism devoid of the typical trappings of pathology. Instead the eating of human flesh is read as a "social weapon" which is used by Hannibal with great verve and panache, transforming that which he deemed an affront to his tastes into something beautiful and worthy of his consumption. Invoking the fundamental principles of Bourdieu's theories on the manner in which class can be seen to dictate taste and vice versa, this essay argues that Hannibal sought to remove himself entirely from such worldly concerns as morality, theology and ethics, and instead posited aesthetic concern as paramount. The pursuit of elegance and beauty is his entire modus vivendi, an approach which he believes compliments God's apathy as he manipulates, controls and ultimately destroys all around him. Therefore while we may still question from a philosophical perspective the efficiency of the claim that its only cannibalism if we are equals, we cannot escape the knowledge that while the bite of the cannibal kills, his taste is all consuming.

NOTES

1. Other examples of a priori concepts include time and space. Kant posits that such concepts existed before human experience of them, yet are vital for our understanding.
2. Case in point being the preparation of the limbs of both Gideon and Bedelia, the death and subsequent arrangement of the body of Sheldon Isley.

WORKS CITED

Allen, Douglas E. and Aderson, Paul F. 1994. "Consumption and Social Stratification: Bourdieu's Distinction." *Advances in Consumer Research,* 21, 70–74.
Allison, Henry E. 2001. *Kant's Theory of Taste: A Reading of the Critique of Aesthetic Judgment.* New York: Cambridge University Press.

Avramescu, Cătălin. 2011. *An Intellectual History of Cannibalism.* Translated by Alistair Ian. New Jersey: Princeton University.

Bourdieu, Pierre. 2007 (1979) *Distinction. A Social Critique of the Judgement of Taste.* Translated by Richard Nice. New York: Routledge.

Bradley, Peri. 2016. "Introduction." In *Food Media and the Contemporary Culture. The Edible Image,* edited by Peri Bradley, 1–8. Hampshire: Palgrave Macmillan.

Burke, Edmund. 1757. "Philosophical Enquiry into the Origin of Our Ideas of the Sublime and Beautiful." http://cnqzu.com/library/Philosophy/neoreaction/_extra%20authors/Burke,%20Edmund/Burke%20Edmund-Of%20the%20Sublime%20and%20Beautiful.pdf.

Carey, John. 2006. *What Good are the Arts?* London: Faber & Faber.

Daniel, Carolyn. 2006. *Voracious Children. Who Eats Whom in Children's Literature?* New York: Routledge.

Falkenstein, Lorne. 2004. *Kant's Intuitionism: A Commentary on the Transcendental Aesthetic.* Toronto: University of Toronto Press.

Fuchs, Michael. 2015. "Cooking with Hannibal: Food, Liminality and Monstrosity in Hannibal." In *European Journal of American Culture.* 34: 97–112.

Gronow, Jukka. 1993. "What is Good Taste'? *Social Science Information,* 32 (2), 279–301.

Harris, Thomas. 1999. *Hannibal.* London: William Heinemann Ltd.

Harris, Thomas. 2006. *Hannibal Rising.* London: William Heinemann Ltd.

Hume, D. 1910. Of the Standard of Taste. In C. W. Eliott (Ed.), *English Essays from Sir Philip Sidney to Macaulay.* P F Collier & Son, 215–236. (Original work published 1757) Retrieved from http://bradleymurray.ca.

Hunter, I.Q. and Kaye, Heidi. 1997. "Introduction." In *Trash Aesthetics: Popular Cultural and Its Audience,* edited by Deborah Cartmell, I.Q. Hunter, Heidi Kaye and Imelda Whelehan. London: Pluto Press.

Kozin, Alexander V. 2012. "The Man and the Cannibal. A Moral Perspective on Eating the Other." In *The Rhetoric of Food. Discourse, Materiality, and Power,* edited by Joshua J. Frye and Michael S. Bruner, 206–221. New York: Routledge.

Lewis Williams, David. 2002. *The Mind in the Cave. Consciousness and the Origins of Art.* London: Thames and Hudson. Kindle edition.

Lupton, Deborah .1996. *Food, the Body and the Self.* London: Sage Publications.

McCraw, Benjamin. 2016. "What Is So Bad About Eating People." In *Hannibal Lecter and Philosophy,* edited by Joseph Westfall, 31–42. Chicago: Open Court.

Metz McDonnel, Erin. 2016. "Food Porn: The Conspicuous Consumption of Food in the Age of Digital Reproduction." In *Food, Media and Contemporary Culture. The Edible Image* edited by Peri Bradley, 239–265. Hampshire: Palgrave Macmillan.

Pavelichm, Andrew. 2016. "The Light from Friendship." In *Hannibal Lecter and Philosophy,* edited by Joseph Westfall, 123–134. Chicago: Open Court.

Reed Danahay, Deborah. 2005. *Locating Bourdieu.* Indiana: Indiana University Press.

Seymour, Diane. 2004. "The social Construction of Taste." In *Culinary Taste. Consumer Behaviour in the International Restaurant Sector,* edited by Donald Sloan, 1–22. Burlington: Elsevier Butterwork-Heineman.

Taylor, Jacqueline. 2011. "Hume on Beauty and Virtue." In *A Companion to Hume,* edited by Elizabeth S. Radcliffe, 273–292. Oxford: Wiley Blackwell.

Tsien, Jennifer. 2012. *The Bad Taste of Others: Judging Literary Value in Eighteenth Century France.* Pennsylvania: University of Pennsylvania Press.

Ullyatt, Tony. 2012. "To Amuse the Mouth: Anthropophagy in Thomas Harris's Tetralogy of Hannibal Lecter Novels," *JLS/TLW* 28: 4–20.

Westfall, Joseph. 2016. "Hello, Dr Lector." In *Hannibal Lecter and Philosophy,* edited by Joseph Westfall, xi–xx. Chicago: Open Court.

Westfall, Joseph. 2016. "I, Cannibal." In *Hannibal Lecter and Philosophy,* edited by Joseph Westfall, 15–30. Chicago: Open Court.

Stranger in a Strange Land

Hannibal *as an Adaptation of Stoker's and Browning's* Dracula

SIMON BACON

This essay will argue that because of certain casting choices in *Hannibal*, the television series unknowingly bears a strong relation to Bram Stoker's *Dracula* and, consequently, talks less of the monster from within, as Thomas Harris' original novels did. Instead, it in fact manifests 21st-century American anxiety about invader/immigrants from the Old World who are consuming those in the New World.

The casting of Mads Mikkelsen as Hannibal Lecter was possibly one of the most dramatic changes in Bryan Fuller's television adaptation of Thomas Harris' novels. While the origin story of the epicurean serial killer remains largely unchanged, the perceived foreignness of the actor can be seen to dramatically change the positioning of the character of Hannibal within his chosen environment. Earlier cinematic adaptions chose actors that spoke perfect English/American to play the cannibal killer, allowing him to be totally at home amongst those he was about to dispatch, but Mikkelsen's strong Northern European accent marks him as "a stranger in a strange land," changing him from an internalized killer to one that comes from outside. In fact, Hannibal's construction as a mysterious outsider from the Old World who holds many in thrall around him, changes those around him to be like himself (Will Graham). Killing others is reminiscent of an earlier gothic narrative, that of *Dracula* by Bram Stoker, and indeed its first cinematic adaptation of the same name by Tod Browning from 1931.[1] The present essay will compare the two narratives to highlight points of similarity and give examples of how Hannibal embodies similar anxieties around transgressive behavior and outsiders in contemporary America, in the same ways that Dracula did for Victorian Britain. It will also investigate what the cannibal's ongoing elusiveness—Hannibal consistently evades

213

capture or escapes, while Dracula was eventually pursued and destroyed by the forces arrayed against him—says about twenty-first century America's relationship with its "monstrous" immigrants.

Making a Monster

Before identifying the correspondences between the two narratives of *Dracula* and *Hannibal* it is worth pointing out those between the two main characters first. In many ways Hannibal Lecter *is* Dracula, as Paul Meehan notes. "Like Dracula, Lecter is a predatory killer who murders casually and without a hint of conscience. Both physically consume parts of their victim's bodies and both have superhuman powers of mind that allow them to dominate their prey."[2] Similarly both come from Eastern Europe, though Lecter's passage from the Old World to the new sees him transform "from a World War II orphan into a cannibalistic avenger who hunts down and eats the Nazi collaborators responsible for his family's demise."[3]

From this point on, their respective paths diverge as Hannibal quite literally eats his way into the heart of America by becoming representative of America itself. This is due more to the cinematic adaptations of Harris' work, and in particular *Silence of the Lambs* (Demme: 1991). Tod Browning's *Dracula* achieved the same for Stoker's villain, though making him representative of all that America was not. Just as the choice of Bela Lugosi defined the look of vampires for generations to come, so too did Anthony Hopkins in the role of Hannibal, and received an Academy Award for his performance. Hopkins portrayed the killer "with courtly European manners, an unblinking crocodilian stare, an otherworldly distance, and a cultured British accent that occasionally slides into hisses calculated to induce pleasurable shudders in his America audience."[4] This was consolidated in its sequel, *Hannibal* (Scott: 2001), which builds on the cannibal's self-confidence and makes much of Lecter's "hisses, smiles, winks, and puns,"[5] but also consolidating his ability to show a surface of sophistication and respectability, beneath which beats the heart of a monster. In this aspect Lecter configures the true American monster, one which looks exactly the same whether they are wearing the mask or not.

Hopkins makes Lecter both foreign and familiar, feared and fated; as Simpson observes, Hannibal "*is* American in spirit as he speaks to one of our [America's] grandest, most cherished national narratives. He is the European immigrant that comes to America, the land of opportunity, to succeed in his chosen trade—which happens to be murder.... Lecter *is* America."[6] Interestingly, unlike Lugosi, Hopkins was not the first actor to play the serial killer—English actor Brian Cox played him "with soft spoken malevolence"[7] in Michael Mann's *Manhunter* (1986), an adaptation of Harris's *Red Dragon*. But his performance did not tap into the popular psyche in the way that Demme's villain did. Cox's performance preceded the sudden acceptance of serial killers as media superstars; as David Schmidt notes, there was a "sea change in public attitudes wrought by *The Silence of the Lambs*. After the success of that film, and after the initial controversy about it had died down, the fame of serial killers became an accepted part of the contemporary American cultural landscape."[8] Hopkins' portrayal of Lecter became the template for all later depictions of high functioning serial killer psychopaths, from Patrick Bateman in *American Psycho* (Harron: 2000) to Dexter Morgan in the television series *Dexter* (Lindsey: 2006–2013). This came into play even more strongly for anyone taking on the role of Hannibal after Hopkins, and indeed even portrayals of the killer as a young man, as happened in *Hannibal Rising* (Webber: 2007) where Gaspard Ulliel took on the role, suffer because of this. This makes the choice of Danish actor Mads Mikkelsen taking the role a daring one. Mikkelsen does not try to imitate Hopkins' version of Lecter at all, but wears his Old World credentials far more obviously. Hopkins' educated English could easily swoop into a Southern drawl when imitating Clarice Starling, but Mikkelsen is never anything other than Northern European. It is this that ties his interpretation to Stoker's, and indeed Lugosi's, vampire Count and correlates his unfolding story more than any of the earlier versions to that of one of the seminal gothic texts, *Dracula*.

Strangers Abroad

As mentioned above, there is already a correlation between the vampire Count and the serial killing cannibal, but Lecter from the television series resonates with very particular aspects of the Transylvanian aristocrat that hint at a stronger connection than just that of being the main protagonists of hugely popular novels about mass murders from Europe. Lecter from Fuller's series differs from earlier interpretations of the role in two main ways, his sound and his look—he sounds European (though not Lithuanian as Lecter actually is) and he dresses impeccably. Dracula in Browning's film is constructed similarly and like Hannibal both these aspects have an effect on their new surroundings. In relation to this, Abigail Burnham Bloom notes that Dracula "is a complete outsider.... He looks, dresses, and sounds different from everyone he meets.... He upsets the natural order of their lives [his victims] by mesmerizing them and seducing them; and consequently he puts the future of England at risk."[9] The latter part of this quote will be addressed further in the essay, but the voice is interesting as

Stoker posits that his vampire is doing all he can not to be recognized as a stranger as he longs to not only to go to London, the heart of the Empire, but to pass through its streets as though he belonged there, to be as English as those around him. At least that is what he says to Jonathan Harker who has visited him in his lair, though beneath that it is more a call for him to have power over those that would denigrate him:

> Well I know that, did I move and speak in your London, none there are who would not know me for a stranger. That is not enough for me. Here I am noble; I am boyar; the common people know me, and I am master. But a stranger in a strange land, he is no one; men know him not—and to know not is to care not for. I am content if I am like the rest, so that no man stops if he sees me, or pause in his speaking if he hear my words, to say, "Ha, ha! A stranger!" I have been so long master that I would be master still—or at least that none other should be master of me.[10]

Arguably Mikkelsen's Lecter would equally have similar problems with those who looked down on him, or treated him as anything other than their equal, if not their better. Lugosi's film version emphasizes the aristocrat's inability to fit into society. As Robert Spadoni says of Lugosi's vocal style in the film:

> From the "mellifluously thick Hungarian accent," to the "liquid, if sepulchral, voice," to the "stately, slightly over-ripe readings," to the "succulently foreign intonations," writers have suggested that Lugosi's voice constitutes within the film an entity with a material weight and density, one that even has its own smell and taste.[11]

While some have argued that this was Lugosi's normal speaking voice and nothing was affected for the film, he had lived in America for some years by 1931 and had also played the role on stage prior to making the film, so it is more likely that he chose this distinctive intonation for dramatic effect, and indeed to signify the sinister and outsider status of the vampire. Thus, Lugosi was so successful in this that such an Eastern European drawl signifies all things vampiric up to this day as J. Gordon Melton observes, "The film [*Dracula*] would influence all vampire films that came after it, and Lugosi would be the standard against which all later vampires were judged."[12]

Mikkelsen as Hannibal Lecter produces something very similar to Lugosi in reimagining the nature of evil through giving it substance through using his own speaking voice. As noted by Kevin Fitzpatrick, he purposely chooses to not follow what had gone before. "A naturally Danish actor, Mikkelsen understandably makes no attempt to ape the classic performance of Hopkins, crafting a civilized, cultured (and thickly-accented) beast all his own."[13] This was a conscious decision of the director:

> "With Anthony Hopkins, his accent was very hard to pin down or pinpoint his origin, but for me, casting a foreign actor was the way to go because Hannibal is foreign," Fuller told Indiewire. "He is other. He's an exotic. That was something that Mads brought to the character, with this erudite quality of experience and worldliness."[14]

This use of an outsider's voice links Lecter from the series directly to Browning's Dracula and is reinforced by its sparsity and precision. This was true of Lugosi and also of Mikkelsen, who says of his own performance, "I try to eliminate words as much as possible. There is a tendency to underestimate the power of what we can do without words. Sometimes you can make a scene even more powerful and precise without dialogue."[15] This scant use of dialogue and a focus on the face of the actor also formed a large part of Lugosi's presence on film with close ups of his face and extra lighting for his eyes. Browning "even used spot lighting to highlight his eyes and eye makeup. Lugosi's performance brought Bram Stoker's accent on Dracula's gaze in the 1897 novel into a powerful cultural image."[16] Bryan Fuller achieves something of the same effect as "his cinematographers uses Mikkelsen's frankly amazing face to great effect, with chiaroscuro somehow showing both his placid mask and the beast underneath. Even when he's not doing much—cooking, staring, delivering speeches on God and amorality—he is terrifying."[17]

The sound of Dracula is then reinforced by his look, which bears little relation to Stoker's vision of the vampire, and who barely mentions his clothes and never talks of a cape or evening dress. In fact, this came from the stage show where the distinctive costume worn throughout the play meant less clothing changes, allowed the vampire to be easily identified visually as well as allowing for it to mysteriously disappear (the high collared cape hiding the actor from the audience when he turned his back and banished down a trapdoor on stage). In Browning's film it achieved something of the same, and as Auerbach notes, Lugosi "is the first to separate himself by his costumes and mannerisms from the actors who encompass him,"[18] while also harking back to earlier cinematic villains/heart throbs such as Lon Chaney as the Phantom of the Opera and Rudolph Valentino. Consequently, many critics have noted his "impeccable evening dress"[19] and "Lugosi's sleek, handsome look."[20] These aspects of Browning's *Dracula*, the almost hyper-sophistication of dress and the foreignness of his voice, both mimic and critique the power structures in the society within which he insinuates himself, even more so when that same society is powerless to stop him taking victims. Rogers notes these qualities "undermined the authority of a hierarchical, class-structured society that empowered propertied men above all groups,"[21] and it is this more than anything that threatened British Victorian society just as Lecter is seen to undermine the elite and the mighty of contemporary America. Mikkelsen's Lecter dresses immaculately, and has been featured in many men's fashion magazines such as *Esquire*[22] and *Gentlemen's Gazette*,[23] and as London McGuire notes "he's a well-groomed, flawlessly-dressed, calculating genius who just so happens to have a peculiar appetite."[24] McGuire goes into greater detail:

Hannibal accompanies three-piece suits with wide, Windsor-knotted ties. It's the power suit, but not the clumsy, cumbersome power suit that moguls like Trump wear. Instead, it's a hybridization of the modern fit with bygone patterns and hues, peaked lapels that harken back to more sophisticated, refined days—when power was earned less by yelling and more by speaking eloquently, and when men didn't take shortcuts by exposing their sockless ankles.[25]

But even McGuire observes the way that it simultaneously fits in yet also marks him out as oddly other. "For how complete and formulated his entire style is, there's also something just slightly off."[26] Mikkelsen's Lecter, like Lugosi's Dracula before him, enacts what Homi Bhabba calls mimicry,[27] where the surface qualities of a dominant culture, the superficial details that mark out its power, are copied by those who are subordinate but in a way that reveals that power for what it truly is—Lecter does exactly this, taking the supreme examples of what a culture believes marks it out as civilized, sophisticated and superior, and shows them as the camouflage of the monstrous, barbarous and cannibalistic. Consequently, the more general similarities between the two serial killers, Dracula and Hannibal Lecter, that already existed have become more focused and specific in Bryan Fuller's television series, particularly in the choice of Mikkelsen as the cultured and consummately coutured cannibal. These individual correspondences reinforce the similarities between the two narratives from which each of the killers comes, though comparing a single novel/film to a television series that is comprised of 39 episodes (over 27 hours of story development) will necessarily not be a precise science.

Correspondences, Collusions and Coincidences

As mentioned above, the more obvious disparities between the two narratives prohibits a straightforward like-for-like comparison, so a cautious study highlighting more general similarities leading to a focused examination of points of particular correspondence would possibly be a better approach.

In a very general sense, *Dracula* tells the story of an Eastern European traveling West to the heart of the dominant empire of the times, wanting to blend in so that he can pursue his own nefarious ends without being recognized. In the film, he ingratiates himself into high society, meets the circle of Dr. Seward while at the opera, and begins his reign of terror. However, one of the group in particular fascinates him in that she is something like himself, and rather than kill her he attempts to make her join him in his endeavor. However, he is thwarted in this by the intervention of a man of similar character, intellect and mental strength to himself, and who saves the woman and who causes the outsider to return home. This is an extremely loose interpretation of the plot of Stoker's novel, but it immediately begins to resonate with *Hannibal* and certain characters and situations within it.

Of course *Hannibal* begins with Lecter already accepted into American society, but the prequel film *Hannibal Rising* (mentioned above) shows his journey from Eastern Europe, Lithuania, and traveling to America, and the major world power after the Second World War. Curiously, Stoker himself identified America as a rival to the then waning British Empire. He has Dr. Seward describe the American member of the group as follows: "If America can go on breeding men like that, she will be a power in the world indeed."[28] Equally, the series does not portray the latter parts of Lecter's narrative when he is captured and then escapes to Europe, and so the correlation between the two narratives will necessarily focus on the scenes when Dracula's and Hannibal's true natures/intent were still undiscovered. Both characters were readily accepted into high/wealthy class society— Dracula, as a foreign aristocrat, is initially accepted by the group of socialites around Mina Seward (Harker in the book), her father, Dr. John Seward, her fiancé John Harker, and her friend Lucy Weston.[29] In fact, the vampire insinuates himself so successfully into their group in the film that the two girls have the following conversation after meeting him:

> LUCY: [doing an impression of Dracula] It reminds me of the broken battlements of my own castle in Transylvania.
> [chuckles]
> MINA: Oh, Lucy, you're so romantic!
> LUCY: Laugh all you like. I think he's fascinating.
> MINA: Oh, I suppose he's all right. But give me someone a little more normal.
> LUCY: Like John?
> MINA: Yes, dear, like John.
> LUCY: [dreamily] Castle…. Dracula…. Transylvania!
> MINA: Well, Countess! I'll leave you to your count and his ruined abbey!
> [both giggle]
> MINA: Good night, Lucy.
> LUCY: Good night, dear.[30]

Much the same could be said about Hannibal, who is found equally fascinating but not quite "normal" by many characters who become enthralled by him. Like *Dracula*, when the series begins, we see Lecter fully integrated into high society (not quite aristocracy, but almost the American equivalent). He is a practicing psychiatrist—somewhat likening him to Dr. Seward as a professional—which gives him social and financial access to almost any part of society to which he wishes to enter. He is a patron of the arts, a culinary expert who holds lavish gourmet soirees in his apartment (Dracula prefers his food more simply presented) and dresses immaculately, obviously using the most expensive tailors—he is Count Dracula but with more patience, and a longer game plan. Both men have already begun their murderous plans. In the film Dracula has already killed a flower girl in London and is about to begin his nightly visits to extract blood from Lucy; Hannibal has already begun his reign of murder under the guise of the Chesapeake Ripper.

After these initial periods of acceptance in their respective narratives, the two characters' paths diverge slightly in that upon the arrival of Professor Van Helsing in *Dracula*, it is quickly ascertained that they are dealing with a vampire, and who it might be, while in *Hannibal*, Lecter is actually called in by the FBI to assist in the investigation concerning the Chesapeake Ripper. However, the major relationships established in each situation oddly mirror the other. The first of these is between Dracula and Professor Van Helsing, and Hannibal and Jack Crawford.

Count Dracula and Abraham Van Helsing are configured as opposites with the professor of the dark arts being seen as the dark lord's nemesis, and not unlike the relationship established by Conan Doyle four years earlier in 1893 between his fictional detective Sherlock Holmes and his nefarious enemy Professor Moriarty in *The Final Problem*.[31] However, the notion of the two opposing characters being doppelgängers in some way is even stronger in Stoker's novel, with the final designation of which one is good and which one is evil largely down to their respective presentations to the audience, both the group of vampire hunters and the readers of the novel. Dracula is purposely marked out as the Other, but, as Burnham Bloom notes, in regard to Browning's film

> Van Helsing is different as well. When first shown on the screen, the camera focuses on his eyes, just as it had Dracula's eyes when he first appeared. Like Dracula, Van Helsing, is foreign and speaks English with an accent. By exaggerating the similarities between Dracula and Van Helsing, they become worthy opponents. The connection between Van Helsing and Dracula makes them alter egos or doubles who engage in battle against each other.[32]

Erik Butler takes this further and draws on the larger amount of written evidence in Stoker's novel which confirms how similar they are:

> Van Helsing resembles the Count … [he] can say, do, command whatever he wants…. Like Dracula (who calls Harker his "friend" back in Transylvania) Van Helsing seems unduly concerned with underlining the amicable relations between himself and others (especially "friend John"[Seward]) … his intimate relationship to Seward goes back to a mysterious incident that looks like a quasi-vampiric encounter ("that time when you such from my wound…"). Indeed, the younger man refers to the foreigner as his "master" (154)—the same term that Renfield employs when speaking of the Count.[33]

Carol Senf also sees this in terms of creating an ambiguity between human and monster, good and evil in the story[34]—Van Helsing is immediately indicated as good since he is human, while Dracula cannot be considered as such as he is a monster, yet their similarities reveal the Professor to exhibit as many monstrous qualities as the vampire. The two father figures here vie for control over their respective children, there will only be one master and, as mentioned above, Dracula does not share that privilege with anyone. This ties directly into the relationship between Hannibal Lecter and Jack Crawford, and constructs a battle of wills between the two men to see who will control not just what the audience thinks but also the lives of those around them, in particular Will Graham.

Jack Crawford is the Head of the Behavioral Unit of the FBI and as such is in charge of the forces arrayed against the Chesapeake Ripper, aka Lecter, not unlike Van Helsing's position against Dracula. As with Van Helsing, the relationship between the two foes is intense, and as with Stoker's professor, the forces of "good" are more concentrated on those of "evil" than the other way round. As Alana Bloom in the television series notes of her "master," "Jack's obsessed with the Chesapeake Ripper and he's grooming Will to catch him."[35]

Of course, Jack has no idea that the killer he is after is in his midst, whereas Van Helsing ascertains who he is fighting quite quickly, though Browning's film shows more interplay between the two characters and the audience sees them engaging in polite conversation before the Professor unveils his definitive proof—Dracula has no reflection in the mirror in the top of a cigarette box. Series one of *Hannibal* then works as something of an extended version of this opening encounter between the Professor and the Count, where Jack and Lecter begin to grasp the nature of who they are sparring with. Jack does much of this blind, and so even though he is using various agents, Alana Bloom and Will Graham, to pursue his prey the identity of his focus is still unknown—not dissimilar to Dracula's invisibility during much of the pursuit of him by the crew of light. As Butler notes, "the Count is a shape-shifting creature who materializes only when closing in for the kill; his potential for destruction is based on his ability to conceal his whereabouts and activities until it is time to strike."[36] *Hannibal's* stretching of this opening encounter between good and evil allows Fuller to explore not only the opening shots between the two "masters" but extend it to the breaking point, as if the moment of (self) recognition between the sworn enemies lasted forever—well, most of the first two series—and it was these events that followed which were caught in that flash of instant dislike as their eyes met. To this end, Hannibal is then hired by Jack to assess and help control the mental stability of Will Graham, and the two masters then become locked in a battle over who controls the special investigator.

In many ways the struggle over the heart and mind of Will Graham is more important to Crawford than that of his own wife, who Hannibal sees on a professional basis in regard to her potentially terminal cancer. Yet Crawford's use of Graham always smacks of the intentional—as is seen in the character's use of Clarice Starling in *The Silence of the Lambs*—and there is the lingering sense of the young investigator being used as bait, an ambivalence which is nominated in Crawford's exchange with Lecter's former mentor Dr. Bedelia Du Maurier:

> **JACK:** How far do you think Doctor Lecter would go in his therapy to treating a patient a patient? Specifically, Will Graham.
> **MAURIER:** Hannibal refers to Will Graham more as a friend than a patient.
> **JACK:** How far do you think he'll go in treating a friend?[37]

Graham, on some level, is used by both masters—Lecter sees him as a way of showing his dominance over Crawford and the normative society he protects and represents, but Jack sees him as a way into defining and capturing Hannibal's true identity. This is something which Jack finally does at the end of season two when he tries to arrest Lecter, and which marks the moment, in relation to Dracula, when Van Helsing and the Count have finally broken their eye contact and know the other for what they truly are:

> **CRAWFORD:** I want to thank you, Dr. Lecter, for your friendship.
> **LECTER:** The most beautiful quality of a true friendship is to understand and be understood with absolute clarity.
> **CRAWFORD:** Then this is the clearest moment of our friendship.[38]

As in *Dracula*, the moment of mutual recognition between foes does not mark the end of the battle between them, but marks the moment when others are more openly used/controlled to score points against the other. In *Hannibal* this is most clearly seen in the struggle for the control of Graham, whose status in the narrative becomes increasingly like that of Mina Harker in Stoker's novel.

Many later versions of *Dracula* make Mina the true focus of the unfolding narrative—Francis Ford Coppola's *Bram Stoker's Dracula* (1994) does this by showing her as the reincarnated wife of the Count and the main motivation for nearly all the vampire's subsequent actions. Stoker's novel portrays her slightly differently and in a way that configures her as something not so unlike the vampire itself. Writers such as Senf posit Mina as representing the figure of the New Woman in Stoker's text—a name given to a woman who strove for equality with men through attending universities and seeking employment in professional jobs, both formerly the sole reserve of men. This leaves her both as a figure of British womanhood, and so to be cherished, but equally as one who exhibits a worrying amount of autonomy and needs to be controlled. This need to contain Mina constructs her as something foreign or different to the company of men that comprise the vampire's foes, or as Senf observes "like Dracula, she is an outsider, an alien distrusted by the dominant group."[39] Part of this distrust is configured by the knowledge she collates throughout the narrative facilitated by her secretarial skills, which see her as the conduit of all the information in the story, and of the various devices through which it is transmitted: the telegraph, stenograph, photograph, etc. As such, even more than Van Helsing, she has a complete picture of the vampire killer's undead foe, and one that is subsequently both enhanced and compromised by her special bond with Dracula. This comes about appropriately through a "shared meal" where the Count and Mina literally consume parts of each other:

> his right hand gripped her by the back of the neck, forcing her face down on his bosom. Her white nightdress was smeared with blood, and a thin stream trickled down the man's bare breast, which was shown by his torn-open dress. The attitude of the two had a terrible resemblance to a child forcing a kitten's nose into a saucer of milk to compel it to drink.[40]

Mina herself denies any complicity in her intimate meeting with the Count, only ever talking about the event and its aftermath in negative terms, but it creates an almost unbreakable link between the two. As Van Helsing notes:

> If it be that she can, by our hypnotic trance, tell what the Count see and hear, is it not more true that he who have hypnotize her first, and who have drink of her very blood and make her drink of his, should, if he will, compel her mind to disclose to him that which she know?[41]

Afterwards, Mina increasingly starts to take on vampiric features, with her eyes hardening and her teeth becoming sharper. The novel only really talks about these changes in Mina in terms of an outside influence forcing an unwanted metamorphosis upon the young woman, but it can equally be read as a catalyst for a release of Mrs. Harker's inner nature so that she might become her true self. In this way her interactions with the vampire allow her to become increasingly different but also increasingly herself, both constructions being oppositional to the dominant patriarchal society within which she lives. Consequently, she is positioned between the two masters, Dracula and Van Helsing, being part vampire but also part of the hunters trying to capture him. She is equally used by both sides to try and confound, undo and destroy the Other—Van Helsing hypnotizes her to ascertain the whereabouts of the vampire and Dracula uses her to listen into the plans of the hunters. These are all aspects and features of Will Graham and his intimate relationships with Hannibal Lecter and Jack Crawford.

Graham's relationship with Crawford is interesting for, as mentioned above, it can be viewed as both a friendship and a manipulative use of a susceptible victim to catch Lecter. Not unlike Van Helsing, superficially he seems almost too effusive in his acts of care, while a closer look at what he says infers something else. Early on in the first series Crawford confesses to a colleague that he will send his "friend" Graham into situations that he can not necessarily control: "Alana, I wouldn't put him out there if I didn't think I could cover him. [pause] All right, if I didn't think I could cover him 80%."[42] And in the next episode prepares his "lamb" to go into the lion's den:

> GRAHAM: Therapy doesn't work on me.
> CRAWFORD: Therapy doesn't work on you because you won't let it.
> GRAHAM: And because I know all the tricks.
> CRAWFORD: Well, perhaps you need to un-learn some tricks. Why not have a conversation with Hannibal? He was there. He knows what you went through. Come on, Will. I need my beauty sleep![43]

Crawford's feigned concern for Will gets the young investigator into the presence of Hannibal, and almost immediately the fight for control of his mind begins:

> GRAHAM: Jack thinks I need therapy.
> LECTER: What you need is a way out of dark places when Jack sends you there.
> GRAHAM: Last time he sent me to a dark place I brought something back.[44]

But Jack's plan appears to go awry with Hannibal pointing out to Will just how little concern for his "friend's" health is motivating his master at the FBI, also intimating that if Crawford is using Graham, then Lecter is courting him.

> GRAHAM: Jack hasn't abandoned me.
> LECTER: Not in discernible way. Perhaps the same way gods abandon their creations. You say he hasn't abandoned you, but at the same time wandering around Wolf Trap in the middle of the night.
> GRAHAM: Well this should be interesting. Please, doctor, proceed.
> LECTER: Jack gave you his word he would protect your head space, yet he leaves you to your mental devices.
> GRAHAM: You trying to alienate me from Jack Crawford?[45]

Once again the difference between a novel/single film and a television series come into play and the battle for Will's mind becomes a greatly elongated version of that for Mina's. Unlike Dracula though, Hannibal does not require the sharing of blood to bond with his prey, but rather a sharing of the mind so that the two become joined in some way, as he says to Will, "You catch these killers by getting into their heads, but you also allow them into your own."[46] For Hannibal then, this communion of minds does not happen in one cathartic scene as in Stoker where the vampire "forces" Mina to drink his blood, while her husband sleeps helplessly in the bed next to them. It occurs over a period of time so that Will does not fully realize what is going on, though this still happens under the helpless gaze of

Jack Crawford. As with Mina, there is some ambiguity between how much the changes that begin to occur in Will are ones forced upon him or are rather a release of his own repressed urges. And while those around the young investigator see him as increasingly unstable, or even hysterical—a term/condition often given feminine or feminizing connotations from its original psychoanalytic definitions—Hannibal sees it as an act of liberation, releasing the "real" person within, as seen from this following dialogue from the end of the first series:

> LECTER: Perhaps you didn't come here looking for a killer. Perhaps you came here to find yourself. You killed a man in this very room.
> GRAHAM: I stared at Hobbs and the space opposite me assumed the shape of a man filled with dark and swarming flies. And then I scattered them.
> LECTER: At a time when other men fear their isolation, yours has become understandable to you. You are alone because you are unique.
> GRAHAM: I'm as alone as you are.
> LECTER: If you followed the urges you kept down for so long, cultivated them as the inspirations they are, you would have become someone other than yourself.
> GRAHAM: I know who I am. I'm not so sure I know who you are anymore.[47]

Interestingly, and unlike Mina in *Dracula*, the forces of good arrayed around Crawford do not separate Will from his dark master and the unfolding narrative between them becomes a visible representation of the inner, unseen turmoil that the English woman went through in Stoker's novel. However, Graham is not necessarily a totally helpless or willing victim to Hannibal's design, and as with Mina, he has moments of lucidity and resistance to what is happening to him—something, arguably, Crawford knew he would do—as seen at the start of series two when he says to Lecter: "What you did to me is in my head, and I will find it. I'm going to remember, Dr. Lecter, and when I do, there will be a reckoning."[48] However, this reckoning is a long time coming, and as with Mina, Graham has to almost lose himself to regain something of the self he once was. Rather aptly it is when he kills someone with Hannibal, when he is most like him, that he strikes:

> LECTER: This is all I ever wanted for you, Will. For both of us.
> GRAHAM: It's beautiful.
> [They embrace, and Will throws them both off the cliff][49]

The series finishes on this note, leaving an ending full of unease and portents, just as Stoker's tale ends with the shadow of the vampire's earlier warning hanging in the air:

> You think to baffle me, you—with your pale faces all in a row, like sheep in a butcher's. You shall be sorry yet, each one of you! You think you have left me without a place to rest; but I have more. My revenge is just begun! I spread it over centuries, and time is on my side.[50]

So too does *Hannibal*. The insatiable appetite of the enemy within can never be stopped and mere physical death will never contain or limit him.

The End?

The correlations between Count Dracula and Hannibal Lecter are many, and that has only been reinforced by Bryan Fuller's television adaptation of Harris' novel and its casting of Mads Mikkelsen in the lead role. What the series has also done, however, is also strengthen the ties between Stoker's and Harris' narratives. While there are many obvious differences shown in Fuller's version—the trips to and from Transylvania/Eastern Europe that bookend the action in *Dracula* are left out and the inclusion of other killers and the far higher body count in *Hannibal*—the similarities are fundamental and integral parts of impetuous and final meaning of each story. Both stories are based on the battle of wills between the forces of good and evil with their fight for control over the body and mind of the innocent victim/sacrificial lamb as final justification for their respective causes—if the victim becomes a predator then the predator is not evil just a force for personal autonomy and the rights of the individual. Ultimately then, both narratives look toward the ambiguity of the categories of good and evil, right and wrong. Yet while Stoker only hints at it in the figure of the vampire, Fuller makes it explicit in his depiction of Hannibal. Much of this is tied up in each author's, director's, creator's use of otherness within their works and how it is deemed to be threatening, monstrous, or a critique of the home society.

In Stoker's late Victorian tale, as Tabish Khair observes, Count Dracula "is a member of a separate (aristocratic) 'race' set on consuming innocent victims … and establishing an empire within the British Empire."[51] This reverse colonialism is further seen in the vampire's racial threat that is configured in his "diabolical attributes" (Ibid) that mark him as mainly Jewish but with an equal otherness that was attributed to black or Asian groups[52] and even anti–Christian.[53] However, as Raphaella Delores Gomez notes, this Otherness within Dracula is created by the forces of Imperialism—i.e., Van Helsing—without any, or very little, reference to the voice of the one being othered. Browning's *Dracula* utilizes and changes this, and while Stoker's narrative spoke of the fear of those obviously demarcated as outsiders, Hollywood wanted to focus that more closely on Europe and to encourage American isolationism—there were already large amounts of European immigrants entering America by the 1930s and indeed Bela Lugosi himself was one of those fleeing his home nation of Hungary. Lugosi's vampire is distinctly old-world European trying to suck the life out of the new, young and vibrant world, i.e., America. His voice marks him out as clearly other, as does his dress, but there is something about his exoticism that attracts those of impressionable mind. Hannibal takes on much of this signification and his voice and dress clearly mark him out as different, yet unlike Dracula, he is not a creature from the past but one firmly placed in the future. As such his costume is not so much anachronistic or out of place, but achingly stylish and impeccably tailored—like the Count, he is a consummate consumer who spends his undead money/capital so that he can purchase more. This shifts Mikkelsen's Lecter from just the odd looking/sounding outsider to one who camouflages and mimics the excess of the society within which he has become embedded. Lugosi in Browning's film might attend the opera—where oddly his dress blends in perfectly—but Mikkelsen's Lecter is on first name terms with the directors of the orchestra—and subsequently feeds them the organs of a particularly bad flutist at a dinner party.

Hannibal's otherness then speaks both of the inherent barbarism of the society within which he lives but also of the monster hiding behind the mask of respectability and normalcy. Christian iconography has nothing of the effect upon him that it does on Dracula, but he speaks of a dark religious other that is waiting to strike at the heart of American society, an accepted other that is a rotten apple and, as seen in his relationship with Will, one which will infect others. Hannibal's links to Stoker's *Dracula* then becomes an all too clear reminder that in the twenty-first century the threat of the outsider no longer come from beyond the borders but from the next door neighbor, or work colleague, or even more worrying, from those in positions of power over us.

NOTES

1. It is worth noting that the novel and the film diverge quite significantly at certain points as the film is based on the Balderston-Deane play of the novel rather than the novel itself. Consequently, Renfield and not Jonathan Harker, is shown going to Transylvania to facilitate the vampire's journey to England, and characters such as Lucy Westenra and Dr. Seward have their significance greatly changed or reduced, while Lord Godalming and Quincey Morris completely disappear. However, the significance and personality traits utilized here for character studies of Van Helsing and Mina are largely consistent and/or supportive between the texts.

2. Paul Meehan, *The Vampire in Science Fiction Film and Literature* (Jefferson, NC: McFarland, 2014), 252. It is worth noting that while Meehan points to the similarities between the characters of Stoker's Count Dracula and Harris' Hannibal Lecter it is only in a very general way.

3. Ian Olney, *Euro Horror: Classic European Horror Cinema in Contemporary American Culture* (Indianapolis: Indiana University Press, 2013), 193.

4. Phillip L. Simpson, "Lecter for President…Or, Why We Worship Serial Killers," Bob Batchelor (ed.) *Cult Pop Culture: How the Fringe Became Mainstream, Volume 1: Film and Television* (Santa Barbara: Praeger, 2012), 91.

5. *Ibid.*, 92.

6. *Ibid.*, 95.

7. Keith Uhlich, "Hannibal: The TV show that went too far," *BBC Culture*, last modified September 28, 2015. http://www.bbc.com/culture/story/20150828-hannibal-the-tv-show-that-went-too-far.

8. David Schmid, *Natural Born Celebrities: Serial Killers in American Culture* (Chicago: The University of Chicago Press, 2005), 115.

9. Abigail Burnham Bloom, *The Literary Monster on Film: Five Nineteenth Century British Novels and Their Cinematic Adaptations* (Jefferson, NC: McFarland, 2010), 173.

10. Stoker, *Dracula,* 22.

11. Robert Spadoni, *Uncanny Bodies: The Coming of Sound Film and the Origins of the Horror Genre* (Berkeley: University of California Press, 2007), 63.

12. J. Gordon Melton. *The Vampire Book: The Encyclopedia of the Undead* (Canton: Visible Ink Press, 2011), 437.

13. Kevin Fitzpatrick. "Our Lunch With Hannibal Lecter: Mads Mikkelsen Dishes the Details on NBC's New Horror Series," Screen Crush, 4 April, 2013. Accessed 1 September, 2016. http://screencrush.com/hannibal-lunch-preview/?trackback=tsmclip.

14. Kevin Fallon, "Mads Mikkelsen On Playing the Tasty New Hannibal Lecter," The Daily Beast, 4 April, 2013. Accessed 1 September, 2016. http://www.thedailybeast.com/articles/2013/04/04/mads-mikkelsen-on-playing-the-tasty-new-hannibal-lecter.html.

15. Mulkerrins, Jane. "Mads Mikkelsen on Hannibal: 'He is not a person, he is the Devil,'" *The Daily Telegraph*, last modified May 7, 2013, http://www.telegraph.co.uk/culture/tvandradio/10035991/Mads-Mikkelsen-on-Hannibal-He-is-not-a-person-he-is-the-Devil.html.

16. Gary Don Rhodes, *Lugosi: His Life in Films, on Stage, and in the Hearts of Horror Lovers* (Jefferson, NC: McFarland, 2006), 30.

17. Sian Cain, "Hannibal: farewell to the best bloody show on TV," *The Guardian*, last modified August 17, 2015, https://www.theguardian.com/tv-and-radio/2015/aug/27/hannibal-finale-bryan-fuller-best-show-on-tv.

18. Nina Auerbach, *Our Vampires, Ourselves* (Chicago: University of Chicago, 1996), 113.

19. Erik Butler, *The Rise of the Vampire* (London: Reaktion Books, 2013), 51.

20. Rhodes, *Lugosi*, 16.

21. David Rogers, "Introduction," *Dracula: Bram Stoker* (London: Wordsworth Classics, 1993), xiv.

22. Jordan Porteous, "How the New Hannibal Lecter Became the Best-Dressed Man On TV," *Esquire*, last modified May 15, 2013, http://www.esquire.co.uk/culture/film/news/a3899/hannibals-style-mads-mikkelsen/.

23. A. J. Shapira, "Stylishly Executed—The Clothes of Hannibal & How to Dress Like Lecter," *Gentlemen's Gazette*, last modified September 15, 2015, https://www.gentlemansgazette.com/suits-hannibal-lecter-how-to-style/.

24. London McGuire, "Fashion and Food According to Dr. Hannibal Lecter," *Criminalelement.com*, last modified October 25, 2013, http://www.criminalelement.com/blogs/2013/10/fashion-and-food-according-to-dr-hannibal-lecter.

25. *Ibid.*

26. *Ibid.*

27. Homi Bhabba, *The Location of Culture* (London: Routledge, 1994), 121–131.

28. Stoker, *Dracula,* 186.

29. In the book Jonathan Harker is originally held captive by the Count but in the film he is replaced by the character Renfield.

30. Browning, *Dracula*, 1931.

31. Arthur Conan Doyle, *Sherlock Holmes: The Final Problem and Other Stories* (London: Harper Collins, 2012).

32. Burnham Bloom, *The Literary Monster,* 174.

33. Erik Butler, *Metamorphoses of the Vampire in Literature and Film: Cultural Transformations in Europe, 1732–1933* (Rochester: Camden House, 2010), 120.

34. Carol A. Senf, *The Vampire in Nineteenth Century English Literature* (Madison: University of Wisconsin Press, 1988), 59.

35. *Hannibal*, "Sorbet," 1.07, created by Bryan Fuller (New York: NBC, May 9, 2013). Television.
36. Butler, *Metamorphoses*, 119.
37. *Hannibal*, "Relevés," 1.12, created by Bryan Fuller (New York: NBC, June 13, 2013). Television.
38. *Hannibal*, "Mizumono," 2.13, created by Bryan Fuller (New York: NBC, May 23, 2014). Television.
39. Senf, *The Vampire*, 71.
40. Stoker, *Dracula*, 305.
41. Stoker, *Dracula*, 351.
42. *Hannibal*, "Apéritif," 1.01, created by Bryan Fuller (New York: NBC, April 4, 2013). Television.
43. *Ibid.*
44. *Hannibal*, "Amuse-Bouche," 1.02, created by Bryan Fuller (New York: NBC, April 11, 2013). Television.
45. *Hannibal*, "Coquilles," 1.05, created by Bryan Fuller (New York: NBC, April 25, 2013). Television.
46. *Hannibal*, "Savoureux," 1.13, created by Bryan Fuller (New York: NBC, June 20, 2013). Television.
47. *Ibid.*
48. *Hannibal*, "Kaiseki," 2.01, created by Bryan Fuller (New York: NBC, February 28, 2013). Television.
49. *Hannibal*, "The Wrath of the Lamb," 3.13, created by Bryan Fuller (New York: NBC, August 29, 2015). Television.
50. Stoker, *Dracula*, 333.
51. Tabish Khair, *The Gothic, Postcolonialism and Otherness: Ghosts from Elsewhere* (London: Palgrave Macmillan, 2009), 59.
52. Harold L. Malchow, *Gothic Images of Race in Nineteenth-Century Britain* (Stanford: Stanford University Press, 1996), 149.
53. Nathalie Bartlett and Bradley Bellows. "The Supernatural Ronin: Vampires in Japanese Anime," in Carol Margaret Davison (Ed.) *Bram Stoker's Dracula: Sucking Through the Century, 1897–1997* (Toronto: Dundurn Press, 1997), 193.

Works Cited

Auerbach, Nina. *Our Vampires, Ourselves*. Chicago: University of Chicago, 1996.
Bartlett, Nathalie and Bradley Bellows. "The Supernatural *Ronin*: Vampires in Japanese Anime." In *Bram Stoker's Dracula: Sucking Through the Century, 1897–1997*, edited by Carol Margaret Davison, 283–320. Toronto: Dundurn Press, 1997.
Bhabba, Homi. *The Location of Culture*. London: Routledge, 1994.
Bram Stoker's Dracula, directed by Francis Ford Coppola. Los Angeles: Columbia Pictures, 1992. Film.
Burnham Bloom, Abigail. *The Literary Monster on Film: Five Nineteenth Century British Novels and Their Cinematic Adaptations*. Jefferson, NC: McFarland, 2010.
Butler, Erik. *Metamorphoses of the Vampire in Literature and Film: Cultural Transformations in Europe, 1732–1933*. Rochester: Camden House, 2010.
_____, *The Rise of the Vampire*. London: Reaktion Books, 2013.
Cain, Sian. "Hannibal: Farewell to the Best Bloody Show on TV," *The Guardian*, last modified August 17, 2015, https://www.theguardian.com/tv-and-radio/2015/aug/27/hannibal-finale-bryan-fuller-best-show-on-tv.
Conan Doyle, Arthur. *Sherlock Holmes: The Final Problem and Other Stories*. London: HarperCollins, 2012.
Dracula, directed by Tod Browning. Universal City: Universal Pictures, 1931. Film.
Fallon, Kevin. "Mads Mikkelsen On Playing the Tasty New Hannibal Lecter," *The Daily Beast*, 4 April, 2013. Accessed 1 September, 2016. http://www.thedailybeast.com/articles/2013/04/04/mads-mikkelsen-on-playing-the-tasty-new-hannibal-lecter.html.

Fitzpatrick, Kevin. "Our Lunch with Hannibal Lecter: Mads Mikkelsen Dishes the Details on NBC's New Horror Series," *Screen Crush*, last modified April 4, 2013. http://screencrush.com/hannibal-lunch-preview/?trackback=tsmclip.

Gomez, Raphaella Dolores. "Dracula Orientalized." In *Dracula and the Gothic in Literature, Pop Culture and the Arts,* edited by Isabel Ermida, 69–90. Leiden: Brill Rodopi, 2016.

Hannibal, directed by Ridley Scott. Beverley Hills: Metro Goldwyn Meyer, 2001. Film.

Hannibal, "Apéritif," 1.01, created by Bryan Fuller. New York: NBC, April 4, 2013. Television.

_____, "Amuse-Bouche," 1.02, created by Bryan Fuller. New York: NBC, April 11, 2013. Television.

_____, "Coquilles," 1.05, created by Bryan Fuller. New York: NBC, April 25, 2013. Television.

_____, "Sorbet," 1.07, created by Bryan Fuller. New York: NBC, May 9, 2013. Television.

_____, "Relevés," 1.12, created by Bryan Fuller. New York: NBC, June 13, 2013. Television.

_____, "Savoureux," 1.13, created by Bryan Fuller. New York: NBC, June 20, 2013. Television.

_____, "Kaiseki," 2.01, created by Bryan Fuller. New York: NBC, February 28, 2013. Television.

_____, "Mizumono," 2.13, created by Bryan Fuller. New York: NBC, May 23, 2014. Television.

_____, "The Wrath of the Lamb," 3.13, created by Bryan Fuller. New York: NBC, August 29, 2015. Television.

Hannibal Rising, directed by Peter Webber. Beverley Hills: Metro Goldwyn Meyer, 2007. Film.

Khair, Tabish. *The Gothic, Postcolonialism and Otherness: Ghosts from Elsewhere.* London: Palgrave Macmillan, 2009.

Malchow, Harold L. *Gothic Images of Race in Nineteenth-Century Britain.* Stanford: Stanford University Press, 1996.

Manhunter, directed by Michael Mann. Beverley Hills: Metro Goldwyn Meyer, 1986. Film.

McGuire, London. "Fashion and Food According to Dr. Hannibal Lecter," *Criminalelement.com*, last modified October 25, 2013, http://www.criminalelement.com/blogs/2013/10/fashion-and-food-according-to-dr-hannibal-lecter.

Meehan, Paul. *The Vampire in Science Fiction a Film and Literature.* Jefferson, NC: McFarland, 2014.

Mulkerrins, Jane. "Mads Mikkelsen on Hannibal: 'He is not a person, he is the Devil,'" *The Daily Telegraph*, last modified May 7, 2013. http://www.telegraph.co.uk/culture/tvandradio/10035991/Mads-Mikkelsen-on-Hannibal-He-is-not-a-person-he-is-the-Devil.html.

Olney, Ian. *Euro Horror: Classic European Horror Cinema in Contemporary American Culture.* Indianapolis: Indiana University Press, 2013.

Porteous, Jordan. "How the New Hannibal Lector Became the Best-Dressed Man On TV," *Esquire*, last modified May 15, 2013, http://www.esquire.co.uk/culture/film/news/a3899/hannibals-style-mads-mikkelsen/.

Rhodes, Gary Don. *Lugosi: His Life in Films, on Stage, and in the Hearts of Horror Lovers.* Jefferson, NC: McFarland, 2006.

Rogers, David. "Introduction," *Dracula: Bram Stoker.* London: Wordsworth Classics, 1993. i-xix.

Schmid, David. *Natural Born Celebrities: Serial Killers in American Culture.* Chicago: The University of Chicago Press, 2005.

Senf, Carol, A. *The Vampire in Nineteenth Century English Literature.* Madison: The University of Wisconsin Press, 1988.

Shapira, A. J. "Stylishly Executed—The Clothes of Hannibal & How to Dress Like Lector," *Gentlemen's Gazette*, last modified September 15, 2015, https://www.gentlemansgazette.com/suits-hannibal-lecter-how-to-style/.

Silence of the Lambs, directed by Jonathan Demme. Los Angeles: Orion Pictures, 1991. Film.

Simpson, Phillip L. "Lector for President…Or, Why We Worship Serial Killers." In *Cult Pop Culture: How the Fringe Became Mainstream, Volume 1: Film and Television*, edited by Bob Batchelor, 83–96. Santa Barbara: Praeger, 2012.

Spadoni, Robert. *Uncanny Bodies: The Coming of Sound Film and the Origins of the Horror Genre.* Berkeley: University of California Press, 2007.

Sperry, Paul. "America has suffered a terror attack every year under Obama," *New York*

Post, last modified June 16, 2016, http://nypost.com/2016/06/16/america-has-suffered-a-terror-attack-every-year-under-obama/.

Stoker, Bram. *Dracula* [1897]. London: Signet Classics, 1996.

Uhlich, Keith. "Hannibal: The TV Show That Went Too Far," *BBC Culture*, last modified September 28, 2015. http://www.bbc.com/culture/story/20150828-hannibal-the-tv-show-that-went-too-far.

Pygmalion of a Broken Mind

Physical and Mental Desire in Will Graham and Hannibal Lecter's Relationship

OLIMPIA CALÌ

> Ars adeo latet arte sua. miratur et haurit pectore Pygmalion simulati corporis ignes.[1]—Ovid & Knox, 2005, 252–253

This essay will analyze the relationship between Hannibal Lecter (Mads Mikkelsen) and Will Graham (Hugh Dancy) in the NBC TV series *Hannibal* (2013–2015) starting from the assumption that, for the cannibal serial killer, Will Graham's broken mind is a sort of white canvas he wants to transform into a piece of art that can reflect himself and his personality. While in Thomas Harris' novels Will Graham is a secondary character, in the TV series Graham is the main protagonist and audience surrogate. Besides, the relationship between Graham and Lecter is the focus of the whole story. In their first meeting, Hannibal starts to study Will's behavior because is fascinating by his empathic skills and his imagination and because he also secretly sees in his new patient someone that could become similar to him. For this reason, Hannibal starts to push Will to his limits, manipulating his mind and his thoughts until Will cannot understand what is real and what it is not. While Hannibal should help Will to heal from his mental disease, Hannibal instead makes him feel worse and develops a symbiotic relationship in which Will needs him even though he understands that Hannibal is dangerous to his mind.

In order to write this essay, I considered the three seasons of *Hannibal* in their entirety. In fact, if watched in totality, *Hannibal* is the long tale of Hannibal's design to transform Will into a killer like him. When he is on a crime scene and uses his empathy skill to reconstruct the events, Will always says, "*This is my design.*" When he uses his imagination, Will does not simply place himself in the killer's shoes, but literally *becomes* him. He in fact recreates in his mind what happened, acting as he would do if he was the murderer: this is the reason why Hannibal believes that he would be capable of ruthless murder. Every design that Will collects since he starts to collaborate with Jack Crawford is one little step closer to the greater design that Hannibal is projecting in order to transform him into a beast. In the second season episode "Mukozuke" (Rymer, 2014), Will physically feels the effect of this metamorphosis when he has an hallucination in which he sees his body take the semblance of a Wendigo, a mythological creature known for being a cannibal and a symbolic representation of Hannibal and his nature. The Wendigo (or even the stag that sometimes appears to Will) is the manifestation of Will's subconscious, an unconscious association with Hannibal from their first meeting (Arien, 2013).

Season by season, the narrative style becomes more metaphorical, and it grows to an elevated language similar to Dante's *Divine Comedy*. The first season is told in an everyday language as the *Inferno*, and the second uses a medium level like *Purgatorio*. The third season, as *Paradiso*, use a more elevated language, full of metaphors and oneiric sequences, as the ones shot in Hannibal's mind palace or Will's hallucinations, that increasingly blend themselves with reality in a way that is difficult to distinguish even for the spectators. Besides, if the audience tries to think using Hannibal's ethic, one can observe that he acts with Will as Virgilio did with Dante: his purpose is to be the guide who makes Will become cruel and a murderer, capable of taking pleasure in killing people (Manseau, 2001).

This essay will analyze how the relationship between Hannibal Lecter and Will Graham is structured, and how it develops in the three seasons of the show, assuming that the diegetic time of the story is a journey into the deepest and darkest corner of two souls that are bonded to each other. Andrew Scahill (2016) uses the term "preboot" to define the nature of *Hannibal*, because as a *reboot* it repeats characters and situations that spectators know from other *media* (books and movies), but simultaneously like a *prequel*, the story is settled before the original events and yet the chronological continuity is abandoned and remixed to create something new. For this reason, I have chosen to base my analysis only on the interactions that Will and Hannibal have in the TV series, without referring to differences and similarities to the original books or movies.

Who Is the Cannibal in the Room?
Predator and Victim at the Mirror

Empathy is one of the basic features of human communication and socialization, because we put ourselves in the position to understand what other people are experiencing and acting consequently. Mirror neurons are considered by most scientists (Gallese & Goldman, 1998; Iacoboni, 2009) as an active part of the empathy process; in the particular case of Will Graham, these play an important role in helping him to solve murder cases in which he is called to give help.

> "The problem Will has is too many mirror neurons. Our heads are filled with them when we are children ... supposed to help us socialize and then melt away. But Will held on to his, which makes knowing who he is a challenge. When you take him to a crime scene, Jack, the very air has screams smeared on it. In those places, he doesn't just reflect; He absorbs."—"Buffet Froid" [Dahl, 2013].

"Empathy" is the key word we have to use to understand how Will Graham's mind works (Hoffman, 2001; Iacoboni, 2009). As Hannibal explains to Jack Crawford, Will is constantly about to lose his rationality. Sometimes, it seems that his mirror neurons cannot understand what is real and what is not, so they carry Will into a parallel world in which he *is* the murderer. This process is clear from the first scene of the show: Will stands at the center of crime scene, closes his eyes, and goes backward to the exact moment of the murder. Even the colors change on the screen to underline the beginning of this process. The screen becomes hotter, a signal of the emotional changing into Will's mind: the scene is now settled inside his head, while, in state of *trance*, he tries to recreate the true course of events. The stress that Will feels when he empathizes with serial killers is both physical and emotional, a sensation that can let him lose touch with reality, which will happen during the series.

To empathize on a deep level with people is a strong experience for Will's mental health, and sometime it seems that he is not capable of handling it. Jack Crawford, the FBI Agent who recruits him, clearly knows how painful is for Will put himself in a killer's shoes, but at the same time, he needs him as a useful source for his work. In order to avoid further damaging Will's mind, he recommends Will sees Hannibal Lecter, a psychiatrist who can help him to maintain the contact with reality.

The first conversation between Will and Crawford sheds a light on Will's personality and partially explains what has happened in the scene before, the one in which we have seen him use his empathy in order to reconstruct a crime scene.

> JACK: I see. May I? Where do you fall on the spectrum?
> WILL: My horse is hitched to a post that is closer to Asperger's and autistics than narcissists and sociopaths.
> JACK: But you can empathize with narcissists—and sociopaths.
> WILL: I can empathize with anybody. It's less to do with a personality disorder than an active imagination.
> JACK: Um can I borrow your imagination?—"Apéritif" [Slade, 2013a].

What Jack Crawford sees as a gift, Will Graham believes to be a curse. By absorbing other personalities, he risks erasing his own. For this reason, Jack sends Will to a psychiatrist who can help him to face his problems. Neither Jack nor Will could imagine the true horrors that await them within Hannibal's mind palace.

During first season, Hannibal really tries to help Will to face his hallucinations, but at a certain point he begins to set a trap that imprisons Will, who is completely at his mercy because he has begun to trust him after their first meeting.

At the first, Will does not want to be psychoanalyzed, but soon his sessions with Hannibal become a habit because he benefits from talking with him. When the struggle for having killed Garret Hobbs becomes a real obsession, Hannibal presses Will to admit his darkest truth regarding the death that haunts him:

> **HANNIBAL:** It wasn't the act of killing Hobbs that got you down, was it? Did you really feel so bad because killing him felt so good?
> **WILL:** I liked killing Hobbs.—"Amuse-Bouche" [Rymer, 2013].

This is the moment in which Hannibal's design starts: his purpose is to make Will understand that the feeling coming from killing people could be good. One of the actions that Hannibal takes in order to make sure that Will needs him is to treat his physical symptoms and eventual illness (encephalitis) as if they do not exist, falsifying medical reports with Dr. Sutcliffe's help (Dahl, 2013). In this behavior we can recognize some symptoms of the Munchausen syndrome by proxy: this syndrome, classified as child abuse that usually is diagnosed in mothers who tries to make their children feel sick in order to gain attention from other people. In Hannibal's case, the act of hiding the truth about Will's mental conditions from him and others (i.e., Jack Crawford and Alana Bloom) is done to make sure that Will continues to need him as psychiatrist and keeps doubting himself. Hannibal is not Will's mother, but he is in a dominant position, because Will's mind is ductile and easily manipulated.

Despite all the suffering that Hannibal causes, Will develops a bond with him, a devotion that is similar to Stockholm syndrome. In order to survive, Will has to love the man who is torturing him and accept everything Hannibal is going to do to him. While he is in prison, he asks to see Hannibal; at the end of second season, when the authorities are ready to arrest him, Will warns Hannibal to escape. Their relationship is a succession of love and hate manifestations ruled by the obsession that they have for one another. In order to be Hannibal's friend (and equal), Will must accept and embrace his evil nature, and Hannibal helps him to take this journey. Together they descend to Hell and then rise up to their personal Paradise.

What Hannibal guesses immediately is the fact that he and Will are more similar than it seems. This peculiarity is visually represented in many scenes in which they do the same thing at the same moment; for example in the episode "Hassun," they get dressed before Will's trial begins (Medak, 2014). Sometimes they are facing each other during the analysis sessions and strike similar poses. They chase each other, until, in episode 3x06 ("Dolce") they are represented as the two Wendigo's antlers, as they have become one single entity (Natali, 2015). Besides Hannibal is a sort of concrete mirror of what Will would like to be: he in fact makes real what Will either imagines or subconsciously desires.

To understand why Will and the other characters are so fascinated by Hannibal, we have to analyze the identity he has built to hide his cannibalistic side. To anyone who meets him for the first time, Hannibal Lecter appears to be an elegant man, an aesthete who surrounds himself with beautiful and perfect things. He also indulges in drawing, an appreciation of classical music, and he proves himself an excellent cook. Cooking for him is a performative art, if we consider how attention pays in this activity and how assembles his dishes make them similar to pieces of art. Looking at the way he kills people, we can observe that even murders are for Hannibal a form of fine art, since when he does not eat his victims he gives them the appearance of grotesque sculptures or famous paintings.

Hannibal's veneration for bodies has something that is more aesthetical that clinical: cannibalism is considered a form of dominion, but Hannibal uses it as a way to honor people that, otherwise, would be only dead bodies. The care that he uses when he dissects and cooks his victims is a perverse form of respect. Garrett Hobbs, in a dialogue with his daughter Abigail, seems to reflect Hannibal's philosophy:

> **Mr. Hobbs:** They're a lot like us. And we're gonna honor every part of her. Her hide is gonna make a beautiful rug. Her leg bones we can carve into knives. None of her is gonna go to waste. Just like we talked about. Start at the sternum. Keep the blade pointed up. Damage the organs, you ruin the meat.
> **Abigail:** I don't know how I'm gonna feel about eating her after all this.
> **Mr. Hobbs:** Eating her is honoring her. Otherwise, it's just murder.—"Potage" [Slade, 2013b].

However, the way Hannibal chooses to honor Will is different: discovered how fragile and broken his mind is, he decides to make him his masterpiece, shaping him in his own image and desire. This process recalls the Pygmalion archetype, which takes his name from the Greek myth of Pygmalion, a man who grew sick of women's lack of morality and made an ivory statue that became alive thanks to Aphrodite. Afterwards, a modern Pygmalion well known in literature is Professor Higgins, the main character of Bernard Shaw's comedy *Pygmalion* (1912), who uses his skills to help a common poor girl, Eliza Doolittle, to act as a noblewoman (*The Project Gutenberg E-text of Pygmalion, by George Bernard Shaw*, n.d.). In both cases, we are in front of people who want to change or shape other people, much like Hannibal does. The difference is that unlike the previous stories, the change is perceived as an improvement (or at least is not made by using violent and sadistic methods); Hannibal wants to make Will worse than he is, by transforming him into someone that takes pleasure from killing. However, this is just our moral perception of Hannibal's design, because to him, everything that comes from killing and eating people is good, so transforming Will into a serial killer and making him discover his real nature is a sort of gift.

Sociologists have used Pygmalion's name to define an experiment (Rosenthal & Jacobson, 1968) to demonstrate that having higher expectations in people leads to an increase in performance. This dynamic is not really a pathology, but what is certain is that the story of Hannibal that uses and manipulates Will's weak mind following his desire and his ideal of friend and partner in crime, recalls Pygmalion's myth.

Even the ancestral and archetypical desire of giving life is partially recalled. Hannibal wants to recreate Will's personality in his own image, and uses this expression to echo the biblical story of world creation: "And God said, 'Let us make man in our image, after our likeness'" (*Bible Gateway passage*, n.d.). There is evidence that, in some ways, Hannibal himself feels close to God, even if he does not explicitly declare a belief in Him. The part of God he seems to admire is the one that can create and destroy at will. He discusses this with Will at the end of the series' second episode:

> **HANNIBAL:** Killing must feel good to God too. He does it all the time. And are we not created in his image?
> **WILL:** That depends who you ask.
> **HANNIBAL:** God's terrific. He dropped a church roof on 34 of his worshippers last Wednesday night in Texas, while they sang a hymn.
> **WILL:** And did God feel good about that?
> **HANNIBAL:** He felt powerful.—"Amuse-Bouche" [Rymer, 2013].

The God whom Hannibal is talking about is typified as the Old Testament God, who uses his power to punish men and is vengeful against those that do not obey him. Hannibal's power is stated by his medical knowledge: with it, he can decide if people that surround him may live or die, as he does when Bella Crawford ask him to kill her to avoid pain from her cancer in the episode "Takiawase" (Semel, 2014).

Paradoxically, we don't have any representations of Hannibal like this interpretation of God, but we see him symbolically crucified when Will, from his prison, tries to kill him "by proxy" (Rymer, 2014). Hannibal is visually represented as if he was the Jesus Christ (victim) of a Giotto painting, but around his neck there is a noose, like the one that Judas (the betrayer who sold Jesus) used to kill himself.

Hannibal does not assimilate himself to God (or if he does, he does not clearly say it), but his charisma makes people believe and have faith in him even when he shows the dark side of his soul (for example in the case of Bedelia Du Maurier, who stays at his side even when she understands his danger). Will himself, while discovering how evil Hannibal can be, continues to orbit around him, as a planet attracted by an invisible force of gravity which is impossible to resist.

"Is Hannibal in love with me?" Attraction, Love and Desire in Will Graham and Hannibal Lecter's Relationship

Will discovers the depths of Hannibal's love for him over the course of three seasons of the show, and the audience bears witness to the surprising nature and depth of these feelings. Since their first meeting, none of what Hannibal has done to Will could be classified as an explicit demonstration of love. Throughout the series, Hannibal drives him to madness, imprisons Will by accusing him of being the Chesapeake Ripper, and leaves him bleeding to near death at the end of the second season. These are far from typical televisual representations of love and devotion.

Bryan Fuller, *Hannibal*'s developer and showrunner, has often spoken about Hannibal and Will's relationship, especially because fans have always had questions about its validity within the story; near the end of the show, Will asked "Is Hannibal in love with me?" (Navarro, 2015). His words confirm something between the two characters has been going apparent from the first episode:

> "I would argue that HanniGraham is already in play—just not physically. Hannibal is absolutely intrigued by Will Graham and has genuine feelings for him. And Will Graham, at this stage of their relationship, trusts Hannibal more than any other person. There is a genuine intimacy to how these two men have connected" [Arien, 2013].

Hannibal's desire for Will is not explicitly physical, which therefore may cause some confusion in spectators who need televisual proof of physical contact to establish a TV relationship. In Hannibal and Will's relationship, we instead have to consider principally the mental component: the attraction that Hannibal—first as a doctor, and then as a man—feels for Will's broken mind.

A clinical case like the one of Will Graham would probably be interesting for every psychiatrist. It's therefore easy to imagine how strong is the attraction that a person like Hannibal Lecter can feel for it. Will's broken mind has a strong attraction for Hannibal, because he wants to manipulate and use it in order to transform him into his image. While is losing his mind, Will follows Hannibal's instructions (Dahl, 2013) and tries desperately to orientate himself in a time and in a place

"Seven sixteen PM. I'm in Baltimore, Maryland. And my name is Will Graham.,"
"My name is Will Graham. It's 1:17 AM. W-We're in Greenwood, Delaware. And my name is Will Graham."
"It's 7:05 PM. I'm in Baltimore, Maryland. My name is Will Graham" [Dahl, 2013].

This is represented as if Will is throwing an anchor to cling to a reality that continues to slip away. Whenever he feels confused, he looks for Hannibal's help.

The show may not represent physical desire between the two men, but given Fuller's description of "HanniGraham," the unconventional love between Lecter and Graham manifests itself in other forms, notably the symbiotic nature of their professional and doctor/patient relationship. Hannibal might want to kill Will and eat his body to honor it, but to realize his design he needs Will alive. All the murders he commits as Chesapeake Ripper are his way to court and pay homage to Will, a way to attract his attentions.

Before Freddie Lounds describes Will and Hannibal with the name of "murder husbands" (3 × 09—"...And the Woman Clothed with the Sun") (Dahl, 2015), Hannibal himself has not displayed any qualms in considering Will part of his family. He therefore shows resentment when he discovers that, after his imprisonment, Will has built another family in which he is not included.

"I smell dogs ... and pine and oil beneath that shaving lotion. It's something a child would select, isn't it? Is there a child in your life, Will? I gave you a chance if you recall" [Dahl, 2015].

Hannibal's chance of a family with Will was Abigail Hobbs, the girl they have in part considered their daughter after her father's death by Will's hand. For a long time, Abigail had been part of their life, until, at the end of second season, she and Will were wounded by Hannibal. While Hannibal tried to make her accept her killer and manipulative nature, Will tried to protect her, not believing that she had helped her father to kill his victims. In them Abigail sees two surrogate paternal figures and she find comprehension (and perhaps love).

Abigail becomes part of Will's memory palace, the imaginary place where the man flees when he is trying to escape from reality. Hannibal's memory palace is a psychological technique that helps people to file a large number of information. Besides that, Hannibal says that he can refuge there even for long times and stay alone with his thought. In this mental construction Will can be calm and safe from his hallucinations, and he can imagine a happy life with Abigail (in a scene he imagines teaching her how to fish).

Hannibal's memory palace, in which he has buried his memories and his secret, is more majestic, "even by the Medieval standards," a real labyrinth that is difficult to decipher, in the same way it is difficult understand the psychiatrist's behaviors. In the third season, we see Will trying to explore it in order to reconnect their minds and find out the location of the runaway Hannibal. Will is the only one who Hannibal allows to penetrate his mind, maybe because he feels closer to him than anyone else.

Hannibal's attempt to draw Achilles and Patroclus (Brancato & Fuller, 2014) can be seen as another clear reference of his and Will's relationship, because the two mythological characters were represented as a pair of lovers.[2] The homoerotic implication is actually only one of the multiple meanings that this drawing can assume (Hoare, n.d.). Patroclus (who represents Will) at certain point of Iliad wears Achilles's armature (Hannibal) and dies while he's doing it. Will, in the TV series, is accused of being the Chesapeake Ripper, an identity that, as we know, belongs to Hannibal. Besides that, Will tries several times to kill people with the same coldness and lucidity demonstrated by Hannibal, similar to wearing his clothes. The only moment in which Will is really capable of doing it is in the final murder of Dolarhyde's Red Dragon, when he can finally empathize with Hannibal and understand how he feels when kills someone.

Indeed, we never see Will or Hannibal build solid relationships outside of their own symbiotic partnership; this may be because the one they have, regardless of explicit or implicit homoerotic implications, is so totalizing that there is no space for anyone else (Casey, 2015, 2018). They are soulmates, intimately bound by a destiny that weaves together life, death, love and hate.

Will and Hannibal metaphorically consume their love when they kill Dolarhyde's Red Dragon (Rymer, 2015). They do it together and for the very first time, Will feels that the pleasure that he gets from this act is not a shame and gives him power (Casey, 2015, 2018). Thus, Hannibal's design is now complete. He wanted Will to become like him and understand the contentment that he could take from killing.

HANNIBAL: See. This is all I ever wanted for you, Will. For both of us.
WILL: It's beautiful—(3×13 The Wrath of the Lamb) [Rymer, 2015].

These two sentences are the closest to a love declaration from Hannibal, and are followed by their fall off a cliff and into the waters below. In the end, it does not matter if they survive or not, their journey is now complete. They are together, in good and bad times.

Notes

1. "Art concealed artfulness. Pygmalion gazed in amazement, / burning with love for what was in likeness a body" (translated by Charles Martin, 2010. *Metamorphoses: a new translation, contexts, criticism*. New York: W.W. Norton).

2. Greek thespian Aeschilus (525 B.C.–456 B.C.), in a tragedy which came to us just in fragments, represents the two heros bonded in the traditional pederast relationship in which an adult male (*erastes*) is involved with a younger male (*eromenos)*. In this case Achilles is identified as the *erastes* and Patroclus is his *eromenos*.

Works Cited

Arien. (2013, June 20). *Blogger interviews Bryan Fuller (mild-ish spoilers for Hannibal season 2 and beyond)*. OhNoTheyDidn't: LiveJournal. https://ohnotheydidnt.livejournal.com/78904651.html.

Bible Gateway passage: Genesis 1:26—New International Version. (n.d.). Bible Gateway. Retrieved February 10, 2020, from https://www.biblegateway.com/passage/?search=Genesis+1%3A26&version=NIV.

Brancato, C., & Fuller, B. (2014). *Tome-Wan*. http://livingdeadguy.com/wp-content/uploads/2015/04/H212-Tome-wan-Web.pdf.

Casey, J. (2015). Queer Cannibals and Deviant Detectives: Subversion and Homosocial Desire in NBC's Hannibal. *Quarterly Review of Film and Video, 32*(6), 550–567. https://doi.org/10.1080/10509208.2015.1035617.

Casey, J. (2018). Afterthoughts on "Queer Cannibals and Deviant Detectives," Inspired by Hannibal Season 3. *Quarterly Review of Film and Video, 35*(6), 583–600. https://doi.org/10.1080/10509208.2018.1499346.

Dahl, J. (2013, May 30). *Buffet Froid* [Crime, Drama, Horror, Mystery, Thriller]. Dino De Laurentiis Company, Living Dead Guy Productions, AXN: Original X Production.

Dahl, J. (2015, July 30). *...And the Woman Clothed with the Sun* [Crime, Drama, Horror, Mystery, Thriller]. Dino De Laurentiis Company, Living Dead Guy Productions, AXN: Original X Production.

Gallese, V., & Goldman, A. (1998). Mirror neurons and the simulation theory of mind-reading. *Trends in Cognitive Sciences, 2*(12), 493–501. https://doi.org/10.1016/S1364-6613(98)01262-5.

Hoare, J. (2014). *Hannibal Season 2 is homoerotic, deal with it*. SciFiNow. Retrieved February 10, 2020, from https://www.scifinow.co.uk/news/hannibal-season-2-is-homoerotic-deal-with-it/.

Hoffman, M. L. (2001). *Empathy and Moral Development: Implications for Caring and Justice*. Cambridge University Press.

Iacoboni, M. (2009). *Mirroring People: The Science of Empathy and How We Connect with Others* (First edition). Picador.

Manseau, P. (2001, February 16). Hannibal Lecter's Harrowing of Hell. *Killing the Buddha*. https://killingthebuddha.com/mag/exegesis/hannibal-lecters-harrowing-of-hell-2/.

Medak, P. (2014, March 14). *Hassun* [Crime, Drama, Horror, Mystery, Thriller]. Dino De Laurentiis Company, Living Dead Guy Productions, AXN: Original X Production.

Natali, V. (2015, July 9). *Dolce* [Crime, Drama, Horror, Mystery, Thriller]. Toscana Film Commission, Dino De Laurentiis Company, Living Dead Guy Productions.

Navarro, G. (2015, August 20). *The Number of the Beast Is 666* [Crime, Drama, Horror, Mystery, Thriller]. Dino De Laurentiis Company, Living Dead Guy Productions, AXN: Original X Production.

Ovid, & Knox, B. (2005). *Metamorphoses: A New Translation* (C. Martin, Trans.; Reprint edition). W. W. Norton & Company.

The Project Gutenberg E-text of Pygmalion, by George Bernard Shaw. (n.d.). Retrieved February 10, 2020, from https://www.gutenberg.org/files/3825/3825-h/3825-h.htm.

Rosenthal, R., & Jacobson, L. (1968). Pygmalion in the classroom. *The Urban Review, 3*(1), 16–20. https://doi.org/10.1007/BF02322211.

Rymer, M. (2013, April 11). *Amuse-Bouche* [Crime, Drama, Horror, Mystery, Thriller]. Dino De Laurentiis Company, Living Dead Guy Productions, AXN: Original X Production.

Rymer, M. (2014, March 28). *Mukozuke* [Crime, Drama, Horror, Mystery, Thriller]. Dino De Laurentiis Company, Living Dead Guy Productions, AXN: Original X Production.

Rymer, M. (2015, August 27). *The Wrath of the Lamb* [Crime, Drama, Horror, Mystery, Thriller]. Dino De Laurentiis Company, Living Dead Guy Productions, AXN: Original X Production.

Scahill, A. (2016). Serialized killers: Prebooting horror in Bates Motel and Hannibal. In A. A. Klein & R. B. Palmer (Eds.), *Cycles, Sequels, Spin-offs, Remakes, and Reboots: Multiplicities in Film and Television*. University of Texas Press.

Semel, D. (2014, March 21). *Takiawase* [Crime, Drama, Horror, Mystery, Thriller]. Dino De Laurentiis Company, Living Dead Guy Productions, AXN: Original X Production.

Slade, D. (2013a, April 4). *Apéritif* [Crime, Drama, Horror, Mystery, Thriller]. Dino De Laurentiis Company, Living Dead Guy Productions, AXN: Original X Production.

Slade, D. (2013b, April 18). *Potage* [Crime, Drama, Horror, Mystery, Thriller]. Dino De Laurentiis Company, Living Dead Guy Productions, AXN: Original X Production.

Gender/Animal Suits

Adapting *Buffalo Bill from* The Silence of the Lambs *to NBC's* Hannibal

Evelyn Deshane

In Rachel Carroll's *Adaptation in Contemporary Culture*, she states that the act of adapting a text is marked with a particular "desire to return to an 'original' textual encounter; as such, adaptations are perhaps symptomatic of a culture's compulsion to repeat."[1] The compulsion to repeat is often brought on by a particular trauma of the original adaptation, a way in which the textual fidelity was violated or the audience's expectations not met. Therefore, all adaptations are as celebratory as they are fundamentally traumatic. For the work of Thomas Harris, this is especially so when he writes about LGBTQ characters. Many scholars like Jack[2] Halberstam, Marjorie Garber, and K.E. Sullivan have interpreted Buffalo Bill as a transgender woman[3] since Jame Gumb (birth name) applies for gender affirmation surgery at John Hopkins but is rejected by the board. It is this rejection from the medical institution that spurs the subsequent killing of women so Jame can make a "woman suit" and become what he always desired, but was denied.[4] The most iconic image we have of Buffalo Bill—that of Jame dancing to "Goodbye Horses" in front of a mirror with genitals tucked—has been used as a punch-line in numerous comedies (*Family Guy* and *Clerks 2* are notable examples) since this moment, and as transgender scholars Julia Serano and Joelle Ruby Ryan note, the image itself and the figure of Buffalo Bill has become synonymous with transmisogyny. In her dissertation on transgender characters in film, Joelle Ruby Ryan documents that the "transgender monster" figure we see in Buffalo Bill has a long cinematic history, one that is plagued by notions of borders, boundaries, and hybridity. She writes,

The Transgender Monster is a recurring stereotype in the transgender media canon, most commonly seen in slasher films but occasionally in dramas, suspense and action films as well. While previously the demarcation between *animal and human* was cast

243

as monstrous, historical developments and the tastes of audiences changed this. Audiences began to fear not some mythical animal-human hybrid creature that does not exist in reality, but the very real people who live right next door.[5]

The "very real people who live right next door" to Ryan becomes the seemingly normal family in *The Texas Chainsaw Massacre*, the suburban family in 1980s slasher horror films, and the character of Jame Gumb in *The Silence of the Lambs*, whom Clarice figures out is the killer before anyone else. The normalcy of what's on the outside (masculine gender presentation, heterosexual family life) becomes contrasted through the liminal state of being a trans woman or a cross-dresser. The boundaries between male/female and heterosexual/homosexual become blurry, and therefore, end up representing the real "villain" of these films because of the way in which these characters echo back the anxieties of the particular era in which the film/book was made. When Harris wrote Buffalo Bill, and subsequently when Jonathan Demme directed the film version, both were reacting to the strong Reagan-era and hyper-masculine images in the media along with playing into a standard trope in 1980s slasher cinema where the killer was always a little bit feminine and usually queer in some way.[6] But as the source material ages and the audience changes, so does the political and social climate which the image exists in.

In 2013, when Bryan Fuller steps up to modernize and adapt the Lecter story for NBC, he becomes aware of the backlash to Buffalo Bill and the way in which the culture's image of transgender people, especially that of transgender women, has changed. Since he is also an LGBTQ writer, and sensitive to the audience's strong emotions involving representation (as demonstrated with his gender- and race-swapped cast and his social media engagement), he opts out of the despairing depiction of Buffalo Bill as a transgender woman. Since the TV show still needs a monster-of-the-week, he needs to write something, and so, like Ruby, Halberstam, and Garber have noted in the lineage of this type of "transgender monster" figure, Fuller goes backwards, towards what came before. Historically, as Jack Halberstam notes in his book *Skin Shows* "the nineteenth-century monster is marked by racial or species violation while Buffalo Bill seems to be all gender. If we measure one skin job against the other, we can read transitions between various signifying systems of identity."[7] Before gender was the be-all and end-all that disrupted the orderly system of binary oppositions, the division was between human and animal marked a monster as such. It's the tension and divide between human/animal, rather than man/woman or cis/trans, that Fuller then plumbs to recreate Buffalo Bill into his character of Randall Tier.

In episodes nine ("Shiizakana") and ten ("Naka-Choko") from the second season of NBC's *Hannibal*, the story of Randall Tier, a former patient of Doctor Lecter now turned serial killer, takes the main focus. His murders are just as over-the-top and grotesque as the show has previously done, except that in order to kill, Tier must become an animal through the use of his exoskeleton suit. Tier's last name means "animal" in German, thereby already categorizing him as an "animal" in a playful yet blunt reference. As a symbol, Tier questions the very limitations of the categories human and animal in the same way Buffalo Bill questions the ones between male and female, both drawing on the same surface artifact (skin or animal suit) in which to enact their performance of an identity. When Fuller goes to represent Tier on the screen, however, he does not rely on the basic "page-to-screen"[8] adaptation Demme used to represent Buffalo Bill; there is no dancing to "Goodbye Horses" that can become a shortcut for laughing at the pathetic queer villain. Instead, through Fuller's sensitive use of psychiatric language and storytelling techniques (such as POV-camera focus and mirroring Tier with the lead, Will Graham), he has managed to adapt the character of Buffalo Bill from a "pathetic transsexual"[9] suffering from gender dysphoria to a disturbed young man with an "otherkin"[10] status suffering from species dysphoria. Because this adaptation effectively rewrites all other canonical interpretations of Buffalo Bill as a rather problematic transgender woman, and does so not only in content but in *form*, Fuller retroactively alleviates the previous character's "wound" on a generation of gender-variant and LGBT viewers.

Adapting the Real

As K.E. Sullivan and Joelle Ruby Ryan point out, Buffalo Bill was adapted by Thomas Harris from a real-life source. Years before he would pen the *Hannibal* Tetralogy, Thomas Harris was a journalist who often covered crime stories. His depiction of Hannibal is based on one of the many criminals he interviewed in his career, and he's admitted that while shadowing the FBI, he learned of the criminal Ed Gein.[11] Gein was a Wisconsin farmer who was a grave-robber and often made items like a lampshade or bowls from skin and bones he collected.[12] Though he is only on record for killing two people, his case has become notorious for the state of his house, and as K.E. Sullivan argues, the way in which he engaged with his crimes when he was caught. When suggested by the police that he was keeping these skin suits so he could become a woman, Gein replied passively. Sullivan quotes a large section of the interview which is worth repeating again to demonstrate just how susceptible to suggestion Gein was:

> **Q:** "Do you have any recollection, Eddie, of taking any of those female parts, the vagina specifically, and holding it over your penis to cover the penis?"

A: "I believe that's true."

Q: "You recall doing that with the vaginas of the bodies of other women?"

A: "That I believe I do remember; that's right."

Q: "Would you ever put on a pair of women's panties over your body and then put some of these vaginas over your penis?"

A: "That could be."[13]

As Ryan has rightly expressed earlier, what ends up being adapted in the transgender monster trope is the anxiety from a culture that does not like its boundaries, especially that of male/female, violated in any way. The police questioning Gein were already deeply influenced by the threat of McCarthyism and homosexuality, and when confronted with someone who had lived so far outside the law, the automatic ideological jump they made was to accuse someone like Gein of more than just moral transgressions of murder, but gender ones too.[14] Moreover, because Gein acted so passively to these accusations, he effectively became a cipher; anything that people threw at him in terms of labels stuck, and therefore, his legacy has been adapted in film, television, and books over and over again. Adaptation scholar Thomas Leitch notes that, when sources for movies and books are drawn from real-life people or incidents, they can become almost free-floating in the culture, to be used at anyone's discretion when the right time comes up. The label "based on a true story" for these types of productions indicate

> a source text that both is and is not a text, one that carries some markers common to most source texts, but not others. Most source texts have authors and publishers who have sold the adaptation rights in return for a given amount of money and a screen credit. But a "true story" is authorless, publisherless, agentless. Because the description maybe claimed or not at the filmmaker's pleasure, it appears only when it is to the film's advantage.[15]

In a similar manner, Robert Bloch drew on Gein for Norman Bates, Tobe Hooper for Leatherface in *The Texas Chainsaw Massacre*, and as I've mentioned earlier, slasher horror films also borrowed and used the idea of Gein decades later. Carroll J. Clover, gender and horror specialist, remarks that this particular relationship between the feminine-man (or transgender woman) killer in these stories is often paired with a strong masculine woman (whom Clover dubs the "final girl") to emphasize their differences even more. "The final girl is boyish," Clover writes. "Just as the killer is not fully masculine, she is not fully feminine—not, in any case, feminine in the way of her friends."[16] The filmmaker and director's advantage in representing these two opposing gender forces expresses another facet of anxiety in the culture at large. As Clover notes in her *Men, Women, and Chainsaws*, films from the slasher era also express feminism's influence and the changing gender politics of the second wave feminist movement.[17]

The Silence of the Lambs film came out in 1991, only a year after Judith Butler's *Gender Trouble*, and both end up representing shadow-aspects of one another. The depiction of Buffalo Bill takes Judith Butler's theory of performativity where there is "no gender identity behind the expressions of gender; that identity is performatively constituted by the very 'expressions' that are said to be its results" and externalizes it completely through the skin suit itself.[18] As Jack Halberstam observes, in *The Silence of the Lambs*, the "interiority of gender [becomes] a surface effect [...] engineered into an identity" which is then made into a literal performance through a dance to "Goodbye Horses."[19] Similarly, in *Vested Interests*, Marjorie Garber notes that Buffalo Bill's story is "a fable of gender dysphoria gone horribly awry."[20] The exteriorization of the self on the body, and worn as a hide, becomes something artificial in the eyes of most readers or viewers; there is nothing behind Buffalo Bill's performance other than deviance itself. Even Hannibal Lecter himself echoes these claims of Bill's inauthenticity when he calls Jame "not a real transsexual" in the film.[21] It's this claim—that Jame Gumb's feelings of gender dysphoria aren't real—and not the fact that Jame Gumb is the killer of the movie—that seems to be the most upsetting for many LGBTQ theorists and trans right activists.

Of course, the violence that Buffalo Bill does in the film is something that was protested when the movie first came out. At the 1992 Oscars, a protest by Queer Nation groups broke out where they kicked, yelled, and slapped "Fag" stickers on the large standing Oscar statues. As reporter Neal Broverman notes, "Queer Nation and many other LGBT people were furious at Hollywood for what they saw as a pattern of demented, homicidal queer characters."[22] In addition to the trans woman killer of Buffalo Bill, Oliver Stones' *JFK* (which contained homicidal gay men seemingly responsible for the president's death) and *Basic Instinct* (which had Sharon Stone play a bisexual killer) were also up for awards. As Jack Halberstam notes, and as I would also argue, Queer Nations arguments—of violence and its correlation to the transgender/queer person and how it presents a negative image of transgender/queer life—isn't as problematic as the ideological core of these works, especially that of *The Silence of the Lambs*. As Halberstam notes in his other work called *Female Masculinity*, positive images or representations, especially in relation to queer content, are inconsequential. He writes that

> [t]he desire for positive images places the onus of queering cinema squarely on the production rather than the *reception* of images. It also makes representation into a kind of unmediated event that shows either truth and reality or else skewed versions of them. But representation and its effects are never so simple.[23]

Indeed, to think that all depictions of the transgender person will be positive is to deny the trans person the right to failure, and that right to failure is just as important (which Halberstam expands on in his book *The Queer Art of Failure*). Failure itself is a very real process when it comes to applying for gender affirmation surgery as well. As Dan Irving and Jay Prosser note in their work, transgender surgery of often fraught with conflicting narratives that the trans person must enact in order to be taken seriously in their gender.[24] Jame Gumb's struggle within John Hopkins and with Hannibal Lecter himself is actually quite an accurate depiction, since many trans people are denied medical care for superfluous reasons.[25] What becomes most problematic in much of the criticism against Buffalo Bill, then, isn't that the character exists and is violent—it's that Jame Gumb was not listened to. It's this assumption of the fake gender and the inauthentic rendering of the feelings of gender dysphoria that matter.

When Fuller and company at NBC are tasked with adapting Buffalo Bill and the work of Thomas Harris, it's the feelings of the fans and of LGBTQ people they listen to in order to heal the prior adaptation's wound.

Gender Feelings

Many adaptation scholars have used fidelity as a critical mode to engage with—or disavowal entirely—an adaptation. Whether or not the director/screenwriter has followed the book in a typical "page-to-screen"[26] adaptation is often closely studied, and any faults of the cinematic production itself is often contrasted with the source text, where the source itself is always elevated. If something is based on a real-world source, such as Ed Gein, fidelity as a critical tool can become even stronger. Even if, like Leitch mentions, the set and staging can be rooted in a historical moment, the film itself "can no more be accurate records of the historical events they purport to represent than a film adaption can be an accurate record of any particular source text" especially since these films "do not claim to tell the truth"[27] audiences and some scholars still seek the point of origination, and in many ways, uphold that origin point above all other adapted elements. Because the claims against Gein's representation are ones about certain marginalized identity groups, these claims to fidelity to an original source become even stronger because, like I've stated before, trans scholars like Julia Serano and Joelle Ruby Ryan worry that the reproduction of this trope (in Serano's words, of the "deceptive transsexual"[28] or in Ryan's of the "transgender monster"[29]) is done so uncritically, and therefore adds to the initial pain of misrecognition in the cinematic universe, which compounds the trauma of being misrecognized in the medical field. The jokes about Buffalo Bill dancing are harmful, not because they could possibly misrepresent Gein, but due to a poverty of representation in film and media, they mis-represent *all* transgender women, and therefore add to the transmisogyny in a wider cultural narrative.

Bryan Fuller sees and understands this. When interviewed by *Esquire* about his process of reboots and screen-writing, Fuller stated that he wanted to redo almost everything because our social milieus have changed. He states,

> We are a different society just because of that awareness and also a different society for other awarenesses, too. Gender identity, which has become so common in our conversations now, is something you wouldn't have really talked about 15 years ago. Transvestites and transsexuals and transgendered people were still marginalized in such a way that it was still a comedic topic because of the perceived absurdity of that person's situation.[30,31]

When it came to doing Buffalo Bill on NBC's *Hannibal*, there was a copyright issue in the way (the De Laurentiis company does not own the rights for *The Silence of the Lambs*) but I believe that was a minor concern in Fuller's motivation to not represent the transgender killer archetype on-screen.[32] As an LGBTQ writer, Fuller is sensitive to these types of issues of representation *and* as a fan of the original books, he's also more in-tune with the language of emotion fans used to communicate. As I've written about previously, Fuller has addressed fans' outrage over Beverly Katz's death as something to address and revise (through later works), rather than something to ignore.[33] Because fans work in an economy that deals primarily with emotion, especially in fandom production where likes and kudos are exchanged for fan material,[34] and Fuller is also a fan, he can engage with the prior criticisms of Buffalo Bill and learn to adapt. Moreover, because adaptation itself is a process of "cultural memory"[35] work that deals in affect, Fuller becomes the perfect candidate in which to write—and also rewrite—the figure of Buffalo Bill into Randall Tier, a man who longs to be an animal, suffering from "species dysphoria."[36] More than that, Fuller also gives Randall Tier the space to become who he was always meant to become—a full transformation from human to animal—something of which was denied to Buffalo Bill entirely.

The term dysphoria comes from the Greek meaning "difficult to bear"; when placed in reference to someone's gender, it means their gender is difficult to bear.[37] As a psychiatric and medical term, gender dysphoria becomes important in understanding and sympathizing with a transgender person. The term *dysphoria* stands out as something different when compared to a similar psychiatric term of *dysmorphia*. *Body dysmorphia* is often used in conjunction with eating disorder patients who in spite of being thin, still see themselves as fat.[38] Dysmorphia becomes a contortion of reality, where the patient's worldview is compromised through delusion; in treatment, eating disorder patients with this diagnosis are not listened to because it is believed their version of reality is flawed. Dysphoria, on the other hand, locates the patient's illness or ill feelings on the body itself. Their perspective is privileged and not treated as inherently incorrect; their gender feelings are listened to and considered something real.

When Fuller writes Randall Tier, he uses this exact same medical language. Tier ends up suffering from a "species dysphoria" where his human body becomes difficult to bear and contains an internal map that does not match the outside.[39] This language places the audience—and the rest of the team, especially Will Graham—inside Tier's perspective, sympathizing with his position. Furthermore, when Randall Tier first appears on screen, the audience does not see him at all.[40] On screen, a man at a truck stop walks slowly across a parking lot, the tension mounting as he moves. Camera angles, the music by Brian Reitzel, and genre alone signal to us that this truck driver is about to be attacked, and most likely, attacked by an animal. This assumption is confirmed as soon as the truck driver is pulled from his cabin amidst the sounds of screams, snapping bones, and guttural moaning. As blood falls down the windshield, the audience realizes he has been attacked by something much larger and stronger than a wolf or other forest dwelling creature. This assumption is further teased out by the camera panning to the moon in the background. From wolf to werewolf, our gaze is coded to assume a supernatural answer; never once do we believe that a human has done this, and this is an important distinction since it makes us align with the way in which Randall Tier sees himself.

Once the lab team arrives in the morning, they realize that the truck driver has not been eaten. "The viscera's exposed," a lab tech states, "the belly's laid bare. But there is no sign of gnawing." Another lab tech reiterates that they "found the same wound patterns on a series of livestock attacks in the area," where the bodies had immense "laceration, dismemberment—yet everything accounted for."[41] From here, everyone draws the conclusion that the attack couldn't have been an animal, since animals eat what they kill. Scholar and writer Emmanuel Levinas traces this fundamental distinction between animals and humans (and what is eaten versus what is not) to Biblical passages in his essay "The Name of a Dog or Natural Rights." He writes that the "flesh torn by beasts in the field [and the] remains of the bloody struggles between wild animals" is not fit for human consumption; rather, if humans wish to eat flesh they must "sublimate" their urges to devour into "hunting games."[42] Animals destroy, then consume *without thought*, whereas humans enact a structure—or ritual—by which to consume our food (especially flesh/meat). Since both these attacks on human and animal bodies have *not* been consumed at these crime scenes, the detectives realize they can't be dealing with an animal, but someone who still feels as if "he is watched over by God."[43] The sheer violence of the act itself is still troubling to the investigators because there is no order to it; this killing has not been "sublimated by intelligence into hunting games."[44] The violence—and then the rejection of the bodies as abject "jettisons"[45]—points to someone who kills to kill and merely uses the bodies as a means to an end; they are, like Ryan and Halberstam have noted, someone who is a hybrid creature and pushes back against boundaries until he becomes "a man who wants to be an animal."[46] As the investigation goes on, Tier becomes coded in the same psychiatric language as transgender patients are coded in, and he confesses that he once suffered from an "identity disorder" but he is now cured:

> I had an identity disorder. The doctors told me that the internal map of my body didn't match reality. [...] I know who I am now—and I'm doing much better. I'm socializing. I'm taking my medication. I'm employed. And I work very hard. I am proof that mental illness is treatable.[47]

Language like gender dysphoria works on making the transgender patient intelligible in the medical field, which in spite of allowing the patient's worldview to be validated, still frames them in a dichotomy of sick/healthy. And as Dan Irving, Jay Prosser, and even Judith Butler note, the creation of a diagnostic category for the transgender patient ends up producing an idealized patient and accompanying idealized trans narrative along with them. These ideals are often hard to live up to and it's these ideals that often hold back transgender people from surgery itself. Since Tier longs to be an animal, but there is no form of transition from one species to another, a similar rejection or rupture of the institutional support happens in the NBC episode. Tier must confess to his aberrations in therapy and then admit that he's been cured to Jack Crawford and Will Graham. What becomes telling, though, is that in this version of the storyline, Tier—unlike Buffalo Bill—is accepted by Hannibal Lecter. The speech he gives to Jack Crawford about being cured has been supplied directly by Lecter the night before and is meant to be a kind of performance piece for Will Graham to be in touch with his own inner animal.[48] To Lecter, seeing Tier's development from a sad boy obsessed with teeth to a full-blown ritual killer who has engineered and exoskeleton suit is "beautiful" and he encourages Tier to "revel in what you are."[49] Tier's feelings of species dysphoria, unlike Buffalo Bill's feeling of gender dysphoria, are given validation by the very institution (Hannibal Lecter, the psychiatric and medical institution) that once rejected Jame Gumb. Moreover, as a writer, Fuller composing this character using sympathetic language and camera techniques that allow us into Tier's head allows room for Tier to be seen as another marginalized group—that of otherkin.

In Danielle Kirby's book *Fantasy and Belief,* she defines the otherkin community as "a loosely affiliated network of individuals who believe that they are to some degree nonhuman."[50] In her assessment of the otherkin community, she discovers that the groups themselves are "communities only in the most minimal sense of the term: association is premised upon a singular shared philosophy or belief without the necessary pragmatic basis such as geography, history, or common situation."[51] Otherkins are together because of a sole attribute that defines them; more than a species dysphoria, but a central *belief* that they do not belong in the classification of human.[52] Kirby's book works on validation that community structure, and therefore the identity group that goes along with it in much the same way Fuller's depiction seeks to humanize Tier's otherkin status as a way to *retroactively* heal the damage done by ignoring Buffalo Bill's gender status.

In Rachel Carroll's work on affect and emotion in adaptation studies, she turns to the term "retrospectatorship" derived from Patricia White's work as a way to extract analysis from various interpretations formed through repeated viewing, or repeated adapted elements in certain works. Retrospectatorship becomes an act of viewing a film (or book or piece of media) again and understanding both unconscious and conscious influences on the way in which the original viewing was experienced, which like all forms of spectatorship, "engages [the viewer in] subjective fantasy, revises memory traces and experience[s]."[53] For Carroll, retrospectatorship "offers a valuable framework within which to conceptualize repetition, as a mode of cultural experience, and its relation to memory and affect; premised on an acknowledgement of affective investment, it might be adapted to contribute to a rethinking of fidelity as something other than a critically suspect sentiment."[54] What Carol does here is to validate the emotions that arise from a particular viewing, but she locates them in a temporal (and Halberstam would perhaps argue) a queer context. Emotions are valid, but sometimes they are particularly potent the first time we engage in spectatorship. Similarly, emotions may become stronger with repeated viewings, or we may blur the memory of the event, or we may blur the culture's memory of the event with our own. Retrospectatorship also offers a unique way in which to view the process of adaptation as continually repeating a storyline or trope in order to produce a desired outcome; it's the entire reason why we reboot series, and for *Hannibal*, it's why Bryan Fuller signed on to this project—but also why he changed so much of it so drastically. As a fan, Fuller wanted to engage in material he'd grown up with, but as an LGBTQ person and someone who listens to fan criticism, he didn't want to reproduce the negative feelings that Buffalo Bill produces (even if, when he watched the film the first time, he may not have had those feelings). By adapting Buffalo Bill into Randall Tier, and allowing for Tier to become a valid participant in his own story, he allows a new set of viewers to have their own retrospectatorship experience in the Hannibal universe by changing the ideological core of the hybrid monster trope itself. If we allow for Tier—and his feelings—to exist in this version of the adapted universe, it effectively means that in some way or another, Buffalo Bill and Jame Gumb are valid too.

Conclusion: Even Steven

"Even Steven," Will Graham states when he presents the body of Randall Tier to Hannibal Lecter in the following episode "Naka-Choko." Graham's remark refers to murder itself: "I sent someone to kill you, and now you sent someone to kill me. Even Steven." In past episodes, Graham and Lecter have battled it out through this constant act of killing/not killing. For Graham, Lecter has always been a polluting force since Lecter spends so much time breaking down borders. Whether it's between what's good and evil or what's animal and human, Lecter knows that there is "one thin barrier between us."[55] Lecter's mission has always been to tear down the barrier of all binaries and revel at what's in between. Up until this point of the show, Will Graham has represented someone who fought to keep those boundaries clear. He solves cases and puts order where there was once chaos. Now, through the act of killing Tier, Will Graham has become the killer he fears and that Lecter desires, but Graham embraces this as an act of performativity—something that is not fixed, only temporary, but still important for survival.

Since the 1990 release of her *Gender Trouble*, Judith Butler has been criticized within the transgender community for her dismissal of gender identity when she wrote, "[t]here is no gender identity behind the expressions of gender; that identity is performatively constituted by the very 'expressions' that are said to be its results."[56] The idea of gender as merely a performance or a becoming was read in the same way as most people read Buffalo Bill's gender in *The Silence of The Lambs*: it's not real and to think there is such a thing is to be fundamentally flawed. Butler eventually responded to criticism from the trans community by writing the article (and subsequent chapter in *Bodies that Matter*) called "Undoing Gender." In this article, she defends her reading of gender performativity while legitimizing a transgender person's desire—and struggle for recognition within the medical system.[57] When she criticizes the gender performance that doctors expect in order to allow transition, she does not criticize trans people. Rather, she encourages them to embrace a "strategic" gender where they can perform the narratives the doctors want, but still find their own expression for their identity as well.[58] In many ways, what Butler advocates for here is *adaptation*. Transition itself is a kind of adaptation on the physical body, and by allowing for transgender people—and others with potentially "monstrous" body types like Tier—to speak within the Hannibal universe, Fuller manages to take the negative emotions from Harris and Demme's work and provide an alternative queer reading. For Butler, Fuller, and the characters inside the NBC *Hannibal* universe, the distinctions between male/female and human/animal blur through the episodes of "Shiizakana" and "Naka-Choko"; whenever someone performs, they become what they perform. Nothing is inauthentic, because everything from Will Graham's fever dreams of the Ravenstag to Tier's exoskeleton suit is real by virtue of it being represented in the storyline itself.

Graham's final call of "Even Steven" also refers to his relationship to Randall Tier. When Graham presents the body, the animal costume that Tier once wore is no longer present. The skin—the hide that he has used to transform himself—is no longer needed because that night, Graham sets up a new display of the corpse alongside the fossils that Tier worked with in his day job. For the price of his own survival and allowing his inner-animal to come out, Graham allows Tier to finally become what he always felt he was. "I gave you what you want," Will Graham says to the spirit of Randall Tier in "Naka-Choko." "This is who you are. What you feel finally matches the reality of what I see."

Randall Tier, the man who wanted to be an animal, has now reached his end goal. Unfortunately, this final transformation ends up becoming a death—a literal "monument" inside a museum using the bones of long extinct creatures. Fuller's new interpretation of Buffalo Bill may still end in a death, but it's a death that wasn't made into a deceptive or pathetic trope, and it's a death that focuses on bridging an emotional and possibly romantic relationship between Will Graham and Hannibal Lecter. Fuller does not suppress or vilify the queer—he revels in it, just like Tier.

For Rachel Carroll and many other adaptation scholars, the source text is only the first stop. Adaptation is another process of becoming, and authors like Harris and Fuller are constantly figuring out the best way to convey the emotions needed. The best becomings don't happen alone, either—they require an audience. Bryan Fuller and Martha De Laurentiis, in their own way, also become privy to the uniqueness of becoming through their re-imagining and adapting of the Buffalo Bill storyline. Buffalo Bill no longer dances alone to "Goodbye Horses" only to be killed by Clarice Starling; instead, Randal Tier is transformed as a gift, and a warning, to Will Graham. Will Graham now has Randall Tier's ghost as his audience, and Tier's final words to remind him about the ultimate act of transformation.

"This is my becoming," Tier states, "and it's yours."[59]

NOTES

1. Carroll, Rachel, *Adaptation in Contemporary Culture: Textual Infidelities* (NY: Bloomsbury Academic, 2009). 1.

2. Halberstam has published several books under different names due to transgender status. I will refer to him using he/his pronouns and credit him as Jack Halberstam in the essay, though some books were published as Judith and will retain the original name in the Bibliography.

3. Many people have called Buffalo Bill many different names relating to the gender identity of the character. For the purpose of this essay, I refer to Buffalo Bill as the character/monster and Jame Gumb as the trans person. I also interpret these actions as a transgender woman, and opt to use the term "trans" or "transgender" rather than transsexual or anything else because the term transgender acts as an umbrella term and is considered to be more favourable in trans communities. Some of my sources, however, use the older language of "transsexual" and I've kept their citations or quotations intact.

4. Harris, Thomas, *The Silence of the Lambs* (NY: St. Martin's Press, 1988), 360.

5. Ryan, Joelle Ruby, "Reel Gender: Examining the politics of trans images in media and film" (PhD diss, University of Ohio, 2009), 180.

6. Clover, Carol J, *Men, Women and Chainsaws: Gender In Modern Horror Films* (Princeton: Princeton University Press, 1992), 40.

7. Halberstam, Jack, *Skin Shows* (Durham: Duke University Press, 1995), 6.

8. Carroll, Rachel, *Adaptation in Contemporary Culture: Textual Infidelities* (NY: Bloomsbury Academic, 2009), 36.

9. Serano, Julia, *Whipping Girl: A Transsexual Woman On Sexism and The Scapegoating of Femininity* (Berkeley: Seal Press, 2007), 40.

10. Kirby. Danielle, *Fantasy and Belief: Alternative Religions, Popular Narratives, and Digital Cultures* (Toronto: Equinox, 2013) 1.

11. Webb, Sam, "Revealed: The Mexican Doctor who chopped up his gay lover and was the inspiration for the fictional Hannibal Lecter" *Daily Mail Online* (31 July 2013, Accessed: August 13, 2016).

12. Sullivan, K.E, "Ed Gein and the figure of the transgendered serial killer," *Jump Cut: A Review of Contemporary Media* (No. 43, July 2000). 38–47.

13. *Ibid.*

14. Ryan, Joelle Ruby, "Reel Gender: Examining the politics of trans images in media and film" (PhD diss, University of Ohio, 2009), 182.

15. Leitch, Thomas, *Film Adaptations and its Discontents* (Baltimore: John Hopkins University Press, 2007), 281–2.

16. Clover, Carol J, *Men, Women and Chainsaws: Gender In Modern Horror Films* (Princeton: Princeton University Press, 1992), 40.

17. *Ibid.*

18. Butler, Judith, *Gender Trouble: Feminism and the Subversion of Identity* (New York: Routledge, 1990), 25.

19. Halberstam, Jack. *Skin Shows* (Durham: Duke University Press, 1995), 168.

20. Garber, Marjorie, *Vested Interests: Cross Dressing and Cultural Anxiety* (NY: Routledge, 1997), 116.

21. *The Silence of the Lambs*, Dir Jonathan Demme, 1991, Orion Pictures.

22. Broverman, Neal, "Violent Gay Protests at the Oscars: Could it Happen again?" *The Advocate* (27 February 2016. Web. Accessed: Aug 12 2016).

23. Halberstam, Jack, *Female Masculinity* (NY: Duke University Press, 1998), 179. Emphasis mine.

24. Prosser, Jay, *Second Skins: The Body Narratives of Transsexuality* (NY: Columbia University Press, 1998). 1–9.

25. Irving, Dan, "Normalized transgressions: Legitimizing the transsexual body as productive," *Radical History 100* (Winter 2008), 40–57.

26. Carroll, Rachel, *Adaptation in Contemporary Culture: Textual Infidelities* (NY: Bloomsbury Academic, 2009). 36.

27. Leitch, Thomas, *Film Adaptations and Its Discontents* (Baltimore: John Hopkins University Press, 2007).282–3.

28. Serano, Julia, *Whipping Girl: A Transsexual Woman On Sexism and The Scapegoating of Femininity* (Berkeley: Seal Press, 2007), 40.

29. Ryan, Joelle Ruby, "Reel Gender: Examining the Politics of Trans Images in Media and Film" (PhD diss, University of Ohio, 2009). 180

30. Wood, M. Jennifer, "Bryan Fuller on Pushing Daisies, Dead like Me, and Being Cancelled," *Esquire Online* (19 March 2015, Accessed: Aug 13 2016).

31. Though the initial question was posed in relation to Fuller's gay character on *Dead Like Me* that was edited out, I believe that Fuller's position as a queer writer influences everything he produces, including material where he was not the source creator.

32. Since the show has been cancelled, Fuller has discussed having Lee Pace play Buffalo Bill, since Pace has already done work as a trans woman character in *Soldier's Girl*. Though this is not the best way to adapt the role by trans representation standards (most trans activists, like Jen Richards from *Her Story*, would want a trans actor to play the role), Fuller does demonstrate the same type of sensitivity that I argue for in this paper, since he's viewing the character of Jame Gumb/Buffalo Bill 1) as a trans woman and 2) deciding to cast an actor that already has a history with playing these roles, thus showing a lineage and interpretation he's drawing from. See the article by Kyle Daly in the Bibliography for more details on the original interview.

33. Deshane, Evelyn, "Hannibal's Refrigerator: Bryan Fuller's Response to Fan's Critical Rage," *Transitions, Endings, and Resurrections in Fandom*, Edit Rebecca Williams (2017).

34. Turk, Tisha. "Fan Work: Labor, Worth, and Participation in Fandom's Gift Economy," in "Fandom and/as Labor," edited by Mel Stanfill and Megan Condis, special issue, *Transformative Works and Cultures*, no. 15. http://dx.doi.org/10.3983/twc.2014.0518.

35. Carroll, Rachel, *Adaptation in Contemporary Culture: Textual Infidelities* (NY: Bloomsbury Academic, 2009). 37.

36. "Shiizakana," Hannibal: Season Two, Dir. Michael Rymer, Perf. Caroline Dhavernas, Laurence Fishburne, Mads Mikkelsen, Hugh Dancy, Alliance Films (September 2014). DVD.

37. Butler, Judith, "Undiagnosing Gender." *Transgender Rights*. Ed. Paisey Currah, Richard M. Juang, and Shannon Price Minter (Minneapolis: University of Minnesota Press, 2006), 276.

38. Deshane, Evelyn, "The Other Side of The Mirror: Eating Disorder Treatment and Gender Identity," in Trans Rights: The Time is Now for the *LGBTQ Policy Journal at the Harvard-Kennedy School* (Volume VI 2015–2016), 93–94.

39. "Shiizakana," Hannibal: Season Two, Dir. Michael Rymer, Perf. Caroline Dhavernas, Laurence Fishburne, Mads Mikkelsen, Hugh Dancy, Alliance Films (September 2014). DVD.

40. There is a reason aside from narrative for this lack of appearance. The suit that the actor playing Randall Tier wore was too big and bulky to get on screen gracefully. Fuller opted to show less of the animal, knowing that like in the film *Jaws*, the audience would make up the difference according to VanDerWerff's article on *AV Club*.

41. "Shiizakana," Hannibal: Season Two, Dir. Michael Rymer, Perf. Caroline Dhavernas, Laurence Fishburne, Mads Mikkelsen, Hugh Dancy, Alliance Films (September 2014). DVD.

42. Levinas, Emmanuel, "The Name of a Dog or Natural Rights," *Difficult Freedom: Essays on Judaism*, Trans. Sean Hand (London: The Athlone Press, 1990) 151.

43. *Ibid.*

44. *Ibid.*

45. Kristeva, Julia, *The Powers of Horror: An Essay on Abjection*, Trans. Leon S. Roudiez (NY: Columbia University Press, 1994) 2.

46. "Shiizakana," Hannibal: Season Two, Dir. Michael Rymer, Perf. Caroline Dhavernas, Laurence Fishburne, Mads Mikkelsen, Hugh Dancy, Alliance Films (September 2014). DVD.

47. *Ibid.*

48. VanDer Weff, Todd, "Hannibal's Bryan Fuller on the Intimacy Between Will and Hannibal," *The AV Club* (April 26 2014. Web. Accessed: November 1 2015).

49. "Shiizakana," Hannibal: Season Two, Dir. Michael Rymer, Perf. Caroline Dhavernas, Laurence Fishburne, Mads Mikkelsen, Hugh Dancy, Alliance Films (September 2014). DVD.

50. Kirby, Danielle, *Fantasy and Belief: Alternative Religions, Popular Narratives, and Digital Cultures* (Toronto: Equinox, 2013) 1.

51. Kirby, Danielle, *Fantasy and Belief: Alternative Religions, Popular Narratives, and Digital Cultures* (Toronto: Equinox, 2013) 6.

52. *Ibid.*

53. White, Patricia in Carroll, Rachel, *Adaptation in Contemporary Culture: Textual Infidelities* (NY: Bloomsbury Academic, 2009). 43.

54. Carroll, Rachel, *Adaptation in Contemporary Culture: Textual Infidelities* (NY: Bloomsbury Academic, 2009). 43.

55. "Shiizakana," Hannibal: Season Two, Dir. Michael Rymer, Perf. Caroline Dhavernas, Laurence Fishburne, Mads Mikkelsen, Hugh Dancy, Alliance Films (September 2014). DVD.

56. Butler, Judith, *Gender Trouble: Feminism and the Subversion of Identity* (New York: Routledge, 1990), 25.

57. Butler, Judith, "Undiagnosing Gender." *Transgender Rights.* Ed. Paisey Currah, Richard M. Juang, and Shannon Price Minter (Minneapolis: University of Minnesota Press, 2006), 267.

58. *Ibid.*, 277.

59. "Naka-Choko," *Hannibal: Season Two*, Dir. Vincenzo Natali, Perf. Caroline Dhavernas, Laurence Fishburne, Mads Mikkelsen, Hugh Dancy, Alliance Films (September 2014). DVD.

Works Cited

Broverman, Neal. "Violent Gay Protests at the Oscars: Could It Happen again?" *The Advocate.* 27 February 2016. Web. Accessed: Aug 12 2016.

Butler, Judith. *Gender Trouble: Feminism and the Subversion of Identity.* New York: Routledge, 1990. Print.

_____. "Undiagnosing Gender." *Transgender Rights.* Eds Paisley Currah, Richard M. Juang, and Shannon Price Minter. Minneapolis: University of Minnesota Press, 2006. Print.

Carroll, Rachel. *Adaptation in Contemporary Culture.* Ed. Rachel Carroll. NY: Continuum.

Clover, Carol, J. *Men, Women and Chainsaws: Gender In Modern Horror Films.* Princeton: Princeton University Press, 1992.

Daly, Kyle. "Bryan Fuller says Hannibal could still return, talks Silence of the Lambs Casting." *The TV Club.* 1 September 2015. Web. Accessed: August 12 2016.

Deshane, Evelyn. "Hannibal's Refrigerator: Bryan Fuller's Response to Fan's Critical Rage." *Transitions, Endings, and Resurrections in Fandom.* Editor Rebecca Williams. 2017.

_____. "The Other Side of the Mirror: Eating Disorder Treatment and Gender Identity." *Trans Rights: The Time is Now. The LGBTQ Policy Journal at the Harvard-Kennedy School.* (Volume VI 2015–2016). Print.

Garber, Marjorie. *Vested Interests: Cross-Dressing and Cultural Anxiety.* NY: Routledge, 1997. Print.

Halberstam, Jack. *Female Masculinity.* Durham: Duke University Press, 1998.

_____. *The Queer Art of Failure.* Durham: Duke University Press, 2011.

_____. *Skin Shows: Gothic Horror and the Technology of Monsters.* Durham: Duke University Press Books, 1995.

Harris, Thomas. *The Silence of The Lambs.* Durham: St. Martin's Press, 1988. E-Book.

Irving, Dan. "Normalized transgressions: Legitimizing the transsexual body as productive." *Radical History 100.* (Winter 2008). 40–57.

Kirby, Danielle. *Fantasy and Belief: Alternative Religions, Popular Narratives, and Digital Cultures.* Toronto: Equinox, 2013. Print.

Kristeva, Julia. *The Powers of Horror: An Essay on Abjection.* Trans. Leon S. Roudiez. NY: Columbia University Press, 1994. Print.

Leitch, Thomas. *Film Adaptations and its Discontents.* Baltimore: John Hopkins University Press, 2007.

Levinas, Emmanuel. "The Name of a Dog or Natural Rights." *Difficult Freedom: Essays on Judaism.* Trans. Sean Hand. London: The Athlone Press, 1990: 151–53.

"Naka-Choko." *Hannibal: Season Two*. Dir. Vincenzo Natali. Perf. Caroline Dhavernas, Laurence Fishburne, Mads Mikkelsen, Hugh Dancy. Alliance Films, September 2014. DVD.

Ruby, Joelle, Ryan. *Reel Gender: Examining the Politics of Trans Images in Film and Media*. PhD Diss. Ohio: Bowling Green State University, 2008.

Serano, Julia. *Whipping Girl: A Transsexual Woman on Sexism and the Scapegoating of Femininity*. Berkeley: Seal Press, 2007.

"Shiizakana." *Hannibal: Season Two*. Dir. Michael Rymer. Perf. Caroline Dhavernas, Laurence Fishburne, Mads Mikkelsen, Hugh Dancy. Alliance Films, September 2014. DVD.

The Silence of the Lambs. Dir. Jonathan Demme. 1991. Burbank, CA: Orion Pictures. DVD.

Slethaug, Gordon. *Adaptation Theory and Criticism*. NY: Bloomsbury Academic, 2013.

Sullivan, K.E. "Ed Gein and the figure of the transgendered serial killer." *Jump Cut: A Review of Contemporary Media*. No. 43, July 2000, pp. 38–47.

Turk, Tisha. "Fan Work: Labor, Worth, and Participation in Fandom's Gift Economy." *Fandom and/as Labor*. Edited by Mel Stanfill and Megan Condis, special issue, *Transformative Works and Cultures*, no. 15. http://dx.doi.org/10.3983/twc.2014.0518.

VanDerWerff, Todd. "Hannibal's Bryan Fuller on the Intimacy Between Will and Hannibal." *The AV Club*. April 26 2014. Web. Accessed: November 1 2015.

Webb, Sam. "Revealed: The Mexican Doctor who chopped up his gay lover and was the inspiration for the fictional Hannibal Lecter." *Daily Mail Online*. 31 July 2013. Web. Accessed: August 13 2016.

White, Patricia. *Uninvited: Classical Hollywood Cinema and Lesbian Representability*. Bloomington and Indianapolis: University of Indiana Press, 1999.

Wood, M. Jennifer. "Bryan Fuller on Pushing Daisies, Dead like Me, and Being Cancelled." *Esquire Online*. 19 March 2015. Web. Accessed: Aug 13 2016.

Queer(y)ing Adaptation

Bryan Fuller's Hannibal
as Slash Fiction Gothic Romance

Evan Hayles Gledhill

Hannibal is densely layered television show; with visual intertextual references to its source novels, to previous adaptations, and to its own fandom. Through the on-screen examination of the distinctions between participation and observation, and detailed discussion of the responsibilities accorded each role, the series asks its audience to consider the divide between the enjoyment of spectacle and the endorsement of the actions on screen. Will Graham's vivid re-imaginings of the crimes he investigates insert him into the murderous role, confusing identities between observer and participant. In the Gothic tradition form and content are often unstable carriers of multiple meanings that invite—even insist upon—audiences' contemplation of the nature of meaning itself, and in *Hannibal* this self-reflexive exploration takes the form of psychotherapy on screen; a running commentary on ideas of audiences, consumption, and unreliable perspective, as psychiatrist Bedelia Du Maurier (Gillian Andersen) and Will Graham debate their roles as victims of, spectators for, or participants in Lecter's murder spree. The "implication" of the audience in the events on screen is heightened by the intertextual references to fan practices off screen. There is complexity in Fuller's active engagement with his fans, with the media that report on cultural trends and review his productions, and with the text itself, though this can be overstated in fan and critical discussions surrounding the show.

At heart, *Hannibal* is a gothic romance, a genre that explores unhealthy power dynamics in romantic attachments. Just as in the most famous gothic romances, *Hannibal* features a powerful man who bonds with, and seeks to control, a person who has less social standing than he does as a cultured, white, male European. In *Jane Eyre*, the eponymous protagonist resists Rochester's suggestion that she become his mistress; knowing he has a wife already, she runs away from his sphere of influence, and only returns once she knows that he has lost his ability to control her. In *Wuthering Heights*, Heathcliff's obsession with Cathy leads him to try and control her, and then to exert this control over the next generation of their families as well. Likewise, psychiatrist and serial killer Hannibal Lecter (Mads Mikkelsen) develops a close relationship with FBI profiler Will Graham (Hugh Dancy), while lying to him repeatedly, and manipulates him to break all his other professional and emotional ties; as Will says, "you don't want me to have anything in my life that's not you" ("Tome-wan"). Hannibal's need for dominance will brook no competition.

With the traditional narrative of the gothic romance transformed into a relationship between men, gender norms and expectations are de-naturalized, enabling a critique of the social expectations of gender roles that normalize and excuse abusive behaviors in intimate relationships. In describing this adaptation of Harris's novels as "slash fiction,"[1] the particular strain of fandom dedicated to same-sex romance, Fuller very deliberately positions himself within a tradition of what Judith Fetterley calls "resistant" reading practices,[2] and as an outsider to mainstream cultural production. Yet, the series is aired by a mainstream television channel that is part of a traditional broadcast media network. By combining the gothic romance with the traditions of slash fiction, Fuller is attempting to challenge normative values of and in quality television series, and queer fiction's place in the margins of the mainstream.[3] However, the very unstable nature of meaning, established by Fuller's own design, sometimes works against this goal, especially as the series is once again turned back into fanfiction by its own fans; all reinterpretations can be said to exploit, rather than explore, the power dynamics that underpin gothic romance. While there are arguments that exploring these ideas in fiction provides catharsis, are we simply romanticizing the very behavior the gothic narrative brings to our attention for condemnation?

Arthouse and Courthouse: Form and Context

Fuller states in an interview that, with *Hannibal*, "we are not making television, we are making a pretentious art house movie from the 80s."[4] While humorous, this comment reveals the intersections at the heart of this gothic production—deliberately distancing itself from the culturally debased form of television, while reveling in the transgressive idea that television is a worthy medium for visual art; sending up the pretentions of art, while enjoying its rich aesthetics and symbolism, and marrying them to highly generic televisual formatting traditions such as the police procedural. As we shall see with slash, explored in the next section, and in the gothic tradition also, this "resistant" position to cultural norms offers a gendered and class-based critique, but not necessarily from an intersectional perspective that also takes account of race. (This is not to argue that the gothic and slash fiction are always and inescapably genres of resistance, there is a long tradition of conservatism and nostalgia in gothic fiction, for example.)

Just as novel reading was initially looked upon as a passive, feminine pastime, so too was the watching of serialized television popularly linked to the feminine domestic sphere, and housewives watching at home. Television has only relatively recently become acceptable, in terms of artistic worth, by mainstream "masculine" standards of cultural quality. Despite the fact that television production roles were dominated by men, the associations of femininity in content and context meant that taking television seriously as an art form was critically rare until, as Michael Kackman notes, "an influential generation of feminist television scholarship took the medium's low cultural value as a provocative starting point, exploring the overt gendering of its pathologised, culturally subordinate viewers and its mediation of the public and private spheres."[5] Though quality television sees increasing complexity developing in the serialized format, such as narrative arcs lasting across seasons rather than a series of stand-alone episodes, it would be naïve to suggest that the definition of "quality" is simply due to technical improvements or more nuanced storytelling. It was only once television became an accepted form for middle-class masculine viewers that the era of "quality" television officially began.[6] It was gritty dramas and police procedurals that first attract the label in the 1980s.[7] Much quality television of the new millennium follows this traditional male-centric value structure; series such as *The Wire* (2002–2008), *Breaking Bad* (2008–2013), and the *Red Riding* trilogy from the UK (2009–2010) focus on majority male casts, dealing with criminal and violent subject matter. Quality shows with female leads, or domestic settings, such as *The Big C* (2010–2013) and *The Fall* (2013–2016) tend to have shorter runs on air, and attract a smaller audience. Men's narratives are still viewed as universal, whereas stories about women are often considered as representative only of the interests of women.[8]

When the feminine traits of a pathologised form are retained by male creators and authors, or in narratives that center male perspectives and concerns, then the cultural associations of femininity are often read as queer. This queerness in *Hannibal's* visual presentation echoes Fuller's deliberate introduction of queerness into the central relationship between two men. Blending aspects from three of the four original books by Harris across three seasons, Fuller's adaptation makes significant departures from the original story. He changes the race and gender of central characters, and the emotional weight of their relationships. The interactions between Will Graham and Hannibal Lecter in the novels are certainly based on mutual fascination and respect for each other's intellects, but there is no hint at a romantic connection; Lecter's attempts on Graham's life are a direct response to the investigations into his crimes, rather than to any emotional turmoil. In Fuller's adaptation, Lecter is a lonely monster, who in Will Graham "for the first time in a long while, [sees] a possibility of friendship" ("Fromage"). Lecter rejects other offers of friendship, from a fellow serial killer and a neurotic patient, because each is only attracted to part of the truth of him—one the violence, and the other the charm. This other serial killer, Tobias Budge, portrayed by black actor Demore Barnes, is presented as less successful as a criminal than Hannibal, and less attractive as a friend, but is this reflecting upon or reinforcing hierarchies of race in American culture. Hannibal maintains a seemingly friendly relationship with colleagues Jack Crawford (Laurence Fishburne) of the FBI behavioral sciences division, and fellow psychiatrist Dr. Alana Bloom (Caroline Dhavernas). However, as his therapist Bedelia Du Maurier (Gillian Anderson) observes, Hannibal maintains the wearing of his "person suit" throughout ("Sorbet"). Will is the only one offered the opportunity to know Lecter's true self intimately and survive, and thus only Will seems to have a truly personal and emotional connection to him.[9]

What is important about how *Hannibal* negotiates these themes is the intense focus upon aesthetics and the centrality of the emotional lives of its characters, which are culturally aligned with ideas of femininity, though the program still centers male characters and violent content. These qualities are shared with previous detective fictions that draw on the forensic sciences, particularly Patricia Cornwall's novels about Kay Scarpetta (1990–2015) and the British television show *Silent Witness* (1996–2015), in which the central characters were female pathologists and medical examiners. The crime genre, like the gothic, has a strong history of female creative excellence, and stories that examine lived experience from a female perspective. It can be argued that these are "feminine" genres that have been elevated in critical perception after their adoption by men.

However, cultural markers of masculinity, in turn, denote queerness in women and the transformation of Alana's wardrobe reflects such stereotypes also after she forms a relationship with Margot Verger (Katherine Isabelle): Alana is no longer styled in feminine wrap dresses and with loose flowing hair, but begins to wear suits, pins her hair into a bun or chignon, and takes to wearing trousers. Alana is not "manly," or presented as butch, but she is certainly masculinized, whereas Margot retains her feminine style. Alana's story suggests that a woman's masculine attributes are indeed pathological. The only openly queer relationship screened in *Hannibal* is between Alana and Margot, yet the formation of this relationship, and its emotional depth, is largely unexplored onscreen. That Alana was positioned in the first two seasons as a heterosexual love interest for Will and Hannibal, making no reference to bisexuality, suggests to the audience that her change in gender preference might be related to the trauma of her abuse at Hannibal's hands, and emotional betrayal by Will. That plays into damaging cultural stereotypes about lesbianism as a negative reaction against men, rather than a positive choice towards women, that continues to insert male presence into a woman-focused experience and lifestyle. In the depiction of a relationship between two women. Fuller unfortunately reverts to the dominant mode that marginalizes women's stories. However, as masculinity is so closely related to power, and its abuses, in this series Alana's styling makes sense as she plots revenge on Hannibal. To take on the power that she needs to dominate the powerful man, she avails herself of the trappings of masculinity. I argue that femininity in men is only pathologised because women represent a lesser social status, however as masculinity is linked to violence and dominance, perhaps it is always already pathological?

Slash and Slice: Murder and Sexuality on Screen

I categorize the relationship between Hannibal and Will as consistently queer, rather than gay. By contrast, though Margot and Alana's relationship is not accorded much screen time, and thus the emotional depths of the relationship remain unexplored, they clearly have a sexual relationship, and their status as partners is socially accepted by their friends and colleagues. Though Will and Hannibal form an intense bond—Hannibal sends Will "a valentine written on a broken man" ("Primavera"), they often talk like lovers, and Hannibal suggests to Will "I gave you a child, if you recall" ("…And the Woman Clothed with the Sun…"), but there is a lack of any kind of physical intimacy. Until they conspire to commit a shared murder, in killing Francis Dolarhyde (Richard Armitage), Will and Hannibal have an antagonistic relationship, rather than a partnership.

In the central queer relationship of this series, the intimate bodily act that forms an emotional bond is presented not as sexual activity, but violence. This is a motif with a history in queer cinema. In *New Queer Cinema: The Director's Cut* (2013), B. Ruby Rich explores the late twentieth century movie subgenre of "lethal lesbians," and claims that "the proof that the women on screen are lesbians is precisely that they commit murder together […] killing replaced sex as consummation" in a gory reinterpretation of the

Boston Marriage.[10] The same cultural history she traces in representations of lesbian couples, from true crime stories to supernatural vampire horror, can be traced in depictions of male murderous pairings on screen. Through the many adaptations of the real-life Nathan Leopold and Richard Loeb murder case—from Alfred Hitchcock's *Rope* (1948) to *Murder by Numbers* (dir. Barbet Schroeder, 2002)—the historical gaps between crime thrillers are filled with horror genre offerings like *Interview with a Vampire* (dir. Neil Jordan, 1994). Thus, D.A. Miller suggests, in his discussion of the representation of homosexuality in *Rope*, these films "excite a desire to see, [while] it inspires a fear of seeing"[11] by substituting the sexual with the fatal.

In her description of the role murder plays in the depiction of intimacy in the lethal lesbian films, Rich could easily be describing the central relationship in *Hannibal*;

> the audience enters into the "friendship" and eventually recognises their crime as a frenzy of fulfilment, a commitment ceremony taken to an extreme […] the protagonists kill with and for each other, either to seal their bond, or to avoid being separated, or both. Murder is a joint activity […] these are artisanal killings, handmade, and atavistic. […] It is these scenes of bonding between the protagonists that are most interesting, not the scenes of violent murder that are mostly overdetermined.[12]

The artistic posing of corpses, the making of gourmet cuisine and musical instruments from the bodies; murders in *Hannibal* are certainly "artisanal." Characters kill with and for each other in a myriad of ways. Murder for Hannibal is how he bonds with others; yet he retains power over them, and controls the narrative to protect his alibi. He secures Abigail's trust, and her silence, after she kills someone; manipulates Bedelia's experience with a patient with whose death she is involved. He excluded Budge, the friendly serial killer, because mutual knowledge of each other's methods and victims provides Hannibal with no advantage, in fact leaving him open to discovery by others through Budge. The joint murder of Francis Dolarhyde by Hannibal and Will is presented as a very different form of bonding: it is the finale of the relationship and the series, both an over-determined murder scene, full of slow-motion graphic bodily wounding and CGI-generated blood, and a scene of bonding. Eye-contact and body language between the killers is emphasized, as is their co-ordination in their attack. After the act, they cling together physically as the camera pans them, to an especially composed power-ballad—the unsubtly titled "Love Crime" by Siouxie Sioux ("The Wrath of the Lamb").

To explain the substitution of sex with violence, Rich makes a connection between blood and femininity, which has a long history in feminist and lesbian media.[13] However, this reading of biologically essentialist ties between blood, bodies, and womanhood does not map for depictions of men who kill in romantic partnership. Neither do the adaptations of the

Leopold and Loeb story appear in a clear grouping, as do the films identified by Rich, but are scattered through cinematic history across half a century. However, a strong subcultural tradition of fictional works, such as novels and stage plays, centers upon this true crime story to create a continuum of queer male bonding expressed through violence.[14] The Leopold and Loeb narrative as "slash fiction" therefore suggests a better model for the mutation of sex into violence for male couples.

"Slash" is a genre of fanworks devoted to the erotic, romantic and/or sexual pairing of characters not represented in the original, or canonical, work as being involved with one another. Slash is very often, though not exclusively, queer, and usually masculine, with same-sex female fiction dubbed "femslash." The name developed from the common practice in fanzines, and then online forums, to describe the content of stories with the names of the protagonists separated with an oblique, commonly termed a slash. Although fanfiction has a long history it has come to prominence in the new millennium in part because the era of digital communications makes it easier for fans to create and find communities online in which to share and create. The popularity of slash makes clear that the audience for representations of romance between men is broad, with a large audience of heterosexual and bisexual women, as well as gay men. The creators of *Hannibal* deliberately engaged the pre-existing fan audience with concerted promotional efforts in online fan spaces such as Tumblr, where their interactions with fans and corporate accounts for other shows demonstrated detailed understanding and appreciation of fan community norms and mores.[15] Further, Fuller brings references to slash fiction created about the television series across the "fourth wall" that usually separates the fictional representation from its audience. The intertextual referencing around this series thus acknowledges a shared creative world involving creators and audience, and a set of expectations around narrative progress and relationship development in fan communities. The inclusion of fandom references could be seen as a reward, an "Easter egg" for fans, or read as a warning.

It is important to note the dynamics already at work in online fan communities. There is much discussion in fan studies and in fan communities about the race, class and gender dynamics of fandom, and particularly in slash fiction. Quantitative analysis of archived fanfiction by a member of the fan community shows how heavily skewed towards white characters fan productions have traditionally been.[16] Though fandom often positions itself as a subculture of resistant reading, it uncritically duplicates the gendered and racial hierarchies of mainstream culture. Fuller's adaptation follows these norms; though he includes more women and people of color in the television series than appeared in the novels, they are often in roles that put their opinions, abilities and goals in opposition to white characters.

In the third season of the show, journalist Freddie Lounds (Lara Jean Chorostecki) is accused on screen of having called Graham and Lecter "murder husbands" in the press ("…And the Woman Clothed with the Sun"). This is a popular term in fan discourse around the show that Fuller co-opted into the fictional realm. In deploying the term through a character who is involved in tampering with evidence and sting operations involving the dissemination of false information Fuller appears to be suggesting that the active audience is somewhat like the unscrupulous journalist, who not only looks for meaning and clues in situations, but sometimes leads and manipulates those situations to produce the same.

Further, Fuller "genderbent" the character of Freddie, who is male in Harris's novels, and updates their publication from a tabloid paper to an online news site. The distinctions between ideas of "real" journalism and online "gossip" forums are invoked in these changes, undermining the female Lounds' credibility as a writer to an even greater extent than her male paparazzi predecessor. Lounds' immersion with the FBI cases involving Will Graham usually ends up with morally dubious decisions being made about the nature of truth, and the boundaries between participant and analyst being blurred: Dr. Frederick Chilton (Raúl Esparza) suffers a fate worse than death because Freddie and Will collude. Yet, this can also be read as two white characters callously disregarding the safety of a man they see as lesser, again we must ask if this is reflecting upon or reinforcing the dominant norms?

Categorizing slash as a resistant reading practice that disrupts or challenges norms, much fan discussion about the practice builds on two culturally dominant ideas; that authorial intent is tied to dominant cultural norms that are subverted by rewritings, and that queer representation is missing from mainstream media. While both may be true, authors of fictions resistant to dominant ideologies are also influenced by dominant norms. The "female gothic" of *Jane Eyre* highlighted the need for women to have financial independence from men, and respect as autonomous individuals, but this respect only extended so far. Jane, a white middle-class European woman with an education, achieves a level of emancipation that Bertha, the Caribbean woman with no formal education, does not. Bertha expressed her independence of spirit in less socially acceptable ways, and was incarcerated and declared mad. In creating more roles for women, and casting people of color in roles previously played by white actors, Fuller depicts a diversity of bodies, but does this reflect an inclusion of a diversity of perspectives? Positioning a black actor, a Latino actor and a female actor in the roles of the untrustworthy or incompetent professionals, is this exploring or exploiting dominant cultural stereotypes? Hannibal is dangerous as an embodiment of white, male power, yet he is also romanticized and his victory over these "adversaries" in his escape in the finale of the series.

Fuller clearly suggests that what he has drawn from Harris's original texts is not necessarily inherent in the original novels, that gendered modes of communication are judged differently, and that interpretation is not always welcomed by the subject. Recognizing the subjective nature of both reading and creating introduces another layer of uncertainty to our interpretation of the roles of creators and consumers, another lens through which to consider the text. In Fuller's embrace of the term slash, he blurs of the boundary between traditional adaptation in a popular medium and a subcultural practice among fans in limited distribution fanzines or password-protected web forums. NBC, the network television company who fund and distribute the show, bought the rights to the material that is adapted. Thus the television production has a measure of traditional creative legitimacy and protection from accusations of plagiarism that fan authors do not have, but there are limits to the access to the original texts that meant Fuller was unable to work with certain characters created by Harris which is not a limitation experienced by fan-produced work.[17] Fuller thus recognizes that in working with this creative material, and with the network, he is working with two commercial brands; "Hannibal Lecter is a franchise character."[18] The extent to which *Hannibal* is a disruptive intervention into mainstream media is therefore debatable; how controversial can an officially sanctioned adaptation be? Does legal legitimacy mean that this is a canonical work in the franchise? *Is the fandom, through its interactions with the series producers in fannish spaces such as Tumblr, seeking a form of official legitimacy, or is Fuller seeking fannish rebel status for corporate-approved slash that re-inscribes both a traditional hierarchy of production in the media and, at times, problematic hierarchies of race and gender?*

These questions of "legitimacy" then ask us to consider what it is that is being "legitimated," or what is being brought within the boundaries of normative culture that was once outside. As raised above, *Hannibal* is not just queer in its presentation of sexuality and gender, but also in its use of violence. As Rich notes, however sympathetic the "lethal lesbians" are to the audience, they always end up dead or in prison and the normative world is re-established.[19] In *Hannibal*, the female same-sex couple ends up on the run from the male same-sex couple, and at times have pursued the murder of at least one of these men—this is not progressive. The ending of *Hannibal* is "ambiguous" did the "murder husbands" survive the fall? Unlike *Thelma and Louise*, they were falling over water after all. Do we celebrate Will's execution of two serial killers, or mourn that he felt he couldn't live with or without Hannibal? Fanfiction can be a space to explore all the complexity of a morally difficult genre that deliberately provokes our questioning about the morality of love and sexual politics. However, it can also be an escapist zone, where real world consequences of queer sexuality, or even murder, no longer apply. Is the coffee shop AU a redemptive space where we don't have to pathologies the queer as murderous? Or does it seek to ignore and erase the long history of violence attached to a particular cultural figure? Is casting Jack Crawford as the "bad guy" deliberately getting in the way of a romance, an exploration of a form of fatherly normativity, or is it reflecting a dangerous urge to displace the abusive behavior of Hannibal onto another character to reduce the problematic elements of the slashed pairing? It is essential to note that, as Fuller "racebent" the character of Crawford in casting Fishburne, that a fannish rewrite to shift abusive and violent power from the white European to the black American plays into distinctly racist tropes, and current power dynamics at work in current news media. This also deliberately ignores the power dynamics depicted on screen that clearly suggest Hannibal's white male privilege is significant in protecting him from suspicion; it is naïve to think that Jack would be afforded anything like that level of leeway.

Slash is obviously not a wholly problematic nor a wholly revolutionary mode in which to create. Slash fiction, like many other forms of adaptation, provides the opportunity to compare and contrast different authors' interpretations of the same characters; with its creative focus on the emotional and sexual lives of the characters, "both fans and academics agree, slash represents a way of rethinking and rewriting traditional masculinity."[20] Thus, it can be argued that what enables Fuller's adaptation to explore monstrous masculinities in new ways is the transformation of the relationship between Hannibal and Will through being "slashed" as fanfiction. As noted by female fans, slash depictions of relationships between men have the potential be read as

> not tainted by sexism, with expectations of a given role, because the one is female and the other male ... [one partner] can be less or more strong or skilful ... but his weakness is not perceived as something that makes him in essence inferior or different. It has a different cultural meaning.[21]

While the author of the above observation interprets this as enabling a "tourist approach" to gender experience for the audience, this reading also offers the opportunity to see traditionally "feminine" experiences universalized; through their representation in the body of a white man (still) assumed to be a neutral everyman in Anglo-American media. Traditional motifs of abusive heterosexual relationships within the gothic, such as gaslighting, hysteria, and "forced seduction," are experienced in *Hannibal* by a man who physically conforms to traditional masculine norms. Will

Graham wears plaid shirts and is often unshaven, his hobbies and skills include fixing mechanical engines; his ability to fulfill normative masculine physicality is further reinforced when Freddie Lounds makes suggestive comments about the size of his penis.

When a man like Will takes on the role, and personality traits, traditionally assigned to heroines within gothic romance these signify very differently than they would for a normative woman. Behavioral attributes often encouraged in women, even venerated, are pathologised in a man; for example, Will's ability to connect with others is labeled an "empathy disorder." His "feminine" attributes—such as empathy, and a desire for domesticity—are not inherently pathological when embodied by a man, they are merely decreed so by a system that demands men and women react in different ways to sustain power dynamics between the two genders. It is his femininity that also makes Will vulnerable to abuse, both through systematic exploitation and by individual's elevated by, and invested in, normative hierarchies of power.

Gender, Genre and Pathology

Depictions of abusive relationships between men and women are a traditional aspect of the "female gothic," but in *Hannibal* the transformation of the central pairing to a same-sex couple opens up new reading positions and possibilities. When a male character is feminized, gender roles are no longer naturalized by essentialist assumptions about embodiment but are individualized, and judgments made about their action, and the actions of others against them, may be perceived quite differently. Will is weak because gothic heroines are, he conforms to his genre—but because he is not actually a woman, it is harder to read it as normalized, as natural. Will is white because he must have enough privilege to have a genuine choice—just as Jane Eyre has choice. How much choice did Bertha have in marrying Rochester? Part of the role of the gothic is the recognition that freedom of choice is part of the hierarchies of power it critiques. The circumscription of choice throws into relief the traditional romance narrative, and how abusive it is.

That femininity makes a person vulnerable to exploitation is the very design and function of societal norms that privilege and reward traditionally masculine-coded behaviors. Will is coded, by contrast to other men in the series, as feminine; self-sacrificing in the pursuit of justice, as he is selfless in his loves. Hannibal and Jack represent different forms of masculinity. Hannibal is most overtly a controlling abuser who uses his position of privilege within society to get away with murder. As a rich, educated white man,

Hannibal has the resources to hide his crimes, but also is repeatedly offered the benefit of the doubt by law enforcement. Jack is, by contrast, a sympathetic but often unhelpful ally to Will and women targeted by killers, as a well-meaning representative of an institution for the enforcement of traditional social power whose own individual power is circumscribed as his authority is questioned even within the institution to which he has devoted his life. How much choice does Jack have, as a black man how much of his power comes from his position within an institution rather than as an individual? Jack refuses to listen to Will's warnings about Lecter because he is worried about their credibility; within social hierarchies, black men and feminized men are seen as inherently less credible than a powerful white man. Will's only ally once accused of murder is the scientist Beverly Katz (Hetienne Park), who can be persuaded to set aside the seeming truths of mediated forensics, to trust in Will's "gut instincts," and then to follow her own.

Intuition and emotional intelligence, coded as feminine on screen and off, are pitted against logic and deductive reasoning, coded as masculine. Though urged to take her evidence and suspicions to Jack, Beverly has lost faith in his leadership (a plot device that further sets characters of color in opposition to truthworthiness and collaboration), and in pursing Lecter alone—at home in the domestic sphere—she ends up his victim also: like Miriam Lass (Anna Chlumsky) and Alana Bloom, she finds the systems of society let her down, and leave her open to the worst excess of masculine dominance. Jack is hampered by his investment in traditional hierarchies, by the limitations of traditionally masculine models of rational engagement. Will's "feminine" attributes of empathy and creative thinking are essential to the working of the social order, represented by Jack Crawford's success in catching criminals.

Fuller's adaptation exaggerates both Will Graham's abilities and the gruesome nature of the violent crimes he investigates with the FBI, when compared to the original source material of Harris's novels, and these exaggerations are linked to gender perceptions of particular behaviors. Just as is recorded by real world crime statistics, in the series sadistic serial killing and brutal violence is typically performed by men: there are so few female serial killers that there is no conclusive data on their trends and behaviors. Fuller chooses to depict female killers on *Hannibal* as performing a twisted form of normative feminine behavior; an acupuncturist and practitioner of alternative healing methods seeks to end her patients' pain in "Takiawase," and a woman desperate to build a family leads young runaways to murder their original families in "Oeuf." This sounds very much like a parallel for Will's own experiences in empathy and domesticity, but the structure of the narrative keeps Will away from the women: in "Ouef," Will bonds with the male children rather than the mother figure, and in "Takiawase" as he is imprisoned he is not a participant in the investigation. However, the only other female murderer in the series, Georgia Madchen, is revealed to not be a serial killer at all but suffering from a delusional disorder. Georgia and Will are directly aligned, in their experiences of being promised protection by the FBI and being betrayed by Lecter, and through their experiences of neurological illness ("Buffert Froid"). This is a rather neat solution to the "problem" that in feminizing Will, the adaptors align him with gendered behaviors that make him less likely to kill. The solution is to suggest that a break from reality could drive Will to do such a thing, or a protective—maternal—drive. This also serves to distance Will from the male killers he doubles with in the recreations of the violent murders, linking himself to them through the phrase "this is my design." That these scenes are mediated through Will's unreliable perception destabilizes his gendered alignment with violence.

Hannibal, as a series, asks complicated questions about victimhood and agency. How much control do individuals have within a system, and in relation to each other? It initially seems to disavow interpretative ambiguity, with the reliance on forensic science echoing series like *CSI*, but as the series progresses representations of mental illness, the manipulation of forensic evidence, the abuse of psychiatric drugs and memory techniques, and the impact of individual desire and personality, are all drawn into the plot. By the time of Dolarhyde's murder, Will Graham's agency in the decision-making process has been circumscribed, if not entirely undermined, by his feminized position. Jack and Hannibal each ask him "whose man" he is ("Mizumono"), suggesting her has little agency of his own. Will's positioning throughout the third series, as emotionally compromised and manipulated by Hannibal, reintroduces a moral ambiguity. What constitutes free will (pun intended)?

The manipulation inherent in patriarchal demands of women's self-transformations, framed as self-determined yet influenced by pressure towards cultural expectation and historicized norms, is presented on screen in the interactions between Hannibal and Will. This exaggerated parallel is made clear as Will's relationship to Hannibal is mirrored in Bella Crawford's relationship to Jack, which is presented as a traditional, even positive, example of heterosexual romance and love. Yet Bella is not really Bella Crawford at all. Hannibal asks "Are you an Isabelle or an Annabelle?," and she answers that her name is in fact Phyllis ("Coquilles"). Jack tells the tale of his renaming her, in affection, "beautiful woman" in Italian. Yet "Bella" is the catcall she received in Italy where they met, inscribing the popular view that men's unsolicited opinions of women's appearance are both complimentary and worthy of notice by the woman herself. We never hear Phyllis's original, full name. The role she plays in the wider world, as a Peace Corps agent and representative of the UN, is not presented on screen, unlike the process of her transformation into Jack's wife. Intercut with the scene of Bella's funeral we are shown her wedding, bookending her life, which thus starts only at the moment she accepts her new role, title, and identity as defined by Jack. She is Mrs. Jack Crawford. The traditional heteronormative romance, this suggests, leaves no space for a woman's individual identity, her agency, her choices. This is reinforced as Hannibal refuses to let Phyllis decide the means of her own death, and he resuscitated her because her husband's emotions are more important than her self-determination. "I couldn't do it to you, Jack" ("Mukosuze").

In the transformation of Phyllis we see a normative model for the abnormal process experienced in Will's developing relationship with Hannibal, which foregrounds and examines the disturbing side of a loss of identity, a transformation into a dependent half of a two-person unit of monstrous identity. Will's hobbies are co-opted by Hannibal who creates forensic evidence out of the fishing lures Will constructs ("Savoureux"). Will is encouraged to view himself as damaged and abused, but his attention is (mis)directed towards the father figure, Jack ("Trou Normand"). Finally, Will loses even physical sovereignty, as he is drugged and orally penetrated by Hannibal with a feeding tube ("Kaiseki"). These actions all have the aim of distancing Will from the institutions of justice, rather than directly bringing him closer to Hannibal himself. This is the same process that real survivors of abusive relationships recount; their abusers aim is not to create a positive emotional bond between them, but to ensure that their victim has no other bonds outside the relationship, and no trust. Will's only safety from the destructive megalomania of Hannibal's monstrous masculinity is his alignment with the greater systemic masculine power of patriarchal institutions; Will seemingly has no agency of his own in this process. Will's role in the public sphere gives him visibility and legitimacy, so he is most vulnerable in the domestic realm traditionally associated with femininity.

Lecter always maintains that he is acting for Will's own good, that he knows Will's true nature and how to make him happy: "I only want what is best for you" ("Tome-wan"). He denies Will choice and agency even in this. Will, however, notes that friendship demands an equality in position, but that the patient and psychiatrist relationship (sub-textually, the predator/prey dynamic) denotes a power imbalance in their interactions ("Sakizuke"). This echoes twentieth-century feminist arguments that there can be no such thing as a fully consenting heterosexual relationship under patriarchy because of the imbalance of power between the genders.[22] Will becomes aware of the manipulation, and eventually takes action, agreeing with Chiyoh's (Tao Okamoto) assessment that "If you don't kill him, you're afraid you're going to become him" ("Contorno"). By the end of the process Will Graham is no longer as he was at the start of the story; just as Phyllis was, he is transformed—into Mr. Hannibal Lecter. It is at home where the worst damage is done.

Daddy Dearest

The family dynamics in *Hannibal* echo older the gothic texts, such as *Jane Eyre* and *The Turn of the Screw*, in which the family is often perceived by the father figure as a haven to which he wants to retreat, or which he wants to protect, but is often a setting for fear and danger for women and children. Three particular sets of monstrous family dynamics that outline these undercurrents are explored on screen, focused around the gothic "heroine" Will Graham. The first traumatic situation is engineered by Hannibal, who endangers the family of serial killer Garrett Jacob Hobbs (Vladimir Jon Cubrt), and then manipulates the surviving, and traumatized, daughter Abigail Hobbs (Kacey Rohl)) and Will into forming a familial bond. In the second family dynamic, Will is seduced by Margot Verger, as she attempts to beget a legitimate heir to reduce her brother Mason's financial power over her. Hannibal utilizes his position as psychiatrist to all three to inflame Mason's jealousy, with violent results. Finally, Will forms a heteronormative relationship with Molly (Nina Arianda) once he believes himself free of Lecter's influence, and Hannibal again uses a surrogate to disrupt the relationship with violence. Hannibal takes everything from Will that has meaning in normative society; his children, his home, the trust of the father-figure, his reputation within systemic institutions, and his opportunity for heteronormative romance; "I bond with Abigail, you take her away. I bond with barely more than the idea of a child, you take it away. You saw to it that I alienated Alana, alienated Jack" ("Tome-wan"). All Hannibal offers in return is himself.

The gendered dynamics of these tropes of power negotiation and autonomy within the family are particularly clear in the relationship Will develops with Abigail Hobbs. Abigail is both the victim of her father's serial murders, and his (perhaps coerced) accomplice. Lecter manipulates Will's instincts and Abigail's search for an ally, as she is investigated by the FBI, to develop a family dynamic between the three of them as part of his seduction of Will; "we are her fathers now" ("Trou Normand"). When Will refuses Hannibal's monstrous seduction, Lecter recreates the Hobb's family trauma: incapacitating Will (the mother), he makes him watch as he slits Abigail's throat, literally stepping into her father's place.

274 Hannibal for Dinner

Hannibal's destruction of the child Abigail, and his attempted murder of Jack, are an attempt to destroy Will's limited, domestic, sphere of influence, having already destroyed his public image through the accusation of murder. Yet Will still forgives him, pursues him, then leaves his reconstituted family with Molly for him. In the couple's unhealthy attachment to each other we can see echoes of *Wuthering Heights*, in their devotion despite the distance between them, and the promise of an alternative life after disaster, perhaps *Jane Eyre*. However, in reading the older texts, many have interpreted them as straightforward romance narratives, rather than specifically gothic romance. In the many adaptations of *Wuthering Heights* on film very few reference the second generation and Heathcliff's horrendous cruelty to his wife, his son, and his niece and nephew. He is usually portrayed as a romantic lead, by an attractive young star, and not shown as the monstrous older man who torments his family. In adaptations of *Jane Eyre*, Rochester is rarely depicted uttering his most terrifying lines from the book, the ones that inspire Jane to leave, lines like "Jane! Will you hear reason? [...] because if you won't I'll try violence."[23] The depiction of his first wife is reduced to a screaming madwoman, which reflects Rochester's description of her, yet he has already been proven a liar, so why should we trust his version of events?

Gender difference is important to the characters in these novels, not just their adaptors and readers. In *Wuthering Heights*, Cathy is drawn between the freedom she finds with Healthcliff on the moorland, and the pressure to be traditionally feminine, and be rewarded with stability, pretty dresses, and warm fires in an upper-class home. Jane Eyre knows that her troubles being poor throughout her life are in part because she is female; she is not valued highly by the relatives who must look after her, and she has few opportunities to earn money respectfully as a nineteenth century middle-class woman. Despite the great deal of detail that the Brontë sisters went to in outlining the specific problems that their heroines faced due to cultural expectations of gendered behaviors, when a narrative has a "marriage plot" a happy ending is seen to sweep away all the previous difficulties. However, I'd suggest instead a reading that highlights them—the only solution for women in the older narratives is to ally themselves with men, and it is only by luck that they find one who will not control and subjugate them. The lure of the dominant and powerful man, the need for a protector as a feminine person who is judged and mistreated by a society that undervalues their talents—these are not romantic elements of the stories, but elements of the gothic horror that sees women trapped in the home, that makes the domestic a site of power negotiations. Exploring the romance through slash, we can gain a new perspective on the gothic aspects of the "marriage plot." We see Will's domination by Hannibal as entirely a product of Hannibal's actions, of his deliberate manipulation of Will's temperament. Will is not "naturally" considered to be in the weaker position in the power struggle, as a woman might be, but is clearly shown to have been manipulated into this position. So too were the gothic heroines in whose footsteps he treads as he sleepwalks, goes hunting for despicable felons in underground tunnels, and protests his innocence against an unjust system.

Conclusion

The fantastical elements of Fuller's adaptation that make it a gothic romance with elements of a thriller, rather than Harris's thriller with elements of gothic horror, makes Will a gothic heroine. That the relationship between the two men is never consummated sexually, demonstrably not for censorious reasons through the inclusion of Margot and Alana's relationship, adds ambiguity that prevents this from simply being read as a story about a gay abusive relationship. Had Fuller romanticized such a relationship, it would have been decried as a callous and exploitative series. This distance he sets up is at once the dangerous space that enables free play and the useful space of uncertainty and metaphor. Queer once meant strange or peculiar, which is what Bryan Fuller has certainly made his series that. We should not try to normalize that; queer can mean not quite "true," at an odd angle, and looking at the normative gender roles and ideas of romance from this perspective reveals the strangeness of "normal."

When we buy into the romance, and revel in the gothic horror, we are complicit and also recognize our own manipulation, like Bedelia. If we accept this as a positive love story, we accept everything this tells us about our ideas about how the feminine is (de)valued culturally. That's not to say that the only resistant reading position is one of complete repudiation; we are as enmeshed in this society as Alana or Jack, and thus we must explore and examine our interest and attraction to the monster.

Notes

1. Ross Scarano, "Bryan Fuller knows you're reading into *Hannibal's* homoeroticism, and he thinks it's hilarious," *Complex*, September 16, 2014, accessed September 9, 2015, http://www.uk.complex.com/pop-culture/2014/09/bryan-fuller-hannibal-interview-slash-fiction.
2. Judith Fetterley, *The Resisting Reader: A Feminist Approach to American Fiction* (Bloomington: Indiana University Press, 1978).
3. Quality television is a phrase to be used with qualifiers, about who determines this quality and by what metrics. It is used here as an industry recognised label for a specific set of shows and producers, without an acceptance that its terminology is reflective of the author's judgement of "quality." For a nuanced examination of the term and its usage, see Newman and Levine (2011).

4. Eric Thurm, "Hannibal Showrunner: 'we are not making television. We are making a pretentious art house movie from the 80s,'" *The Guardian*, June 3, 2015, accessed September 9, 2015, http://www.theguardian.com/tv-and-radio/2015/jun/03/hannibal-tv-showrunner-bryan-fuller.

5. Michael Kackman, "Quality Television, Melodrama, and Cultural Complexity," *Flow* 9.1 (2008), accessed September 27, 2015, http://flowtv.org/2008/10/quality-television-melodrama-and-cultural-complexity michael-kackman university-of-texas-austin/.

6. Geraldine Harris, "A return to form? Postmasculinist television drama and tragic heroes in the wake of *The Sopranos*," *New Review of Film and Television Studies* 10:4 (2014): 443–463, accessed 12 December 2015, doi: 10.1080/17400309.2012.708272.

7. Ashley Sayeau, "As Seen on TV: Women's Rights and Quality Television," in *Quality TV: Contemporary American Television and Beyond*, eds. Janet McCabe, Kim Akass (London: I.B. Tauris, 2007), 52–61.

8. The recent exception to this might be Netflix series *Orange Is the New Black*; as a prison drama it echoes the content and form of the long running criminal dramas, but with a majority female cast it is disrupting the norms of the genre.

9. Bedelia's survival is conditional, as Hannibal will not kill her until he also has the opportunity to eat her, and he promised Alana that he would eventually kill her too ("Mizumono").

10. B. Ruby Rich, *New Queer Cinema: The Director's Cut* (London: Duke University Press, 2013), 114.

11. D.A. Miller, "Anal *Rope*," in *Inside/Out: Lesbian Theories, Gay Theories*, ed Diana Fuss (New York: Routledge, 1991): 131.

12. Rich, *New Queer Cinema*, 110–111.

13. Rich, *New Queer Cinema*, 114.

14. Mark Lynn Anderson, "Psychoanalysis and Fandom in the Leopold and Loeb Trial," in *Twilight of the Idols: Hollywood and the Human Sciences in 1920s America* (University of California Press, 2011), 51.

15. Nistasha Perez, "The Creation of Official Tumblr Accounts in Online Fannish Spaces: Examining Integration of Fannish Practices by Media Corporations," paper presented to *Fan Studies Network Conference 2014*, Regent's University, London, September 27, 2014.

16. Lulu, "Fandom's Race Problem and the AO3 Ship Stats," Slow Dance of the Infinite Stars blog, August 13, 2016, accessed September 1, 2016, http://centrumlumina.tumblr.com/post/148893785870/fandoms-race-problem-and-the-ao3-ship-stats.

17. Eric Goldman, "Hannibal: How Bryan Fuller Approached the Iconic Character," *IGN Entertainment*, April 3, 2013, accessed August, 2016, http://uk.ign.com/articles/2013/04/04/hannibal-how-bryan-fuller-approached-the-iconic-character-and-why-clarice-starling-cant-appear-red-dragon-the-silence-of-the-lambs?page=1 .

18. Goldman, Hannibal, 3.

19. Rich, *New Queer Cinema*, 113.

20. Shoshanna Green, Cynthia Jenkins and Henry Jenkins, "'Normal Female Interest in Men Bonking': Selections from The Terra Nostra Underground and Strange Bedfellows," in *Fans, Bloggers and Gamers: Exploring Participatory Culture*, ed by Henry Jenkins (Durham: Duke University Press, 2006), 71.

21. Cat Anestopoulo, quoted in Green, Jenkins and Jenkins, *Normal Female Interest*, 68.

22. Carole Pateman, "Women and Consent," *Political Theory*, 8.2 (May, 1980) 149–168.

23. Charlotte Brontë, *Jane Eyre: An Autobiography* (Paris: Baudry's European Library, 1850), 230.

Works Cited

Anderson, Mark Lynn. "Psychoanalysis and Fandom in the Leopold and Loeb Trial." In *Twilight of the Idols: Hollywood and the Human Sciences in 1920s America*. 49–69. University of California Press, 2011.

Brontë, Charlotte. *Jane Eyre: An Autobiography*. Paris: Baudry's European Library, 1850.

Fetterley, Judith. *The Resisting Reader: A Feminist Approach to American Fiction.* Bloomington: Indiana University Press, 1978.

Goldman, Eric. "Hannibal: How Bryan Fuller Approached the Iconic Character." *IGN Entertainment.* April 3, 2013. Accessed August, 2016. http://uk.ign.com/articles/2013/04/04/hannibal-how-bryan-fuller-approached-the-iconic-character-and-why-clarice-starling-cant-appear-red-dragon-the-silence-of-the-lambs?page=1.

Green, Shoshanna, Cynthia Jenkins and Henry Jenkins. "'Normal Female Interest in Men Bonking': Selections from The Terra Nostra Underground and Strange Bedfellows." In *Fans, Bloggers and Gamers: Exploring Participatory Culture*, edited by Henry Jenkins. 61–88. London: Duke University Press, 2006.

Harris, Geraldine. "A return to form? Postmasculinist television drama and tragic heroes in the wake of *The Sopranos.*" *New Review of Film and Television Studies* 10:4 (2014), 443–463. Accessed December 12, 2015. doi: 10.1080/17400309.2012.708272.

Kackman, Michael. "Quality Television, Melodrama, and Cultural Complexity." *Flow* 9.1 (2008). Accessed September 27, 2015. http://flowtv.org/2008/10/quality-television-melodrama-and-cultural-complexity-michael-kackman-university-of-texas-austin/.

Lulu. "Fandom's Race Problem and the AO3 Ship Stats," *Slow Dance of the Infinite Stars blog*, 13 August 13, 2016. Accessed September 1, 2016. http://centrumlumina.tumblr.com/post/148893785870/fandoms-race-problem-and-the-ao3-ship-stats.

Miller, D.A. "Anal Rope." In *Inside/Out: Lesbian Theories, Gay Theories*, edited by Diana Fuss. 119–141. New York: Routledge, 1991.

Newman, Michael Z., and Elana Levine. *Legitimating Television: Media Convergence and Cultural Status.* London: Routledge, 2011.

Pateman, Carole. "Women and Consent." *Political Theory* 8.2 (1980) 149–168.

Perez, Nistasha. "The Creation of Official Tumblr Accounts in Online Fannish Spaces: Examining Integration of Fannish Practices by Media Corporations," paper presented to *Fan Studies Network Conference 2014*, Regent's University, London. September 27, 2014.

Rich, B. Ruby. *New Queer Cinema: The Director's Cut.* London: Duke University Press, 2013.

Sayeau, Ashley. "As Seen on TV: Women's Rights and Quality Television." In *Quality TV: Contemporary American Television and Beyond*, edited by Janet McCabe and Kim Akass. 52–61. London: I.B. Tauris, 2007.

Scarano, Ross. "Bryan Fuller knows you're reading into *Hannibal*'s homoeroticism, and he thinks it's hilarious." *Complex*, September 16, 2014. Accessed September 9, 2015. http://www.uk.complex.com/pop-culture/2014/09/bryan-fuller-hannibal-interview-slash-fiction.

Thurm, Eric. "*Hannibal* Showrunner: 'We are not making television. We are making a pretentious art house movie from the 80s.'" *The Guardian*, June 3, 2015. Accessed 9 September 2015. http://www.theguardian.com/tv-and-radio/2015/jun/03/hannibal-tv-showrunner-bryan-fuller.

An Art Form That Honors Aesthetic and Taste

The Art of Murder and the Art of Television in Hannibal

MICHAEL FUCHS

In the spring of 2014, the *New York Times* ran a feature titled "Television Tests Tinseltown," in which television's "new golden age" was celebrated. Among the indicators for this golden age, the introduction listed the "many A-list directors, writers and actors [who] choos[e] series over films" and the fact that "water cooler chat ignor[es] Oscar contenders to discuss shows like *Mad Men*."[1] In view of the debates which have surrounded "quality television" for the past decade, none of these ideas seem particularly new, let alone groundbreaking or astounding. However, in his contribution to the discussion, film and music critic Armond White claims, "Film is a visual art form and television is merely a visual medium." He continues,

> It's generally accepted that television is a producer's, or show runner's, format, where content is developed to support advertising, but all this talk about "television's gold age" overlooks the fact that television has never proven to be a medium for artists—or auteurs—who express themselves personally and, primarily, visually.[2]

As White laments the "time watching the classics in old-school movie houses," he not only rhetorically apes the thousands of trolls frequenting internet discussion forums, but it also becomes obvious that his (or the implied troll's) idea of movies, and watching movies, is limited to the theatrical experience, possibly even the theatrical experience at least two score years ago.[3] Ironically, a year before White's opinion piece, in which the physical space of the movie theater would play a key role in the conceptualization of film, was published, several Austrian and German movie theaters had screened the first two episodes of the third season of *Game of*

Thrones (HBO, since 2011) for free the day after their release in the United States (in a promotional effort by the pay TV provider Sky Germany). And less than a year after White had decried television by unfavorably comparing the medium to the movie houses of the days of yore, American and British IMAX theaters showed the final two episodes of the fourth season of the fantasy show.

My point here is, however, not to discredit White and explain that his differentiation between film and television does not stand up to scrutiny in the age of streaming services, mobile viewing, 4K Blu-rays, and home theaters. Rather, my contribution to this volume is interested in a more fundamental question White's opinion piece raises: Is television art? Or, maybe more to the point, *can* television be art? Of course, any straightforward answer to these questions is bound to stir up heated discussions, not the least because "art" is hard, if not impossible, to define. After all, wise minds such as Ludwig Wittgenstein have brooded over this issue and concluded that the spectrum of cultural artifacts and performances considered "art" is too diverse to come up with a satisfying definition of the phenomenon.[4] In view of these contrivances, I will not tackle the issue of television's artistic merits head-on, but rather demonstrate that *Hannibal* taps into the visual grammar of the visual arts.

By discussing *Hannibal*'s indebtedness to "real" art, I do not mean to suggest that television may only become artistic when a show consciously seeks to locate itself within the history of the visual arts (or any other "true" art form). A brief anecdote Elana Levine offers in the book *Legitimating Television* (2012) seems telling in this context: After completing her first university course on television, she "eagerly registered for TV Aesthetics and Criticism the following semester." Her sizzling anticipation of studying the artistic merits of television was, however, short-lived, for Levine was "confronted with a course that focused on television broadcasts of the arts—opera, theater, classical music." Of course, this approach implied an understanding of television in which "the question of aesthetics could only be paired with television when true art forms were involved."[5]

While my essay and the course Levine took back in the day share an interest in the coupling of television and "true" arts, my argument will center on the ways in which *Hannibal*'s visual style remediates painting. Just as fictional murderer Francis Dolarhyde's devouring of William Blake's painting *The Great Red Dragon and the Woman Clothed in the Sun* (1805–1810) represents and effort to tap into the ritualistic cannibalistic function of assimilating the spiritual force of the consumed, *Hannibal*'s incorporation of not simply an older medium, but an accepted art form, can be viewed as an effort to stake a claim to cultural legitimacy by remediating "high-brow" cultural artifacts. Indeed, Jonathan Freedman has argued that this form of pandering to literati and cultural elites is typical of popular culture: "[T]he embedding of a moment from high culture in the effluvia of mass culture," he has remarked, endows pieces of popular culture with "a cognate legitimacy."[6] As much subversive power as this transgressive gesture may hold (in terms of potentially countering established cultural hierarchies), Freedman has astutely pointed out that popular culture's cannibalizing of "high" culture for purposes of cultural legitimation implies accepting the elite's taste culture. In other words, if popular culture requires the legitimacy of "high" culture, the referencing, or even straight-up incorporation, of "high" culture in popular culture perpetuates ideas surrounding popular culture's inferior status and its need for cultural legitimation.

This notion of television's striving for cultural acceptance undergirds not only many academic discussions of television today, but also my exploration of *Hannibal*'s artistry. While one could argue that my discussion of how a television series' visual style references traditions in painting reproduces "patterns of taste judgement" and "nudg[es television] closer to more established arts and cultural forms," my guiding argument revolves around the question of how the show tries to transcend binary oppositions, including those binaries pertaining to cultural hierarchies. Accordingly, my essay will focus on *Hannibal*'s murder scenes and food designs. As I will argue, the series' crime and food scenes draw attention to them as set pieces of a television show. Thus, these visual excesses threaten to tear down the imaginary wall separating the diegetic from the extradiegetic world, as the lines between the artist within the storyworld (i.e., Hannibal) and outside the storyworld (i.e., the showrunner and the directors) disappear. In this way, Hannibal's art not only metaleptically transforms into *Hannibal*'s art, but also becomes representative of televisual art in the early twenty-first century. At the same time, however, the careful visual designs, characterized by their excesses, do not only draw viewers into the show, but also break the illusion and ask viewers to distance themselves form the on-screen events and engage cognitively with the images in Brechtian fashion. This conscious resumption of disbelief emerges as key to *Hannibal*'s meaning, as the show raises the question in how far this aesthetic distance is desirable or acceptable when confronted with the repugnant (albeit artistic) handiwork of (fictional) murderers.

Television (as) Art

Historically, television studies primarily developed out of communication studies and British cultural studies. Although early television scholarship emerging from the former discipline did not lack a critical edge, academics working in the field were mostly parked in departments and schools interested in answering "questions of more or less direct utility to the communications industry" and imparting upon students "the crafts of reporting, advertising and public relations."[7] The cultural studies approach, championed by John Fiske's writings of the mid–1980s, on the other hand, focuses on television "as an outgrowth of an ideological system." In this system of power, television is merely one of various cultural texts playing their respective role "in the maintenance or contestation of that system."[8] While the medium of television has often been perceived as an arbiter of the status quo, its intricate relationship with cultural studies grew out of historical circumstances. After all, American television raised public awareness of the plight of African Americans in the 1960s, since television allowed millions of Americans across the country to witness how "Birmingham police used dogs and high-pressure water hoses on the demonstrators." The circulation of these images "resulted in national and international outrage."[9] Television's "powerful and visceral images … permeated many levels of American social and political reality" during this tumultuous time in American history.[10] As a result, television and discourses of power have become nearly inseparable.

Considering the deprecatory—if not even hostile—attitude some television scholars adopt toward television aesthetics, it may seem somewhat ironic that the cultural studies scholar Raymond Williams introduced the concept most closely aligned with the aesthetics of television—"flow." Turning on the television in a Miami hotel room after crossing the Atlantic in an ocean liner, the British academic was bombarded by what he perceived as "a single irresponsible flow of images." This experience was totally at odds with watching television back home in the United Kingdom. Flow, Williams concluded, "is planned," evidenced by "the replacement of a … series of timed sequential units by a … series of differently related units in which the timing, though real, is undeclared." Accordingly, Williams diagnosed a fusion of disparate elements, as he likened watching American television to

> having read two plays, three newspapers, three or four magazines, on the same day that one has been to a variety show and a lecture and a football match. And yet in another way it is not like that at all, for though the items may be various the television experience has in some important ways unified them.[11]

Since the concept of flow "can be bent in the most diverse directions," it has easily adapted to the changing environment of the televisual landscape in the post-network era.[12] While Williams' original conception was tied to the structure of individual channels (or, arguably, the lack of a structure), planned by the network, modern televisual flow is controlled by viewers, as they zap from channel to channel, between live programming, Netflix,

Hulu, HBO On Demand, and Amazon Video, transforming the flow into a movement across multiple channels and platforms instead of the effortless movement between individual programs on a single channel.

However, already a decade before Williams introduced his seminal concept, a book commissioned by CBS proclaimed television the eighth art.[13] This somewhat rash assertion of television's artistic qualities was refined in the 1970s when literary scholars increasingly colonialized the then-new medium. Among these pioneers was Horace Newcomb, back then a relatively young man with a Ph.D. in American literature who came to be known as "Mr. Television." Newcomb's *TV: The Most Popular Art* (1974) was a seminal book in many respects. One of its principal accomplishments was singling out the art and aesthetics of seriality, which Newcomb saw most obviously manifested (and nearly perfected) in one of the lowest forms of television—soap operas. As Newcomb put it, "With the exception of soap operas, television has not realized that regular and repeated appearance of a continuing group of characters is one of the strongest techniques for the development of rich and textured dramatic presentations."[14]

Newcomb's foundational ideas about the serialized art of telling stories still echo today in scholarly works such as Jason Mittell's. Mittell has recently developed a "poetics" of television, which merges the narrative potentials of the medium with their ideological underpinnings.[15] Indeed, Mittell's book offers a variety of approaches to study the "poetics" of *Hannibal*, its narrative "complexity," and, accordingly, the show's artistic character. *Hannibal* thrives on serio-episodic storytelling, the show employed paratexts to make viewers invested in the show, showrunner Bryan Fuller embraced the role of a television auteur—one could go through all of the points Mittell considers characteristic of complex television and apply it to *Hannibal* in some way.

Although *Complex TV* (2015) repeatedly tackles televisual style, Mittell eschews the terms "television art" and "television aesthetics." However, he explicitly makes use of Neil Harris' concept of "operational aesthetic"—moments in which television meta-reflexively draws attention to its production, circulation, and reception. As Mittell explains, "We watch [complex television] not just to get swept away in a realistic narrative world (although that certainly happens) but also to watch the gears at work, marveling at the craft required to pull off such narrative pyrotechnics." "The operational aesthetic," he continues, "is heightened in spectacular moments within narratively complex programs, specific sequences or episodes that we might consider akin to special effects."[16]

In contrast to Mittell's emphasis on narrative, my essay will explore *Hannibal*'s visual style and how it opens up at least two (seemingly contradictory) approaches to understanding and appreciating the show.

Accordingly, my interest is more akin to an aesthetic category John Caldwell had introduced two decades before Mittell's book was published, televisuality. Caldwell was interested in the specific "looks" of television programs and concluded that "one of the chief directorial tasks in primetime is to construct coherent stylistic worlds." While Caldwell dismissively wrote about the "ideology of stylistic excess," which "pervade[d] ... American television and mass culture" of the 1980s, he still acknowledged that "signs of excess are rooted in the very broad cultural and pictorial traditions that practitioners can ... bring to bear in producing shows."[17]

In film studies, visual excess has repeatedly been linked to spectacle, which "directly solicits spectator attention ... and ... emphasiz[es] the direct stimulation of shock or surprise."[18] On the other hand, Kristin Thompson has argued that visual excess invites "the spectator to linger over devices longer than their structured fiction would warrant." The resultant increased alertness to stylistic aspects allows viewers to gain aesthetic distance, as they are "no longer constrained by conventions."[19] These two opposing views on one phenomenon not only show two extremes of interacting with a cultural artifact, but they are also entrenched in the opposition between the mind and the body. The first type (i.e., the—more or less—direct address of the human body) is traditionally connected to "lower" forms of cultural expression, whereas the latter type presents a more critical, intellectual kind of response, which is typically linked with "high" culture.

Hannibal *as Art Aficionado and Artist*—Hannibal *as Art*

The novel *Red Dragon* (1981) consciously plays on this opposition. In the book, Francis Dolarhyde records his horrific deeds on film. As Dolarhyde watches the recording of his second vicious attack on an American family, the narrator comments:

A bouncing blur in a harsh movie light became a bed and Charles Leeds thrashing, Mrs Leeds sitting up, shielding her eyes, turning to Leeds and putting her hands on him, rolling toward the edge of the bed, legs tangled in the covers, trying to rise. The camera jerked toward the ceiling, molding whipping across the screen like a stave, and then the picture steadied, Mrs Leeds back down on the mattress, a dark spot on her nightdress spreading and Leeds, hands to his neck and eyes wild rising. The screen went black for five beats, then the tic of a splice.

The camera was steady now, on a tripod. They were all dead now. Arranged. Two children seated against the wall facing the bed, one seated across the corner from them facing the camera. Mr and Mrs Leeds in bed with the covers over them. Leeds propped up against the headboard, the sheet covering the rope around his chest and his head

lolled to the side. Dolarhyde came into the picture from the left with the stylized movements of a Balinese dancer....
     [I]n the film's ensuing scene he lost all his grace and elegance of motion, rooting pig-
like with his bottom turned carelessly to the camera. There were no dramatic pauses,
no sense of pace or climax, just brutish frenzy.

Watching the film unfold in front of his very eyes, Dolarhyde detects "[t]wo
major flaws": "the film did not actually show the deaths of the Leedses and
… his own performance was poor toward the end. He seemed to lose all
his values." Dolarhyde understands that his primal drives took over and he
lost control; however, he is certain that "with experience," he will "maintain
some aesthetic distance, even in the most intimate moments."[20]

     The use of "aesthetic distance" is crucial here, for the expression high-
lights Dolarhyde's desire to create something of lasting value. He seeks
to immortalize the moment of death in a motion picture and believes
that this project may only be achieved once he can overcome his bodily
urges. Sarah Cardwell has explained that in traditional aesthetic theory,
"'Under-distancing' is a critical flaw, which can arise from the work, or
from the observer who fails to grasp the necessary requirements of aesthetic engagement."[21] Dolarhyde seems to be aware of this expectation to
remain at a critical distance from the artwork in order to truly appreciate it.
Yet he is located in a complex position, simultaneously artist and beholder.
For the artist inside of him to create what Dolarhyde considers beautiful,
the artist needs to put all his passion into his work, which makes it nearly
impossible to maintain the critical distance his rational self desires. As a
result, Dolarhyde begins to grasp that while his movie may be "wonderful,"
it is "not as wonderful as the acts themselves."[22] Accordingly, whereas intel-
lectuals may strive for critical distance, Dolarhyde's down-to-earth understanding suggests that direct, visceral reactions to a piece of art do not
necessarily undermine its value; indeed, from a certain perspective, this
bodily response may surpass a more critical approach, since it establishes a
more intimate relationship with the artifact; a kind of becoming-art.

     This brief episode from the first entry in the Hannibal Lecter fran-
chise illustrates that the arts and discourses surrounding the arts have
always played a central role in the Hannibalverse. As a result, scholars have
repeatedly studied this topic. For example, in his article "Eating Blake"
(1999), Nicholas Williams focuses on the iconic scene in *Red Dragon* in
which "Dolarhyde, having already murdered two families … adds to his
list of crimes a comparatively minor but still chilling act of artistic dese-
cration," as Thomas Harris' lowly mass culture thriller similarly devours
the high art of William Blake. Williams remarks that this gesture of cannibalistic incorporation allows Harris to query "the status of high art by
suggesting that its aura of presentness can never actually survive literary

representation."[23] Thomas Fahy has explored the meaning of classical music in the *Silence of the Lambs* adaptation (1991), concluding that "[t]he juxtaposition of Lecter's explosive violence with his affinity for J.S. Bach's *Goldberg Variations* … undermines … ideas about culture as civilizing."[24] In *Making Murder* (2009), Philip Simpson tracks allusions in Thomas Harris' novels. Although he includes references to popular culture, most of the intertextual and intermedial traces he discusses in more detail would traditionally be aligned with art (e.g., painting, classical music, and "great" works of literature).[25] Michelle Leigh Gompf's *Thomas Harris and William Blake* (2013) makes its goal explicit in the title, as she traces the connections between Harris and Blake in an attempt to explore the theme of binary oppositions (e.g., good vs. evil; taste vs. no taste), which unites the two texts.[26] But these are merely some of the more explicit scholarly explorations of art and/in the Hannibal Lecter universe.

The television show embraces the dialogue with the arts introduced in the novels. Tellingly, Titan Books' companion to the series is titled *The Art and Making of* Hannibal (2015) and proclaims "*Hannibal* stands alone in the television landscape," as the show is "notable not only for the high calibre of performances" but also for its "finely-tuned aesthetic vision."[27] In addition, Bryan Fuller has repeatedly invoked the show's artistic character. For example, in an interview with the British newspaper *The Guardian*, he stressed, "We are not making television. We are making a pretentious art film from the 80s."[28] This paratextual emphasis on *Hannibal*'s visual (and sound) design not only testifies to the efforts put into these aspects of the show, but also draws the viewers' attention to these elements. Indeed, this underlining of the series' artistic character continues in the show itself. As early as the first episode, Will Graham quips, "Whoever killed Elise Nichols did not paint this picture," upon seeing Hannibal's first victim in the narrative now.[29]

But Will's diagnosis of the crime scene's careful design is merely the beginning. Angela Ndalianis has astutely observed that "the walls of [Hannibal's] home are littered with Old Master prints and paintings …; his bedroom includes an exquisitely designed Edo-period samurai warrior armor piece; and in his study hangs a triptych of ukiyo-e prints form early 19th-century Japan." However, "Hannibal's vision and taste for art and aesthetics," she continues, "move beyond those of on-looker to active creator," as viewers

witness his artistic flair not only in the numerous sketches he draws, but also in the victims he transforms into artistic displays that announce to the world the virtuosic performances of Hannibal the serial killer, otherwise known as the Chesapeake Ripper. The actual embodiment of "Wound Man"—a popular image of the 15th and 16th centuries that represented the fusion of art and science, and which showed the body pierced by a variety of weapons that a physician might have treat—first appear in "Entrée" (1:6).... In "Mukozuke" (2:5), Hannibal experiments with contemporary art: the body of Beverly Katz, the crime lab scientist, is found dissected vertically into six pieces and displayed in glass cases in a composition reminiscent of Damien Hirst's animal works, particularly *Mother and Child (Divided)* [Tate Gallery, 1993].[30]

Ndalianis wrote her article prior to the start of the third season; if she had penned it a year later, she would have most definitely pointed out that season three makes the connections to the arts even more explicit. When Dolarhyde interrogates Dr. Frederick Chilton toward the end of season three, he asks, "Will you tell the truth now? About me? About my work? My becoming? My art?" He continues, "Is this art?" while showing an image of Blake's *Great Red Dragon* on a screen. The concluding question insinuates that Chilton fails to understand Dolarhyde's art despite his attempts at explaining that his art "pushe[s] the world so much further."[31] This brief exchange between Chilton and Dolarhyde in *Hannibal*'s penultimate episode functions as a crescendo to the aestheticization of murder in the show, as if the series were to say that by now, viewers should have come to understand that the murder scenes are not just simple gory visual effects, but rather important ingredients to the show's generation of meaning. Indeed, Dolarhyde emphasizes that his murders are motivated by an artistic impulse, while his video recordings serve to "ensure that their design has been properly executed," as Jack Katz has described the meticulous planning behind violent actions—and their consequent execution.[32] In addition, by explicitly acknowledging Blake's influence on Dolarhyde, the show refers back to an earlier moment in its serial narrative when Will and company hunted for Lecter and discovered that he had roamed the streets of Italy two decades prior.

In Palermo, Will and Jack (and viewers) learn that Hannibal came to be known as "Il Mostro," the monster of Florence, twenty years earlier. Commendatore Rinaldo Pazzi explains, "It was his custom to arrange his victims like a beautiful painting." As Pazzi shows Will a photograph of the murder scene from the 1990s, he continues, "Twenty years ago, I was dwelling on a couple found slain in the bed of a pickup truck in Impruneta. Bodies placed garlanded with flowers." Will remarks, "Like a Botticelli." Looking at an image of the painting, Pazzi highlights, "The garlanded nymph on the right, the flowers streaming from her mouth—match," and goes on to relate that it took him some time, but he eventually "f[ou]nd the inspiration Il Mostro used." Once he had uncovered the killer's source of creative influence, he

stood before the original *Primavera* day after day. And most days, [he]'d see a young Lithuanian man, as transfixed by the Botticelli as [he] was; as transfixed as [he] imagined Il Mostro would be. And every day [he] saw him, he would recreate the *Primavera* in pencil, just as he did in flesh.[33]

Although Pazzi's words imply that Lecter copied the painting—both on a piece of paper and in the flesh, the situation proves more complex, as Hannibal's postmodernist play with art history examines the relationship between copy and original. After all, Lecter did not simply copy the painting, but he excised one part of it and re-created it in a different medium. Hannibal's ludic performance of killing transformed into a murder scene (immortalized in photographs) becomes a new, original cultural artifact that establishes a dialogic relationship with the past.[34] Thus, beyond the bodily attack on the victims performed during the killings and the visual attack on onlookers, the murder scene attacks three ideas traditionally aligned with the arts.

First, it queries an original's originality. Resonating with Roland Barthes's ideas, Hannibal's crime scene suggests that its "origin ... is indiscernible."[35] Since Lecter's piece of art results from a double homicide, this idea bears the troubling suggestion of the authorities' inability to find him. Indeed, this implication is echoed in Will's observation that Hannibal "doesn't leave evidence."[36] This impossibility of tracking down the creator of the grisly scene is interrelated with the question of authorship. Whereas the police try to track down Lecter, from an aesthetic perspective, assigning his name to the painting in flesh and blood would be "a pure gesture of inscription," which "traces a field without origin."[37] In other words, while mere survival instincts drive Hannibal's attempts to evade the authorities (at least for some time; after all, he allows Jack to arrest him), Lecter's elusiveness also seeks to remove the creator from his creation and, accordingly, allow audiences to appreciate the work of art without the specter of the author haunting it. Of course, these first two points assume that the murder scene alluding to Sandro Botticelli's *La Primavera* (c. 1482) (and many other murder scenes) can be considered a work of art, to begin with—and this is the third point of Lecter's inquiry into the nature of art: Can we approach a murder scene from an aesthetic vantage point? Joel Black has answered this question with a resounding "yes," going so far as to assert that "our customary experience of murder ... is primarily aesthetic, rather than moral, physical, natural, or whatever term we choose as a synonym for the word *real*."[38]

Food, Murder and Art

Unlike Black's emphasis on the aesthetic engagement with murder scenes, Ndalianis claims that *Hannibal* "attack[s] ... the audience" by exploiting the multimodal medium of television to "absorb the 'viewer' on the level of the sensorium."[39] In "Cooking with Hannibal," I presented a similar argument, suggesting that the show's succulent food seeks to "creat[e] an affective response and whet viewers' appetites."[40] This affective response is supported by food's "primacy in our lives," which "precedes literacy."[41] However, Hannibal's sophisticated and deliberate presentation of meals not only target these direct bodily responses, but also cognitive and aesthetic ones.

This additional dimension of Hannibal's actions becomes most explicit in the season three episode "Secondo." In this episode, Hannibal and Bedelia have Professor Sogliato for dinner, the Italian scholar who questioned Lecter's knowledge of Dante in an earlier episode. During the dinner, Sogliato makes it clear that he does not trust Hannibal and thinks little of him. Suddenly, Lecter thrusts an ice pick into Sogliato's head. The professor goes blind and starts laughing in an uncontrolled fashion rather than dying right away—obviously Lecter knew what part of the brain he was aiming for. Hannibal sighs and remarks, "That may have been impulsive." However, Bedelia puts him straight, responding, "You'd been mulling that 'impulse' ever since you decided to serve punch romaine." Indeed, as Lecter clarified a few minutes earlier, punch romaine was "served to first-class guests on the *Titanic* during their last dinner."[42] As soon as Hannibal selected this specific drink, it was clear that his upper-class guest was to meet a fate similar to the (majority of the) *Titanic*'s passengers.

This brief scene demonstrates that Hannibal carefully chooses his meals for maximum symbolic effect. However, his presentation of food requires nearly as much attention to detail as its selection. For example, in the season two premiere, Jack Crawford dines at Lecter's place. In typical *Hannibal* fashion, one of the show's elaborate food preparation scenes precedes the actual meal, as Hannibal slices raw fish, dips sea urchin in lemon juice, and carefully designs the plates to the tune of Franz Schubert. As Hannibal serves the first course, he explains, "This course is called mukōzuke: Seasonal sashimi, sea urchin, water clam, and squid," before continuing, "Kaiseki—a Japanese art form that honors the taste and aesthetic of what we eat."[43]

On the basis of Hannibal's definition, "kaiseki" could well be considered the show's underlying aesthetic principle, targeting both the mind and the body. This veiled meta-commentary suggests similarities between the artist in the storyworld (i.e., Hannibal) and the artist in charge of the diegesis (i.e., Bryan Fuller). Tellingly, in *The Making and Art of* Hannibal, Jesse McLean stresses that "Bryan Fuller shares Hannibal Lecter's rarefied aesthetic sensibilities."[44] Lecter thereby becomes a stand-in for the show's "creator" and his aesthetic standards. Indeed, Mittell has argued that *Hannibal* was among the shows that made 2014 "the year when television direction began to eclipse (or at least match) its writing," implying that—much like movies—directors have become the most important source of creative input in television. Tellingly, in his brief assessment of the best shows of 2014, he describes *Hannibal*'s season two finale as "the most sustained example of *avant garde* filmmaking [he's] ever seen on television."[45] By referring to filmmaking, Mittell uses a shortcut to describe what Robin Nelson has called the "enhanced visual style" which characterizes many contemporary television shows. In particular, Nelson has singled out the "density of visual texture," which asks viewers to explore images in detail.[46]

Indeed, as Hannibal serves the Japanese dish, the camera lingers (albeit only momentarily) on the tasteful and artistically arranged plate. This image becomes suspended in time and transforms the show's moving images into a freeze frame. These moments when the images' movement comes to a halt allow viewers to gaze at the calculated staging of food and/or human corpses. However brief these moments may be, they produce liminal, intermedial spaces between television and the visual arts, in particular the traditions of the still life and the tableau vivant.

The still life is a painting genre in which inanimate objects are displayed. From the pork loin with Cumberland sauce of red fruits in "Amuse-Bouche" to the venison entrecote served with seared foie gras in "Cotorno"; from the foie gras au torchon with a late harvest of Vidal sauce and figs to the coratella con carciofi presented in "Secondo"; from the langue d'agneau en papillotes with a sauce of duxelles and oyster mushrooms to the escargot bourguignonne seen in a flashback in "Antipasto"; from the jamón ibérico in "Buffet Froid" to the truite saumonée au bleu in "Su-zakana"; and from the osso buco with risotto in "Sakizuke" to the braised roast baked in clay in "Futamono," Hannibal's dishes not simply show inanimate objects, but present them in careful arrangements, meticulously designed, visually akin to artworks.

However, Susan Stewart has refined the basic understanding of the painting genre, remarking that "still life is a configuration of consumable objects." Since Hannibal's meals garnished by human ingredients are made to be eaten, his food designs tap into the idea of configuring consumables in a specific manner. As Stewart continues, "In the depiction of still life, attention is devoted to objects."[47] Lecter's extravagant plate designs featuring pieces of human meat thus explore the question of how a human subject may become an object. Accordingly, Hannibal's inclusion of human beings among the consumables questions clear-cut binaries between consumer and consumed.

Yet instead of simply depicting a brutal and merciless dog-eat-dog world, Hannibal rather subverts these oppositions with style, re-integrating humans into the food chain and, thereby, undermining human exceptionalism. This questioning of the differentiation between the meat of human and nonhuman animals is made most explicit at the dinner party which concludes the season one episode "Sorbet." In characteristic *Hannibal* fashion, the preparation of the fancy dinner is turned into an audiovisual spectacle, as Hannibal carves various types of meat to classical music. A tilting shot across the dinner table reveals different kinds of carpaccio, galantine, and other meat products. Hannibal toasts to the higher-ups of society gathered around his table, "Before we begin, you must all be warned—nothing here is vegetarian!"[48] While scholars such as Jennifer Brown have argued that "[t]he cannibal has become the reviled image of overindulgence, overspending, and overexploitation of resources," *Hannibal*'s preeminent cannibal outs the presence of these cannibalistic traits in the other diners and consequently symbolic into literal cannibals.[49]

In addition, eating human meat emphasizes both the omnipresence of death in the show and the interrelations between life and death *Hannibal* philosophically addresses. The term "still life" captures this idea, because as soon as life has come to a halt, it becomes inanimate, and thus comes to share important traits with death. Arguably, the French expression for "still life," "nature morte" (dead nature), even further highlights the complex interconnections between (still) life and death the genre exploits, for "dead nature" is immortalized (i.e., never dead) through the process of painting. This netherworld between death and immortality becomes even more palpable in the show's murder tableaux, which pervert the tableau vivant into a tableau mort (or "meurant"). To be sure, the tableau vivant ("living picture") is a style present across the visual arts in which life is frozen in time. Since these images are often staged, scholars have considered the tableau vivant inherently intermedial, as it combines the stage-like setting of the theater with the visual arts.[50] Accordingly, tableaux vivants are theatrical performances stuck in time; fleeting moments captured and sculpted into permanence.

Rinaldo Pazzi's death scene exemplifies this process. In the episode "Cotorno," Pazzi seeks out Lecter—going by the name of Dr. Roman Fell—at his workplace, the Palazzo Capponi museum. The inspector explains that the police were unable to find "any sort of note" from Fell's predecessor—no "farewell note, suicide note," whatsoever. Hannibal is well aware that he met the inspector several years ago ("We shared a fondness for Botticelli," he tells Bedelia a little later) and that "all the elements of epiphany were present" in the inspector. However, Lecter still calmly responds that "[t]he going assumption is that he eloped with a woman—and her money." Pazzi counters, "What is the going assumption regarding Professor Sogliato?" and continues, "[N]o one has spoken to Professor Sogliato since he declined your invitation to dinner." As Pazzi is about to leave with a knowing grin on his face, Lecter wonders whether he is "a Pazzi of *the* Pazzi," remarking that the inspector "resemble[s] a figure at the Della

Robbia rondels in [the Pazzi] family's chapel at Santa Croce." When Hannibal mentions Francesco de' Pazzi, who famously "attempted to assassinate Lorenzo the Magnificent," the evocation of the past encounter between Francesco de' Pazzi and Lorenzo de' Medici functions as a cautionary warning to Rinaldo Pazzi and foreshadows things to come later in the episode. After all, it was not the mere assassination attempt on Lorenzo's life that secured the attempted coup d'état's place in history, but rather the depictions of and myths surrounding the hangings of five conspirators, including Francesco. Tellingly, later in the episode, Lecter shows Inspector Pazzi a woodcut showing Francesco hanging outside the Palazzo della Signoria. Lecter explains, "By all accounts, Francesco was led astray by thirty pieces of silver from the hand of the Papal banker," as he establishes an analogy to Rinaldo Pazzi's selling of Lecter to Mason Verger before anesthetizing the policeman. After a brief interrogation, Lecter cuts open Pazzi's abdomen and throws him out of the Palazzo's window. As the rope tied around Pazzi's neck tightens and the body recoils, the inspector's bowels squash to the street below. While the images are very dark and thus do not necessarily trigger much of a reaction, the splashing sound and the knowledge that it is Pazzi's intestines that smacked to the ground generate an affective response in viewers. Surprisingly, Crawford calmly stands only a few feet from the puddle of blood and looks up toward Hannibal. The brief moment from Jack's perspective showing Pazzi hanging from the window, supposedly dead, emanates an uncanny and awkward calmness. The brutality of Hannibal's uncomfortably serene attack comes to an effective standstill, caught in the image of Pazzi's death, which remediates artworks from the past.[51]

In addition, the suddenness of Lecter's attack, supported by several quick cuts (especially "quick" for *Hannibal*, which is slow-paced and generally employs relatively long takes) demonstrates how close life and death, in fact, are. While the split-second difference between being alive and dead becomes manifested in the Pazzi murder scene, Hannibal's "tree of life" in the season two episode "Futamono" makes the close (and mutual) relationship between the seeming binaries of life and death even more explicit: In this episode, Will tells Crawford that the Chesapeake Ripper is a cannibal; he "kills in sounders of three or four in quick order" because "if he waits too long, the meat spoils." Sheldon Isley, the human around which the "tree of life" was formed, tellingly misses all of his innards but the lungs and seems to form one of the bases of what Lecter refers to as a "life-enhancing event"—a dinner party. However, since Hannibal is well aware of the connections Will (and Jack, by this point) has established between Lecter and past murders, he keeps the human ingredients for himself to enjoy.

Although Lecter does not serve human meat at the dinner party, the murder tableau addresses the interconnections between life and death in great depth, as death comes to emblematize a kind of "creative destruction." Isley was a Baltimore city councilor who "brokered a woodlands development deal despite the disapproval of the EPA," lab rat Jimmy explains. He continues, "[Isley] paved an important nesting habitat for endangered song birds," and goes on, "Here's the exciting part: Treeman actually bears fruit."[52] In other words, Isley impudently killed the birds, along with dozens of other nonhuman species, to create a parking lot for the city of Baltimore (i.e., to animate the city). Lecter, well aware of the irony, not only murders the city councilor (for having killed nonhuman beings), but turns him into a nutrient for various forms of nonhuman life as well as a source of protein for the cannibalistic doctor. However, this tableau does not simply conclude with the transformation of the consumer into the consumed. Instead, the hybrid "treeman" figure becomes reintegrated into the circle of life and transcends binary oppositions. While Isley may no longer be quite man and while he may be dead, his body has become part of a living structure. By ending Isley's life, Hannibal transforms the inanimate body into an animating structure, while the motionless body is re-animated by *Hannibal*, the television show.

In this way, these momentary glimpses of murder scenes frozen in time also emphasize the interrelation between stillness and motion in moving image media. Brigitte Peucker has remarked that in film, "tableau vivant moments … remind us … that the 'motion picture' is the first medium able to animate visual representation, to make painting 'come to life.'"[53] Similarly, *Hannibal*'s tableaux draw viewers' attention to television's (and also film's) reliance on individual images, which are continually replaced at a rate of 24 to 30 frames per second.

Killer Art

Accordingly, *Hannibal*'s intermedial nature highlights the show's position in a long line of cultural artifacts pondering the line separating life from death. The moving image (whether in film or television) seems the ideal vehicle for querying this issue, because—to quote the title of Laura Mulvey's most recent monograph—in these media, death occurs twenty-four times a second. Yet beyond this meta-reflexive acknowledgment of the medium's nature, *Hannibal* truly revels in the display of wounded, fragmented, and distorted human bodies. Following Joel Black, the excessive display of violence targets "the idea of art itself."[54] In this way, the show reflects not only on the value and meaning of art, but also on the artistic merits of television.

By combining singular "moments of beauty or meaning," as Mulvey

has put it, with the affective potentials of serial narration, *Hannibal* questions binaries that traditionally separated—and still separate, in the minds
of many—popular culture from "high culture." Instead of the clear opposition between "high" and "low" culture, *Hannibal*'s visual style highlights
how "impurity and uncertainty displace … traditional oppositions."[55] Similar to how the show's titular monster "def[ies] categorization," as Dr. Alana
Bloom describes Hannibal in the third season, the series does neither truly
belong to television nor the visual arts, as traditionally conceived.[56] I do not
mean to put *Hannibal* on a pedestal and suggest that it simply stands out
from other television shows, though. Rather, *Hannibal* acknowledges that
television is hybrid by its very nature. While the "flow" blurred the distinctions between individual programs as well as commercials and other types
of programming for Raymond Williams, creating a hybrid audiovisual
landscape where everything merges, John Caldwell understood that defining television's "essential qualities" goes hand in hand with "overlook[ing]
the fact that television includes a great deal that comes from elsewhere."[57]
In this way, Caldwell underlined the unclear lines separating individual
media; that "all mediation is remediation," as Jay David Bolter and Richard
Grusin have concluded.[58]

In fact, the show plays out this deconstruction (for the lack of a better term) of opposites through its two main characters, Hannibal Lecter
and Will Graham. Hannibal is the intellectual, who is distanced and in control.[59] Aside from his (literal) cannibalism, Hannibal is the perfect consumer of "high" culture—literate, with exquisite taste, and aspiring toward
creating art himself. Will, on the other hand, is the type of recipient who
"get[s] too close," since his "pure empathy" allows him to "assume [any]
point or view."[60] Will tries to be reserved, to see the world from a detached
point of view, but he simply can't. Like the consumers of "body genres," he
is constantly directly affected by cultural artifacts (-slash-murder scenes)
he is confronted with.[61] For Will, there is no such thing as aesthetic distance; for him, the perception of any given murder scene "arrives like experience—sudden and entire."[62]

In his satiric condemnation of (primarily German) aesthetic theory "On Murder Considered as One of the Fine Arts" (1827), Thomas De
Quincy remarks, "Murder … may be laid hold of by its moral handle, …
and *that*, I confess, is its weak side; or it may also be treated *aesthetically*, …
that is, in relation to good taste." After seeing a murder (scene), he continues, "We dry up our tears, and have the satisfaction to discover, that a trans-
action, which, morally considered, was shocking, and without a leg to stand
upon, when tried by principles of Taste, turns out to be a very meritorious
performance."[63] *Hannibal* plays out these opposing views on murder; Will
repeatedly faces moral dilemmas and is affected by the crime scenes (and

his own shooting of a killer), whereas Hannibal stands aloof beyond issues of morality while nourishing his hunger for human meat and satisfying his refined taste by killing people. In this way, *Hannibal*—like De Quincey two hundred years prior—raises the question of what an aesthetic response to murder, in fact, means. What can we say about a culture that celebrates the "Corpse Art of *Hannibal*," praises the show's "Most Beautifully Gruesome Crime Scenes," and includes eight crime scenes among the "74 Times [That] 'Hannibal' Was the Most Stunningly Beautiful Show on Television"?[64]

Of course, *Hannibal* is merely a television show and not depicting real-life crime scenes. However, the series still raises this fundamental question of how to approach murder—both in fictional form and also in real life. Tellingly, at the end of the series, the two main characters representing two opposing views on murder plunge into the Atlantic Ocean in each other's arms. This highly symbolic moment suggests that the two approaches to art do not exclude one another. In fact, *Hannibal*'s conclusion implies that the two perspectives cannot exist without one another; the critical, distanced understanding of cultural artifacts cannot ignore the affective and emotional dimensions of cultural phenomena. And in this respect, there is also no difference between a television show and "fine" art—both may trigger affective responses, but they may also generate aesthetic ones.

In his seminal work *The Principles of Art* (1938), Robin George Collingwood railed against mistaking entertainment for art, but he also acknowledged that not all portrait paintings are inherently art. For a portrait to become art, he claimed, it must be "something more" than simple mimicry.[65] Collingwood provided several additional ways of differentiating between art and its others. At the end of the day, however, these differences are tentative, at best. Television, "real" art—there is no difference, suggests *Hannibal*.

Notes

1. Anon., "Television Tests Tinseltown."
2. White, "Film Is Art."
3. *Ibid.*
4. Wittgenstein, *Philosophical Investigations*, §66.
5. Newman and Levine, *Legitimating Television*, 159.
6. Freedman, "Autocanonization," 214; 213.
7. Boddy, "Loving a Nineteen-Inch Motorola," 5.
8. Gray and Lotz, *Television Studies*, 36–37.
9. Perry, "Civil Rights Coverage," 45.
10. Everett, "Civil Rights Movement."
11. Williams, *Television*, 92–93; 96.
12. Buonanno, *The Age of Television*, 32.

13. Shayon, *The Eighth Art.*
14. Newcomb, *TV*, 254.
15. Mittell, *Complex TV.*
16. *Ibid.*, loc. 889–891.
17. Caldwell, *Televisuality*, 77; 21; 92.
18. Gunning, "The Cinema of Attractions," 58–59.
19. Thompson, "Cinematic Excess," 516; 523.
20. Harris, *Red Dragon*, 60–61.
21. Cardwell, "Television Aesthetics," 34.
22. Harris, *Red Dragon*, 60.
23. Williams, "Eating Blake," 137; 155.
24. Fahy, "Killer Culture," 33.
25. Simpson, *Making Murder*, 121–128; 173–179; 214–221.
26. Gompf, *Thomas Harris and William Blake*, 18.
27. McLean, *Making of* Hannibal, 10.
28. Thurm, "Hannibal showrunner."
29. "Apéritif."
30. Ndalianis, "*Hannibal*," 280–281.
31. "The Number of the Beast Is 666."
32. Katz, *Seductions of Crime*, 300.
33. "Primavera."
34. Jameson, *Postmodernism*, 17.
35. Barthes, *S/Z*, 164.
36. "Primavera."
37. Barthes, "The Death of the Author," 143.
38. Black, *Aesthetics of Murder*, 3; italics in original.
39. Ndalianis, "*Hannibal*," 279.
40. Fuchs, "Cooking with Hannibal," 107.
41. Bower, "Watching Food," 10.
42. "Secondo."
43. "Kaiseki."
44. McLean, *Making of* Hannibal, 36.
45. Mittell, "Best Stuff of 2014"; italics in original.
46. Nelson, *State of Play*, 11; 113.
47. Stewart, *On Longing*, 29; 55.
48. "Sorbet."
49. Brown, *Cannibalism*, 214. For a more detailed discussion of the use of food in "Sorbet," see Fuchs and Phillips, "Eat, Kill, … Love," 209–211.
50. See, for example, Paech, *Die Einbildungen des Jean-Luc Godard*, 45.
51. "Cotorno."
52. "Futamono."
53. Peucker, *The Material Image*, 26.
54. Black, *Aesthetics of Murder*, 5.
55. Mulvey, *Death 24x a Second*, 28; 12.
56. "The Great Red Dragon."
57. Caldwell, *Televisuality*, 110.
58. Bolter and Grusin, *Remediation*, 54.
59. On Hannibal's control, see Fuchs and Phillips, "Eat, Kill, … Love," 206–208.
60. "Apéritif."
61. Williams, "Film Bodies," 3–6.
62. "Contorno."
63. De Quincey, *On Murder*, 7; 11; italics in original; capitalization adopted from original.
64. Schnelbach, "Ranking the Corpse Art"; Rowles, "11 Most Beautifully Gruesome Crime Scenes"; Dalton, "The Most Stunningly Beautiful Show On Television."
65. Collingwood, *Principles of Art*, 45.

WORKS CITED

Anon. "Television Tests Tinseltown: Introduction." *The New York Times*. Last modified April 3, 2014. Accessed August 3, 2016. http://www.nytimes.com/roomfordebate/2014/04/03/television-tests-tinseltown.

"Apéritif." Written by Bryan Fuller. Directed by David Slade. In *Hannibal: Season 1*. Santa Monica, CA: Lions Gate, 2013. Blu Ray.

Barthes, Roland. "The Death of the Author." In *Image—Music—Text*. Edited and translated by Stephen Heath, 142–148. New York: Hill & Wang, 1978.

____. *S/Z: An Essay*. Translated by Richard Miller. New York: Hill & Wang, 1974.

Black, Joel. *The Aesthetics of Murder: A Study in Romantic Literature and Contemporary Culture*. Baltimore, MD: Johns Hopkins University Press, 1991.

Boddy, William. "Loving a Nineteen-Inch Motorola: American Writing on Television." In *Regarding Television—Critical Approaches: An Anthology*. Edited by E. Ann Kaplan, 1–11. Frederick, MD: University Publications of America, 1983.

Bolter, Jay David, and Richard Grusin. *Remediation: Understanding New Media*. Cambridge, MA: MIT Press, 1999.

Bower, Anne L. "Watching Food: The Production of Food, Film, and Values." In *Reel Food: Essays on Food and Film*. Edited by Anne L. Bower, 1–13. New York: Routledge, 2004.

Brown, Jennifer. *Cannibalism in Literature and Film*. Basingstoke: Palgrave Macmillan, 2013.

Buonanno, Milly. *The Age of Television: Experiences and Theories*. Translated by Jennifer Radice. Bristol: Intellect, 2008.

Caldwell, John Thornton. *Televisuality: Style, Crisis, and Authority in American Television*. New Brunswick, NJ: Rutgers University Press, 1995.

Cardwell, Sarah. "Television Aesthetics: Style and Beyond." In *Television Aesthetics and Style*. Edited by Jason Jacobs and Steven Peacock, 23–44. London: Bloomsbury, 2013.

Collingwood, Robin George. *The Principles of Art*. Oxford: Oxford University Press, 2013.

"Cotorno." Written by Tom de Ville, Bryan Fuller, and Steve Lightfoot. Directed by Guillermo Navarro. In *Hannibal: Season 3*. Santa Monica, CA: Lions Gate, 2015. Blu Ray.

Dalton, Dan. "74 Times 'Hannibal' Was The Most Stunningly Beautiful Show On Television." *BuzzFeed*. Last modified June 10, 2015. Accessed August 3, 2016. https://www.buzzfeed.com/danieldalton/i-gave-you-a-rare-gift.

De Quincey, Thomas. *On Murder Considered as one of the Fine Arts*. London: Penguin, 2015.

Everett, Anna. "Civil Rights Movement and Television." In *Encyclopedia of Television*. Edited by Horace Newcomb. Chicago: Fitzroy Dearborn, 1997. DVD-ROM.

Fahy, Thomas. "Killer Culture: Classical Music and the Art of Killing in *Silence of the Lambs* and *Se7en*." *Journal of Popular Culture* 37, no. 1 (2003): 28–42.

Freedman, Jonathan. "Autocanonization: Tropes of Self-Legitimation in 'Popular Culture.'" *Yale Journal of Criticism* 1, no. 1 (1987): 203–217.

Fuchs, Michael. "Cooking with Hannibal: Food, Liminality and Monstrosity in *Hannibal*." *European Journal of American Culture* 34, no. 2 (2015): 97–112.

____, and Michael Phillips. "Eat, Kill, … Love? Courtship, Cannibalism, and Consumption in *Hannibal*." In *What's Eating You? Food and Horror on Screen*. Edited by Cynthia J. Miller and A. Bowdoin Van Riper, 205–219. New York: Bloomsbury, 2017.

"Futamono." Written by Andy Black, Bryan Fuller, Scott Nimerfro, and Steve Lightfoot. Directed by Tim Hunter. In *Hannibal: Season 2*. Santa Monica, CA: Lions Gate, 2014. Blu Ray.

Gompf, Michelle Leigh. *Thomas Harris and William Blake: Allusions in the Hannibal Lecter Novels*. Jefferson, NC: McFarland, 2013.

Gray, Jonathan, and Amanda Lotz. *Television Studies*. Cambridge: Polity Press, 2012.

"The Great Red Dragon." Written by Nick Antosca, Steve Lightfood, and Bryan Fuller. Directed by Neil Marshall. In *Hannibal: Season 3*. Santa Monica, CA: Lions Gate, 2015. Blu Ray.

Gunning, Tom. "The Cinema of Attractions: Early Film, its Spectator, and the Avant-Garde." In *Early Cinema: Space—Frame—Narrative*. Edited by Thomas Elsaesser and Adam Barker, 56–62. London: British Film Institute, 1986.

Harris, Thomas. *Red Dragon*. In *Red Dragon | The Silence of the Lambs*, 1–278. London: Peerage Books, 1991.

Jameson, Fredric. *Postmodernism; Or, the Cultural Logic of Late Capitalism*. Durham, NC: Duke University Press, 1991.

"Kaiseki." Written by Bryan Fuller and Steve Lightfoot. Directed by Tim Hunter. In *Hannibal: Season 2*. Santa Monica, CA: Lions Gate, 2014. Blu Ray.

Katz, Jack. *Seductions of Crime: Moral and Sensual Attractions in Doing Evil*. New York: Basic Books, 1988.

McLean, Jesse. *The Art and Making of* Hannibal. London: Titan Books, 2015.

Mittell, Jason. "Best Stuff of 2014." *Just TV*. Last modified December 30, 2014. Accessed August 3, 2016. https://justtv.wordpress.com/2014/12/30/best-stuff-of-2014/, 16 July 2016.

___. *Complex TV: A Poetics of Contemporary Television*. New York: New York University Press, 2015. Kindle edition.

Mulvey, Laura. *Death 24x a Second: Stillness and the Moving Image*. London: Reaktion, 2006.

Ndalianis, Angela. "*Hannibal*: A Disturbing Feast for the Senses." *Journal of Visual Culture* 14, no. 3 (2015): 279–284.

Nelson, Robin. *State of Play: Contemporary 'High-End' TV Drama*. Manchester: Manchester University Press, 2007.

Newcomb, Horace. *TV: The Most Popular Art*. New York: Anchor Books, 1974.

Newman, Michael Z., and Elana Levine. *Legitimating Television: Media Convergence and Cultural Status*. New York: Routledge, 2012.

"The Number of the Beast Is 666." Written by Jeff Vlaming, Angela Lamanna, Bryan Fuller, and Steve Lightfoot. Directed by Guillermo Navarro. In *Hannibal: Season 3*. Santa Monica, CA: Lions Gate, 2015. Blu Ray.

Paech, Joachim. Passion; *oder die Einbildungen des Jean-Luc Godard*. Frankfurt: Deutsches Filmmuseum, 1989.

Perry, Linda M. "Civil Rights Coverage." In *Encyclopedia of Television*. Edited by Michael D. Murray, 44–45. Phoenix, AZ: Oryx Press, 1999.

Peucker, Brigitte. *The Material Image: Art and the Real in Film*. Stanford, CA: Stanford University Press, 2007.

"Primavera." Written by Jeff Vlaming and Bryan Fuller. Directed by Vincenzo Natali. In *Hannibal: Season 3*. Santa Monica, CA: Lions Gate, 2015. Blu Ray.

Rowles, Dustin. "Ranking the 11 Most Beautifully Gruesome Crime Scenes on NBC's 'Hannibal.'" *Pajiba*. Last modified 13 June 2013. Accessed August 3, 2016. http://www.pajiba.com/seriously_random_lists/ranking-the-11-most-beautifully-gruesome-crime-scenes-on-nbcs-hannibal-nsfw.php.

Schnelbach, Leah. "Ranking the Corpse Art of *Hannibal*." tor.com. Last modified July 30, 2015. Accessed August 3, 2016. http://www.tor.com/2015/07/30/ranking-the-corpse-art-of-hannibal/.

"Secondo." Written by Angelina Burnett, Bryan Fuller, and Steve Lightfoot. Directed by Vincenzo Natali. In *Hannibal: Season 3*. Santa Monica, CA: Lions Gate, 2015. Blu Ray.

Shayon, Robert Lewis, ed. *The Eighth Art: Twenty-Three Views of Television Today*. New York: Holt, Rinehard, and Winston, 1962.

Simpson, Philip L. *Making Murder: The Fiction of Thomas Harris*. Santa Barbara, CA: Praeger, 2009.

"Sorbet." Written by Jesse Alexander and Bryan Fuller. Directed by James Foley. In *Hannibal: Season 1*. Santa Monica, CA: Lions Gate, 2013. Blu Ray.

Stewart, Susan. *On Longing: Narratives of the Miniature, the Gigantic, the Souvenir, the Collection*. Durham, NC: Duke University Press, 1993.

Thompson, Kristin. "The Concept of Cinematic Excess." In *Film Theory and Criticism*. 6th Ed. Edited by Leo Braudy and Marshall Cohen, 513–524. New York: Oxford University Press, 2004.

Thurm, Eric. "Hannibal showrunner: 'We are not making television. We are making a pretentious art film from the 80s.'" *The Guardian*. Last modified June 3, 2015. Accessed August 3, 2016. https://www.theguardian.com/tv-and-radio/2015/jun/03/hannibal-tv-showrunner-bryan-fuller.

White, Armond. "Film Is Art, Television Is a Medium." *The New York Times*. Last modified April 3, 2014. Accessed August 3, 2016. http://www.nytimes.com/roomfordebate/2014/04/03/television-tests-tinseltown/film-is-art-television-is-a-medium.

Williams, Linda. "Film Bodies: Gender, Genre, and Excess." *Film Quarterly* 44, no. 4 (1991): 2–13.

Williams, Nicholas M. "Eating Blake; Or, An Essay on Taste: The Case of Thomas Harris's *Red Dragon*." *Cultural Critique* 42 (1999): 137–162.

Williams, Raymond. *Television: Technology and Cultural Form*. Abingdon: Routledge, 2003.

Wittgenstein, Ludwig. *Philosophische Untersuchungen/Philosophical Investigations*. Edited by G. E. M. Anscombe, P. M. S. Hacker, and Joachim Schulte. Translated by P. M. S. Hacker and Joachim Schulte. 4th Ed. Malden, MA: Wiley-Blackwell, 2009.

The Rise of the Showrunner in *Hannibal*

Bryan Fuller as Simultaneous Fan Author and Legitimate Auteur

KYLE A. MOODY

Bryan Fuller and his work on *Hannibal* represents a newer kind of fan creator relationship with the text. In particular, since Fuller is adapting existing text to craft a metatextual prequel to the existing canon, *Hannibal* represents a postmodern televisual experience that is unique in its narrative with preexisting media. Conversely, Fuller's relationship with fans as a showrunner reflects and embodies the show's peculiarness and self-awareness. This can best be represented through his social media accounts, particularly his use of Twitter to engage with the impassioned fanbase. The "spreadable media" (Jenkins, Ford, & Green, 2013) on display in the work reflects Fuller's intention to address fan concerns throughout production while also promoting the ideologies of his content. In short, Fuller is emblematic of the new model of showrunner, one closer to the Alan Ball model than the David Chase model in Brett Martin's book *Difficult Men* (Martin, 2014). The use of social media as emblematic of this new auteur model is illustrative of Fuller's role as an intermediary between Hollywood producer and fan fiction creator.

Introduction

Bryan Fuller began work on *Hannibal* before its air date in 2013, as a love letter to Thomas Harris's work on Hannibal Lecter and Will Graham. He envisioned the project as a unique synthesis of his idiosyncratic sensibilities linked to the greater work of Harris and Hannibal Lecter as cultural figures. What Fuller brought to the project was his own cult fan-base and engaged audience, which anticipated a blend of artistic influences and snappy dialogue that stood out from other televisual programming. Since Fuller oversaw all the production components and writing that went into *Hannibal*, he was the show's main visionary a role that is frequently labeled as "showrunner."

The role of the showrunner has long been a disputed one in the world of television, which itself has undergone heavy transformations (see Hilmes, 2013). In his seminal book *Difficult Men*, Brett Martin links the changing role of the showrunner of a television program to the increased sophistication of narrative in televisual programming (Martin, 2014). From the work done by Norman Lear on hot-button shows of the 1970s like *All in the Family*, producer Aaron Sorkin in the heyday of 1980s American primetime dramas like *Dynasty*, and the eventual culmination with aspiring filmmaker-turned-showrunner David Chase on the epochal drama *The Sopranos*, Martin captures the intensity of the very nature of production of television. More importantly, Martin links the increasing need for content by premium cable providers to the burgeoning movement of highly personalized and dramatically engaging dramatic stories produced by idiosyncratic showrunners like Chase (Martin, 2014).

Indeed, while this essay will largely focus on Fuller's role as the showrunner for a broadcast television program, it is incumbent that the stage for Fuller's rise as a distinct auteur also be linked to the growth of specialty, niche programming that gained prestige and critical acclaim on non-broadcast network and streaming platforms. Without the rise of HBO's slate of programming by Chase, *Deadwood* creator David Milch, and *Six Feet Under/True Blood* showrunner Alan Ball, the ground for *Hannibal* on NBC in the United States may not have been plowed.

Fuller as a showrunner was immediately recognizable to his fans through his years of work in genre programming. Works like *Star Trek: Deep Space Nine, Voyager*, and *Heroes* all bore his imprint in different ways (Later, 2018). Fans would often cite episodes of his as series favorites, especially as the credited writer for the *Heroes* season one episode "Company Man," long thought to be the pinnacle of the series. His focus on nonlinear storytelling as a means of character development would become a hallmark of his writing, particularly in the second season of *Hannibal* and its unique flashback structure for specific episodes and the season's narrative arc.

The role of the showrunner has changed over time as well (Hilmes, 2013; Martin, 2014; Sepinwall, 2013), which makes Fuller's link to *Hannibal* more indicative of an auteurist focus with the change in in televisual storytelling. Much of television's programming history has focused on the role of network executives and cultural shifts as the reason for success behind specific programs (Hilmes, 2013). However, as Martin's text and more recent additions have illustrated, the showrunner behind specific programs has received greater credit for being the guiding light for success in a television setting. Figures like Norman Lear, Aaron Spelling, David Milch, and Steven Bochco were early figures whose unique voices shone through on network television. This is reflective of a cultural shift in television's importance in the American social landscape, where the medium became a point of greater unity and possibility for including diverse perspectives that shifted away from more formulaic content presented through the channel.

Fuller benefited from the growth of cable television as a means of more prestige, adult-oriented storytelling. As HBO and its cable channel competitors like FX and AMC emerged in the early-to-mid 2000s with programs like *The Shield*, *Mad Men*, and *Breaking Bad*, a greater focus was placed on the role of the showrunner in corralling disparate actors and storylines into a new realm of more cinematic serialized narrative. In his work *The Revolution Was Televised*, *Rolling Stone* television critic Alan Sepinwall highlighted the diverse array of voices that emerged in the so-called "Golden Age" of television, now known as "Peak TV" (2013).

It is here that Fuller and his rise as a showrunner worth exploring is noted. Before *Hannibal*, Fuller had broken from the science fiction and fantasy model of genre programming to create narratives of his own. His first creation was a quirky program about a woman who worked for Death on the Showtime cable network titled *Dead Like Me*. This show starred Ellen Muth and Mandy Patinkin as grim reapers working in the Pacific Northwest. Even though it ran for two seasons and received acclaim for its unique voice, Fuller left the program after five episodes, citing creative differences. Next, Fuller was given a series order for *Wonderfalls*, which aired on Fox Network in the United States and starred future *Hannibal* actor Caroline Dhavernas. After it was cancelled following its initial season run, Fuller developed the resurrectionist drama *Pushing Daisies* with fellow *Wonderfalls* alum Lee Pace at its head as a pie-maker with the ability to reanimate the dead through his touch. It was developed as a more whimsical take on the forensics genre, with critics claiming it was a "forensic fairytale" (Neumann, 2018).

The extreme stylization of these programs laid the foundation for Fuller's work on *Hannibal*. *Pushing Daisies* was seen as a "candy-colored, computer-generated bucolic scenery" with a "Technicolor world that seems to exist at right angles to our own" (Mikey Neumann, 2018). Critics also noted "bizarre dialogue" and the use of alliteration and near-duplicate names of both characters (such as Deedee Duffield, Billy Balsam, and Charlotte "Chuck" Charles) and locations (Boutique Travel Travel Boutique, Über Life Life Insurance) (Sepinwall, 2008).

302 **Hannibal for Dinner**

These stylistic touches were also found on *Wonderfalls* and *Dead Like Me*, from the rapid edits and time-lapsed camera movements to unwitting protagonists being directed to their tasks by supernatural or anthropomorphic deities. This type of content soon characterized what made a show a Bryan Fuller program, which extends the idea of *auteur theory* to include the role of the showrunner as one that integrates auteurist tendencies into a more collaborative, long-form effort. By creating a style that could be recognizable regardless of the program, network, or actors involved (though he would reuse actors like Dhavernas, Muth, and Pace across his shows), Fuller is linked to the greater tendencies of auteur theory.

Fan Audiences and the Role of Auteurs

Another shift in the role of showrunners in the twenty-first century was their involvement with fan audiences. Simply put, the showrunners of diverse programming were now more likely to interact with audiences through more participatory media networks and cultures available on platforms like Twitter. *Lost* co-creator and showrunner Damon Lindelof would often interact with fans of his seminal network program through blog sites and Twitter, and as the program ended he began a contentious relationship with his supposed detractors. This shift in relationships comes through the participatory means unlocked through Web 2.0 and independent media creators, as Jenkins has described in his work on convergence (Jenkins et al., 2013). More fans became "produsers" of content, shifting the relationship between producer and consumer roles (Bird, 2011; Jenkins et al., 2013).

However, while there have been discussions of fan fiction authors and creators in this book, this essay will not explore that. Instead, it will explore how Fuller represents a new class of showrunner during his tenure as the showrunner for *Hannibal*. Fuller's role on the program was already unique because *Hannibal* was not wholly his creation. Instead, the series served as an adaptation of/prequel to the existing Thomas Harris Hannibal Lecter books and media. Yet while Fuller did not create the existing intellectual property, one cannot deny that the extreme stylization on *Hannibal* exists as a creation of his own. Therefore, Fuller acts as both showrunner and "fan author" throughout his tenure on the program, which itself straddles the line between a more procedural mystery (at least throughout its first, less serialized season) and the artistic flourishes that were normally viewed on premium cable television during the years before *Hannibal* premiered on NBC.

What makes Fuller's engagement with fans fascinating is that he is himself a fan, an intermediary between the audience and the text of Harris.

He operates in the spaces between the realities of the "canonical" Harris texts and the work of fans that created their own content for the universe of Hannibal Lecter. Fuller then translates that operation into engagement with fans by creating social media content on Twitter that would communicate with second-screen viewers in real-time during broadcasts of the show. He would also tease future release content for fans through Twitter, and engage with the audience to drive their involvement with the series. This is a more common practice today, particularly with the voluminous amount of critically-loved television programs available to consumers across a variety of platforms.

Due to the amount of activity Fuller engaged with while he was showrunner for *Hannibal*, it could be said that he encouraged "fan activism" himself. Fan activism is considered "forms of civic engagement and political participation that emerge from within fan culture itself, often in response to the shared interests of fans, often conducted through the infrastructure of existing fan practices and relationships, and often framed through metaphors drawn from popular and participatory culture" (Jenkins, 2019).

While activism itself may refer to the very nature of the fan engagement, this also implies a level of activity reflective of social justice and awareness of injustice on representative media content. This in turn is reflective of the changing nature of fan engagement through these multiple platforms, which often takes the role from outspoken fan nature to potential "overseer" of content. Again, the convergence of online production allows for fan curation of content to become more prominent.

Queer Fandom as Art and Acceptance

Fuller, an out gay man, often interacted with fans regarding the potential love story of Hannibal and Will Graham. This is where the nature of fan activism and fan fiction takes hold in discussing *Hannibal* as a cultural work since the Harris text and film adaptations do not include specific text regarding the potential amorous pairing. However, since Fuller is admitting that his work occupies a level of fan fiction, his work with "Hannigram" becomes more pronounced as a line between fiction and clear connection with the authorial voice of Fuller.

Fuller's voice is often captured in the elliptical production that *Hannibal* offered to viewers, particularly the sumptuous visuals that accompanied the increasingly dark stories and the dissolution of Will Graham's sanity throughout the three-season narrative. The dreamlike visuals when Will begins to inhabit the point of view of the killer in each episode

grow increasingly opaque and darker, with Will engaging in more macabre acts of violence that are nonetheless beautifully shot. This juxtaposition between violent horror and fantastical production is linked to Fuller's
voice, which would reach its apex here.

That's not to say that he wouldn't approach it with humor. For example, when describing an episode where Hannibal bled on Will, Fuller
tweeted that "Will Graham is covered in #Hannibal's bodily fluids #GayA-
genda" (Fuller, 2014). This illustrated how his humor influenced the critical
and fan reaction to episodes, along with the bigger ideas behind the subversive nature of Will and Hannibal's twisted relationship. The explication of
this was much appreciated by users.

Fuller's use of behind the scenes productions on social media was
another reason he became a more identifiable figure in the production of
Hannibal. The intersection between fan and creator on social media went
deeper than others, and this intersection was linked with Fuller's use of
Twitter as a public platform to engage with fans during the production of
episodes and airing of episodes in America. For example, immediately after
an episode where Hannibal's throat was slit, Fuller tweeted a behind the
scenes picture of Mads Mikkelson with the grisly makeup effect. The cap-
tion read "Will Graham did this to me. #Hannibal #EatTheRude" (Fuller,
2014).

These tweets, captured between 2013 and 2015, reflect a producer using
shifting media to create and foster an excitement with work. Fuller also
emerges with specific details of the production, from discussing particularly well-shot and edited love scenes to highlighting how Hannibal's murder victims were made up on the show. There was special care given to fans
and journalists who could use Fuller's work as entertainment reporting.

This continued out to 2017, when Fuller would continue to use his
platform on Twitter to highlight the troubled legal maneuvering necessary
to bring *Hannibal* back into production. Fuller spoke to his fans (Fannibals) through the platform and would retweet fan art to stoke the fires of
the show. Later, he responded that the show was going through development and retooling in an attempt to reemerge (Fuller, 2017). This estab-
lishment of a fan-sanctioned and production-enabled authorial voice gave
Fuller more credibility regarding his production.

Social Media and the Emergent Showrunner

Fuller would also be the first source to discuss the difficulty of production in the world of "peak TV," where *Hannibal* emerged as a unique voice
within the broadcast spectrum of television. *Hannibal* was often in danger

of cancellation throughout the entirety of its run, with fans turning to Twitter and other social media to proclaim their love of the series. Fuller also used this platform to encourage fans to speak out for their love of *Hannibal*, ostensibly becoming a public cheerleader of his team's work and a vocal producer that would interact with fans when network executives would not or could not. In this way, Fuller represents the showrunner as "fan activist," but also as one who is clearly linked to his audience. This reflects how Gene Roddenberry and original *Star Trek* fans could engage in email correspondence, while simultaneously maintaining a more immediate link with the text.

Hannibal was a program that emerged at a specific point in time, and its depictions of violence beget a discussion regarding art vs. violence in recreations of criminal acts. However, it also emerged as a voice for Bryan Fuller at a time when respect for genre programming was increasing, as evidenced by the critical reception and Emmy victories for fantasy prestige programming such as *Game of Thrones*. While *Hannibal* does not inhabit the same genre as *Game of Thrones*, the programs were notably similar in terms of their representations of graphic violence, intelligent depictions of interactions within fantastical settings, and strong acting. Moreover, much like *Game of Thrones* is largely linked to original author George R.R. Martin, *Hannibal* is linked to the original Harris text, and the televisual adaptation is linked to Fuller's voice. An interesting divergence between Fuller's *Hannibal* and HBO's *Game of Thrones* was Fuller's opposition to depicting sexual violence on screen.

As listed above, Fuller's work often contains explicit diversity within casting, stylistic flourishes accompanied by strong dialogue, and idiosyncratic characterization. The narratives across his programs often exemplify "high concept" production, which is focused on highlighting the unique nature of the television show. In this case, *Hannibal* upended the typified nature of the police procedural by emphasizing the stylistic shifts and artistry on hand in the production.

This is where Fuller's voice within *Hannibal* becomes more important to the growth of the program. While the character of Hannibal Lecter had become iconic due to Sir Anthony Hopkins's performance in *The Silence of the Lambs*, Harris's character and works had largely disappeared from the public eye after the critically and commercially disappointing *Hannibal Rising* was released in 2007. It can be argued that Fuller's involvement in the program was potentially more exciting to an audience. After all, *Hannibal* itself was not a commercial hit (due to a variety of factors), so it behooves the academic community to highlight its successes. Fuller's unique voice was attached to the program, and it is these auteurist flashes that we must examine.

Fans gravitate towards his work because he is a "fan-turned-creator."
He proudly integrates his ideologies into his work. This itself could be
read as an act of fan activism through his involvement with the LGBTQA
community.

When *Hannibal* was canceled, Fuller began work on *Star Trek: Discovery*. When it was beginning production, *Deadline* reported that Fuller
and Kurtzman were looking for a diverse cast including a non-white female
protagonist and a gay character. These choices honor the progressive decisions made by *Star Trek* creator Gene Roddenberry on the original series 50
years ago—he cast a black woman, Nichelle Nichols, and George Takei, an
American of Asian descent, in lead roles. Fuller says it was "absolutely my
goal" to be respectful of Roddenberry's vision and legacy in "creating [*Discovery*] and getting to the heart of what the important themes were to me
as a *Star Trek* fan—how do we get along with people who are different than
ourselves? How do we find common ground? How do move into the future
together? Those themes were implicit in the scripts that I wrote before I left,
and the storylines [I plotted]."

In fact, Alan Ball serves as a worthwhile link to Fuller as a model for
showrunning. Since his tenure as the showrunner for *Six Feet Under*, Ball
has often operated less as an overly controlling leader like David Chase of
The Sopranos or *Mad Men* creator Matthew Weiner. The impact Fuller has
on his fellow writers indicates this sort of prolific, relatable relationship that
drives the link between creators to be of a piece, less a monopoly on creative voices and more a specific team vision. Whether this is because *Hannibal* is not a Fuller original creation is unknown, but Fuller often brings
other ideas and authors into his work. This is reflective of fan wikis and
atmospheres where the creators are part of a larger ecosystem of fan work.

Furthermore, by updating Roddenberry's work in the Prime Universe,
which is the original series timeline, Fuller and Kurtzman were obligated to
link Roddenberry's progressive politics to a modern ideological paradigm.
This paradigm is partly highlighted by Fuller's own experience as a gay man
writing for a series that previously did not have an openly gay human character when he first started writing for *Star Trek: Voyager*, and partly highlighted by the presence of Fuller on Twitter where he admits to encouraging
slash fiction regarding the iconic characters of Captain Kirk and Mr. Spock.
By addressing modern progressive politics within the frame and timeline
of Roddenberry's original series, Fuller continues to reframe Roddenberry's characters and work as relevant to the science fiction community of
fandom.

Finally, Fuller illustrated a willingness to indulge with the fans by
highlighting behind-the-scenes content. This content production and
teasing could easily fit into the production of culture method described

by Peterson and Anand. For example, his knowledge of the work of Nicholas Meyer and his outspoken fandom for Mr. Meyer's work caused him to outwardly accept him through his Twitter account. This highlighting of behind-the-scenes is incredibly important from a fan activism perspective because it allows for fans to speak up during the process of production, which can be cumbersome and expensive. The potential for addressing controversial or non-essential content through early access and behind-the-scenes content has an economic element, which fits neatly with the production of culture perspective spread by Peterson and Anand (2004).

Switching and Attacking the Work

These choices to create a more diverse representation of characters are seen in the depictions of series favorites like Beverly and Freddie Lounds. Switching them from original cisgender heterosexual white men in the text to Asian American and redheaded female, respectively, Fuller attempted to provide greater diversity onscreen to match the modern era in which *Hannibal* was created. This also matches with Fuller's vision of a more equitable society onscreen, which we can see in his future work with *Discovery*.

In reframing Roddenberry's work as a modern progressive text, the incorporation of specific signifiers of progressivism are necessary. This holds true with production of culture texts, where specific images, texts, and details are used to bolster the boundary conditions and accepted reality of the program.

"Every director who comes to the show gets the same lecture," says Fuller. "We are not making television. We are making a pretentious art film from the 80s." This statement is linked to his recreation of existing tropes in *Hannibal*. We can see this in his attempts to make the show more aggressive and hypnotic. Put simply, Fuller was focused on making *Hannibal* a beautiful show with aggressively violent representations. While Harris's original works were notable because of the way they portrayed psychological and social dysfunction, Fuller's show worked to integrate his fascination with artistic aesthetics in the original content. His work on *Hannibal* is notable because it is based on an existing property, and his work subverted or altered several elements of the original Thomas Harris texts (such as Freddie Lounds' fate, gender, and the gender, sexuality, and ultimate fate of Dr. Alana Bloom). Because of his approach to the Hannibal text, Fuller's inversion of the primary text may be seen as an activist approach to representation within a medium or canon. However, unlike *Hannibal*, which existed as its own interpretation of existing material, *Star Trek: Discovery* is a continuation of the Prime Timeline, which necessitates maneuvering within a canon of existing content.

It is within that context that fandom returns to dictate specific rules and regulations regarding the role of Fuller within this medium.

Conclusions

When fans claim to want Fuller to engage with the text, they are themselves asking for Fuller and other creators to engage with the text on their terms. In many ways, Twitter and the public account that Fuller directly controls as his outreach to his engaged followers necessitates a linkage between the fans. An obvious expansion on Jenkins' principles of convergence, it nevertheless necessitates an update due to the fan activist nature inherent with *Star Trek*. Since Roddenberry's original series text was a reaction to the existing social and cultural conditions, it only makes sense that several fans would want to have their own series address the issues of the day.

In conclusion, Fuller's very presence on *Star Trek: Discovery* is itself a work of fan activism, particularly since the property is so valuable for Paramount and CBS. The need to be current with the existing—and potentially new—fandom surrounding the property meant that Fuller's very impact on the property was meant to galvanize a portion of fans. Witness the discussion of the potential four-gendered Andorian race member on the program to indicate how likely the fans would be to demand specific attributes that define the character of the production. This aspect of sexuality and demanding representation is characteristic of fan activism, so Fuller's own statements indicate his likelihood to engage in the practice.

The potential for fan effect is transformative itself, and also possibly hopeful. After all, the show has yet to air, so it is as yet unclear how much of these fan activist suggestions have made it into the production of the program. However, the reaction of these charged fans has necessitated a new model of understanding how the pre-production and production processes includes fan feedback. Adapting older properties to shifting media usually requires a deft touch and elements that tie into the core property ideology, spirit, or otherwise.

Perhaps a new term is required for people like Fuller, who sit at unique intersections within Hollywood and televisual productions in the twenty-first century. Since Fuller has adapted properties in the past (he called his adaptation of *Hannibal* a work of fan fiction), and he himself creates "shipping" through his admissions on Twitter, the term "fan ambassador" may apply to him due to his overlap between the roles. Fan ambassadors are unique in how they intersect the shifting roles of Hollywood and the consumers, as the consumers themselves become producers. Though it has become clichéd to view YouTube as a means of production for amateur creators as continuing policy and site shifts have forced these creators to continue to adapt to changing production guidelines, the site still exists as the main nexus point between content creator and audience. Fan reactions to Fuller's show exist on YouTube as a means of fans creating content to exist within the increasingly interactive narrative of the program.

WORKS CITED

Bird, S. E. (2011). Are We All Produsers Now? *Cultural Studies*, 25(4–5), 502–516. https://doi.org/10.1080/09502386.2011.600532

Hilmes, M. (2013). *Only Connect: A Cultural History of Broadcasting in the United States* (4 edition). Australia: Cengage Learning.

Jenkins, H., Ford, S., & Green, J. (2013). *Spreadable Media: Creating Value and Meaning in a Networked Culture*. New York ; London: NYU Press.

Later, N. (2018). Quality Television (TV) Eats Itself: The TV-Auteur and the Promoted Fanboy. *Quarterly Review of Film and Video*, 35(6), 531–551. https://doi.org/10.1080/10509208.2018.1499349.

Martin, B. (2014). *Difficult Men: Behind the Scenes of a Creative Revolution: From The Sopranos and The Wire to Mad Men and Breaking Bad*. New York, NY: Penguin Books.

Sepinwall, A. (2008, October 1). Sepinwall on TV: "Pushing Daisies" review. Retrieved March 22, 2019, from nj.com website: https://www.nj.com/entertainment/tv/2008/10/sepinwall_on_tv_pushing_daisie.html.

Sepinwall, A. (2013). *The Revolution Was Televised: The Cops, Crooks, Slingers, and Slayers Who Changed TV Drama Forever* (Reissue edition). New York: Gallery Books.

Stanley, A. (2007, October 3). Pushing Daisies—TV - Review. *The New York Times*. Retrieved from https://www.nytimes.com/2007/10/03/arts/television/03stan.html.

Afterword

Dining In—The Legacy
of Bryan Fuller's Hannibal, or,
How Hannibal Inspired Us to Eat Better

NICHOLAS A. YANES

The notoriety of Dr. Hannibal Lecter never sank his teeth into me during my formative years of media consumption. Jonathan Demme's adaptation of *The Silence of the Lambs* was such a hit in 1991 that the slurping sound Sir Anthony Hopkins made while portraying Lecter seasoned my diet of entertainment. Not even being a pre-teen at the time, I didn't fully understand how that sound effect sent shivers down the spines of people who watched the movie.

As with all things that are overwhelmingly popular within modern media, *Silence of the Lambs*'s cinematic success inspired a sequel—*Hannibal* (2001)—and two prequels—*Red Dragon* (2002) and *Hannibal Rising* (2007). These films came and went in the media buffet of the 2000s with little impact. The popularity of *CSI: Crime Scene Investigation* pushed crime stories to focus on the science of solving crimes, and pulled them away from the deconstruction of the psychology of villains. An example of this in the show *Bones* is that the main character, Dr. Temperance "Bones" Brennan, never saw the field of psychology as a real science. The result of this is that I lost interest in shows and movies centered on serial killers and other criminals ... that is until I found Bryan Fuller's *Hannibal.*

By 2013 I had largely moved away from traditional television viewing and was surprised when Hulu (which was free at the time) recommended that I check out this new show from NBC, *Hannibal.* While some would avoid *Hannibal* by simplistically dismissing the show's content and visuals as grotesque, I found that there was a multilayered balance of flavors in

311

this show that reminds me of a quote from the dearly departed Anthony Bourdain.

While in Chiang Mai, Thailand to enjoy a dish comprised of grilled frog, Bourdain explained,

> There's almost an inverse relationship, like the more hideous looking the dish, the more delicious it is. As you probably noticed by now, the food here is not Pad Thai or green curry chicken. There are complex layers of flavor, sophisticated balances, spicy, sour, a little bitter, salty, herby. Color and texture are important. Crispy, soft, cold, hot. It's exactly this interplay between elements that makes Northern Thai food so thrilling and so addictive ["Thailand." *Anthony Bourdain: Parts Unknown*].

Fuller's show was the result of similarly careful interplay of multiple elements. *Hannibal* was more than just a criminal procedural in which the "good guys" won at the end of every episode. It was a show that made viewers understand, empathize, and even admire a cannibalistic serial killer. It was this near perfect balance of macabre subject matter and visuals with beautiful aesthetics that immediately grabbed my attention. Even before my eyes and ears first indulged in *Hannibal*, the contradictory and balanced flavors that comprised the character of Dr. Lecter appetized and inspired Fuller's imagination were being mixed to a sophisticated perfection.

In an interview conducted by *Hannibal* actor Scott Thompson (who played the FBI investigator Jimmy Price), Bryan Fuller stated that he was "intrigued with a gentleman cannibal" (Bryant). Fuller was not only fascinated by the opportunity to do a unique dark comedy, he also saw this as a way to explore serial killers without focusing on women being murdered and sexually assaulted as other shows do: "The reality of it is covered so well on other crime procedural shows where women are frequently raped and murdered. That's something I don't want to do on this show. I find it difficult to derive any entertainment from rape" (Bryant). Fuller's bold choice to artistically glamorize the chivalrous and refined behaviors of Dr. Lecter instead of the violence committed against women and other defenseless people allowed *Hannibal* to take be an oneiric space in which in murders were performance pieces.

As has been examined by the essays in this book, *Hannibal* is a cinematic work of art ripe with subtext academics are hungry to taste. Additionally, *Hannibal* had two lasting impacts on me that will last forever.

First, it was initial show to inspire me to think beyond the main narrative's presentation, to think beyond the plot and dialogue. This is because *Hannibal* was a feast for the senses. This show stood out not just because of the fantastic acting and plot progression, but also through the usage of sound, deep focus, color, set design, wardrobe, and other elements that form a *mélange* of cinema, and all on the small screen of broadcast television.

After all, Mads Mikkelsen was only able to truly embody Dr. Lecter due to the choices made by Christopher Hargadon as the show's costume designer. Hargadon dressed Lecter in suits made of fabrics which were boldly patterned and textured. Each of Lecter's outfits communicated to the world his lust for culture, his attention to detail and precision, and his need to stand out while still confining himself to a traditional professional suit. It is a fashion style which mirrors his artistic approach to killing people and handling their remains. On the other hand, Hugh Dancy's Will Graham is wrapped in clothing that at first roots Graham in a rugged, blue-collar life outside of his work with the FBI. As Graham becomes seduced by Dr. Lecter's worldview, his clothing begins to echo Lecter's wardrobe. While Graham's later clothing is never as bold as Lecter's, it is clear from how Graham is dressed that he is no longer the man audiences met.

In other words, *Hannibal* not only told stories with acting, dialogue, and plot, but also with clothing, lighting, and other visual and audio elements. It is a layered approach to storytelling that gave *Hannibal* a cinematic feel few television shows could emulate.

Second, watching *Hannibal* inspired my friend group to step up our food game. Shows focused on food tend to be competition shows that present cooking as an activity for only elite athletes, while other shows center cooking around diet fads or the sense of place. *Hannibal*, on the other hand, highlighted that every step of production in cooking was a work of art, and it inspired viewers to approach food preparation as an artistic endeavor that could be enjoyed every day. Multiple essays in this book highlight this exact feeling.

For my friends and me, soon after we made watching the latest episode of *Hannibal* a group activity, we found ourselves reflecting on the types of food and beverages we would bring. We became keenly aware of the process that went into a dish's production and presentation, and made sure to share this knowledge with one another. We probably spent too much time thinking of which alcohols would best partner with foods to form combinations that Dr. Lecter would hopefully approve of, though we also reminded ourselves that the world's favorite cannibal was also a fan of similar libations.

We never followed in Lecter's footsteps by eating the rude, but this remains a personal element of *Hannibal*'s legacy. It was not just a network show that thrived to be more than its medium; it was an experience that used murders, cannibalism, and other dark elements of humanity to illuminate the artistry present in everyday life. Like Hannibal himself, the show would not be satisfied with simply acceptable results. It sought the extraordinary and the divine. So too does this volume that you have now concluded.

Kyle and I hope that you have enjoyed this compendium of what we hope will be a continuing look at a show that one can always find some meat on when viewing. This book is more than a collection of fantastic works by academics who loved the show and sought its influences and mythological antecedents. This book is more than a collection of interviews with the talented artists and producers that brought this macabre and beautiful vision to life.

To paraphrase Will Graham, this book is our design.

WORKS CITED

Bryant, Adam. "Exclusive *Hannibal* Video: Go Inside the Deliciously Twisted Mind of Creator Bryan Fuller." *TVGuide.com*, TV Guide, 24 Apr. 2014. https://www.tvguide.com/news/hannibal-post-mortem-video-bryan-fuller-1080858/.

"Thailand." *Anthony Bourdain: Parts Unknown*, CNN, 1 Jun. 2014. http://transcripts.cnn.com/TRANSCRIPTS/1406/01/abpu.02.html.

About the Contributors

Simon **Bacon** is an independent scholar based in Poznan, Poland. He has edited various books, including *Undead Memory* (2014), and *Growing Up with Vampires* (2018), both with Katarzyna Bronk. He edited *Gothic: A Reader* (2018), *Horror: A Companion* (2019), and *Monsters: A Companion* (2020). He has published three monographs, *Becoming Vampire* (2016), *Dracula as Absolute Other* (2019), and *Eco-Vampires* (2020).

Olimpia **Calì** holds a Ph.D. in cognitive science from the University of Messina in Italy, where she is also a teaching assistant in photography and visual culture at the Department of Cognitive Science. Her principal areas of interest concern media and audience studies, both investigated by using a cognitive approach. She has published articles in international journals and has attended several international conferences as speaker.

Sarah **Cleary** holds a Ph.D. in horror. She has dedicated her studies to the juxtaposition between the media and the alleged negative effects of popular culture on children, and splits her time between lecturing and academic consultancy in the media. Her first critical study on horror and censorship was published in 2019. She is a pop culture panelist on a daytime current affairs TV show, the creative director of Horror Expo Ireland and producer of *The Rocky Horror Picture Show* in Ireland.

Evelyn **Deshane** has had creative and nonfiction work published in *The Atlantic*'s tech channel, *Plenitude Magazine*, *Briarpatch Magazine*, *StrangeHorizons*, *Lackington's*, and *Bitch* magazine, among other publications. She received an MA from Trent University's Public Texts Program after completing a gender studies and English literature BAH at Trent years earlier. She completed her Ph.D. in 2019 and writes and teaches in Waterloo, Ontario.

Megan **Fowler** is an English Ph.D. student at the University of Florida. Her research interests include fandom studies, popular culture studies, children's literature, comics studies and queer studies. Her dissertation project deals with queer representation and trauma in contemporary media and fandom spaces. She has given several paper presentations at conferences including MLA, SAMLA and IGA, and has published several essays.

Michael **Fuchs** is an assistant professor in American studies at the University of Graz in Austria. He has coedited six essay collections, most recently *Intermedia Games* (2019), and (co-)authored more than fifty journal articles and book chapters which have appeared in *The Popular Culture Journal*, *The Journal of Popular Television*, the *Quarterly Review of Film and Video*, *The Cambridge History of Science Fiction* (2019), and *Horror Television in the Age of Consumption* (2018).

Evan Hayles **Gledhill** is a sessional lecturer at the University of Reading, where they gained a Ph.D. exploring gothic monstrosity through the lens of queer and disability theory. Their research interests include subjectivity and the body, gender and sexuality in genre fiction, and the history of fandom. Their recent publications include work on Hannibal and the gothic romance and agency, monstrosity and queerness in gothic horror by Poppy Z. Brite.

Anamarija **Horvat** is a postdoctoral fellow at the University of Edinburgh's Institute for Advanced Studies in the Humanities. Her research looks at representations of queer memory in transnational film. Her publications can be found in the *Feminist Media Studies* and *Critical Studies in Television* journals. She is co-founder of the Queer Screens Network, and co-chair of the Feminist and Queer Research workgroup at NECS (European Network of Cinema and Media Studies).

Naja **Later** is a sessional academic at Swinburne University of Technology. She researches intersections between pop culture, politics and history, focusing on horror and superhero genres. She has published research on *Hannibal* in the *Quarterly Review of Film and Video*, *Participations Journal of Audience and Reception Studies* and with Syracuse University Press.

Vittoria **Lion** is a Surrealist writer, painter and Ph.D. student in the University of Toronto Graduate Department of Art. Her thesis focuses on Surrealist animal representations, speculative evolution and psychoanalysis. Her fiction, poetry, visual art and academic work have been featured in *Monstering*, *Peculiar Mormyrid*, *Feral Feminisms* and *Knots: An Undergraduate Journal of Disability Studies*.

Megan **McAllister** is a pastry chef in Dallas. Her research focuses on food symbolism and food sciences. She has worked in many different restaurants and bakeries, including the pastry section in the Dallas Cowboys Stadium during Superbowl XLV. She has spent her time in the Hannibal fandom working with the Fannibal Movement and the fan-run convention FannibalFest.

Samantha **McLaren** is a Scottish writer and artist living in New York City. While earning her master's degree in English literature from the University of Edinburgh, she began researching portrayals of body horror in film, TV and literature, particularly in Bryan Fuller's *Hannibal*. In 2018, she gave a presentation on *Hannibal* and *Twin Peaks* at the Split Screens Festival in NYC.

Kyle A. **Moody** is an assistant professor of communications media at Fitchburg State University in the United States. He has authored multiple book chapters and journal articles, including works that have appeared in *The 100 Greatest Video Games*, *Masculinities in Play* and *The Handbook of Research on Deception, Fake News, and Misinformation Online*. His research focuses on online communities of practice, dissemination and production of information, and the use of false information narratives.

Lorianne **Reuser** is an independent scholar with interests in fantasy and horror. She completed a double major in English literature and Greek and Roman studies at the

University of Calgary. In Dublin, she completed an M.Phil in popular literature at Trinity College, with a focus on nostalgic childhood in Stephen King's novels. She is working on an education degree with the goal of teaching literature.

Lisa **Rufus** lives in Brisbane, Australia. She completed a BA with honors at the University of Queensland in 2014, majoring in film and television studies and writing. Inspired by the beautiful and twisted aesthetic style of Bryan Fuller, she wrote her honors thesis on the television series *Hannibal*. In 2017, she completed an MA in writing at the Swinburne University of Technology.

Nicole Michaud **Wild** is an assistant professor of sociology at Upper Iowa University. Her research interests and publications include work on culture, fandom, media, politics, humor and conspiracy beliefs. She received her Ph.D. from the University at Albany, SUNY, and is a faculty fellow at the Yale Center for Cultural Sociology.

Kirsty **Worrow** is a program leader for media, film and music at Shrewsbury Sixth Form College. She covered *Hannibal* for dailyfandom.com and contributed to *Squee! Projects* on YouTube. Her research interests include horror, gender, celebrity and fan cultures. She has presented papers at Cine-Excess and to the Fan Studies Network and is a contributor to *Media Magazine*.

Nicholas A. **Yanes** earned his Ph.D. in American studies from the University of Iowa. His first book was *The Iconic Obama* and he has (co-)authored several academic articles. Outside of academia, he is a freelance writer who has contributed to CNBCPrime, MGM, ScifiPulse, Sequart, Casual Games Association's (now GameDaily Connect) *Casual Connect* and *GameSauce*, and several other publications. His academic and professional interests center on researching and analyzing the business of entertainment industries.

Index

319